In some languages words tend to be rather short but in others they may be dauntingly long. In this book, a distinguished international group of scholars discuss the concept 'word' and its applicability in a range of typologically diverse languages. An introductory chapter sets the parameters of variation for 'word'. The nine chapters that follow then study the character of 'word' in individual languages, including Amazonian, Australian Aboriginal, Eskimo, Native North American, West African, Balkan and Caucasian languages, and Indo-Pakistani Sign Language. These languages exhibit a huge range of phonological and grammatical characteristics, the close study of which enables the contributors to refine our understanding of what can constitute a 'word'. An epilogue explores the status and cross-linguistic properties of 'word'. The book will be an invaluable resource for scholars of linguistic typology and of morphology and phonology.

The editors
R. M. W. Dixon and Alexandra Y. Aikhenvald are Director and Associate Director of the Research Centre for Linguistic Typology at La Trobe University. Professor Dixon has published five grammars of Australian languages (notably of Dyirbal and of Yidinj), a grammar of Fijian (1988), *A New Approach to English Grammar* (1991), and is currently completing a grammar of Jarawara (Arawá family, Brazil). His theoretical works include *Ergativity* (Cambridge, 1994) and *The Rise and Fall of Languages* (Cambridge, 1997). Professor Aikhenvald has published seven books including a grammar of Modern Hebrew (in Russian) and grammars of two languages from the Arawak family. Her monograph *Classifiers: a Typology of Noun Categorization Devices* was published in 2000. One of the current projects is a grammar of the Manambu language from the East Sepik region of Papua New Guinea. Professor Dixon and Professor Aikhenvald are also the editors of *The Amazonian Languages* (Cambridge, 1999) and *Changing Valency: Case Studies in Transitivity* (Cambridge, 2000).

Word

A cross-linguistic typology

Edited by

R. M. W. Dixon

and

Alexandra Y. Aikhenvald

Research Centre for Linguistic Typology, La Trobe University

CAMBRIDGE
UNIVERSITY PRESS

CAMBRIDGE UNIVERSITY PRESS
Cambridge, New York, Melbourne, Madrid, Cape Town, Singapore, São Paulo

Cambridge University Press
The Edinburgh Building, Cambridge CB2 8RU, UK

Published in the United States of America by Cambridge University Press, New York

www.cambridge.org
Information on this title: www.cambridge.org/9780521818995

First published 2002
Fourth printing 2005
This digitally printed version 2007

A catalogue record for this publication is available from the British Library

ISBN 978-0-521-81899-5 hardback
ISBN 978-0-521-04605-3 paperback

Contents

Contributors

Alexandra Y. Aikhenvald
Research Centre for Linguistic
   Typology
La Trobe University
Victoria, 3086
Australia
e-mail:
a.aikhenvald@latrobe.edu.au

John Boyle
Dept of Linguistics
University of Chicago
Chicago, IL 60637
USA
e-mail:
jpboyle@midway.uchicago.edu

R. M. W. Dixon
Research Centre for Linguistic
   Typology
La Trobe University
Victoria, 3086
Australia
no e-mail

Randolph Graczyk
PO Box 29
Pryor, MT, 59066
USA
e-mail: rgraczyk@acl.com

Alice C. Harris
Department of Linguistics

SUNY Stony Brook
Stony Brook, NY 11794
U.S.A.
e-mail: alice.harris@stonybrook.edu

John Henderson
Dept of Linguistics
University of Western Australia
WA, 6907
Australia
e-mail:
john.henderson@uwa.edu.au

Brian Joseph
Dept of Linguistics
Ohio State University
222 Oxley Hall
Columbus, OH 43210
USA
e-mail:
bjoseph@ling.ohio-state.edu

John Koontz
471, E Rainbow Ct
Louisville, CO 80027-2125
USA
e-mail: john.koontz@colorado.edu

P. H. Matthews
St John's College
Cambridge, CB2 1TP
UK
no e-mail

Knut J. Olawsky
Research Centre for Linguistic
   Typology
La Trobe University
Victoria, 3086
Australia
e-mail:
olawsky@latrobe.edu.au

Robert Rankin
Dept of Linguistics
University of Kansas
Lawrence, KS 66045-2140
USA
e-mail: rankin@ukans.edu

Anthony C. Woodbury
Dept of Linguistics
Calhoun Hall 501
University of Texas
Austin, TX 78712
USA
e-mail: acw@mail.utexas.edu

Ulrike Zeshan
Research Centre for Linguistic
   Typology
La Trobe University
Victoria, 3086
Australia
e-mail: u.zeshan@latrobe.edu.au

Preface

This volume includes a typological introduction, plus revised versions of ten of the sixteen presentations at the International Workshop on 'Word', held at the Research Centre for Linguistic Typology, La Trobe University, 7–12 August 2000. An earlier version of chapter 1 had been circulated to contributors, to ensure that the detailed studies of 'word' in individual languages were cast in terms of the same typological parameters.

All of the authors have pursued intensive investigations of languages, some of them little-known in the literature. They were asked to write in terms of basic linguistic theory – the cumulative framework in which most descriptive grammars are cast – and to avoid formalisms (which come and go with such frequency that any statement made in terms of them will soon become dated and inaccessible).

This volume comes from the third International Workshop organised by the Research Centre for Linguistic Typology. The first, held in 1997, gave rise to the book *Changing valency: case studies in transitivity* (edited by Dixon and Aikhenvald), published by Cambridge University Press in 2000. The second, held in 1998, resulted in the volume *Areal diffusion and genetic relationship: problems in comparative linguistics* (edited by Aikhenvald and Dixon), published by Oxford University Press in 2001.

We owe a special debt of gratitude to Siew Peng Condon, Executive Officer of the Research Centre for Linguistic Typology, for organising the Workshop in a most efficient and caring manner, and to Anya Woods for assisting with preparation of the volume and for compiling the indices in her normal professional manner.

Abbreviations

1	first person	CONT.GO	continuous action while in motion
2	second person		
3	third person		
A	transitive subject function	CV	character vowel
		DAT	dative
ABL	ablative	DEC	declarative
ABS	absolutive	DEF	definite
ACC	accusative	DET	determiner
ACT	active	DIFFSUBJ	different subject
ACTR	actor, subject of active verb	DIM	diminutive
		DIR.OBJ	direct object
ADJ	adjective	DU, du	dual
ADV	adverbial case	e	eyewitness
AG	agentive	EMPH	emphatic
ANIM	animate	ERG	ergative
ANTIPASS	antipassive	exc	exclusive
APPLIC	applicative	F, FEM, f	feminine
APPR	approximative	FOC	focus
ART	article	FP	far past
ASSOC	associative	FUT	future
ATTEN	attenuative	GEN	genitive
AUX	auxiliary	HABIT	habitual
C	consonant	ImmPosIMP	immediate positive imperative
CAUS	causative		
CL	classifier		
CLIT	clitic	IMP	impersonal
COLL	collective	IMPERF	imperfect
COMIT	comitative	IMPFVE	imperfective
COMPL	completive	IMPV	imperative
CONC	concessive	INC, inc	inclusive
CONT	continuous	IND	indicative mood

INF	infinitive	PAT	patient, subject of stative verb
INST	instrumentive		
INSTR	instrumental	PAUS	pausal
INT	intentional	PEJ	pejorative
INTENS	intensifier	PERF	perfect
INTER.VIS	visual interrogative	PERI	peripheral postposition
intr	intransitive	PERS	person
IP	immediate past	PERFVE	perfective
ITER	iterative	PL, pl	plural
IV	intransitive verbaliser	PORT	portative
		POSS	possessive
LOC	locative	PP	past/passive participle
M, MASC, m	masculine		
MD	modalis case	PRES	present tense
n	non-eyewitness	PRES.NON.VIS	present non-visual
N	nasal		
NAR	narrative case	PRO	pronominal
NCL	noun class	PRX	proximity marker
NEG	negative		
nf	non-feminine	PST	past
NOM	nominative	PTCPL	participle
NOMLSR	nominaliser	PURP	purposive
NONACC	non-accomplished	PW	phonological word
NP	noun phrase		
nsg	non-singular	QUOT	quotative
NTR	neuter	RC	relative clause marker
O	transitive object function		
		REC.PAST	recent past
OBJ	object	RECIP	reciprocal pronominal
OBJ.FOC	object focus	REDUP	reduplication
Oc	O-construction marker	REFL	reflexive
		REL	relativiser
ORD	ordinal	REM.P.INFR	remote past inferred
P	possessor		
PART	particle	REM.P.REP	remote past reported
PASSING	do while passing	REM.P.VIS	remote past visual
PAST.PCPL	past participle		
PASTHAB	past habitual	RP	recent past

S	intransitive subject function	tr TV	transitive transitive verbaliser
SAMESUBJ	same subject		
SEMBL	semblative	V	vowel
SG, sg	singular	VERT	vertitive, motion back towards point of origin
SUBJ	subject		
SUBJUNC	subjunctive		
SUPPO	supposedly		
SUUS	reflexive- possessive pronominal	VL VP WK	vialis verb phrase weak
TOP.NON.A/S	topical non-subject	WKNED	weakened

1   Word: a typological framework

R. M. W. Dixon and Alexandra Y. Aikhenvald

In this book we ask how 'word' should be defined. What are the criteria for 'word'? Is 'word', as the term is generally understood, an appropriate unit to recognise for every type of language?

This introductory chapter first looks at what scholars have said about 'word', and then discusses the categories and distinctions which need to be examined. Chapter 2 suggests a number of typological parameters for the study of clitics. Following chapters then provide detailed examination of the notion of 'word' in a selection of spoken languages from Africa, North and South America, Australia, the Caucasus and Greece, together with a discussion of words in sign languages. The final chapter, by P. H. Matthews, asks what has been learnt from these general and particular studies.

This introduction begins by surveying the criteria that have been put forward for 'word', and suggests that one should sensibly keep apart phonological criteria, which define 'phonological word', and grammatical criteria, which define 'grammatical word'. In some languages the two types of word coincide and one can then felicitously talk of a single unit 'word', which has a place both in the hierarchy of phonological units and in the hierarchy of grammatical units. In other languages phonological word and grammatical word generally coincide, but do not always do so. We may have a grammatical word consisting of a whole number of phonological words, or a phonological word consisting of a whole number of grammatical words. Or there can be a more complex correspondence between the two types of word with, say, a grammatical word consisting of all of one and part of another phonological word.

§1 summarises the tradition, §2 discusses linguists who would do without the word and §3 surveys opinions concerning 'what is a word'. In §4 a number of confusions are discussed and then in §5 some suggested criteria are examined. The heart of the chapter is in §§6–8 – proposed definitions for phonological word and for grammatical word (and the status of clitics) – followed by (in §9) examination of the relationship between the two types of word. In §10 we ask whether all kinds of languages have words; in §11 there is brief discussion of the varying social status of 'word' in different languages, and then §12 provides a summary of the results of the introductory chapter. Finally, the appendix gives a

1

brief statement of the criteria for phonological word and for grammatical word (and their relationship) in a sample language, Fijian.

1   The tradition

Many writers have assumed that 'word' is a – or the – basic unit of language. Bolinger (1963: 113) comments: 'Why is it that the element of language which the naive speaker feels that [they] know best is the one about which linguists say the least? To the untutored person, speaking is putting words together, writing is a matter of correct word-spelling and word-spacing, translating is getting words to match words, meaning is a matter of word definitions, and linguistic change is merely the addition or loss or corruption of words.' Bolinger himself takes 'word' as a prime, commenting that it is 'the source, not the result, of phonemic contrasts'.

And, as Lyons (1968: 194) comments: 'The word is the unit *par excellence* of traditional grammatical theory. It is the basis of the distinction which is frequently drawn between morphology and syntax and it is the principal unit of lexicography (or "dictionary-making")'. Indeed, for the Greeks and Romans the word was the basic unit for the statement of morphological patterns; they used a 'word and paradigm' approach, setting out the various grammatical forms of a given lexeme in corresponding rows and columns, with no attempt to segment into morphemes (Robins 1967: 25). (In fact Greek and Latin are fusional languages where it is not an easy matter to segment words into morphemes, without bringing in the impedimenta of underlying forms, morphophonological rules, and the like.)

Much that has been written about the word is decidedly eurocentric. It has sometimes been said that 'primitive languages' do not have words, an opinion which Lyons (1968: 199) explicitly rejects, partly on the basis of Sapir's report that uneducated speakers of American Indian languages can dictate 'word by word'.

However, it appears that only some languages actually have a lexeme with the meaning 'word'.[1] Even in some familiar languages where this does occur it may be a recent development. For instance, in Old English the primary meaning of *word* was (a) for referring to speech, as contrasted with act or thought. There was a second sense, which may then just have been emerging: (b) what occurs between spaces in written language. In the development to Modern English (b) has become the major sense – the one used in this book – with sense (a) still surviving mainly in fixed phrases, e.g. *the spoken word*,

---

[1] Dixon (1977a: 88) states 'every (or almost every) language has a word for "word"'; this is erroneous. Wierzbicka (1996, 1998) has 'word' as a universal semantic primitive, which is said to be realised in every language; this is equally erroneous.

the written word, the Word of God, a word of warning/advice/caution, Can I have a quick word with you? Similar remarks apply to corresponding terms in some other European languages, e.g. *mot* in French and *slovo* in Russian. German also has a noun, *Wort*, with these two senses, but there are here two plural forms – *Worte* for 'speech' and *Wörter* for 'what is written between spaces'.[2]

Over on the other side of the world, *vosa* in Fijian is a verb meaning 'speak, talk' and also a noun, with several related senses: 'language', 'talk, speech' and 'word'. It is likely that we have here a similar line of semantic development to *word* in English.

The vast majority of languages spoken by small tribal groups (with from a few hundred to a few thousand speakers) have a lexeme meaning '(proper) name' but none have the meaning 'word'. This applies to many languages from Australia (including Arrernte, chapter 4 in this volume), Amazonia (including Jarawara, chapter 5) and New Guinea with which we, or our colleagues, are familiar.

2 Doing without 'word'

The idea of 'word' as a unit of language was developed for the familiar languages of Europe which by-and-large have a synthetic structure. Indeed – as will be shown below – some of the criteria for 'word' are only fully applicable for languages of this type.

What about languages from extreme ends of the typological continuum – those of an analytic or of a polysynthetic profile? Reviewing the first edition of Nida's (1944) *Morphology*, Hockett (1944: 255) notes that Nida 'devotes a chapter to the criteria by which words may be recognised. None of these criteria, nor any combination of them, gives any fruitful results with Chinese . . . the real implication is that THERE ARE NO WORDS IN CHINESE. The whole tradition of "words" as worked out with western languages is useless in Chinese.' (However, a quite different opinion is expressed by the leading Chinese linguist, Chao, discussed in §10 and §11 below.)

Some of the polysynthetic languages of North America lack any unit that looks like the sort of word we are used to from European languages. Gray (1939: 146) presents his own definition of word as 'a complex of sounds which in itself possesses a meaning fixed and accepted by convention'. (Note that this would, in fact, also be satisfied by a prefix such as *un-* or a phrase such as

---

[2] It is likely that all languages with an established (non-ideographic) orthographic tradition do have a word for 'word'. Other languages tend to create such a term once they are exposed to writing. The interesting question is how many languages with no written tradition have a lexeme which corresponds to *word* in English, *mot* in French, etc.

The King of England.) Then, in a footnote, he reports a suggestion from
H. J. Uldall that in polysynthetic languages (such as Maidu from north-east
California) 'the word as such is not a relevant part of analysis'. This idea is repeated by Milewski (1951), who argues that in all languages of the world there
are three kinds of morphological unit, morphemes, syntactic groups and clauses.
However, Krámský (1969: 74–5) suggests that Milewski's 'syntactic group'
in polysynthetic North American languages does satisfy criteria for 'word'. It
is clear that the unit 'word' can be recognised in polysynthetic languages, it is
just that it is much longer and more complex than the words linguists were used
to at that time.

It is, however, important to distinguish between the structure of the predicate
and the structure of the verb. This is discussed in §§5–6 of chapter 5, where
it is shown that a language may have fairly complex predicate structure but
relatively simple verb structure (as in English and Fijian), or simple predicate
structure combined with somewhat complex verb structure (as in Dyirbal), or
both complex predicate structure and complex verb structure (as in Jarawara).

There are those who consider 'word', as a general notion, not to be a basic
category of language. The anthropologist Malinowski (1966: 11) insists that
one should analyse utterances, not any smaller units of language taken out of
their context of use. He can then say 'isolated words are in fact only linguistic
figments, the products of an advanced linguistic analysis'.[3]

Other linguists accord a grudging role to 'word'. For Börgström (1954: 276)
'words are utterance-segments consisting of one or more morphemes. Assuming
that there is a procedure for the demarcation of morphemes, it is possible, I
believe, to formulate a set of distribution rules as a procedure for the demarcation
of words.' Writing in the same year, Garvin (1954: 345) is less sure about this:
'in the present state of our techniques one may assume that we know how to
isolate morphemes properly – that is, unequivocally and without unaccountable
residue. It is not so certain that we know how to isolate words, and hence how
to separate morphology from syntax.'

The extreme position is taken by Harris (1946: 161) who presents a procedure
(illustrated for English and Hidatsa) for analysing utterances into morphemes:
'the method described in this paper will require no elements other than morphemes and sequences of morphemes, and no operation other than substitution,
repeated again and again'. The unit 'word' does not feature in Harris' analysis.[4]

---

[3] We also find (perhaps as a further reflection of Malinowski's position) Potter's (1967: 78) statement: 'unlike a phoneme or a syllable, a word is not a linguistic unit at all. It is no more than a
conventional or arbitrary segment of utterances.'

[4] We have noted one instance of *word* in this paper, but this is used in an informal rather than in
an analytic sense. On page 166 Harris is discussing the English sentence *I know John was in* and
talks of 'pronouncing its intonation twice, once over the first two words and again over the last
three'.

3   What is a word?

Matthews commences the section 'What are words?' in the second edition of his seminal textbook *Morphology* (1991: 208) with: 'there have been many definitions of the word, and if any had been successful I would have given it long ago, instead of dodging the issue until now'.

Matthews mentions that the ancient grammarians simply had word as the smallest unit of syntax. But, he comments, to follow that line 'will only turn our larger problem back to front. If words are to be defined by reference to syntax, what in turn is syntax, and why are syntactic relations not contracted by parts of words as well as whole words?'

Some of the definitions suggested for word are horrifying in their complexity and clearly infringe the principle that a definition should not be more difficult to understand than the word it purports to define.[5] There are useful surveys of definitions of 'word' in Rosetti (1947), Weinreich (1954), Ullmann (1957) and Krámský (1969).

Some definitions are simple and appealing. These include Sapir's (1921: 34) 'one of the smallest, completely satisfying bits of isolated "meaning" into which the sentence resolves itself' and Žirmunskij's (1966: 66): 'the word is the most concise unit of language, which is independent in meaning and form'. But each of these is essentially vague; they do not provide definite criteria for deciding 'what is a word' in a given language.

Sweet (1875/6: 474) suggests: 'we may, therefore, define a word as an ultimate or indecomposable sentence'. That is, anything which is a word can make up a complete sentence. Sweet offers as examples of this (from English) *Come!* and *Up?* (meaning 'Shall we go up?'). However, he is then concerned over what to do with forms like English *the* and *a*, which he terms 'half-words'.

Bloomfield (1933: 178) pursues a similar line in his definition: 'a word, then, is a free form which does not consist entirely of (two or more) lesser free forms; in brief, a word is a *minimum free form*' (his italics). This is probably the most oft-quoted definition of 'word' but it is, in fact, scarcely workable. There is further discussion in §5 below.

---

[5] We can quote two rather extreme examples. Firstly, Longacre's (1964: 101) definition, which was conceived within the formal framework of tagmemics: 'a class of syntagmemes of a comparatively low hierarchical order, ranking below such syntagmemes as the phrase and the clause and above such syntagmemes as the stem (as well as above roots which have no external structure and are therefore not syntagmemes). It may be of greatly varied structure... Words tend to be rigidly ordered linear sequences containing tagmemes which (aside from those manifested by stems) are manifested by closed classes of morphemes unexpandable into morpheme sequences and giving only stereotyped bits of information.'

Krámský devotes a whole monograph to discussing 'word'. He surveys past definitions and then comes up with his own (1969: 67): 'the word is the smallest independent unit of language referring to a certain extra-linguistic reality or to a relation of such realities and characterised by certain formal features (acoustic, morphemic) either actually (as an independent component of the context) or potentially (as a unit of the lexical plan)'.

4   Confusions

The word 'word' is used in many ways in everyday speech, and in much linguistic discourse. It is important to make certain fundamental distinctions:
(1) between a lexeme and its varying forms;
(2) between an orthographic word (something written between two spaces) and other types of word;
(3) between a unit primarily defined on grammatical criteria and one primarily defined on phonological criteria.
These are discussed, in turn, in §§4.1–3.

   The (grammatical) word forms the interface between morphology and syntax. Morphology deals with the composition of words while syntax deals with the combination of words. One could imagine slightly different words being required as ideal units for these two purposes. That is, there could be a 'morphological word' and a 'syntactic word' which would perhaps generally coincide but might not always do so. We are not aware of this sort of distinction having been fully justified for any language;[6] but it is certainly a possibility. (In chapter 7, Rankin et al. put forward the idea that the term 'syntactic word' could perhaps be used – in Siouan languages – for a type of word incorporating a relative clause, the whole constituting one phonological word.)

4.1   *Word and lexeme*

Consider the following examples, from English and Latin, of the root or underlying form of a lexeme and its inflected forms, as used in a sentence.

	root or underlying form	inflected forms	
(a)	*look*	*look*	present, non-3sg subject
		looks	present, 3sg subject
		looked	past
		looking	participle
(b)	*lup-* 'wolf'	*lupus*	nominative sg
		lupō	dative/ablative sg
		lupī	genitive sg, nominative pl
		etc.	

---

[6] The possibility of this is mentioned by Di Sciullo and Williams (1987) without, however, the formulation of any explicit cross-linguistic or language-specific criteria. This question is also aired in Gak (1990). Dai (1998) establishes separate units 'syntactic word', 'phonological word', and 'morphological word' in Chinese. He suggests that a compound is one syntactic word and also one morphological word but that it may have different syntactic and morphological structures.

   A number of other types of 'word' have been suggested. For example, Packard (2000: 7–14) lists: orthographic word, sociological word, lexical word, semantic word, phonological word, morphological word, syntactic word, and psycholinguistic word.

The term 'word' is sometimes used in reference to the root or underlying form, and sometimes in reference to the inflected forms. That is we hear, on the one hand things like '*look, looks, looked* and *looking* are forms of the same word', and on the other hand things like 'the lexeme *look* is realised as word-forms *look, looks, looked* and *looking*'.

Bally (1950: 287–9) is so concerned about this ambiguity of usage that he recommends abandoning the label 'mot' in French (and 'word' in English) and instead employing 'sémantème' for the root or underlying form and 'molécule syntaxique' for inflected forms. Lyons (1968: 197) prefers a different course. While recognising that in classical grammar 'word' was used to mean 'sémantème' he notes that modern usage tends to employ 'word' as a label for 'molécule syntaxique' and suggests standardising on this.

We have followed Lyons' suggestion, of using 'lexeme' as the label for 'root or underlying form' and '(grammatical) word' for 'inflected form of a lexeme'. Note that Lyons uses italics for words and capitals for lexemes – thus, the word *looked* is the past tense form of the lexeme LOOK.

Lyons' convention is useful from another viewpoint, for dealing with lexemes that involve two words. These include phrasal verbs in English such as MAKE UP, as in *I made the story up* and *I made it up*. Note that the words of this lexeme are mapped onto two non-contiguous syntactic slots – an inflected form of *make* goes into the verb slot while *up* follows the object NP.[7] That is, the lexeme MAKE UP consists of two words, each of which has its own syntactic behaviour. If we had decided on 'word' as the label for lexeme, there would then be need for a separate notion of 'syntactic word'. We would have had to say that the (lexical) word *make up* consists of two syntactic words, *make* and *up*. This is avoided by describing MAKE UP as a lexeme that consists of two (grammatical) words, an inflected form of *make* and the preposition *up*. (Similar remarks apply to phenomena such as separable preverbs in German and Hungarian.)

4.2   Orthographic word

In many language communities a word is thought of as having (semantic, grammatical and phonological) unity and, in writing, words are conventionally separated by spaces. (In §9 below we investigate the writing convention when phonological and grammatical criteria do not produce the same unit.)

Indeed, in his *Phonemics*, Pike (1947: 89) defines 'word' as 'the smallest unit arrived at for some particular language as the most convenient type of

---

[7] The *up* can move to the left over an object that is a full NP but not over a preposition – *I made up the story* but not **I made up it*. Note the distinction between a phrasal verb like *make up* and one like *pick on*, where the *on* must precede the object NP, e.g. *He picked on his brother* or *He picked on him* but not **He picked his brother on* or **He picked him on*. See Dixon (1982; 1991: 274–8).

grammatical entity to separate by spaces; in general, it constitutes one of those units of a particular language which actually or potentially may be pronounced by itself'. Pike here implies that the ideal orthographic convention is to write spaces between grammatical words. The first part of his definition is circular – spaces are written around a grammatical word and a grammatical word is what is felt to be appropriately written between spaces; that is, no explicit criterion for 'grammatical word' is provided. The second part of his definition is essentially Bloomfield's 'minimum free form', discussed in §5 and §7 below.

Writing conventions are unlikely to be absolutely consistent. In English, for instance, the convention is to write *cannot* as one word but the analogous *must not* as two. There appears to be no reason for this; it is just a convention of the language community.

The Bantu languages of southern Africa have a complex but agglutinative verb structure. Van Wyk (1967: 230) describes different conventions used in these languages for writing word divisions:

(a) disjunctivism – 'according to which relatively simple, and, therefore, relatively short, linguistic units are written and regarded as words';
(b) conjunctivism – 'according to which simple units are joined to form long words with complex morphological structures'.

He exemplifies with the Northern Sotho sentence 'we shall skin it with his knife'. The two ways of writing this are:

(a) *re tlo e bua ka thipa ya gagwe*, according to the disjunctive system;
(b) *retloebua kathipa yagagwe*, according to the conjunctive system.

Van Wyk does not provide an interlinear gloss. However, we have been able to ascertain that *re-* is the 1pl subject prefix, *-tlo-* is the future prefix, *-e-* is a 3sg object prefix, *-bua* is the verb root 'to skin', *ka-* is an instrumental prefix, *thipa* is the noun 'knife', *ya-* is a class 9 prefix (agreeing with the class 9 noun 'knife') and *gagwe* is 'his'.

In fact different orthographic strategies have been adopted for different Bantu languages. Northern Sotho, Southern Sotho and Tswana are written disjunctively while Zulu and Xhosa are written conjunctively. There is no inherent grammatical difference between these languages; it is just that different writing conventions are followed. In the conjunctive system spaces are written between grammatical words (which may be long); in the disjunctive system spaces are written between morphemes within grammatical words. This may have been influenced by the fact that some of the prefixes are bound pronouns and case-type markers, corresponding to free pronouns and prepositions in languages such as English and Dutch (the languages of the Europeans who helped devise these writing systems), which are there written as separate words.

The orthographic conventions used for a language tend to reflect what the language was like at the time when an orthography was first adopted. For example, *knee* was pronounced with an initial *k* when English was first written. A language may undergo considerable changes, few of which get incorporated into the orthography. French, for instance, has shifted from a mildly synthetic structure to one bordering on the polysynthetic. A sentence such as *je ne l'ai pas vu* 'I have not seen it' can be considered a single word, on both grammatical and phonological criteria. But the language is – as a reflection of its history – written disjunctively, with the consequence that speakers will say that the sentence consists of five or six words (see Vendryes 1925: 87–8). This is one of the reasons why linguists have found it harder to decide 'what is a word' for French than for many other languages. (This point is further pursued by Matthews in chapter 11.)

4.3   *Grammatical and phonological aspects*

Before the idea (followed here) that one should deal separately with 'grammatical word' and 'phonological word' and then examine the relationship between the two units, there was confusion about exactly what a word is.

As Ullmann (1957: 46) points out 'since the word is the central element of the language system, it is natural for it to face both ways: not only is it the chief subject matter of lexicology, but it is dependent on phonology for the analysis of its sound-structure, and on syntax for the delimitation of its status in more complex configurations'. But is 'word' primarily a grammatical unit, with some phonological properties; or is it primarily a phonological unit, with some grammatical properties; or is it equally a unit in grammar and in phonology? Ideas have varied.

The majority opinion has been that 'word' is primarily a unit of grammar although, as Matthews (1991: 209) notes 'the word tends to be a unit of phonology as well as grammar. In Latin, for example, it was the unit within which accents were determined'. Jespersen (1924: 92) states 'words are linguistic units, but they are not phonetic units' and Bloomfield (1933: 181) agrees that 'the word is not primarily a phonetic unit', while Meillet (1964: 136) maintains: 'le mot n'admet pas, comme la syllabe, une définition phonétique; en effet la notion de mot n'est pas phonétique, mais morphologique et syntaxique'.

Lyons (1968: 200–1) puts it this way: 'we will continue to assume, with the majority of linguists, that in all languages the morpheme is the minimum unit of grammatical analysis. The question we have set ourselves therefore is this: how shall we define a unit intermediate in rank between the morpheme and the sentence and one which will correspond fairly closely with our intuitive ideas of what is a 'word', these intuitive ideas being supported, in general, by the conventions of the orthographic tradition?' He then adds (p 204): 'in many languages the word is phonologically marked in some way'.

Pike (1947: 90) makes a clear distinction between 'grammatical units', which include 'morphemes, words, clitics, phrases and utterances', and 'phonological units', which include 'phonemes, syllables, stress groups, rhythm groups, intonation groups, utterances, and so on'. Halliday puts forward a similar view, having 'word' as one of the five 'units' in his grammatical theory, the full list being: morpheme, word, group, clause and sentence (see, for example, Halliday, McIntosh and Strevens 1964: 25).

Just a few linguists opt for the opposite position. Newman (1967: 182–3) begins his perceptive study of words and word classes in Yokuts with lists of phonological and grammatical criteria, stating 'morphological criteria serve to supplement the phonological features for delimiting the unit word'. And Wells (1947: 99) states 'because of their insufficiency, the phonemic criteria of a word must be supplemented, for every or nearly every language, by criteria of the second kind . . . the grammatical'.

Utilising phonological and grammatical criteria to define a single unit can, not unnaturally, lead to conflicts and ambiguities. Wells rightly states – working in terms of a single unit 'word' – 'in fact, the word is most solid as a unit in those languages where phonemic and grammatical criteria reinforce each other'.

An alternative position is to provide a set of criteria for deciding 'what is a word' that mix grammatical and phonological features, with no indication of what should be given priority when they do not provide the same result; see, for example, Bazell (1957: 25–6) and Chao (1968), discussed in §5.

We will – in §6 and §7 – suggest definitions for phonological word and for grammatical word, which should in each instance give a clear and unambiguous result. We will also, in §8, briefly discuss clitics, which may constitute a grammatical word but not an independent phonological word (clitics are discussed more fully in chapter 2). Before that it will be instructive to look – in §5 – at some of the types of criteria that have been put forward in the literature.

5   Some suggested criteria

In a short but classic discussion of 'the word' Bazell (1953: 67–8) states that 'criteria may be found which are either necessary, or sufficient, but not both'. If criterion X is necessary but not sufficient for defining 'word' this implies that all words show X but some other units show X as well. If criterion X is sufficient but not necessary this implies that any unit showing X is a word but there are also some words that do not show X.

Bazell then provides examples: 'the vowel-congruence [vowel harmony] of alternating morphs is a sufficient but not necessary criterion of word-unity in Turkish; the presence of at least one vowel is a necessary but not a sufficient criterion of word-status in English. The possibility of pause is a sufficient criterion, in most languages, of word-division'.

Lyons (1968: 200) paraphrases Meillet: 'a word may be defined as the unit of a particular meaning with a particular complex of sounds capable of a particular grammatical employment'. He then points out that this may be a necessary but is by no means a sufficient criterion – a phrase such as *the new book* or affixes such as *un-* and *-able* (as in *unacceptable*) also have these properties.

In contrast, Bloomfield's well-known definition of 'word' as a 'minimum free form' is plainly sufficient but not necessary. As Matthews (1991: 210) points out 'Latin *et* "and" would normally be called a word, and so would English *my* or *the*. But are these words that could occur on their own?' They could do so in a kind of citation ('Did you mean *et* or *aut*?' '*Et*.') but so too could a part of a word. Matthews recalls having heard a dialogue: '(A) "Did you say révise or dévise?". (B) "Re".'

In his grammar of spoken Mandarin, Chao (1968: 146–7) suggests that 'the definition of a word as a minimum free form (free at both ends) has often been felt to be too drastic, and weaker conditions have been proposed instead. In languages with clear and regular phonological marking, it is fairly simple to find word boundaries without trying to find an isolated occurrence of the word as an independent utterance. For example, words in Latin can in most cases be marked off by the penultimate and antepenultimate stress rules. In the Wu dialects, compound words are recognisable from their tone sandhi, which are different within words from the tone sandhi between words . . . In Mandarin, stress and tonal patterns can sometimes be used to mark off words, but potential pauses are more generally available for this purpose'. Note that Chao is here adding one or more phonological criteria to Bloomfield's essentially grammatical criterion.

The possibility of pausing before and/or after has often been suggested as a criterion for 'word'. In the quotation just given Chao appears to consider it as necessary and sufficient for Mandarin, whereas Bazell quoted it as a 'sufficient criterion, in most languages' – that is, if one can pause on either side of a unit it must be a word, but there are some other words, in addition.

In a typical synthetic language a case could be made for 'potential pause' being a necessary but not a sufficient criterion. That is, pauses can be at the boundaries of units which are both (a whole number of) phonological and (a whole number of) grammatical words – and one always has the possibility of pausing at such a boundary – but there may also occasionally be pauses in the middle of a word (typically, at a morpheme boundary which is also a syllable boundary), for example *it's very un-* <pause, perhaps including *um*> *suitable*. (This is discussed further under (f) in §7.) It may be that in analytic languages, such as Chinese, pauses can only occur at word boundaries, never in the middle of a word. And it is certainly the case that the more polysynthetic a language is – that is, the longer its words tend to be – the more likelihood there is of a pause being made in the middle of a word, in addition to between words. This applies particularly to languages which are polysynthetic and agglutinative, less to those that are polysynthetic and fusional.

Where one may pause in natural speech is undoubtedly related to (but not necessarily identical to) where people do pause when dictating. Firth (1957: 5) suggests that one way of discovering the words of a language is 'by slow dictation, using any feeling for word-units the native may have'. Sapir (1921: 33–4) is more definite, stating: 'no more convincing test could be desired than this, that the naive Indian, quite unaccustomed to the concept of the written word, has nevertheless no serious difficulty in dictating a text to a linguistic student word by word'. However, Bloomfield (1933: 178) puts forward a contrary opinion: 'people who have not learned to read and write, have some difficulty when, by any chance, they are called upon to make word divisions'.

An explanation for these differences of opinion may well be that the various scholars were dealing with different types of language. When working on Dyirbal – a mildly synthetic and predominantly agglutinative language from northern Australia – Dixon found that speakers did dictate phrase-by-phrase, or more slowly word-by-word, or more slowly still syllable-by-syllable (never morpheme-by-morpheme). He then worked on Jarawara, a polysynthetic but basically agglutinative language from southern Amazonia. Here a verb form might involve six or more morphemes making up twelve or more syllables. When speakers dictate this language at a pace that the linguist can transcribe they tend to break up long words into feet (disyllabic units) and to pause between these. (A morpheme may span two feet, and a foot may span two morphemes.) As mentioned before, the longer the average length of word in a language, the more likelihood there is of pausing at some specifiable places within the word.

Sapir concludes that the unit word has 'psychological validity' for speakers of American Indian languages with whom he worked, presumably in a similar manner to speakers of English and other European languages – see the quotation from Bolinger at the beginning of §1. This is again a matter which may depend on the typological profile of the language involved; we return to it in §11.

The ideal situation, of course, would be for there to be one or more criteria for 'word' that would apply in all languages and be both necessary and sufficient in each. Vendryes (1925: 55–6) seeks such a universal criterion, just for 'phonetic word'. He assesses accent (or stress) as a possible candidate but finds that while this is fine for some languages it is not adequate for all: 'in certain languages the position of the accent is clearly decided by the word-ending; in others the accent falls upon the final or penultimate syllable, and in others again upon the beginning of the word. But these cases do not exhaust all the possibilities; there are tongues, indeed, in which the variable accent gives no indication of the word-ending. On the other hand, it may happen that there will be only one accent in a group of several words; or, conversely, a single word may have two. Greek and Sanskrit prove that Indo-European possessed what are called enclitics, short words never used independently, but attached to the preceding word'. Note that Vendryes is here confusing two different kinds of unit. Although he sets out to discuss 'phonetic word', he then describes a clitic as a 'short word'. In fact a clitic is something which may have the status of a grammatical word but never that of a phonological word, being generally a stress-less element which attaches to some full phonological word (which does bear stress)[8] – see §8 below, and chapter 2. Leaving aside such instances it is the case that stress is not a significant feature in some languages, and is not then available for deciding 'what is a word'. Vendryes appears to be correct in inferring that accent/stress is not a universal criterion for 'phonological word'.

We have seen that many discussions of 'word' combine grammatical and phonological criteria without any clear statement concerning the relative statuses of these two kinds of criteria. The most sensible course of action is to keep apart the two kinds of criteria and the units which they define.

6   Phonological word

It is clear that there is no single criterion which can serve to define a unit 'phonological word' in every language. Rather there is a range of types of criteria such that every language that has a unit 'phonological word' (which is probably every language in the world) utilises a selection of these.

We can offer the following definition:

> A **phonological word** is a phonological unit larger than the syllable (in some languages it may minimally be just one syllable) which has at least one (and generally more than one) phonological defining property chosen from the following areas:
> (a) *Segmental features* – internal syllabic and segmental structure; phonetic realisations in terms of this; word boundary phenomena; pause phenomena.
> (b) *Prosodic features* – stress (or accent) and/or tone assignment; prosodic features such as nasalisation, retroflexion, vowel harmony.
> (c) *Phonological rules* – some rules apply only within a phonological word; others (external sandhi rules) apply specifically across a phonological word boundary.

Note that there is likely to be a close interaction between these types of features. For example, many phonological rules, under (c), operate in terms of stress

---

[8] Quite a lot of the discussion of word suffers from not recognising the unit clitic and its status with respect to grammatical and phonological criteria for 'word'.

assignment within a word, under (b); the appearance of certain phonemes at certain positions within a phonological word, under (a), may be a consequence of the operation of certain phonological rules, under (c).

We can now briefly discuss these types of criteria, one at a time.

(a) Segmental features. In some Australian languages, for example, a root or suffix may have one or more syllables but every phonological word must involve at least two syllables. In Walmatjari (Hudson 1978: 37–43) a disyllabic verb root may take a zero tense–mood suffix, e.g. *luwa-ø* 'hit!' (the allomorph of imperative for the conjugation to which this verb root belongs is zero), whereas a monosyllabic root must take a suffix that is at least one syllable in extent, e.g. *ya-nta* 'go!' (here the imperative allomorph is *-nta*). In the Mbyá variety of Guaraní (Tupí-Guaraní branch of Tupí family) a monosyllabic root, when used without affixes, is obligatorily reduplicated in order to satisfy the requirement that each word have at least two syllables, e.g. root *hū* 'black' becomes *hūʔhū* as a complete word (Guedes 1991: 44, 49). In other languages each word must have at least two moras; thus, if a word is monosyllabic it must include a long vowel or a diphthong – this happens in Warekena (Aikhenvald 1998: 409) and in Fijian (Dixon 1988a: 25).

Looking now at segmental restrictions, there are languages in which a word-medial syllable may begin with a lateral but a word-initial syllable may not, e.g. the Western Australian language Yingkarta (Dench 1998: 15). One of the most common restrictions is that a word may not commence with *r* (this applies for Tariana, see §2.2 of chapter 2). And there are languages in which a word-medial syllable may end in consonant but every phonological word must be vowel-final, e.g. the Pitjantjatjara dialect of the Western Desert language of Australia (Dixon 1980: 209). Phonotactic possibilities sometimes vary for words of different types; for example, nouns and verbs may show different phonotactic possibilities. In §3.1 of chapter 10, Joseph finds that there are restrictions on final consonants in Modern Greek for words of native origin, but these do not apply to recent loans.

Trubetzkoy (1969: 275) notes that in some languages 'certain distinctive oppositions' occur only in initial or final position: 'This is true, for example, for the aspirated occlusives of the Scottish-Gaelic dialect of Barra Island, the aspirated and recursive consonants of East Bengali, the recursive occlusives and emphatic palatalised consonants of Chechen'.

There are often different possibilities for sequences of phoneme types within a phonological word and across word boundaries; for example, a sequence of two vowels may only occur between words. In some Australian languages each word begins with a single consonant and ends with a vowel or a single consonant so that there can be a sequence of at most two consonants across a word boundary; however within a phonological word there can be a sequence of three consonants (for example, *bulmbun* 'mourning' in Yidiɲ). In contrast, Zoque allows syllables beginning in CCC and CCCC only in word-initial position (Wonderly 1951: 116). In Estonian 'only the first syllable of a word may begin with a vowel; every non-first syllable begins with a one mora consonant ... If a word ending in a vowel is followed by a word beginning with a vowel, the occurrence of the sequence serves as a boundary marker, since only the first syllable of a word may begin with a vowel' (Lehiste 1962: 179–80).

The realisation of vowel clusters between consecutive syllables may vary depending on whether the syllables belong to the same or different phonological words. In Fijian, for instance, certain vowel sequences are pronounced as diphthongs within a phonological word (e.g. the /oi/ in *boica* 'smell') but the same sequence across a phonological word boundary is pronounced as two distinct vowels e.g. *ilo.ilo* 'glass' (where '.' indicates a phonological word boundary within a grammatical word, here the boundary of an inherent reduplication).

Quite apart from the possible positioning of phonemes within a word, their phonetic realisation often depends on position in a word. For example 'in Japanese, where "g" initially is realised as the voiced obstruent *g*, and medially as a nasal *ŋ*, *g* is a positive and *ŋ* a negative non-phonemic boundary signal' (Trubetzkoy 1969: 292). Similarly, the operation of certain phonological rules – see (c) below – can signal boundaries. For instance, in the Papuan language Yimas 'the final nasal plus stop cluster simplification rule only applies at the end of words' while 'initial semivowel formation only applies at the beginning of words' (Foley 1991: 80).

For the Arawak language Bare, Aikhenvald (1996) states that aspirated consonants are only found in word-initial position (most of them come from phonological rules which only apply at this place in the word, e.g. *me-haba* '3pl-fingernail' → *mʰeba* 'their fingernails'). Thus, the presence of an aspirated consonant marks the beginning of a phonological word in Bare. And the presence of a nasalised vowel marks the end of a word, since this is the only structural slot in which nasalised vowels occur. In §3.2 of chapter 4, Henderson shows how the realisation of vowels at word boundaries in Arrernte constitutes a criterion for the recognition of these boundaries.

Meillet (1964: 137–40) has a useful discussion of processes applying at the ends of words in Indo-European languages (and see also Meillet 1970: 43–9). Trubetzkoy (1969: 273–97) provides an incisive discussion of boundary signals, mostly relating to the phonological word.

In some languages, words have special final features when followed by a pause. For example, in Warekena the occurrence of an *-hV* indicates that this must be the end of a phonological word that is followed by a pause (Aikhenvald 1996: 503; 1998: 411). In Semitic languages, such as Biblical Hebrew and Classical Arabic, words have distinctive forms when followed by a pause – see, for example, Gray (1934: 28–9) and Dresher (1994). The occurrence of pausal forms is never likely to constitute a necessary and sufficient criterion for recognising a phonological word, but can be a useful concomitant feature.

(b) Prosodic features. In very many – but not quite all – languages, stress (or accent) provides one criterion for phonological word. Many languages have fixed stress – on the first or last or penultimate or antepenultimate syllable (or mora) of a phonological word. It should then be possible to ascertain the position of word boundaries from the location of stress. (For example, Olawsky shows, in §1.2 of chapter 8, that stress falls on the penultimate syllable in Dagbani; see also the examples given in Bloomfield 1933: 182 and Trubetzkoy 1969: 277–8.) The placement of stress may be linked to the segmental properties of phonemes; for example, in Latin stress falls on the penultimate syllable if it is long and on the antepenultimate if the penultimate is short.

In languages with contrastive stress there will generally be just one syllable with primary stress per word – see Weinreich (1954) on Yiddish, and Joseph and Philippaki-Warburton (1987: 242–3) on Modern Greek. Although here phonological word boundaries cannot be deduced from the position of stress, one can tell from the number of stressed syllables in an utterance how many phonological words it contains (and one can deduce that a word boundary must lie somewhere between two stressed syllables).

However, in some languages stress placement may depend on a combination of morphological and phonological factors. In such cases stress may not be a useful criterion for phonological word.

A tonal system may relate to the syllable or to the phonological word – the latter applies in Lhasa Tibetan (see Sprigg 1955) and to the Papuan language Kewa (Franklin 1971, Franklin and Franklin 1978), for example.

A suprasegmental prosody such as nasalisation or retroflexion will have a syntagmatic extent, and this may be a phonological word. For example, Allen (1957) provides a prosodic account of aspiration in nominals for Hāṛautī (Rajasthani) in terms of the unit 'word'. Among his conclusions is: 'a breathy transition is never followed or preceded by another breathy transition within the same word'. Robins (1957) describes vowel nasality in Sundanese as having prosodic extent. A nasal consonant engenders nasalisation of a following vowel and of all subsequent vowels if separated from it only by a glottal stop or *h*; this continues until a word boundary is reached. (Robins points out that this applies to all nominal words except for loans and onomatopoeics.)

In Terena, an Arawak language, Bendor-Samuel (1966) describes how each word has one of three prosodies – nasalisation, yodisation (involving fronting and raising of all vowels, similar to vowel harmony) or neither nasalisation nor yodisation.

There is in Sanskrit a prosody of retroflexion which extends until the end of a word, under certain conditions. Allen (1951: 940) translates Pāṇini's rule as:

'r̥, r̄, r, ṣ, in spite of intervening vowels, gutturals (including *h*), labials (including *v*), *y* and Anusvāra, change *n* to *ṇ* if followed by vowels, *n*, *m*, *y*, *v*'.

Vowel harmony is a prosody which operates over a certain syntagmatic extent, and this is often the phonological word. In Turkish, for instance, the vowels in certain types of word must either be all front or all back (Bloomfield 1933: 181; Waterson 1956). Trubetzkoy (1969: 285) mentions an associated phenomenon (found in Kazakh and a number of other Turkic languages) which he calls 'synharmonism' – a word can contain only front vowels and palatalised consonants or only back vowels and velarised consonants. This is also found in North-eastern Neo-Aramaic (Jastrow 1997: 352–3).

(c) Phonological rules. In many languages the optimum analysis involves recognising underlying forms for roots and affixes and then a number of phonological rules which apply to generate the surface forms. Each rule applies over a certain syntagmatic extent. Many rules apply just within the phonological word while some apply across a phonological word boundary.

We can first look at rules that only apply within a phonological word. In Hungarian, for instance, a rule of palatalisation assimilates dentals *d*, *t*, *l* or *n* to a following semi-vowel *j*, yielding the corresponding palatal sound, and the rule applies just within a phonological word (Kenesei, Vago and Fenyvesi 1998: 438, 440; Nespor and Vogel 1986: 123–4). In the Australian language Yidiɲ (Dixon 1977a: 42–98; 1977b) some trisyllabic nominals are assigned an underlying form ending with a morphophoneme, e.g. *gajarrA* 'brown possum'. There are the following rules that apply within a phonological word:

(i) If a phonological word has an odd number of syllables then the penultimate vowel is lengthened.

(ii) If a morphophoneme *A* is the last segment of a phonological word, it is omitted; otherwise it is realised as *a*.

We can compare what happens to *gajarrA* with zero suffix (for absolutive case) and with suffix *-gu* (for purposive case).

(1) underlying form *gajarrA*   *gajarrAgu*
      rule (i)   *gaja:rrA* –
      rule (ii)   *gaja:rr*   *gajarragu*

A root plus monosyllabic suffix (such as purposive *-gu*) forms one phonological word. But a disyllabic suffix always commences a separate phonological word. For example, *gajarrA* 'brown possum' plus privative suffix *-gimbal* 'without' gives *gajarrA.gimbal*, a single grammatical word that consists of two phonological words (again using '.' for a phonological word boundary within a grammatical word). To this can be added purposive suffix *-gu*, which is part of the same phonological word as *-gimbal*. Rules (i) and (ii) then apply separately to the two phonological words within this grammatical word.

(2)   underlying form   *gajarrA.gimbalgu*
         rule (i)   *gaja:rrA.gimba:lgu*
         rule (ii)   *gaja:rr.gimba:lgu*

If *gajarrAgimbalgu* had been one phonological word, it would consist of an even number of syllables. Rule (i) would not apply and the surface form would be *gajarragimbalgu; the occurring form is, in fact, *gaja:rr.gimba:lgu*.

In §3.1 of chapter 4, Henderson refers to 'prosodically conditioned allomorphy'. In effect, this involves phonological rules for the realisation of a vowel in a suffix (as *i* or *e*), depending on the number of preceding syllables within the phonological word. Similar rules in Jarawara are mentioned by Dixon in §2 of chapter 5.

In some languages the phonological rules that apply within a phonological word relate to stress or tone, and are thus an extension of (b).

Then there are some languages in which a special set of '(external) sandhi rules' apply across word boundaries. In these languages word boundaries may be recognised partly by the operation of the sandhi rules. Allen (1972) is a detailed account of Sandhi in Sanskrit. Mutation in Celtic languages is a phenomenon of the same general type (see, for example, Gregor 1980: 149–57; Ball 1993: 9–10). (Rice 1990 has a useful discussion of types of phonological rule and the syntagmatic domains over which they apply.)

There can also be unusual, language-particular criteria for wordhood. Henderson (in §3.4 of chapter 4) describes how, in olden days, speakers of Arrernte used a play language style called 'Rabbit Talk'. This involves relocating the initial syllable of a polysyllabic word to the end of the word, and thus indicates word boundaries.

Different types of criteria are relevant to defining the phonological word in different languages. And the relative importance and weighting of criteria differ from language to language. For example, in some languages a rule of vowel harmony may constitute a necessary and sufficient condition for recognising phonological words, whereas in others it may be sufficient but not necessary (see Bazell's remarks on Turkish quoted in §5).

Sign languages employ a different medium of expression from their spoken cousins. Nonetheless, criteria similar to those discussed above have been enunciated. In §2 of chapter 6, Zeshan summarises Sandler's discussion of phonological word in Israeli sign language, including phonological rules which operate within and across phonological words.

7   Grammatical word

For phonological word we could offer only a number of *types of* criteria, no one of which applies in every language. In the case of grammatical word it is possible to put forward universal criteria, although tempered by a number of caveats.

> A **grammatical word** consists of a number of grammatical elements which:
> (a) always occur together, rather than scattered through the clause (the criterion of cohesiveness);
> (b) occur in a fixed order;
> (c) have a conventionalised coherence and meaning.

A few comments are in order on the criteria.

Van Wyk (1968: 546) translates Reichling's (1935) 'two basic criteria for word identity' as 'internal immutability' and 'syntagmatic mobility' – these relate to our (a) and (b). Cohesiveness is a strong criterion. It is sometimes said that in Portuguese a pronominal clitic can intervene between verb root and future tense suffix (a putative exception to (a)). However, the facts are as follows. Future tense marking in present-day Portuguese has developed from a periphrastic form involving the verbal infinitive plus an inflected form of the verb 'have'. The form of the 'have' auxiliary first developed into an enclitic which can follow an object pronominal enclitic added to the infinitive form of a verb (such as *procurar* 'look for'), for example *procurá=lo=ei* 'I will look for it' (where = marks a clitic boundary). An alternative is to place the object pronoun before the verb ('it' is then just *o*), giving *eu* (I) *o* (it) *procurar-ei* 'I will look for it'. In this construction the future tense (plus 1sg subject) form *-ei* has evolved further, to be a suffix to the verb.[9] The important point is that in *procurá=lo=ei* the *=ei* is a clitic, not a suffix.

We can illustrate the criterion of fixed order for Dyirbal, where there are two forms with similar meanings, *bulayi* 'two' and *jarran* 'two, each of two, a pair'. One could say either of:

(3) *Ban*   *yibi*   *bulayi*   *bani-nyu*
     DETERMINER(fem)   woman   two   come-PAST
     The two women came

(4) *Ban*   *yibi*   *jarran*   *bani-nyu*
     DETERMINER(fem)   woman   two   come-PAST
     The two women came

Dyirbal is a language with remarkably free word order. In (3) the four forms *ban*, *yibi*, *bulayi* and *baninyu* can be permuted and occur in any order (e.g. *yibi ban baninyu bulayi*). However in (4) *jarran* must follow *yibi*; here we can only

---

[9] Verbs of the form *procurá=lo=ei* are still freely used in the Portuguese spoken in Portugal, but in Brazil they are confined to the written register and to a formal spoken style which deliberately reflects the conventions of writing (Prista 1966: 60–1).

permute *ban*, *yibi*-plus-*jarran* and *baninyu*. This shows that *bulayi* is a separate grammatical word, the adjective 'two', while -*jarran* is a nominal suffix, with dual meaning. (Further justification is provided at (7–10) below.)

Concerning criterion (b), it is in fact sometimes possible for affixes to occur in alternative ordering within a word, but there must then be a difference in meaning – that is, a change in (b) affects (c), the coherence and meaning of the word. Matthews (1991: 213) provides a nifty pair of examples from English: *nation-al-is(e)-ation* and *sens(e)-ation-al-ise* (these examples are further discussed at (5–6) below). Dyirbal has a rich array of derivational affixes to nouns including the dual suffix -*jarran*, as in (4), and -*gabun* 'another'. These can occur in either order with, of course, a meaning difference. Thus *yibi-jarran-gabun* is 'another two women' (where there have been a number of pairs of women and here is another pair) and *yibi-gabun-jarran* is 'two other women' (where there have been a number of women and here are two more). (See Dixon 1972: 232–3 where a further example is given.) Nedjalkov (1992) illustrates alternative orderings of the affixes 'want to' and 'begin' ('begin to want' versus 'want to begin') in Evenki.

In their seminal account of Siouan (§2 of chapter 7), Rankin et al. show that the order of elements in a word is not according to a fixed template, as it is in most languages. The Siouan languages thus constitute something of an exception to criterion (b).

Criterion (c) indicates that the speakers of a language think of a word as having its own coherence and meaning. That is, they may talk about a word (but are unlikely to talk about a morpheme). Confronted with a word like *untruthfulness*, people may talk in various ways about *true* or *truth* or *untruth* or *truthfulness* or *untruthfulness*s, etc., but scarcely of -*th* or -*ness* (although they may possibly talk about the suffix -*ful*, since it is homonymous with the word *full* which has some semantic similarities, or about *un*-, since this has a clear meaning, of negation). And it must be noted that, while the meaning of a word is related to the meanings of its parts, it is often not exactly inferable from them. *Blackbird* refers to a particular species of bird that is black, not to any black bird. The noun *action* is a nominalisation from *act* but has a shifted meaning – not every instance of 'acting' could be described as an 'action' (e.g. 'She acted in Hamlet' or 'He acted the fool' would not normally be).

Zeshan provides an illuminating account of grammatical word in sign languages, in §2 of chapter 6. Criterion (b), that the parts of a word should occur in a fixed order, has to be modified. Since sign languages make use of several articulators (two hands, facial gestures), it is possible to have simultaneous components. (Zeshan draws an analogy to Semitic languages, which have discontinuous roots – consisting of three consonants – into which grammatical affixes – in the form of two vowels – are placed.) Zeshan shows that criteria (a) and (c) do have straightforward application to sign languages. She also describes (in her §3.1) how compounds involve temporal compression, elimination of repetition, and various processes of assimilation.

Matthews (1991: 213) suggests a further criterion. Whereas syntactic processes may be recursive (e.g. a relative clause within a relative clause, or just saying something like *very very very good*) we find that:

> (d) Morphological processes involved in the formation of words tend to be non-recursive. That is, one element will not appear twice in a word.

But, as Matthews points out, this only applies to some languages (Latin being an example). In Turkish, for instance, a causative derivation can apply twice within a given word, so that two instances of the causative suffix occur in sequence (although with slightly different forms). In Dyirbal an intransitive verb (e.g. *nyinay-* 'sit') can take the comitative derivational suffix *-mal-*, producing transitive stem *nyinay-mal-* 'sit together with'. This can then be made intransitive by adding the reflexive suffix *-rriy-* and then a second token of comitative *-mal-* may be added to this, giving *nyinay-ma-rri-mal-* 'two (people) sit with (a third)' – see Dixon (1972: 98, 246–7). (And one can say things like *re-rediscover* in English, although these are highly marked.)

In §2.2 of chapter 9, Harris examines certain derivational circumfixes in Georgian which exhibit some of the characteristics of recursion, but concludes that they are not truly recursive. However, Rankin et al. (chapter 7) show that locative affixes are recursive in Siouan languages, and that the positioning of locatives can disturb the placement of pronominal affixes.

We also find some instances of a single grammatical category being marked twice in a word. In Yiddish, plural is generally marked just at the end of a word, as in *hant* 'hand', diminutive *hant-l'*, diminutive plural *hent-lex*. There is, however, a class of nouns where plural is marked twice, by suffix *-im* to the root and by the plural form, *-lex*, of the diminutive suffix. (Note that these are hybrid forms, including the Hebrew marker *-im* together with plural diminutive *-lex* of Germanic origin.) Thus we get (Bochner 1984: 414–15):

> *poyer* 'peasant'   *poyer-l'*, diminutive
> *poyer-im*, plural   *poyer-im-lex*, diminutive plural

Aikhenvald (1999a) gives examples of both plural and gender being marked twice – both within a noun and within a verb – in Tariana.

It is generally the case that a word is centred on a root or else on a combination of roots (a compound stem). Various derivational processes may be applied to the root or compound stem, each in its turn forming a derived stem. Thus the examples from Matthews quoted earlier, of *-al* and *-ise* applying either before or after *-ation*, involve the following derivations:

(5)   noun root   *nation*
    add *-al*, deriving an adjective stem   *nation-al*
    add *-ise*, deriving a verb stem   *nation-al-ise*
    add *-ation*, deriving a noun stem   *national-is-ation*

(6)   verb root   *sense*
    add *-ation*, deriving a noun stem   *sens-ation*
    add *-al*, deriving an adjective stem   *sens-ation-al*
    add *-ise*, deriving a verb stem   *sens-ation-al-ise*

Once all derivational processes have applied, the resulting stem takes the inflection appropriate to its word class. *Nationalisation* is a derived noun and can take the plural suffix *-s*; *sensationalise* is a derived verb and takes one of the inflectional suffixes available for verbs in English, *-s*, *-ed*, *-ing* or zero.

In some languages there can be a variant type of grammatical word, with no root at all (or perhaps with a zero root). Dixon provides examples of this from Jarawara, in chapter 5. The 1sg pronoun prefix *o-* can attach to the feminine declarative suffix *-ke*, to form *o-ke*, which is both one grammatical word and one phonological word. And some verbal suffixes may be added to an auxiliary root, *-na-*, but cause the auxiliary to drop if it also bears a prefix; thus, underlying *o-na-bisa* '1sg-AUXILIARY-ALSO' becomes *o-bisa*, one (phonological and grammatical) word which consists just of prefix *o-* and suffix *-bisa*.

In §6 we discussed boundary phenomena, characteristic features of the beginning and end of phonological words in particular languages. Similar features can be recognised for grammatical words. Van Wyk (1968: 554) mentions: 'in Northern Sotho, for example, the negative morpheme *ga-* only appears on initial boundaries of verbs and the relative morpheme on the final boundaries of verbs'. Thus, the negative prefix *ga-* always marks the beginning of a grammatical word in Northern Sotho. Similarly, in English past tense suffix *-ed* (with allomorphs /-t/, /-d/ and /-ɪd/) marks the end of a verb.[10] These are language-particular criteria which can be of great help to a linguist working on a previously undescribed language.

Each language has its own morphological profile. In some cases all affixes are optional but in others a certain type of affix is obligatory – an inflectional system. Just in languages with a single inflectional system on each class of words, there is a further criterion for grammatical word, concerning the distribution of inflections:

(e) There will be just one inflectional affix per word.

---

[10] One must of course be careful to distinguish this *-ed* from an *ed* which is the final part of an unanalysable root. Compare *bak(e)-ed* and *naked*. The different statuses of the *ed*'s is brought out in the phonological realisations: /beikt/ and /neikɪd/.

In Latin each word in an NP must show the appropriate inflection for number and case. The same applies in Dyirbal, but just for case. Harking back to (3–4) suppose that we have NPs:

(7)   *ban   yibi   bulayi*

(8)   *ban   yibi-jarran*

Now, when dative case *-gu* is added to these two NPs we get:

(9)   *bagun   yibi-gu   bulayi-gu*

(10)   *bagun   yibi-jarran-gu*

The dative form of the determiner *ba-n* is *ba-gu-n*, with the dative suffix *-gu* coming between root *ba-* and feminine suffix *-n*. The point to note is that in (9) noun *yibi* 'woman' and adjective *bulayi* 'two' are separate words and each takes the dative suffix *-gu*. But in (10) *yibi-jarran* is one word and it takes a single token of *-gu*, after the dual suffix *-jarran*.

In a language where inflections do not go onto every word of an NP (but only, say, onto the head, or only onto the last word or the first word) this criterion would have to be modified but could still be applicable. In a language such as Turkish or Hungarian, where number and case are separate, obligatory suffixes, the criterion would have to be modified in a further way but again could still be applicable. However, it may not be applicable in languages which permit double case.[11] The criterion may also apply with respect to inflections on verbs.

We can now look at two of the most quoted criteria for word, concerning the placement of pauses and the ability of words to make up complete utterances.

Bloomfield (1933: 180) and Lyons (1968: 202) lay stress on the criterion of uninterruptability:

(f) A speaker may pause between words but not within a word.

Bloomfield (1933: 180) exemplifies this with: 'one can say *black – I should say, bluish-black – birds*, but one cannot similarly interrupt the compound word *blackbirds*'.

This criterion should, however, be treated with caution. Firstly, it is at best a tendency. In a synthetic language one certainly tends to pause more often between words than within words but it is by no means unheard of to pause between morphemes within a word – as mentioned in §5 one does hear things like *it's very un-* <pause> *suitable*. Secondly, this applies better to synthetic

---

[11] Dench and Evans (1988) and Evans (1995) describe true instances of double case marking. Note that some things that have been called 'double case' – by many of the contributors to Plank (1995) for example – involve genitive (a marker of function within an NP) followed by a marker of function within a clause; see Dixon (1998) and Aikhenvald (1999b) for discussion of this.

than to polysynthetic languages – the longer the words of a language are, the more likely there are to be pauses in the middle of them (as mentioned above, this applies especially to languages which are polysynthetic and agglutinative).

The third caveat is the most important. Pausing appears in most cases (although perhaps not in all) to be related not to grammatical word but to phonological word. In English, for instance, there are just a few examples of two grammatical words making up one phonological word, e.g. *don't, won't, he'll*. One would not pause between the grammatical words *do-* and *-n't* in the middle of the phonological word *don't* (one could of course pause between the *do* and *not* of *do not*, since these are distinct phonological words).

The places where expletives may be inserted, as a matter of emphasis, are closely related to (but not necessarily identical to) the places where a speaker may pause. Expletives are normally positioned at word boundaries (at positions which are the boundary for grammatical word and also for phonological word). But there are exceptions – for instance the sergeant-major's protest that *I won't have no more insu bloody bordination from you lot* or such things as *Cinda bloody rella* and *fan fucking tastic*. McCarthy (1982) shows that in English expletives may only be positioned immediately before a stressed syllable. What was one unit now becomes two phonological words (and the expletive is a further word). Each of these new phonological words is stressed on its first syllable; this is in keeping with the fact that most phonological words in English are stressed on the first syllable.

Associated with pause is the phenomenon of 'self-repair'. If a speaker realises that they have made a mistake in the middle of an utterance, they are likely to pause. The mistake will have to be corrected and the utterance resumed. The interesting question is how far (if at all) one has to go back, in this process of repair. Woodbury shows how in Cup'ik (a highly polysynthetic language) 'if a pause or speech error occurs in the middle of a phonological word, the speaker will go all the way back to the beginning of the word and start again' – see (57) in §7.4 of chapter 3.

We can now turn to the criterion of isolatability – Sweet's 'ultimate or inde-composable sentence' and Bloomfield's 'minimum free form':

(g) A word may constitute a complete utterance, all by itself.

When this criterion is examined it is seen to apply neither to grammatical word nor to phonological word. Rather it applies to a combination of these – to a unit which is both a grammatical word and a phonological word. Or to something which is a grammatical word consisting of a whole number of phonological words; or to something which is a phonological word consisting of a whole number of grammatical words. In §5.4 of chapter 3, Woodbury states that every grammatical word in Cup'ik may stand alone as a complete utterance, except for most clitics (which are one grammatical word, but not a separate phonological word).

That is, a grammatical word which is just part of a phonological word may not make up a complete utterance (e.g. *n't* from English *don't*). Nor may a phonological word which is part of a grammatical word (e.g. *gimba:lgu* from Yidiɲ *gaja:rr.gimba:lgu* in (2) of §6).

Even then, criterion (g) has no more than limited applicability – to only *some* words in *some* languages, depending on the conventions for discourse organisation and on other factors; see §11 below.

Note also that, in certain speech situations, part of a word may make up a complete utterance. Matthews' example of an utterance consisting just of 'Re' was mentioned in §5. And we have heard an airline clerk ask a passenger whether they would like a smoking or non-smoking seat, the answer being just 'Non'.

In summary, (a–c) are the main criteria for defining a grammatical word, with the caveats mentioned above. Criterion (d), non-recursiveness, and (e), distribution of inflections, do apply well in certain languages. The principle of uninterruptability, (f), is only a tendency – which may apply more to phonological than to grammatical words – but can be a useful support for the other criteria. And (g), isolatability, is again a tendency which can be of use when it is realised that it only applies to a unit which consists of a whole number of (one or more) grammatical words and also a whole number (one or more) of phonological words.

8   Clitics

The term clitic is often used to refer to something that is a grammatical word but not a complete phonological word (for example, it does not take stress). A clitic is attached to a host phonological word, as a sort of optional extra. There are some items that can have the form either of a clitic or of a full phonological word. For example, *the* in English is generally a proclitic [ðə=] but can, when used contrastively, be accorded a full vowel which is stressed. [ðíː] (as in 'Is that *the* man you saw yesterday?').

Clitics may sometimes form part of a host phonological word for purposes of assignment of prosodic features (such as stress and vowel harmony) and for the application of phonological rules. More often, they are simply added – as an extra, unstressed syllable – to a fully articulated phonological word after all processes and rules have applied. Consider an example from Yidiɲ of verb root *warrŋgi-* 'do all around', past tense *-ɲu* and the clitic with meaning 'now' which has form *=la* after a vowel and *=ala* after a consonant. Recall, from (c) in §6, rule (i), which states that if a phonological word has an odd number of syllables then the penultimate vowel is lengthened. A further rule, (iii), omits the final *-u* of past tense *-ɲu* from a word with an odd number of syllables. We get the following derivation (Dixon 1977a: 237):

underlying form	*warrŋgiɲu*	*=(a)la*
rule (i) applies to an odd-syllabled form	*warrŋgi:ɲu*	*=(a)la*
rule (iii) applies to an odd-syllabled form	*warrŋgi:ɲ*	*=(a)la*
the clitic attaches	*warrŋgi:ɲ=ala*	

If the clitic were attached to the underlying form *warrŋgiɲu* we would have *warrŋgiɲula* which has four syllables and rules (i) and (iii) would then not apply. But these rules do apply to *warrŋgiɲu*, showing that *=(a)la* is added to the phonological word as the very last step in word-building, after all other rules.

One then effectively has two 'levels' of phonological word: (i) that without any clitics; and (ii) that with one or more clitics. Woodbury (in §7.1 of chapter 3) states that, for Cup'ik, (ii) is the phonological word proper (which he labels PW), while (i) is 'a subdomain of the phonological word' (which he calls PW –).

Sometimes if two clitics occur in sequence they may come together to form one phonological word. In Boumaa Fijian, for example, the preposition *i*= 'to' is generally a proclitic to a following noun and so is the common article *a*=, as in *i=vanúa* 'to land' (as opposed to 'to sea') and *a=vanúa* 'the land' (where = indicates a clitic boundary). Note that primary stress goes on the syllable containing the second mora from the end of a word and secondary stress on the syllable containing the fourth mora; here the clitics *i*= and *a*= bear no stress, showing that they are attached to the phonological word *vanúa* after the stress rule has applied. However, when the preposition and article are used together (the article then has allomorph *na*) they make up a phonological word, which has penultimate stress, *í=na vanúa* 'to the [place on] land' (see the appendix to this chapter, and Dixon 1988a: 116, 29). Similar 'clitic-only' words are reported by Aikhenvald for Tariana (chapter 2) and by Woodbury for Cup'ik (chapter 3).

Chapter 2, by Aikhenvald, commences with a comprehensive typology of fifteen parameters in terms of which clitics vary – the kind of host to which they attach, the direction of attachment, etc. The second part of her chapter describes the rich set of proclitics and enclitics in Tariana, comparing their properties with those of prefixes and suffixes. Most of the following chapters include descriptions of the behaviour of clitics in individual languages. Jarawara, in chapter 5, is unusual in not requiring a category of clitics for its grammatical description.

In §3.2 of chapter 6, Zeshan points out that a set of clitics can be recognised for various sign languages. For example, a deictic index can be cliticised to a double-handed host sign; the left hand fully articulates the host sign while, part way through the articulation, the right-hand makes the index clitic.

Most scholars consider Modern Greek to have clitics. However, in chapter 10, Joseph adopts the theoretical stand that the recognition of clitics should be avoided – for this or for any other language. One should simply have words (of a variety of types) and affixes (of a variety of types). Joseph examines the properties of the 'little elements' that are normally classed as clitics in Modern Greek, and suggests that some of them could be treated as a type of word ('prosodically weak or deficient words') and others as a type of affix. Matthews, in the following chapter, comments on this position. (Note that Joseph is the only contributor not to explicitly distinguish between phonological words and grammatical words, and then to look for coincidences and mismatches between them. A major type of mismatch, in many languages, concerns clitics, which each make up one grammatical word but do not constitute a separate phonological word.)

9   Relationship between grammatical and phonological words

Rather few linguists, in writing grammars of languages, have clearly distinguished between phonological and grammatical words. Sometimes the unit word is taken for granted, with no justification or criteria offered. Sometimes criteria are offered but they may mix grammatical and phonological characteristics with no clear discussion of whether these always define the same unit. However, there are sufficient clear descriptions for us to be able to recognise each of three simple types of relationship between the two kinds of word: (a) the units coincide; (b) a phonological word may consist of several grammatical words; and (c) a grammatical word may consist of several phonological words. We discuss these first, before looking at more complex relationships, in (d).

(a) Phonological and grammatical word coincide. Newman (1967) clearly distinguishes phonological and grammatical criteria in Yokuts, implying that these converge on a single unit 'word'. A similar conclusion is explicitly stated by Czaykowska-Higgins (1998) for Moses-Columbia Salish (see the discussion at the end of this section).

A considerable search of grammars has found almost none which provide explicit criteria for phonological word and for grammatical word and state that these coincide. It may be that grammars tend only to mention instances where the two units do not coincide; or that in those languages which have been investigated from this point of view the two units never exactly coincide. More work is needed on this.

(b) Phonological word consists of (usually) one or (sometimes) more than one grammatical words. Many languages have clitics, which are grammatical words that do not constitute a phonological word on their own but must be attached to a phonological word primarily associated with some other grammatical word, e.g. -n't as in English *mustn't*. In Dyirbal there is a clitic -*ma* (marking a clause as a polar interrogative) which is a grammatical word that attaches, as an enclitic,

to the end of the first phonological word of the sentence. For example, the interrogative version of (3) would be *Ban=ma yibi bulayi baninyu* 'Did the two women come?'

Some of the chapters below provide examples of one phonological word consisting of two grammatical words. In Tariana (chapter 2), Cup'ik (chapter 3), Arrernte (chapter 4) and Dagbani (chapter 8) this involves clitics. In Jarawara (chapter 5) the auxiliary verb *-na-* is the core of a grammatical word. It generally takes one or more affixes and then makes up one phonological word (which must have at least two moras). When it occurs without affixes, it encliticises to the preceding non-inflecting verb, e.g. *amó=na* 'he/she sleeps' (and it is a full constituent of this phonological verb, for purposes of stress assignment).

Nespor and Vogel (1986) provide useful discussion of how phonological word and grammatical word boundaries do not coincide, in a number of languages. However, in no case do they provide full criteria for phonological word and grammatical word in a given language.[12]

(c) Grammatical word consists of (usually) one or (sometimes) more than one phonological words. In Yidiɲ we may find one grammatical word consisting of two phonological words; this applies both to nouns, illustrated in (2) above, and to verbs. Foley (1991: 80–7) reports a similar situation in the Papuan language Yimas.

There are a number of types of grammatical construction which typically fall under this heading. A compound is by definition one grammatical word but in many languages the components are separate phonological words. For nominal compounds in Yimas, Foley (1991: 86) notes 'each of the nouns in these compounds constitute a phonological word in themselves, as shown by the individual primary stresses. Yet they form one grammatical word in that there is only one inflection for number'. Similar remarks apply for compounds in Fijian (Dixon 1988a: 22), in Jarawara (§2 of chapter 5) and in Georgian (§5 of chapter 9). Nespor and Vogel (1986: 120) state that in Turkish 'additional evidence that the two members of a compound do not form a single phonological word is provided by vowel harmony'.

These languages are different from English. Bloomfield's definition of word as a 'minimum free form' appears to encounter difficulties with compounds such as *bláckbird* since *black* and *bird* are themselves minimum free forms.

---

[12] There are also a number of errors and inaccuracies in their account. For instance, on page 34 they refer to 'Yidiɲ, a language spoken in Central Australia' and on page 134 to 'Yidiɲ, an Australian language spoken in northeast Queensland'. The same language is referred to and in fact the same data is presented on the two pages; but it is presented in a misleading manner. Nespor and Vogel say that underlying *gumari-daga-ɲu* becomes *gumá:ridagá:ɲu* after a rule of penultimate lengthening has occurred. In fact this is an intermediate stage in derivation, not an occurring form. The surface form is (after further rule application) *gumá:ridagá:ɲ* (Dixon 1977a: 91; 1977b: 28).

He is able to argue that *bird* in *bláckbird* is not the same as *bird* in *bláck bírd* since it does not bear major stress. This argument works for English, and also for Dagbani (see chapter 8). It would not be applicable to Yimas, Fijian, Jarawara or Turkish; for these languages a compound is one grammatical but two phonological words.

Arrernte provides an interesting situation. Henderson (in chapter 4) states that a compound is one grammatical word which consists of two phonological words (since each part of the compound has its own stress). However, the stress patterns on the two parts of a compound differ from those on the same two words in syntactic association; he concludes that the parts of a compound 'constitute distinct phonological words which are conjoined into a single higher phonological word'.

In some languages with verb serialisation, the verbs involved are effectively compounded together – see Foley (1991: 84–5) on Yimas. This is another typical instance where a grammatical word (the serialised verb compound) may consist of several phonological words (the individual verbs involved).

The other typical example of a grammatical word consisting of two phonological words involves reduplication. A reduplicated form is one grammatical word (if it were not it would be simply repetition) but in many languages the reduplication boundary is also a phonological word boundary. We saw under (a) in §6 how a sequence of *o*-plus-*i* forms a diphthong within a phonological word in Fijian but in an inherent reduplication like *ilo.ilo* 'glass' each vowel is pronounced as a separate syllable. (Stress rules support this analysis – see Dixon 1988a: 24.) Similar remarks apply to Jarawara – see §2 in chapter 5. In the Australian language Warrgamay a long vowel may only occur in the initial syllable of a phonological word. The only grammatical words with two long vowels are *ji:ji:* 'bird (generic)' and *bi:lbi:l* 'pee wee (bird species)', words with inherent reduplication (Dixon 1981: 17). This shows that in Warrgamay, as in many other languages, a reduplication boundary is also a phonological word boundary within a grammatical word.

A division between phonological words within a grammatical word may have other types of motivation in individual languages. For example, Dixon shows (in §4.4 of chapter 5) that there are just a few verbal suffixes in Jarawara which commence a new phonological word within a grammatical word if they are preceded by more than a single mora within the grammatical word.

(d) More complex relationships between grammatical and phonological word. We only know of two instances where one type of word does not consist of a whole number of instances of the other type. The first is in Fijian and it involves the derivational prefix *i*-, which is added to a verb and derives a noun, e.g. *sele* 'to cut, slice' → *i-sele* 'knife'. The unusual feature is that *i*- coheres with a preceding common article *a* to form one phonological word with it:

(11)   GRAMMATICAL WORDS   ARTICLE   DERIVED NOUN

$$a \; + \; i\text{-} \quad\quad sele$$

PHONOLOGICAL WORDS   1   2

(The criteria for phonological word and for grammatical word in Fijian are given in the Appendix.)

The grammatical words are *a* and *i-sele*, but the phonological words are *ai* (pronounced as a diphthong, which only happens within a phonological word) and *sele*. Thus the grammatical word *i-sele* consists of one full phonological word (*sele*) and a part of another (*i* from *ai*) while the phonological word *ai* consists of one full grammatical word (the article *a*) and a part of another (the derivational prefix *i-* from the noun *i-sele*).

The early missionaries to Fiji found it hard to decide where to write the word boundary in a phrase like (11). There are three possibilities:

(12)   i. *ai sele*   ii. *a i sele*   iii. *a isele*

Hazlewood (1850), in his grammar, opted for (i), Churchward (1941) criticised this and preferred (ii). Then Milner (1956) went to the other extreme and used (iii). In fact there is merit in each of these alternatives: (i) shows the phonological word, (iii) the grammatical word, while (ii) simultaneously recognises both kinds of word boundary. There are fuller details in the appendix (see also Dixon 1988a: 21–31; 1988b).

The second known example of one type of word consisting of other than a whole number of instances of the other type of word concerns Arrernte, and is described by Henderson in §4.3 of chapter 4. It relates to the VC(C) syllable structure which Henderson posits for this language.

We can now return to the topic of orthographic word, briefly mentioned in §4.2. The question is: if there is a difference between phonological word and grammatical word, where do people prefer to insert a space – between grammatical words or between phonological words? In order to provide a fully informed answer to this we would need an array of studies for individual languages, which is not at present available. But some preliminary remarks may be offered.

In many cases people will place word boundaries around the larger unit. Thus, if a phonological word involves two grammatical words they will write spaces around the phonological word (for example, *mustn't* in English) and not between the grammatical words within the phonological word. And if a grammatical word consists of two phonological words they will write spaces before and after the grammatical word and not between the two constituent phonological words (this applies to reduplication and compounding in many languages).

But what of case (d), in Fijian, where there is no 'whole number of units' inclusion between the two kinds of word? Well, most spontaneous written material (and the Bible translation) in Fijian work in terms of alternative (i) in (12). Similarly, when speakers dictate material or help the linguist transcribe texts they say '*ai* - pause - *sele*' and stoutly maintain that *ai* is one word and *sele* another. This shows that in this instance it is the phonological word which determines word spaces (and that this is the unit which has 'psychological validity' – see §11 below).

We have discussed phonological words and grammatical words as if they were quite separate units, and then investigated the types of relationship between them. In fact, the two kinds of word are always closely intertwined. Each type of morpheme in a language is likely to have its own accentual potentiality (for example, some affixes may bear inherent stress while others lack this), so that the way in which the components of a grammatical word are combined defines its phonological status.

Phonological words of different compositions may show varying prosodic properties. In Modern Greek, if a long phonological word consists of more than one grammatical word it has an obligatory secondary stress, whereas the inclusion of a secondary stress is always optional in a long phonological word which consists of just one grammatical word (Joseph and Philippaki-Warburton 1987: 243).

Czaykowska-Higgins (1998) presents an illuminating discussion of words in Moses-Columbia Salish, showing that although phonological word and morphological word coincide in extent, their internal structures – in terms of phonological and grammatical bracketing – differ. For example, reduplication is a grammatical process of suffixation applying to a 'morphological root' whereas, in terms of phonological processes, the reduplicated portion forms an inherent part of the 'phonological root'.

For each language we can recognise a hierarchy of grammatical units; this is, typically: morpheme, grammatical word, phrase, clause, sentence. There must also be a hierarchy of phonological units; this is, typically: phoneme, foot (in some languages), syllable, phonological word, intonation group, utterance. (An alternative phonological hierarchy is suggested by Nespor and Vogel 1986 and repeated in Hall and Kleinhenz 1999: 9: syllable, foot, phonological word, phonological phrase, intonational phrase, phonological utterance.) The way in which the hierarchies relate varies from language to language. The place at which the two hierarchies are most likely to converge concerns grammatical word and phonological word – these may wholly coincide or else often coincide, for a given language. (This is why it is appropriate to use the term 'word' for units on both hierarchies.)

10   Do all languages have words?

One cannot assume that just because all the languages one knows have 'words' then so must all the languages in the world. However, it does seem likely that every language will have both a phonological word, such as we defined in §6, and a grammatical word, as defined in §7 (that is to say, we cannot imagine a language which does not have these units). In some languages these units may always coincide and in others they generally coincide (note that in languages of types (b–d) from §9 it is only in a minority of cases that phonological word and grammatical word do not coincide). It is not impossible that there would be a language that lacks phonological words and/or grammatical words, but we are not at present aware of one.

As mentioned before, most discussion of 'words' has centred on the familiar synthetic languages of Europe. How about languages of other types? Recall Hockett's comment, quoted in §2: 'THERE ARE NO WORDS IN CHINESE. The whole tradition of "words" as worked out with western languages is useless in Chinese'. Well, the leading grammarian of Chinese, Chao, reaches a different conclusion. He recognises a 'syntactic unit' in Chinese which satisfies our criteria for grammatical word – it has fixed internal structure but 'unlimited versatility' in syntactic constructions; in addition, one may pause at a word boundary, etc. (Chao 1946; 1968: 136–93). See also the comments in §11.

At the other end of the scale we can certainly recognise a unit grammatical word in polysynthetic languages, on the criteria given in §7. That is, the parts always occur together, in fixed order and have a conventionalised coherence and meaning. What makes fieldwork on a polysynthetic language demanding is that one has to quote a complete word (which can be dauntingly long) whenever one wants to discuss its form or function or meaning; it is not acceptable to quote just one part of a word.

There have been few in-depth studies of the unit word in polysynthetic languages, but we can air a few preliminary impressions. Firstly, one is rather more likely than in a synthetic language to find a grammatical word consisting of a number of phonological words. And it may be more possible to pause at phonological word boundaries within a grammatical word. Further work is needed to confirm (or disprove) these initial impressions.

11   The social status of words

Although it is likely that all languages have words (as we have characterised 'word' in this chapter), the social role of words differs widely.

In English and other European languages (with an established tradition of writing) the word is the unit of the language about which people talk and argue. A quite different kind of unit may fulfil this role in other languages. Chao

(1968: 136) explains that in Chinese a unit called *tzyh* (nowadays written *zì*) is the 'sociological' unit of the language, meaning by this 'that type of unit, intermediate in size between a phoneme and a sentence, which the general, nonlinguistic public is conscious of, talks about, has an everyday term for, and is practically concerned with in various ways. It is the kind of thing which a child learns to say, which a teacher teaches children to read and write in school, which a writer is paid for so much per thousand, which a clerk in a telegraph office counts and charges so much per, the kind of thing one makes slips of the tongue on, and for the right or wrong use of which one is praised or blamed. Thus it has all the social features of the common small change of every day speech which one would call a "word" in English'. Chao (1946: 4) mentions that *tzyh* is translated as 'word' by 'most of those who speak in English on Chinese', a footnote adding 'such as Sinologists, missionaries, and Chinese students studying abroad'. But in fact *tzyh* is not a 'word' on any of the accepted definitions; it is a character. As mentioned in §10, Chao provides criteria for a 'syntactic unit' in Chinese (called *cí*, see Packard 2000: 14–20) which satisfies our criteria for grammatical word (it consists of one or more *tzyh*) but states that it 'plays no role in the Chinaman of the street's conception of the subunits of the Chinese language' (1968: 138).

That is, Chinese does have 'word' but this unit has no social status for the language community. In much the same way that speakers of English and other languages talk about words, speakers of Chinese talk about *tzyh* 'characters', which roughly correspond to the grammatical morpheme and/or phonological syllable. This social difference is undoubtedly related, at least in part, to the different writing systems employed by the Chinese and the English.

In languages where people do talk about words, noun and verb may have different statuses. When doing fieldwork on a previously undescribed language one may – in some cases – felicitously cite a noun and ask about its meaning and use. But it is bad practice to do the same for a verb. One should always include at least minimal information about core arguments, asking about 'She hit him' rather than just about 'hit'. A noun generally names a type of object and may be used just for this; but a verb describes an action or state which requires a number of participants and these should be specified.

Languages vary. In Jarawara a noun will not normally be used alone, for naming. When a new species of bird is encountered, a Jarawara would never point it out by just saying its name, e.g. *sasaha*. They would add the copula verb *ama* 'be' or the intransitive verb *wata* 'exist', often with a declarative suffix, feminine -*ke* or masculine -*ka*, indicating the gender of the noun. That is, they would point at the bird and say *sasaha ama* or *sasaha wata* or *sasaha ama-ke* or *sasaha wata-ke* (this particular bird, the hoatzin bird, is of feminine gender).

Many topics remain to be investigated in connection with the unit 'word'. We will mention just two.

(*a*) Sapir (1921: 33–4) talks of the 'psychological validity' of 'word'. Does this relate to a phonological word or to a grammatical word or to both? What does it imply – that 'word' is a cognitive unit? What are the consequences of this? Does the difference between Chinese and English just described relate to a cognitive difference between the language communities?

Work is also needed on the role of 'word' in language acquisition. Studies of how children learn a language appear seldom to first establish what the types of words are for that language, and then to study how children acquire units of the various types.

As Joseph points out (§5 of chapter 10), although phrases can be borrowed, 'borrowing of individual words is by far the most common type of borrowing'. But is it phonological word or grammatical word that is the basis for loans? Preliminary work by Aikhenvald (forthcoming) suggests that, at least in Amazonia, phonological word is the unit which is borrowed.

(*b*) Some societies plainly operate in terms of words. All over the world there is tabooing, and it is generally words that are tabooed (see Rosetti 1947: 43). In indigenous communities of Australia, when an important person dies their name may be tabooed for a while, and so too any common noun or verb which is phonologically similar to it. For example, in 1975 a man called Djaayila died at Yirrkala (in north-east Arnhem Land); his name was tabooed and so too was the verb *djaal-* 'to want, to be desirous of' (Dixon 1980: 28). Note that it is the lexeme which is here being tabooed, in the form of all words based on it. The whole question of tabooing deserves detailed study, on a cross-linguistic basis, from the point of view of the language units concerned.

Bits of language may be endowed with mystical or religious properties, but these are seldom just words. Rather, one has magical spells, pious incantations, and the like. Even a 'password' is more often a phrase than a single word. It may indeed be forbidden to pronounce a certain name (e.g. 'Jehovah') but – as noted in §1 – it is likely that every language has a word '(proper) name' whereas only a minority of languages have a term 'word'.

12   Summary

We have found that although many types of definition have been suggested for 'word', there has often been lack of a clear distinction between lexeme and word form, and/or between phonological and grammatical criteria. We suggest that different sorts of criteria should be kept strictly apart – phonological criteria define phonological word, which is a unit in the phonological hierarchy, while grammatical criteria define grammatical word, which is a unit in the grammatical hierarchy. In some languages grammatical and phonological words coincide so that we have a single unit functioning in both hierarchies. Many languages have clitics which are grammatical words but not independent phonological words and here we have one phonological word consisting of a number of grammatical words. Other languages can have one grammatical word consisting of several phonological words (especially in compounding or reduplication). And there are two known examples of a grammatical word consisting of one-and-a-bit phonological words (and vice versa). Note that in all these languages phonological and grammatical word do coincide most of the time; it is only in a minority of cases that their borders differ.

There is no one criterion that characterises a phonological word in every language. In §6 we defined a phonological word as a phonological unit larger than the syllable with at least one (and generally more than one) defining property from the following areas: segmental features, including word boundary phenomena; prosodic features such as stress and/or tone assignment and vowel harmony; the domain of application of phonological rules.

In §7 we defined a grammatical word as consisting of a number of grammatical elements which always occur together, in a fixed order, and have a conventionalised coherence and meaning. Other useful criteria, in certain languages, can be the non-recursiveness of morphological processes and the distribution of inflections.

The possibility of pause may relate to a phonological word more often than to a grammatical word. Bloomfield's criterion of 'minimum free form' appears to apply to something which consists of one or more grammatical words and also of one or more phonological words (that is, not to a phonological word which is part of a grammatical word, nor to a grammatical word which is part of a phonological word). In similar fashion, in writing there is a tendency to place a word space where there is both a phonological word boundary and a grammatical word boundary.

Appendix Sample outline account of phonological word and grammatical word in Fijian

This account is based on Dixon (1988a: 12–31).

Phonological word

(a) Segmental features. Syllable structure is (C)V and there is no special structure for a word, nor restrictions on what consonants and vowels may go into C and V slots for word-initial and non-initial syllables. However, we do find:

(i) A phonological word must have at least two moras (where a short vowel is one mora, and a long vowel and a diphthong are each two moras). There are some roots of underlying form CV, e.g. *ca-* '(be) bad' as in the transitive verb-form *ca-ta* 'hate, consider bad'. When this is used without an affix the vowel is lengthened, giving *caa*.

(ii) A sequence of *ai, ei, oi, au, eu, ou* or *iu*, within a phonological word, is pronounced as a diphthong. Across a phonological word boundary, such a vowel sequence is pronounced as two separate syllables.

(b) Stress rule. Primary stress goes on the syllable containing the second mora from the end of a phonological word. Secondary stress goes on the syllables containing the fourth and sixth moras from the end (we have no example of a phonological word involving eight moras).

Grammatical word

A grammatical word is centred on a root or a compound stem (combining two roots) and may have prefixes and/or suffixes added to it. The components must appear together, in fixed order, with the word having a conventionalised coherence and meaning (speakers will talk of the form and meaning of grammatical words, called *vosa*).

Note that there are some examples of recursion within a grammatical word (e.g. two occurrences of the prefix *va'a-*; see Dixon 1988a: 197–8). A grammatical word can generally be pronounced by itself.

Relation between grammatical and phonological words

(a) There are instances of a grammatical word consisting of two phonological words:

(i) Compounds, e.g. *sára.vanúa* (lit. 'look+at.place') 'tourist'.

(ii) In a productively or inherently reduplicated word (where at least two moras are involved), the reduplication boundary within the grammatical word is a phonological word boundary. For example *butá'o* 'to steal', *búta.butá'o* 'to steal constantly', where the penultimate stress rule operates independently within each phonological word. (And see the discussion of vowel sequences under *(a)* in §6 above.)

(iii) Whereas one-mora affixes form one phonological word with the root to which they are attached, multi-mora affixes constitute a separate phonological word within the one grammatical word, e.g. the root *talanoa* 'tell' plus transitive suffix *-ta'ina* make up one grammatical word consisting of two phonological words, *tàlanóa.ta'ína* 'tell (stories)'.

(b) There are instances of a phonological word consisting of two grammatical words. For example, preposition *i* 'to, at' plus common article *na* form one phonological word, *í+na*.

If a single-mora grammatical word does not enter into a combination of this type it becomes a clitic to an adjacent phonological word. That is, it does not enter into the stress assignment pattern of the host word, but is added on, as an extra unstressed syllable, after the stress rule has applied.

(c) As described under *(d)* in §9 above, the nominalising prefix *i-* behaves in an unusual way. For instance, in an NP consisting of the common article *a* plus derived noun *i-talanoa* 'story' (formed by adding prefix *i-* to the verb *talanoa* 'tell') the *a* and *i-* form one phonological word (pronounced as a diphthong) while *talanoa* is a separate phonological word. If this is preceded by the preposition *i*, the common article then has allomorph *na* and we get:

(13)   GRAMMATICAL WORDS   PREPOSITION ARTICLE DERIVED NOUN

                                i   =   *na*   +   *i-*   *talanoa*

        PHONOLOGICAL WORDS   1   2

                                 'in the story'

Here the phonological word *inai* consists of all of two grammatical words (preposition *i* and article *na*) plus part of a third grammatical word (the prefix *i-* from derived noun *i-talanoa*).

But note that if anything should intervene between the common article (*a* or *na*) and a grammatical word beginning with the derivational prefix *i-*, the *i-* becomes part of the same phonological word as the root to which it is prefixed, i.e. grammatical and phonological words here coincide. For example:

(14)   GRAMMATICAL WORDS   ARTICLE POSSESSOR DERIVED NOUN

                                  a   =   *ona*   *i-talanoa*

        PHONOLOGICAL WORDS   1   2

                                    'his story'

Here the article *a* becomes a clitic to the following possessor *ona* 'his'. Note that if this NP were preceded by the preposition *i* we would get *i=na ona i-talanoa* 'in this story', where *i=na* is one phonological word consisting of two grammatical words (each a clitic) and *ona* and *i-talanoa* are each both one grammatical word and one phonological word.

References

Aikhenvald, A. Y. 1996. 'Words, phrases, pauses and boundaries: evidence from South American Indian languages', *Studies in Language* 20.487–517.

    1998. 'Warekena', pp 225–439 of *Handbook of Amazonian languages*, Vol. 4, edited by D. C. Derbyshire and G. K. Pullum. Berlin: Mouton de Gruyter.

    1999a. 'Multiple marking of syntactic function and polysynthetic nouns in Tariana', pp 235–48 of *CLS* 35, Part 2.

    1999b. Review of Plank 1995, *Studies in Language* 23.447–54.

    Forthcoming. *Language contact in Amazonia*. Oxford: Oxford University Press.

Allen, W. S. 1951. 'Some prosodic aspects of retroflexion and aspiration in Sanskrit', *Bulletin of the School of Oriental and African Studies* 13.939–46.

1957. 'Aspiration in the Hārautī nominal', pp 68–86 of *Studies in Linguistic Analysis*, by J. R. Firth et al. Oxford: Blackwell.

1972. *Sandhi: the theoretical, phonetic and historical basis of word-junction in Sanskrit*. The Hague: Mouton.

Ball, M. J. 1993. Editor of *The Celtic languages*. London: Routledge.

Bally, C. 1950. *Linguistique générale et linguistique française*. 3rd edition. Berne: Francke.

Bazell, C. E. 1953. *Linguistic form*. Istanbul: Istanbul Press.

1957. 'On the historical sources of some structural units', pp 19–29 *of Miscelánea homenaje a André Martinet: 'Estructuralismo e historia'*. Universidad de la Laguna.

Bendor-Samuel, J. T. 1966. 'Some prosodic features in Terena', pp 30–39 of *In memory of J. R. Firth*, edited by C. E. Bazell. J. C. Catford, M. A. K. Halliday and R. H. Robins. London: Longman.

Bloomfield, L. 1933. *Language*. New York: Holt, Rinehart and Winston.

Bochner, H. 1984. 'Inflection within derivation', *The Linguistic Review* 3.411–21.

Bolinger, D. L. 1963. 'The uniqueness of the word', *Lingua* 12.113–36.

Börgström, C. Hj. 1954. 'Internal reconstruction of Pre-Indo-European word forms', *Word* 10.275–87.

Chao, Y. R. 1946. 'The logical structure of Chinese words', *Language* 22.4–13.

1968. *A grammar of spoken Chinese*. Berkeley and Los Angeles: University of California Press.

Churchward, C. M. 1941. *A new Fijian grammar*. Sydney: Australasian Medical Publishing.

Czaykowska-Higgins, E. 1998. 'The morphological and phonological constituent of words in Moses-Columbia Salish (Nxaʔamxcín)', pp 154–95 of *Salish languages and linguistics: theoretical and descriptive perspectives*, edited by E. Czaykowska-Higgins and M. D. Kinkade. Berlin: Mouton de Gruyter.

Dai, J. X-L. 1998. 'Syntactic, phonological and morphological words in Chinese', pp 103–34 of *New approaches to Chinese word formation: morphology, phonology and the lexicon in Modern and Ancient Chinese*, edited by J. L. Packard. Berlin: Mouton de Gruyter.

Dench, A. 1998. *Yingkarta*. Munich: Lincom Europa.

Dench, A. and Evans, N. 1988. 'Multiple case-marking in Australian languages', *Australian Journal of Linguistics* 8.1–47.

Di Sciullo, A-M. and Williams, E. 1987. *On the definition of word*. Cambridge, Mass.: MIT Press.

Dixon, R. M. W. 1972. *The Dyirbal language of North Queensland*. Cambridge: Cambridge University Press.

1977a. *A grammar of Yidiɲ*. Cambridge: Cambridge University Press.

1977b. 'Some phonological rules in Yidinʸ', *Linguistic Inquiry* 8.1–34.

1980. *The languages of Australia*. Cambridge: Cambridge University Press.

1981. 'Warrgamay', pp 1–144 of *Handbook of Australian languages*, Vol. 2, edited by R. M. W. Dixon and B. J. Blake. Canberra: Australian National University Press, and Amsterdam: John Benjamins.

1982. 'The grammar of English phrasal verbs', *Australian Journal of Linguistics* 2.1–42.

1988a. *A grammar of Boumaa Fijian.* Chicago: University of Chicago Press.

1988b. ' "Words" in Fijian', pp 65–71 of *Lexicographical and linguistic studies, essays in honour of G. W. Turner*, edited by T. L. Burton and J. Burton. Cambridge: D. S. Brewer.

1991. *A new approach to English grammar, on semantic principles.* Oxford: Clarendon.

1998. Review of Evans 1995, *Studies in Language* 22.507–15.

Dresher, B. E. 1994. 'The prosodic basis of the Tiberian Hebrew system of accents', *Language* 70.1–52.

Evans, N. 1995. *A grammar of Kayardild, with historical-comparative notes on Tangkic.* Berlin: Mouton de Gruyter.

Firth, J. R. 1957. *Papers in linguistics, 1934–1951.* London: Oxford University Press.

Foley, W. A. 1991. *The Yimas language of New Guinea.* Stanford: Stanford University Press.

Franklin, K. J. 1971. *A grammar of Kewa, New Guinea.* Canberra: Pacific Linguistics.

Franklin, K. J. and Franklin, J. 1978. *A Kewa dictionary, with supplementary grammatical and anthropological materials.* Canberra: Pacific Linguistics.

Gak, V. G. 1990. 'Slovo [Word]', pp 464–7 of *Lingvističeskij enciklopedičeskij slovar* [*Linguistic encylopaedic dictionary*], edited by V. N. Yartseva. Moscow: Sovetskaya Enciklopediya.

Garvin, P. L. 1954. 'Delimitation of syntactic units', *Language* 30.345–8.

Gray, L. H. 1934. *Introduction to Semitic comparative linguistics.* New York: Columbia University Press.

1939. *Foundations of language.* New York: Macmillan.

Gregor, D. B. 1980. *Celtic, a comparative study of the six Celtic languages: Irish, Gaelic, Manx, Welsh, Cornish, Breton, seen against the background of their history, literature, and destiny.* Cambridge: Oleander.

Guedes, M. 1991 *Subsídios para uma análise fonológica do Mbyá.* Campinas: Editora da Unicamp.

Hall, T. A. and Kleinhenz, U. 1999. Editors of *Studies on the phonological word.* Amsterdam: John Benjamins.

Halliday, M. A. K., McIntosh, A. and Strevens, P. 1964. *The linguistic sciences and language teaching.* London: Longmans.

Harris, Z. S. 1946. 'From morpheme to utterance', *Language* 22.161–83.

Hazlewood, D. 1850. *A Feejeean and English and an English and Feejeean dictionary . . . and a compendious grammar of the Feejeean language . . .* Vewa: Wesleyan Missionary Press.

Hockett, C. F. 1944. Review of *Linguistic interludes* and *Morphology: the descriptive analysis of words* (1944 edition) both by E. A. Nida, in *Language* 20.252–5.

Hudson, J. 1978. *The core of Walmatjari grammar.* Canberra: Australian Institute of Aboriginal Studies.

Jastrow, O. 1997. 'The Neo-Aramaic languages', pp 334–77 of *The Semitic languages*, edited by R. Hetzon. London: Routledge.

Jespersen, O. 1924. *The philosophy of grammar.* London: Allen and Unwin.

Joseph. B. D. and Philippaki-Warburton, I. 1987. *Modern Greek.* London: Routledge.

Kenesei, I, Vago, R. M. and Fenyvesi, A. 1998. *Hungarian*. London: Routledge.

Krámský, I. 1969. *The word as a linguistic unit*. The Hague: Mouton.

Lehiste, I. 1962. 'Acoustic studies of boundary signals', pp 178–87 of *Proceedings of the 4th International Congress of Phonetic Sciences, Helsinki*, edited by A. Sovijarvi and P. Aalto. The Hague: Mouton.

Longacre, R. E. 1964. *Grammar discovery procedures*. The Hague: Mouton.

Lyons, J. 1968. *Introduction to theoretical linguistics*. Cambridge: Cambridge University Press.

McCarthy, J. J. 1982. 'Prosodic structure and expletive infixation', *Language* 58.574–90.

Malinowski, B. 1966. *Coral gardens and their magic*, Vol. 2, *The language of magic and gardening*. 2nd edition. London: Allen and Unwin.

Matthews, P. H. 1991. *Morphology*. 2nd edition. Cambridge: Cambridge University Press.

Meillet, A. 1964, *Introduction à l'étude comparative des languges Indo-Européennes*. University, Alabama: University of Alabama Press.

    1970. *General characteristics of the Germanic langues*, translated by W. P. Dismukes. Coral Gables, Fl.: University of Miami Press.

Milewski, T. 1951. 'The conception of the word in the languages of North American natives', *Lingua Posnaniensis* 3.248–68.

Milner, G. B. 1956. *Fijian grammar*. Suva: Fiji Government Press.

Nedjalkov, I. V. 1992. 'Functions of Evenki verbal suffixes with variable morpheme ordering (comparative approach)', *Languages of the World* 4.20–41.

Nespor, M. and Vogel, I. 1986. *Prosodic phonology*. Dordrecht: Foris.

Newman, S. 1967. 'Yokuts', *Lingua* 17.182–99.

Nida, E. A. 1944. *Morphology: the descriptive analysis of words*. Glendale, Calif.: Summer Institute of Linguistics.

Packard, J. L. 2000. *The morphology of Chinese: a linguistic and cognitive approach*. Cambridge: Cambridge University Press.

Pike, K. L. 1947. *Phonemics: a technique for reducing languages to writing*. Ann Arbor: University of Michigan Press.

Plank, F. 1995. Editor of *Double case: agreement by Suffixaufnahme*. New York: Oxford University Press.

Potter, S. 1967. *Modern linguistics*. London: Deutsch.

Prista, A. da R. 1966. *Essential Portuguese grammar*. New York: Dover.

Reichling, A. J. B. N. 1935. *Het woord: ean studie omtrent de grondslag van taal en taalgebruik*. Nijmegen: Berkhout.

Rice, K. 1990. 'Predicting rule domains in the phrasal phonology', pp 289–312 of *The phonology–syntax connection*, edited by S. Inkelas and D. Zec. Chicago: University of Chicago Press.

Robins, R. H. 1957. 'Vowel nasality in Sundanese: a phonological and grammatical study', pp 87–103 of *Studies in linguistic analysis*, by J. R. Firth et al. Oxford: Blackwell.

    1967. *A short history of linguistics*. London: Longmans.

Rosetti, A. 1947. *Le mot: esquisse d'une théorie générale*. 2nd edition. Copenhagen: Munksgaard, and Bucharest: Intitutul de linguistică română.

Sapir, E. 1921. *Language: an introduction to the study of speech*. New York: Harcourt Brace.

Sprigg, R. K. 1955. 'The tonal system of Tibetan (Lhasa dialect) and the nominal phrase', *Bulletin of the School of Oriental and African Studies* 17.133–53.

Sweet, H. 1875/6. 'Words, logic and grammar', pp 470–83 of *Transactions of the Philological Society for 1875/6*.

Trubetzkoy, N. S. 1969. *Principles of phonology*, translated by C. A. M. Baltaxe. Berkeley and Los Angeles: University of California Press.

Ullmann, S. 1957. *The principles of semantics*. Oxford: Blackwell, and Glasgow: Jackson.

van Wyk, E. B. 1967. 'Northern Sotho', *Lingua* 17.230–61.

    1968. 'Notes on word autonomy', *Lingua* 21.543–57.

Vendryes, J. 1925. *Language: a linguistic introduction to history*, translated by P. Radin. London: Routledge.

Waterson, N. 1956. 'Some aspects of the phonology of the nominal forms of the Turkish word', *Bulletin of the School of Oriental and African Studies* 18.578–91.

Weinreich, U. 1954. 'Stress and word structure in Yiddish'. pp 1–27 of *The field of Yiddish*, 1, edited by U. Weinreich. New York: Linguistic Circle of New York.

Wells, R. S. 1947. 'Immediate constituents', *Language* 23.81–117.

Wierzbicka, A. 1996. *Semantics: primes and universals*. Oxford: Oxford University Press.

    1998. 'Anchoring linguistic typology in universal semantic primes', *Linguistic Typology* 2.141–94.

Wonderly, W. L. 1951. 'Zoque II: phonemics and morphophonemics', *International Journal of American Linguistics* 17.105–23.

Žirmunskij, V. M. 1966. 'The word and its boundaries', *Linguistics* 27.65–91.

2 Typological parameters for the study of clitics, with special reference to Tariana

Alexandra Y. Aikhenvald[1]

The term 'clitic' typically refers to a morphological element which does not have the full set of properties of an independent (phonological) word, and which forms 'a phonological unit with the word that precedes it or follows it' (Matthews 1997: 56) for the purposes of accent or prominence assignment (see Nevis, Joseph, Wanner and Zwicky 1994: xii–xx). And they behave differently from affixes. Sapir (1930: 70) remarked that 'enclisis is . . . neither true suffixation nor juxtaposition of independent elements. It has the external characteristics of the former (including strict adherence to certain principles of order), the inner feeling of the latter'.

The consensus appears to be that clitics are morphemes which are prosodically deficient or unusual in certain ways. Criterial properties of clitics found in the literature invariably include that they are 'loosely phonologically bound to a word', or 'occur in second position' in a clause (Klavans 1985: 117), or 'are phonologically deficient'.

This chapter has two distinct parts. In §1, I propose parameters which help distinguish clitics from affixes, determine the nature of their similarity to other morpheme types and define their independent properties in a given language. These criteria suggest a scalar, or continuum-type, approach – that is, some morphemes turn out to be more affix-like and others to be more word-like. (In the Appendix, these parameters are compared to those which have been proposed in the literature.)

Then, in §2, these parameters are applied to Tariana, an Arawak language from Amazonia. Several subclasses of clitics, with different positions on a clitic–affix continuum, are established, and arguments are provided in favour of phonological words including clitics, and for clitic-only phonological words, as distinct from phonological words with no clitics. §3 is a brief summary.

[1] I am especially indebted to R. M. W. Dixon, Timothy J. Curnow, and Mauro Tosco, for insightful discussion. Special thanks go to the members of the Brito family of Santa Rosa and Iauaretê in northwest Amazonia for teaching me Tariana, and to Pauline Laki, for revealing the beauty of her native Manambu.

1   Parameters for clitics

Clitics occupy an intermediate position between a full-fledged phonological word and an affix, and may fall into different classes depending on their phonological properties and grammatical characteristics. A clitic generally cannot form a phonological word on its own; however, there are some forms which can act either as a clitic or as a full phonological word. *The* in English was mentioned in §8 of the introduction. These are known as 'simple clitics', as opposed to others called 'special clitics' (e.g. Zwicky 1977).

A clitic attaches to a HOST, a morpheme with which it forms one phonological word. Phonological words which include clitics or which consist of clitics only[2] may display phonological peculiarities when compared to phonological words which do not contain clitics.

Clitics can be characterised in terms of:
(A) the direction in which they attach to a host – proclitics before the host and enclitics after it – or the position they occupy within a clitic-only phonological word;
(B) their selectivity: whether they may attach to anything, or must attach to a particular kind of host;
(C) the type of host they attach to; for example, the first word in a clause, the last word in an NP, any noun;
(D) whether they form an independent phonological word or not (covering their relationship with stress);
(E) segmental and phonotactic properties of clitics (compared with other morpheme types);
(F) phonological cohesion (that is, processes occurring on a clitic–host boundary or between clitics);
(G) the relationship of clitics to pauses;
(H) combinations of clitics; and the status of words including clitics, and of clitic-only words;
(I) relative ordering in clitic strings;
(J) position with respect to what can be defined as affixes;
(K) the correlation of clitics with grammatical words;
(L) their syntactic scope;
(M) possibilities of lexicalisation, and semantic and morphological idiosyncrasies;
(N) clitic-specific syntactic rules; and
(O) correlation of clitics with word classes.

These parameters provide us with a scalar definition of clitics: each prosodically deficient morpheme occupies a particular place within a multidimensional continuum, from a fully bound to a fully independent morpheme.

---

[2] Both are termed 'clitic group' by Nespor and Vogel (1986: 149ff).

(A) *Direction.* This parameter provides a binary distinction between proclitics and enclitics. Enclitics appear to be more frequent than proclitics, correlating with the fact that more languages have suffixes than prefixes. Languages with exclusively suffixal morphology – such as Eskimo (Sadock 1991: 75; and discussion by Woodbury in chapter 3), Yagua (Payne and Payne 1990; Payne 1983), or Tucano – tend to have just enclitics. However, this statement is far from universal. In chapter 8, Olawsky shows that Dagbani, a suffixing language, has proclitics rather than enclitics.

There may be further complications in drawing boundaries between enclitic and proclitic. Clitics can be enclitic in one construction type and proclitic in another, e.g. Italian, where clitics precede the finite indicative verb, as in *me=lo=dici* 'you tell me it', but follow imperatives, as in *dimme=lo* 'tell me it'.[3]

There are also a number of examples of endoclitics (also known as 'mesoclisis') whereby clitics appear followed by affixes. In some of such cases – e.g. Beja (Klavans 1979: 73), or Ngiyambaa – clitics can be described as having a set of morphological categories of their own, a property which brings them close to independent words (similar examples from Tariana are provided in §2.4.2).

Unusual positioning of clitics may sometimes be accounted for by a kind of 'historical accident'. This is the case of the well-known 'mesoclisis' in Portuguese (marginal in Brazilian Portuguese, frequent in European Portuguese) whereby the personal clitic effectively goes in between the verbal root and the personal cross-referencing affixes fused with tense, e.g. *escrever-se-ia* 'it will be written'. This construction is thought to have arisen because the tense affixes – which were originally forms of the auxiliary 'have' – became suffixes only recently (see §8 of the introduction, and also Halpern 1998: 121).

(B) *Selectivity.* Clitics can attach to any, or 'almost any' word class, e.g. English cliticised auxiliaries (*'ve*, *'s*) or post-inflectional 'clitic-like' affixes in Yidiny. Or they can be selective in terms of the grammatical class of their host. They can attach specifically to verbs – for instance, cliticised auxiliaries tend to be positioned close to the main verb, as in Kannada or Malayalam, or to noun phrases, as are oblique case markers in Apuriná (also see Halpern 1998, on verbal clitics). Some affixes are not selective, e.g. person–number–gender cross-referencing,

---

[3] In this, and numerous other cases, the order of clitics in a clitic sequence is still the same. A well-known exception is French *il me=le=donne* 'he gives it to me', and imperative *Donne=le moi* 'Give it to me' where the order of arguments of the imperative is a mirror image of that of a non-imperative verb; the imperative also requires a non-cliticised form of a personal pronoun in the addressee function. The form of enclitics may not be the same as that of proclitics – this is the case with pronominal enclitics in Portuguese (Vigário 1999).

negative *ma-* and relative–attributive *ka-* in Arawak languages (Aikhenvald 1999a). Relative selectivity is one of the scalarly defined parameters in determining which morphemes are clitics in a particular language.

Some languages plainly lack clitics with low selectivity. This is the case for Siouan languages which, according to Rankin et al. in §4 of chapter 7, lack clitics 'in the often used sense of unmotivated or accidental attachment of a light constituent to a chance neighbor'. In other languages – such as Dagbani (see table 2 in chapter 8) – all clitics are attached to a host (defined phonologically) with which they may not have any grammatical connection.

(c) Type of host. Clitics can have a fixed position within a clause or an NP, depending on purely phonological factors, or on grammatical properties of the host, or they can be floating.

(c1) Fixed position clitics can be classified according to two principles: (i) phonological position regardless of the grammatical class of the host, and (ii) position depending on the grammatical class of host.

(i) Clitics which are placed regardless of the grammatical class of their host can be second-position clitics (in 'Wackernagel's position'), as in Hittite. They can be sentence-initial, e.g. Kwakwala determiners (Anderson 1992: 202), or sentence-final, as in Wari' (Chapacuran: Everett and Kern 1997: 355). In Chamicuro (Arawak), enclitic definite articles which form part of the preceding word (not part of the noun they modify: Parker 1999: 556) belong to this type.[4]

If clitics are positioned by phonological rules only, they cannot be category-specific and must lack 'any direct constituency with the host word', as stated by Woodbury in §6.2 of chapter 3.

Phonological constraints on positioning a clitic may be complex. The emphatic clitic *fa* in Hausa (Zec and Inkelas 1990: 369–70) must occur immediately after a phonological phrase. There are a few prosodic constraints on its positioning: it appears between a verb and a following object noun phrase only if the noun phrase itself consists of more than one word; however, *fa* can occur after any constituent which is 'intonationally emphasised'.

(ii) Clitics whose position depends on the grammatical class of their host can be:
- pre-head, e.g. pronominal clitics in Romance languages or in Macedonian (Dimitrova-Vulchanova 1995: 75) attaching at the front of the finite verb; the

---

[4] The placement of 'second-position' clitics can be defined in two ways – either after the first phonological word, as in Hittite or Kabyle – or after the first constituent. In Serbo-Croatian both possibilities are attested; however, the second position is defined by a combination of phonological and grammatical factors, since 'following the first content word' is equivalent to following the first phonological word (see discussion in Zec and Inkelas 1990: 367).

Macedonian clitic auxiliary in combination with a pronominal clitic (p 74);
prepositional clitics, as in Russian or Hebrew;
- post-head, e.g. pronominal clitics in Romance languages attaching at the end
  of an imperative, or Finnish *-kin* 'unexpected';
- anticipatory, that is, clitics which phonologically attach to an element immediately preceding their host, chosen by grammatical parameters, as in Yagua
  (Payne and Payne 1990: 365), or Kugu-Nganhcara (Smith and Johnson 2000;
  Klavans 1985: 104), and in Djinang (Waters 1989: 23, 189: where clitics are
  phonologically bound to the word immediately preceding the verb).[5]

A language can distinguish quite a few subclasses of clitics depending on
the type of their grammatical host; Henderson, in §5 of chapter 4, provides an
exhaustive analysis of such subclasses in Eastern/Central Arrernte.

A clitic which is associated with words of a certain class may be positioned
at the end of a phrase which has a member of that word class as its head. That
is, clitics can be phrase-final, as *'s* in English, or the indefinitising–focussing
noun-phrase-final clitic in Kannada (Sridhar 1990: 259). In Malayalam, all clitics occur 'at the end of the element to which they relate', e.g. coordinator *-oo*
'or', or auxiliary verbs that follow the main verb (Asher and Kumari 1997:
380–1).[6]

(C2) Floating clitics with no fixed position are attached to a particular constituent
under a special discourse or other condition. In Kannada (Sridhar 1990: 136,
257–8), the emphatic clitic = *e:* can occur with every type of constituent except
demonstrative adjectives. If it attaches to a noun phrase, it follows case marking
and postpositions, as in the following example (here and below, the clitics under
discussion are underlined).

(1)   gandhiy=e: eddu   bandante
       Gandhi=EMPH   get.up+PAST.PCPL   come+PAST+thus
       It was as though Gandhi himself got up and came

---

[5] Cf. clitic clusters in Macedonian (which are phonologically 'hosted' by the preceding negation,
that is, form a phonological word with it) (Dimitrova-Vulchanova 1995: 75).

[6] Some morphemes – which are affix-like according to their prosodic and segmental properties – can
show unusual syntactic behaviour. When an independent noun grammaticalises as a derivational
affix, it may still retain some of the syntactic properties of a free noun, that is, displaying a certain
mobility which may make it look similar to a clitic. Numerous Romance languages have a suffix
used to form adverbs from adjectives which comes from the accusative form of Latin feminine
noun *mens* 'mind' *-mentem*, e.g. French *-ment*, Portuguese and Italian *-mente*. Synchronically,
in all these languages this suffix requires the feminine form of an adjective, e.g. French *franche-
ment*, Portuguese *franca-mente* 'openly, frankly'. This suffix is productive in these languages.
Only in Portuguese and in Spanish does it display another unusual peculiarity which indicates
its connection with an independent word: it undergoes a process comparable to coreferential
deletion in a sequence of two adverbs, e.g. *sábia- e prudente-mente* (lit. 'wise- and cautious-ly')
rather than *sábia-mente e prudente-mente* 'wisely and cautiously'.

(2)   ka:rinoLagindal=<u>e:</u>   kaybi:sidaLu
         car+GEN+inside+ABL=<u>EMPH</u>   hand+wave+PAST+3F
         She waved from inside the car itself

With negated verbs, the emphatic clitic appears before the negation, attaching
to the preceding verb, as in *ke:Lal=<u>e:</u> illa* (listen+INF=<u>EMPH NEG</u>) 'she didn't
listen'.

Floating clitics which mark speakers' 'attitude' or focus are positioned close
to a constituent which is emphasised; see Sadock (1995: 267–8) for an example
from West Greenlandic. The interrogative clitic *=ne* in Latin displays 'floating'
properties: it can attach to a word which is being questioned; if a clause is being
questioned, it attaches to the verb (Nespor and Vogel 1986: 161).

Floating clitics do not always express emphasis, focus or other discourse
categories. The clitic in Zoque which marks past tense may attach to members of
most lexical categories (Jan Terje Faarlund, p.c.). In Apurinã (Arawak: Facundes
2000), a number of floating clitics can attach to various grammatical classes,
depending, apparently, on which of them is focussed; these include a frustrative
marker, a predicative marker, two perfectives and an emphatic marker. Floating
verbal enclitics in Tariana go onto the predicate, unless another constituent is
in focus (see §2.4.2).

Languages can combine clitics of different kinds. Hittite has fixed second
position clitics and also emphatic 'floating' clitics which go onto an emphasised
constituent. Warekena has sentence-initial proclitics, and also proclitics associated with a specific constituent (for instance, negation – Aikhenvald 1998).
See also discussion in chapters 3, 4, 8, 9 and 10 below.

The position of a clitic may correlate with a change of meaning. In Kannada,
the interrogative clitic *=a* is sentence-final if it marks a yes-no question; if a
particular constituent is questioned, it attaches after that constituent, and thus
behaves as a floating clitic.

(D) *Relationship with phonological word.* The lack of independent stress, and
incapability of forming a phonological word on its own, is typically considered
a definitional property of a clitic. As Zwicky (1985: 286) puts it, 'if an element
counts as belonging to a phonological word for the purposes of accent, tone or
length assignment, then it should be a clitic'. Clitics are described as underlyingly unstressed, as in European Portuguese where they do not even affect
the stress placement in a phonological word (Vigário 1999). Olawsky considers
this a definitional property of clitics in Dagbani (see table 2 in chapter 8).

Underlyingly unstressed clitics can acquire stress by phonological rules (and
see the discussion of accented enclitics in Siouan by Rankin et al. in §3.1 of
chapter 7). Clitics can take the stress of 'another clitic in a sequence' in Modern
Greek (Joseph and Philippaki-Warburton 1987: 211–12, 243): 'when one or

at most two enclitics increase the distance between the stressed syllable and the end of the phonological word, another stress is assigned to the penultimate syllable of the whole unit'; in example (3) a secondary (weaker) stress appears on the clitic *mù*.

(3)   ďóse=mù=to
         give.IMPV.SG=me:GEN.CLIT=it:ACC.CLIT
         Give it to me

Similarly, in Tuareg Ahaggar, *e=kăy=əɣhəlăɣ* (IMPFVE=2sg=love:IMPFVE) 'I will love you' (Prasse 1972: 34), the second person direct object clitic = *kăy* carries the primary stress when it follows the imperfective proclitic *e=*.

In Neapolitan Italian, main word stress falls on one of the word's last three syllables; and a string consisting of a verb and two enclitics surfaces with main stress on the first of the clitics (regardless of the stress on the verb) (Peperkamp 1995: 234).

Grammatical words which have accentless variants (Nevis et al. 1994: xviii) – such as English personal pronouns or articles – can form phonological words when stressed, under specific conditions, e.g. *the* in English. Monosyllabic adverbs in the Papuan language Manambu are usually procliticised to the verb, e.g. *bə=yá-na-d* (already=come-REC.PAST-3sgMASC) 'he has already come'; but they surface as independent phonological words when used as a single-word answer to a question. That is, the question 'Is he gone yet?' will be answered *bɔ́* 'yes, he is' (lit. 'already'). Along similar lines, Harris (in §4 of chapter 9 and notes 5 and 6) discusses conditions under which negative and interrogative clitics can be accented in Georgian. And Henderson (§5 of chapter 4) provides evidence in favour of the phonological independence of some clitics, based on their behaviour in 'Rabbit Talk' in Eastern/Central Arrernte.

Clitics can have prosodic properties of their own. Enclitics in Tariana always take secondary stress on the first, second or third syllable (which is weaker than the primary stress and does not have higher pitch).

(E) Segmental and phonotactic properties of clitics. Clitics can differ from affixes and from roots in their segmental structure and phonotactics. Like affixes, they tend to be monosyllabic (as in Romance languages, or in Warekena). Cliticised – or accentless – forms of disyllabic independent words in Bare are monosyllabic. In Tariana – see below – clitics differ from affixes and from independent roots in combinatorial possibilities of consonants.

Zeshan (in §3.2 of chapter 6) gives additional evidence for the loss of syllabicity in clitics in sign languages. Here, a combination of a clitic and its host behaves as one unit for the purpose of assignment of a suprasegmental – this is analogous to the process of forming one phonological word in spoken languages.

Clitics can differ from independent words. Tariana clitics are the only morphemes to form monosyllabic phonological words with a short vowel. In numerous Cushitic and Omotic languages of Ethiopia, clitics – but not roots – can end in consonants (Mauro Tosco, p.c.).

(F) Phonological cohesion. Clitics may differ from affixes with respect to (i) phonological processes at clitic–host boundary, (ii) processes on boundaries between clitics, (iii) processes within clitics, and (iv) processes at the edges of phonological words which include clitics.

It has been claimed that clitics are agglutinative, and subject to automatic phonological rules only. This is indeed the case in a number of languages. However, fusion across clitic-plus-clitic boundaries is found in the so-called contractions in Romance and Germanic languages, e.g. French *au* or Portuguese *na* or German *zum* from *zu + dem*. In Piedmontese, a Western Romance language of northwest Italy (Tosco forthcoming), cliticisation of pronouns results in a variety of clusters which are not admissible word-internally, e.g. /dʒl/ in *cog-lo* /kúdʒ=lu/ 'put him to bed', /tʃt/ in *specc-te* /spétʃ=te/ 'look at yourself in the mirror', /dt/ in *vard-te* /várd=te/ 'look at yourself'. Geminated consonants in Piedmontese only occur on clitic boundaries, e.g. *séte* 'sit!' + *-te* '2sg' gives [sét:e] (Mauro Tosco, p.c.). In Manambu, word-initial *h* deletion accompanied by vowel fusion is specific for a clitic boundary: when the copula *ha* gets encliticised to a noun in a copula complement function in rapid speech, *h* disappears and vowel fusion takes place. Example (4) is a clause pronounced slowly; (5) is the same clause pronounced quickly with *h* deletion and vowel fusion:

(4)   ñəna-kə́   sə́   há-l
        you:sgf-POSS name COPULA-F
        This is your name

(5)   ñəna-kə́   <u>sá=l</u>
        you:sgf-POSS <u>name=COPULA:F</u>
        This is your name

Tariana has a clitic-specific process: 'aspiration floating'. Here, an aspirated consonant in a non-word-initial position loses its aspiration if either preceded or followed by a syllable with another aspirated consonant. This process takes place only on an enclitic boundary. For instance, underlying *dí-pha=khà* (3sgnf-fall=AWAY) 'he fell in the opposite direction' becomes either *dí-pa=khà* or *dí-pha=kà*. The process does not apply across suffix boundaries, e.g. *pana-phé-kha* (leaf-CL:LEAF.LIKE-CL:CURVED) 'a curved feather' cannot be pronounced as **pana-phe-ka* or as **pana-pe-kha*. Phonological cohesion between clitics and their hosts in sign languages is discussed by Zeshan, in §3.2 of chapter 6.

Just a subset of phonological rules which operate on an affix boundary may operate on clitic boundaries. The more processes clitics share with affixes, the more 'affix-like' they are. In Warekena (Aikhenvald 1998: 407, 416–18), the rule of identical vowel loss operates on affix and proclitic boundaries, e.g. *ya=amena=pia* (NEG=sharp=NEG) → *yamenapia* 'not sharp'; *wa-aʧia* → *waʧia* (1pl-stand) 'we stand'. In contrast, the rule of non-identical vowel loss operates only on a prefix boundary, e.g. *a-* + *e* → *e*; e.g. *wa-eda* → *weda* 'we see, perceive'; but not on a proclitic boundary *a* + *e* → *ae*; e.g. *ya=eda=pia* 'he does not see'; *wa-eda* 'then he saw'. Of the numerous processes of vowel fusion on affix boundaries in Tariana, only the process *i* → *y* occurs both on an affix boundary and on an enclitic boundary: if a root-final -*i* is followed by an enclitic -*a*, *i* becomes *y*, e.g. *nawiki* 'person' + =*a* 'emphatic' → *nawíkya* 'really a person'; the same process operates between two enclitics, e.g. *nhésiri=tìki=à* (like=DIM=EMPH) → *nhésiri=tìkyà* '(he) likes (it) really a little'. If a root-final -*i* is followed by an affix-initial *a*, then again *i* becomes *y*, e.g. *dá:pi* 'cipó vine', *Dá:pyari* 'the river of Cipó vine'. Proclitics differ from enclitics in that no boundary processes apply across proclitic boundaries.[7]

Allomorphic variation on clitic boundaries occurs in Serbo-Croatian: here the shape of a following clitic conditions that of a preceding one. The feminine singular accusative clitic *je* becomes *ju* when preceded by another clitic with the shape *je* (see Anderson 1995, on this process of dissimilation). Idiosyncratic allomorphy of clitics is found in standard Italian: clitics *mi*, *ti*, *si* surface as *me*, *te*, *se* before *ne*, *lo*, *la*, *li*, *le*.

Specific intra-clitic phonological processes are not very common, but they are attested. For instance, regressive vowel assimilation in Tariana affects only the last two syllables of a clitic: thus, -*naku* 'topical non-subject' becomes -*nuku*, and -*nuka* 'present visual' becomes -*naka* in the speech of the younger generation.

Word-boundary phenomena may operate differently with words which contain clitics than with other words. According to Mauro Tosco (p.c), Piedmontese dialects which raise final unstressed *e* to *i* do not do so with clitics, for example, *sét:e* 'sit down' (discussed above) does not become [sét:i]. That is, phonological words including clitics behave differently from phonological words of other kinds – see §2.4.4.

(G) *The relationship of clitics to pauses.* Restrictions on how one can pause in the middle of a word which includes clitics depend on what the clitics are. Clitics which can be realised as full phonological words ('simple' clitics) often behave

---

[7] An example of special phonotactics on clitic boundaries in West Greenlandic is provided by Sadock (1995: 266). In dialectal French the insertion of [z] occurs between clitics, as in *donnez-moi-z-en* 'give me some' (see further examples in Halpern 1998: 105).

in exactly the same way as other words (non-clitics) as far as pause-marking goes. This is the case in Warekena and in Bare, the two Arawak languages which have segmental markers for 'pause', such as *hV* syllable insertion (see Aikhenvald 1995: 11 for more detail on Bare). So-called independent clitics in Warekena – such as *eya* 'the one mentioned in the previous text'; *eni* 'this; near demonstrative'; *eta* 'that; distant demonstrative'; *iʃi* 'what'; *e* 'this, just mentioned' – can be used as independent phonological words (with or without a pausal marker -*hṽ*), if they are focussed or topicalised, or if used headlessly. But of the four types of pausal marking in Tariana, only one occurs on an enclitic boundary. No pauses can occur on affix boundaries, or on proclitic boundaries.

(H) Combinations of clitics; and the status of words including clitics, and of clitic-only words. A phonological word which consists just of clitics (a 'clitic-only' word) may be similar to phonological words of other types – see the example from Boumaa Fijian in §8 of chapter 1. But it can also be different from phonological words of other sorts in its prosodic properties, and in the ways in which it correlates with a grammatical word. There is ample evidence in favour of 'clitic-only' words. In Tariana, a sequence of a proclitic and an enclitic forms a phonological word different from words of other types. In such a word, the proclitic always bears the primary stress (that is, such a word always has initial stress). And it cannot contain more than two enclitics – see §2.4.4.

In Warekena (Arawak: Aikhenvald 1998: 406) the sequence proclitic + enclitic(s) behaves similarly to clitics: it can form an independent phonological word if focussed, as in (6),[8] or it can be cliticised to the following verb, as in (7).

(6)   y<u>á</u>=mia   yué=pia-hã   nimá-hã   e-píʧi
       NEG=PERFVE   for=NEG-PAUS   3pl+with-PAUS   eat-OBJ.FOC
       He didn't have anything to eat with them (his children)

(7)   y<u>á</u>=mia=ni-tse=pia-hã   dába   ʃá=wa
       NEG=PERFVE=3pl-know=NEG-PAUS   where   go=NONACC
       They did not know where to go

Phonological words containing clitics can behave differently from clitic-less words. In a host + clitic group in Modern Greek, the rule of stress readjustment applies differently from how it applies in words of other structures: in the clitic group the original stress does not shift to any other syllable, while it does so in compounds. Rabbit Talk in Eastern/Central Arrernte (see §5 in chapter 4)

---

[8] Stress in Warekena is contrastive. Clitic groups are a subclass of words with stress on the first syllable. An independent phonological word consisting of a proclitic with a clitic can be used in a pausal form (marked with -*hV*: see discussion in Aikhenvald 1996).

demonstrates differences between words which contain clitics and those that do not. (Also see Vigário 1999, for further evidence on the separate properties of clitic-only words in European Portuguese, and the summary in Halpern 1998: 103).

A clitic group does not have to be coextensive with a syntactic constituent or with a grammatical word – which is to be expected of a prosodically defined constituent. Neither does it have to be coextensive with a phonological word of any other type. Woodbury, in §7.1 of chapter 3, demonstrates that a phonological word without clitics (PW –) can be interpreted as a subdomain of a phonological word including clitics (PW).

(1) Relative ordering in clitic strings. Clitics tend to attach to their host in an idiosyncratic order.[9] In Hittite, the order of second position clitics is as follows:

> sentence connectives *nu, ta* – quotative = *wa(r)*= – dative/accusative plural – third person nominative; accusative singular – first, second person dative/accusative singular, third person dative singular – reflexive – local, emphatic particles (Friederich 1974).

Sentence-final clitics in Wari' (Chapacuran: Everett and Kern 1997: 355) fall into five position classes: (1) temporal particles, (2) the emphatic particles; (3) the referent particle *quem*, (4) the emphatic particle *-ta*, (5) the emphatic particles with restricted use (other than those in position 2).

In Warekena, aspectual clitics (e.g. *-mia* 'perfective') in a clitic sequence are followed by relativiser *-ri*, which is followed by the personal O/S_0 enclitics. Figures 1 and 2 show clitic ordering in Tariana. And see §7 of chapter 7 on the rules for ordering clitics in Siouan languages.

The order of clitics can sometimes be explained semantically – for instance, indirect object clitics preceding direct object clitics, and first or second person clitics preceding third person clitics in Greek, could both be accounted for by a topicality scale (Haberland and Van der Auwera 1990). This principle could also account for the order of verbal clitics in Kabyle Berber (host – indirect O – direct O) which is the mirror image of the order of their independent counterparts (verb – direct O – indirect O).

Clitic ordering can be accounted for by 'phonological' weight; for instance, in Tagalog (Schachter and Otanes 1972), monosyllabic clitics precede disyllabic ones. In Tariana, 'heavy' (two- or three-syllable long) clitics tend to attach to the first component of a serial verb.

But in a great many cases, explanations for clitic ordering are not readily available. This can be compared to idiosyncratic ordering of affixes in polysynthetic

---

[9] This is also known as 'clitic clustering' – see, for instance, examples in Dimitrova-Vulchanova (1995: 74–5).

languages. In this respect, clitics show some similarities to affixes, but still form a class of their own.

(J) Position with respect to what can be defined as affixes. In most languages, clitics usually occur outside all affixes. However, enclitics may sometimes occur before suffixes, as in the Portuguese conditionals quoted in A above. In Albanian, pronominal clitics are proclitics to indicative forms and enclitics to the imperative; however, in the imperative they precede the plural inflection (Sadock 1991: 56). In Platense Spanish, plural inflection can occur after the clitic pronoun, as in *tire=me-n=lo* (throw=TO.ME:CLITIC-PL=IT:CLITIC) 'throw this to me' (see Sadock 1991: 57).

If clitics have morphological categories of their own, these morphological markers can occur inside clitics (see Klavans 1979, for the discussion of examples). In some varieties of Brazilian Portuguese, the diminutive *-zinho* – which arose as the result of a reanalysis of an epenthetic *z* and the regular diminutive *-inho* (masculine), *-inha* (feminine) – inflects for number and for gender, e.g. *aquel-e-zinh-o* (this-MASC-DIM-MASC) 'that little one masculine', *aquel-a-zinh-a* (this-FEM-DIM-FEM) 'this little one feminine', *aquel-e-zinh-o-s* (this-MASC-DIM-MASC-PL) 'these little ones masculine'. In West Greenlandic, the clefting demonstrative nasalises a final consonant of the word preceding it (unlike any suffix) (Sadock 1995: 264). And we will see in §2.4.1 that in Tariana some nominal clitics have partially suppletive number marking (§2.4.1).

This special morphology can account for what only appears to be 'endoclisis', that is, derivational or other affixes intervening between clitics. This makes clitics appear similar to independent grammatical words. However, in most cases clitics have only a subset of the grammatical categories characteristic of full grammatical words, that is, they are both phonologically and grammatically unlike other 'words'.

(κ) The correlation of clitics with grammatical words. A clitic often constitutes a grammatical word; this is what defines simple clitics in Zwicky's terms (e.g. Slavic pronominal clitics, auxiliary clitics, question clitics, etc; cf. Dimitrova-Vulchanova 1995). In Tiriyó, a Carib language from Brazil, all clitics are grammatical words (Meira 1999: 113). In Tariana, as we will see in §2, all the proclitics can be grammatical words, and most enclitics cannot be. And, as Matthews reminds us in §4 of chapter 11, 'the words in Greek originally called "enclitics" were, to repeat, words', or, alternatively, '"clitics" were in certain cases "roots"'.

Clitics may have special morphology of their own – see J – and thus form independent grammatical words. This is the case for the Tariana nominal diminutive enclitic *=tuki* with a partially suppletive plural *=tupe*, or nominal past masculine =*miki-ri*, feminine =*miki-ru*, and plural -*miki*; these can be considered not only phonologically but also grammatically deficient, if compared to modifiers of other classes.

The mismatches between grammatical and phonological words (see §9 of chapter 1) are most often accountable for by clitics which form a phonological word with their host, but can be considered a grammatical word in their own right. For instance, in Awa Pit (Barbacoan: Curnow 1997), postpositions and discourse clitics are enclitics to the last word of a noun phrase and/or of a clause, and are independent grammatical words; a phonological word containing clitics consists of more than one grammatical word. Similar mismatches are discussed for Cup'ik by Woodbury (see §8 of chapter 3), and by Henderson for Eastern/Central Arrernte (see §6.1 of chapter 4). Mismatches of this sort are by no means universal – Rankin et al. show (in §4 of chapter 7) that phonological words in Siouan languages are always coextensive with grammatical words, no matter whether they contain clitics or not.

A word including clitics, and a clitic-only word may – or may not – be co-extensive with a grammatical word (also see Nespor and Vogel 1986: 151–63). Of three kinds of words including clitics in Tariana, only one coincides with a grammatical word. Just one of the clitic-only words is also a grammatical word (see §2.4.4, and table 5 there).

(L) *Syntactic scope of clitics.* Clitics differ in their scope: a clitic marking negation or a polar question may have scope over an entire clause, while one marking emphasis or 'also' may have scope over a phrase or perhaps just over a word. The interesting scope effect of English *n't* – when compared with its non-cliticised counterpart – has been noted by Sadock (1995: 267): *you can't stay* means 'you must leave', and it does not mean 'you can [not stay]', that is 'you can leave'; when *you cannot stay* can have either meaning (at least for some native speakers). Fixed position clitics whose scope is a phrase are sometimes called 'phrasal affixes'.

The scope of a clitic can be a whole clause or a sentence, e.g. Kannada interrogative enclitic; or it can be a noun phrase, as in the case of cliticised adpositions. Fixed position clitics (see C) tend to have scope over the constituent to which they attach. As mentioned above, in Kannada, when the interrogative enclitic attaches to the end of the clause, it is used for questioning the whole clause; when it is used to question a particular noun phrase, it attaches to the end of this noun phrase.

However, this scope effect is not the exclusive property of a clitic. In Tariana, variability in placement of nominal suffixes (underlined) results in scope change, e.g. *[[nu-kapi-<u>má</u>]-da]* (1sg-hand-CL:SIDE.OF-ROUND) 'one palm of my hand' and *[[nu-kapi-<u>dá</u>]-ma]* (1sg-hand-ROUND-CL:SIDE.OF) 'one side of my finger' (a similar example for Dyirbal is given in §7 of chapter 1). Only some verbal enclitics in position 19 (see figure 2) allow variability of ordering, (a) as a kind of afterthought (then there may be a pause) and (b) depending on what aspect of the activity is focussed on. In this respect Tariana clitics are somewhat similar to independent words in that change of order has to do with emphasis and focus.

(8)   di-sapé=sinà=sità=<u>pità</u>=[...]=nikì
        3sgnf-speak=REM.P.INFR=PERFVE=<u>REPETITIVE</u>=COMPLETIVE
        He had <u>completely</u> (finished) speaking again (one stresses the complete
            extent of the action as opposed to something different)

(9)   di-sapé=sinà=sità=<u>nikì</u>=[...]=pità
        3sgnf-speak=REM.P.INFR=PERFVE=<u>COMPLETIVE</u>=REPETITIVE
        <u>Again</u>, he had completely (finished) speaking (one stresses the
            repetition of the action as opposed to something different)

(M) *Lexicalisation, and semantic and morphological idiosyncrasies.* In many languages clitics do not display any semantic or morphological idiosyncrasies. Zeshan points out that clitics do not form idiosyncratic combinations with their host in sign languages (§3.2 of chapter 6). But this is not always the case (pace Zwicky and Pullum 1985).

In Piedmontese, the third person proclitic object *l* has been reanalysed as a part of copula verb 'have' (*a l'ha:* Tosco forthcoming: 19–22); cf. Pullum (1997) on lexicalisation of *to* contractions, e.g. *wanna, gonna,* in English. In Latin, *atque* 'and' (from *at* 'but' and *=que* 'and') and *=cumque* '-soever' as in *quodcumque* 'whatsoever' are both formed with the clitic *=que* 'and' (see other examples in Sadock 1991: 60). The emphatic clitic in Kannada (Sridhar 1990: 136, 257–8) displays idiosyncratic behaviour: when it occurs with reduplicated forms, it conveys the meaning of collectivity or exhaustiveness; with verbs, it means repetitive action. When it occurs with the non-past continuous form of the verb, it conveys the meaning of 'immediate succession' (Sridhar 1990: 259), and it lexicalises with reduplicated verbs to indicate repetitive aspect (Sridhar 1990: 286).

In Tariana, numerous postpositions are historically verbs of motion accompanied by a fossilised subordinating enclitic (see Aikhenvald 2000), e.g. *di-rukú-ita-ka* (3sgnf-go.down-CAUSATIVE-SUBORDINATE) 'downwards from him'. Lexicalised idiomatic combinations containing clitics are found in Cup'ik – see discussion in §6.1 of chapter 3.

(N) *Clitic-specific syntactic rules.* Clitics can be syntactically unusual – that is, special rules may apply to them which do not apply to other morpheme types. Examples of this include 'clitic climbing' and 'clitic doubling' in Romance and

Slavic languages. Clitic doubling is a process whereby a clitic and a non-clitic referring to the same argument are allowed to co-occur in one clause (Halpern 1998: 107–8).

(o) Correlation with morphological classes. Some word classes tend to be prosodically deficient, and display at least some properties associated with clitics. These include pronominal arguments (see, for instance, Shaul 1983 on Tepiman, and Halpern 1998), discourse markers (often subsumed under an umbrella term 'particles' – see Zwicky 1985; or called function words), auxiliary verbs, interrogatives, conjunctions, adpositions and adverbs. In sign languages, clitics include pronouns, deictics and determiners – see §3.2 of chapter 6.

Personal pronouns frequently go through a stage of cliticisation before they become cross-referencing or agreement markers – see Chafe (1977) on this path of development for third person verb agreement in Iroquoian; Steele (1977) on Uto-Aztecan, and Haiman (1991) on Romance languages.

In some languages all members of a word class may share the phonological property of being prosodically deficient – that is, none of them is capable of forming a phonological word on its own. This is the case for discourse markers in Hixkaryana (Carib: Derbyshire 1985: 21–3), and Awa Pit (Curnow 1997).

Along similar lines, cliticisation is a usual stage in the development of auxiliaries as the result of their grammaticalisation out of full verbs (Heine 1993: 55–6). In many languages auxiliaries are clitics – this applies to Kannada and Malayalam, among other languages.[10]

Adverbs often become pre-verbs, and go through a stage of cliticisation – see the examples from Svan and from Georgian in Harris and Campbell (1995: 94–6).

It is often assumed that when affixes develop out of full lexemes they go through a stage of cliticisation. Verbs often get cliticised in compounds; they may then also acquire a more general meaning. In Nahua, a branch of Uto-Aztecan, constructions involving the verb *nemi* 'live, walk' have changed so that in some languages, e.g. Tetelcingo Nahuatl, Michoacan Nahuatl and North Pueblo Nahuatl, *nemi* has become a clitic verb meaning 'go around doing', while in Huasteca Nahuatl the clitic *nemi* has been reanalysed as a habitual marker (Harris and Campbell 1995: 64). In Tariana and in Tucano, compounded verbs get grammaticalised as aktionsart and aspect markers; they then become enclitics, e.g. Tariana *-sitá* 'finish' → *=sità* 'anterior'; *-mayá* 'cheat' → *=mayà* 'almost do something' (Aikhenvald 2000).

---

[10] The auxiliary can cliticise onto the main verb (as in Malayalam), or onto the subject pronoun, as appears to be the case in a number of West African languages (Heine 1993: 76). This cliticisation may result in further evolution of clitics into affixes, and the development of new paradigms (e.g. tense paradigm in Hausa: Heine 1993: 76–7; and the development of an old conjugated auxiliary into a set of subject pronoun suffixes in Muskogean languages described in Haas 1977).

Adpositions are often cliticised. Case relations can be expressed with affixes, with adpositional clitics or with adpositions as independent phonological words. Affixes usually go on every word in a noun phrase, or they may appear at the rim of a noun phrase, or just on the head of a noun phrase, while clitics tend to appear just on the rim of a noun phrase (depending on how they are positioned – see A above).

Prosodic 'deficiency' as a class-specific characteristic is typical for closed classes. However, there is no language with an open word class, every member of which can be prosodically deficient.[11]

It may appear that – historically – clitics represent an intermediary stage of a development path, from 'full' words to 'full' affixes. Historical and comparative studies show, however, that this is not the case – see §7 in chapter 7. We hypothesise that clitics with low selectivity – that is, those that can attach to any constituent, by phonological rules – will tend to be diachronically more stable than clitics which attach to some particular grammatical host. This requires further investigation which goes beyond the scope of this chapter.

Clitics often present orthographic problems. Established orthographies may fail to treat them in a consistent way. For instance, in Italian pronominal proclitics are written as separate words, but enclitics are written together with their host. Rankin et al. (chapter 7) demonstrate the difficulties which Ella Deloria, a linguist and a collaborator of Frans Boas, had in consistently writing enclitics in her native Dakota. Similarly, the Tariana tend to write some disyllabic clitics separately, and some together with their host; most monosyllabic clitics are not written separately.

We will now discuss properties of words and of clitics in Tariana.

2   Words and clitics in Tariana

2.1   Typological properties of Tariana

Tariana is morphologically complex and highly polysynthetic, in both nouns and verbs. It combines head-marking with some dependent-marking. Like most other Arawak languages, it is mostly suffixing, with a few prefixes. Both nouns and verbs have just one prefix position, with over a dozen post-root positions reserved for suffixes and enclitics. Tariana is agglutinative with some fusion, mostly restricted to prefix + root or root + suffix boundaries. Open classes are nouns, adjectives and verbs; there is a semi-open class of adverbs. Any constituent can occupy the predicate slot. The constituent order is syntactically 'free' (that is, the order of constituents depends on their focussing and topicality), and predominantly verb-medial.

---

[11] A putative exception to this could be cliticised inflectional verb forms in Verb Second position, and cliticisation of the verb forms in certain environments (see Anderson 1993).

Table 1 *Morphemes classes and their stress in Tariana*

	underlying primary stress	secondary stress	phonological word	grammatical word
roots	yes	yes (under certain conditions)	yes	
prefixes	no	no	no	
suffixes	some yes, some no	yes (under certain conditions)	no	
proclitics	possible	no	possible	yes
enclitics	no	always	only aktionsart predicate enclitics	

2.2   Phonological word in Tariana

A phonological word in Tariana is defined by a combination of prosodic and segmental parameters outlined below. Only the primary stress (of pitch accent type) is word-defining; other parameters can be considered subsidiary.

(1) primary stress (one per word);

(2) segmental property: a phonological word cannot begin with the flap *r*;

(3) syllable structure: a monosyllabic phonological word contains a long vowel;

(4) secondary stress: indicative of the structure of a phonological word; may be more than one per word;

(5) nasalisation spread: operates within the boundaries of a phonological word;

(6) post-tonic vowel reduction: indicative of word-final position;

(7) pause marking.

All these parameters also apply to clitic groups. Proclitics which can occur as independent words form an exception to (3). Two more properties are indicative of words containing clitics: aspiration floating and regressive vowel assimilation (F in §1). See §2.4.4.

Morphemes in Tariana divide into 'roots', affixes (prefixes and suffixes) and clitics (enclitics and proclitics; following parameter A under §1 above). All roots have underlying stress (e.g. *hanú* 'big', *má:ʧi* 'bad', *maʧá* 'good') which is contrastive. They always form phonological words. Prefixes are underlyingly unstressed, and suffixes are either stressed or unstressed. Suffixes consisting of more than one syllable may acquire secondary stress (depending on the properties of the root) (see Aikhenvald forthcoming).

Proclitics cannot take secondary stress. They may form a phonological word on their own (§2.4.1). Out of over sixty enclitics, only one group may function as independent phonological words (see §2.4.2). Table 1 summarises these properties.

Prefix	1. Possessive prefix (five persons in singular, three in plural), or negative *ma-*, or relative *ka-*
	2. ROOT

Suffixes { 3. Gender-sensitive derivational suffix
4. Classifier as a derivational suffix (may be more than one)
5. Plural marker

Enclitics { 6. Pejorative =*yana* (± plural suffix *-pe*)
7. Approximative =*iha* 'more or less'
8. Diminutive =*tuki* (or diminutive plural =*tupe*); augmentative =*pasi* (± plural suffix *-pe*)
9. Tense (past singular masculine =*miki-ri*, f =*miki-ru*, pl =*miki*; future =*pena*)
10. Extralocality and restrictivity (=*wya* 'the one left out; extralocal: participant in a place distinct from where the speech act is'; =*mia* 'only').

Suffixes { 11. Oblique *-se* 'locative'
12. Oblique case *-ne* 'comitative-instrumental'
13. Contrastive *-se*

Enclitics { 14. Coordinative =*misini*, =*sini* 'also'
15. Focussed A/S =*ne*
16. Topical non-Subject =*nuku*

Figure 1 Noun structure in Tariana

2.3   Grammatical word in Tariana

A grammatical word in Tariana is centred on a root; there are just a few compounds which consist of two roots. Proclitics are grammatical words (see §2.4.1). The components must appear together, with the word having a conventionalised coherence and meaning. The structure of a nominal word (covering most adjectives and nouns, and pronouns of all sorts) is given in figure 1.

A minimal nominal word can consist just of a root, or of prefix + root (depending on the type of the root: whether it is alienably or inalienably possessed), or of root + gender-sensitive suffix. Other markers are obligatory if the sort of meaning they denote needs to be expressed (for instance, plural is obligatory with human referents; classifier as an agreement marker is obligatory if a noun or an adjective is used as a modifier etc).

Not all nouns can have all positions filled (e.g. 1 is only for inalienably possessed prefixed nouns and 3 is only for humans). Positions 4 and 10 can be filled more than once, and allow variable order (see examples under L in §1). Some positions cannot be filled simultaneously, e.g. a noun cannot be marked for oblique case and for the focussed subject case simultaneously.[12]

---

[12] But note that 15 and 16 can be filled simultaneously, creating an instance of marking two syntactic functions: see Aikhenvald (1999b).

| Prefix | 1. Cross-referencing prefixes (A/S$_a$) (three persons in singular and in plural), or negative *ma-*, or relative *ka-* |

2. ROOT

Suffixes

- 3. Thematic syllable
- 4. Causative *-ita*
- 5. Negative *-(ka)de*
- 6. Reciprocal *-kaka*
- 7. *-ina* 'almost, a little bit'
- 8. Topic-advancing *-ni*, or passive *-kana*, or purposive non-visual *-hyu* or visual *-karu*
- 9. Verbal classifiers
- 10. Benefactive *-pena*
- 11. Relativisers or nominalisers

Enclitics

- 12. Intentional 'be about to' *=kasu*
- 13. Mood (imperative, declarative, frustrative, conditional, apprehensive, interrogative fused with evidentiality and tense)
- 14. Aspect 'zone' I
  - 14a. Habitual prescribed *=hyuna* 'what you do and what you ought to do'
  - 14b. Customary *=kape*
  - 14c. Habitual repetitive *=nipe*
  - 14d. Anterior *=nhi*
- 15. Evidentiality and tense, e.g. *=mhana* 'non-visual-remote.PAST'
- 16. Epistemic *=da* 'doubt', *=pada* 'isn't it true that'
- 17. Aktionsart (manner or extent of associated action, e.g. 'split open', 'step on and feel pain', 'wag one's tail', 'away')
- 18. Degree (augmentative (also meaning 'indeed'), diminutive, approximative ('more or less'))
- 19. Aspect 'zone' II
  - 19a. Prolonged, ongoing=*daka* 'yet, still'
  - 19b. Perfective *=sita* 'already accomplished'
  - 19c. Repetitive *=pita* 'once again'
  - 19d. Completive *=niki* 'totally, completely'
- 20. Switch-reference and clause-chaining markers
- 21. Emphatic enclitics *=a/=ya*, *=wani*; evidence *=sõ*

Figure 2 Verb structure in Tariana

Some categories – e.g. plural – can be marked recursively, that is, more than once, since enclitics in positions 6, 8 and 9 require an additional number marker, thus creating a situation comparable to endoclisis – see J above. In the following example, brackets show clitics which require a separate number marking: *nha-má-pe=[yanà-pe]=[tùpe]=[mìki]* (they-CL:FEM-PL=[PEJ-PL]=[DIM:PL]=[NOM.PAST:PL]) 'the little bad dead female ones'. These enclitics cannot occur as independent phonological words.

The structure of the verbal word is given in figure 2. A minimal verbal word consists of positions 1, 2 and 3. Position 1 has to be filled for transitive and intransitive active verbs. Other positions have to be filled if the corresponding meaning needs to be expressed.

Not all enclitics can co-occur; for instance, imperative does not co-occur with evidentiality and tense (full details are found in Aikhenvald 1999b and forthcoming). Variable ordering is allowed for position 19 (see examples (8–9) in §1), and this has a pragmatic effect. Suffixes never come in between enclitics, and categories are not marked recursively. Of all the verbal enclitics, only aktionsart enclitics can be used as independent phonological words when in contrastive focus; they are different from other enclitics in some other ways as well.

Tariana also has serial verbs and complex predicates (Aikhenvald 1999c) consisting of more than one grammatical and phonological word but occupying one predicate slot. Suffixes in positions 5–11 go onto the first grammatical word and characterise a serial verb construction or a complex predicate as a whole.

2.4   Clitics in Tariana

2.4.1 Proclitics Proclitics are a small class of four members, with low selectivity (parameter B). Most of them are FIXED POSITION CLITICS whose position does not depend on the grammatical class of their host (parameter C). For this reason they are not included in the noun structure (figure 1) or the verb structure (figure 2). Proclitics are contrasted with prefixes in table 2.

The adverb *kay* 'thus', *kwa/kwe* 'interrogative–distributive' and connective *ne* 'then; there' are sentence-initial proclitics which form one phonological word with the following word. The negative *ne* is procliticised to the following numeral 'one', e.g. *ne=pa-ita* (NEG=one-CL:ANIM) 'non-one', interrogative, e.g. *ne=kwaka* (NEG=what) 'nothing', or a verb, e.g. *ne=mema-kade-pidana* (NEG=NEG+sleep-NEG-REM.P.REP) '(he) did not sleep'.

Proclitics can form independent phonological words if contrastive (D); then they acquire a primary stress. If they form a phonological word on their own, they constitute the unique kind of phonological word without a long vowel. Example (10) shows *kay* 'thus' as a proclitic, and in (11) it is an independent word.

(10)   kay=ná-ni   ná-yha   nemháni=pidanà
        thus=3pl-do 3pl-swim 3pl+walk=REM.P.REP
        Thus (lit. having done thus), they drowned

(11)   káy dú-ni   di-kesi-pé=nukù   du-kalité=pidanà ...
        thus 3sgf-do 3sgnf-friend-PL=TOP.NON.A/S 3sgf-tell=REM.P.REP
        After she acted this way (not any other way), she told his friends ...

A phonological word consisting of a proclitic and an enclitic is the first word in (12). Verbal enclitics can attach to all the proclitics except for the negative

Table 2 *Properties of proclitics compared to prefixes*

properties	proclitics (four)	prefixes (eleven)
B. Selectivity	low	high
C. Type of host	any sentence-initial word (*ne* 'then, there', *kwe/kwa* 'interrogative', *kay* 'thus') numeral 'one', interrogative, verb (*ne* 'negative')	subtypes of nouns and verbs which take prefixes
D. Phonological word	possible; the only monosyllabic phonological words in Tariana with short vowels	no
E. Segmental properties	cannot contain any long or nasal vowels; monosyllabic	
F. Phonological cohesion	no phonological boundary processes	vowel fusion and metathesis on the boundary
G. Pauses	no pauses after	
H. Combining with other clitics	do not combine with other proclitics; do not combine with enclitics (*ne* 'negative'); combine with verbal enclitics (*ne* 'then, there', *kwe/kwa* 'interrogative', *kay* 'thus'); combine with nominal enclitics (*ne* 'then, there')	proclitics precede prefixes prefixes cannot go onto enclitics
I. Relative ordering in clitic string	precede enclitics	not applicable
J. Position with respect to affixes	precede affixed words	not applicable (there is only one prefix position per word)
K. Grammatical word	are grammatical words	no
L. Scope	clause: *ne* 'then, there', *kwe/kwa* 'interrogative' negated constituent: *ne* 'negative' predicate or clause: *kay* 'thus'	grammatical word
M. Lexicalisation	*kay* 'thus' forms a fixed expression with the verb 'do'	often lexicalise with nouns and verbs
N. Special syntactic rules	*ne* 'negative' and *ne* 'then, there' can be independent clauses *kay* 'thus' can be the predicate	no
O. Word class	*kay* 'thus' member of a semi-closed class of adverbs *ne* 'then, there' is a member of semi-closed class of connectives *kwe/kwa* 'interrogative' and *ne* 'negative' are classes on their own	not applicable

ne – which is more selective than the others – if the proclitic is focussed and/or contrastive, as in (12). No more than two enclitics can attach to one proclitic – see §2.4.3.

(12) <u>né=pidanà</u>   dihá   itá-whya=nè   dísa
      then=REM.P.REP   the   canoe-CL:CANOE=AG   3sgnf+go.up
      dí-nu
      3sgnf-come
      Then the canoe came upstream

The proclitic *ne* 'then, there' can attach to the nominal enclitic *-nuku* 'topical non-subject'; *né=nukù* (then=TOP.NON.A/s) is used if sequencing is topical, i.e. is what the story is about – see (13). It forms one phonological word and one grammatical word with the proclitic.

(13) <u>né=nukù</u>   nhá   na-kúna   nhéta=pidanà
      then=TOP.NON.A/s   they   3pl-take.with.hand   3pl+drag=REM.P.REP
      And <u>then</u> they took (a piece of gold they found) with their hands

Table 2 shows that proclitics are similar to prefixes in just two ways: in their segmental structure, and in the restriction against having a pause after them. All four proclitics share the following properties:
• the capacity for forming an independent phonological word and a grammatical word;
• the lack of phonological boundary processes;
• their position with respect to affixes and enclitics.
They differ from prefixes with respect to other parameters.

2.4.2 Enclitics Enclitics in Tariana are a largish, albeit heterogeneous class. We first discuss NOMINAL ENCLITICS; then we consider PREDICATE ENCLITICS.

Nominal enclitics are highly selective fixed position clitics whose position depends on the grammatical class of their host (noun phrase). No nominal enclitic – except for =*tuki* 'diminutive' – can form an independent phonological and grammatical word. However, *tuki* has different properties as a nominal enclitic and as an independent word: it is in free variation with =*tiki* and distinguishes singular and plural only as an enclitic; when used as an adverb it can be repeated: *tuki-tuki, tuki-tiki* or *tiki-tiki*.

The morphemes =*miki-* 'nominal past', =*yana* 'pejorative' and =*pasi* 'augmentative' are good candidates to be grammatical words, since each of them requires number marking. The enclitic =*miki-* also requires gender marking. Each of these three clitics is a fusion of a number of grammatical elements, and satisfies criteria for a grammatical word. They could be grouped together with adjective modifiers since they show gender and number agreement. They are contrasted with nominal suffixes in table 3.

Predicate enclitics are contrasted with verbal suffixes in table 4. Tense-evidentiality enclitics (position 15) display low selectivity, while the aktionsart enclitics (position 17) are highly selective.[13]

Tense-evidentiality enclitics are floating. Their position does show some correlation with the grammatical class of their host. They can go onto any constituent in the clause, if it is in contrastive focus and preposed to the predicate. This is the case in (14) where the tense-evidentiality enclitic goes onto the first constituent. If no constituent is contrastive, they go onto the predicate.

(14)   matʃá-peri=<u>sinà</u>   du-kalité
        good-CL:COLL=<u>REM.P.INFR</u>   3sgf-tell
        She (mother) says good things (contrary to what a misbehaving
            girl might think)

Of predicate enclitics, only aktionsart enclitics can be used as independent phonological and grammatical words. When independent, they belong to the class of adverbs. This is similar to how proclitics are used in Tariana.

In (15) *thepi* 'INTO.WATER' is an enclitic, and is not contrastive.

(15)   du-hwá=<u>thepì</u>   du-á   du-aphuá=pidanà
        3sgf-fall=<u>INTO.WATER</u> 3sgf-go   3sgf-dive=REM.P.REP
        She (the girl transformed into a snake-woman) fell into water diving

In (16) it is used as an independent word and is contrastive:

(16)   <u>thepí</u>   di-rúku   di-á
        <u>INTO.WATER</u>   3sgnf-go.down   3sgnf-go
        Into water he went (contrary to all expectations)

These enclitics – unlike other predicate enclitics – can appear as one-word responses to a 'clarification' question. Such a question – to clarify (15) or (16) – is (17). The answer is (18).

(17)   kaní=nihkà   ná:?
        where=INTER.VIS.PAST   3pl+go
        Where did they (the fish, or the girl) go?

(18)   <u>thepí</u>
        INTO.WATER
        Into water

---

[13] There are several more classes of predicate enclitics which are not included here, for the sake of pedagogic simplicity; full details are provided in Aikhenvald (forthcoming).

Table 3 *Nominal enclitics compared to suffixes*

properties	nominal enclitics (about twelve)	nominal suffixes (over one hundred)
B. Selectivity	high (noun phrase)	high (noun)
C. Type of host	fixed position; host noun phrase	nouns and adjectives
D. Phonological word	only =*tuki* 'diminutive' can be	no
E. Segmental properties	lack long and nasal vowels, can consist of one, two or three syllables; idiosyncratic restrictions on consonants	lack long and nasal vowels, can consist of one, two or three syllables
F. Phonological cohesion	fewer boundary processes than affixes; idiosyncratic process within clitics and in word-final position	vowel fusion and metathesis on the boundary
G. Pauses	one type of segmental pause-marking available (in between enclitics)	no pause
H. Combining with other clitics	only =*nuka* 'topical non-subject' combines with proclitic *ne*= 'then, there'; can be followed by floating enclitics	not applicable
I. Relative ordering in clitic string	fixed position in nominal clitic strings	not applicable
J. Position with respect to suffixes	follow suffixes; may precede suffixes (see figure 1); do not allow variable position	may follow enclitics; allow variable position
K. Grammatical word	=*tuki* 'diminutive', =*miki*- 'nominal past', =*yana* 'pejorative' and =*pasi* 'augmentative'	no
L. Scope	noun phrase	grammatical word
M. Lexicalisation	no	yes
N. Special syntactic rules	no	no
O. Word class	=*tuki* 'diminutive' is an adverb =*miki*- 'nominal past', =*yana* 'pejorative' and =*pasi* 'augmentative' are adjectival modifiers	not applicable

Table 4 *Predicate enclitics compared to suffixes*

properties	predicate enclitics (about 50)		suffixes (about fifty)
	aktionsart	tense-evidentiality	
B. Selectivity	high: main verb	low	high
C. Type of host	fixed position: main verb	floating: can go onto the predicate or onto any focussed constituent	verb
D. Phonological word	if focussed; may be monosyllabic with a short vowel	no	no
E. Segmental properties	similar to suffixes in length and in the lack of long vowels; idiosyncratic restrictions on consonants		lack long vowels, idiosyncratic restrictions on consonants
F. Phonological cohesion	fewer boundary processes than affixes; phonological processes within clitics and in word-final position		numerous boundary processes
G. Pauses	one type of segmental pause-marking available in between enclitics		no
H. Combining with other clitics	do not combine with proclitics; occupy position 17	combine with proclitics; occupy position 15 (figure 2)	not applicable
I. Relative ordering in clitic string	fixed position		not applicable
J. Position with respect to suffixes	follow suffixes		not applicable
K. Grammatical word	yes	no	no
L. Scope	main verb	sentence or verb complex	not applicable
M. Lexicalisation	yes	no	yes
N. Special syntactic rules		no	not applicable
O. Word class	adverbs	not applicable	not applicable

Most aktionsart enclitics consist of two syllables; monosyllabic enclitics, such as *hu* 'away', constitute an instance of a monosyllabic phonological word with a short vowel. In this they behave similarly to proclitics. Note that all other monosyllabic phonological words must have a long vowel.

Segmental pause-marking in Tariana involves (i) the insertion of a final syllable *hã*; (ii) vowel raising and centralisation and raising without lengthening: *a* to *ɨ*; (iii) vowel raising and centralisation with lengthening: *a* to *ɨː*; and (iv) vowel lengthening with lowering (if applicable): *i* > *eː*, *e* >*aː*, *a* > *aː*. Only the latter can occur before a predicate enclitic, e.g. *díraː-pidanà* (3sgnf+drink-REM.P.REP) 'he drank . . .' Other kinds of pausal marking occur at the end of a phonological word.

Aktionsart enclitics may form idiomatic combinations with their host, unlike enclitics of other types, but similar to suffixes. Most of these occur with just a few verbs because of their idiosyncratic semantics, e.g. =*dhala* 'touch the surface, unsticking or scratching it'. Some occur with just one verb – this is the case of =*khuli* 'rub against someone in a friendly way, e.g. a cat, or a dog', used only with the verb -*peta* 'for an animal to wag its tail in greeting'.

Predicate enclitics have one property reminiscent of gaps in paradigms: imperative, apprehensive and interrogative – which are fused with evidentiality and tense – block all other enclitics.

2.4.3 Clitics in Tariana: a comparison Proclitics, nominal enclitics and predicate enclitics in Tariana share only a few properties. Like proclitics, enclitics in Tariana form a phonologically defined class. Nominal enclitics are fixed position enclitics: they appear attached to nouns or to noun phrases. They are highly selective. The enclitic =*tuki* 'diminutive' is more similar to an independent root than other nominal enclitics since it can also appear as an independent phonological and grammatical word, albeit with different grammatical properties; it has a suppletive plural form. Three enclitics are somewhat similar to independent roots in that they mark number (=*yana* 'pejorative' and =*pasi* 'augmentative') or gender fused with number (=*miki-* 'nominal past'), but less similar than =*tuki* since they cannot be used on their own.

Nominal enclitic =*nuku* 'topical non-subject marker' is the only nominal enclitic capable of forming a phonological word which consists exclusively of clitics, since it can attach to the proclitic connective *ne*= 'then'. It is thus similar to floating enclitics. Unlike floating enclitics, *ne*=*nuku* forms one grammatical word (=*nuku* indicates that the connective is topical). The association of floating enclitics with their phonological hosts – which can be proclitics – depends on whether a particular host is focussed.

Predicate enclitics fall into a number of classes. Of these, aktionsart enclitics are fixed position enclitics with high selectivity. They always attach to the main

NOMINAL ENCLITICS

• =*nuku* 'topical non-subject'
•   =*yana* 'pejorative',
=*miki-* 'nominal past',
=*pasi* 'augmentative'
•=*tuki*

•other nominal enclitics

like a suffix ←————————————————————————→ **like a root**

•Aktionsart enclitics
•Floating enclitics

PREDICATE ENCLITICS

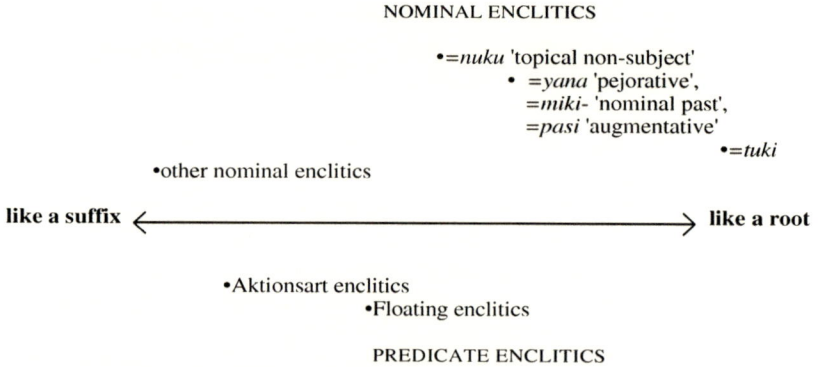

Figure 3 Properties of clitics in Tariana

verb, and thus are similar to suffixes. They can form a phonological word and a grammatical word of their own, if focussed. They can also form idiomatic combinations with the verb.

Tense-evidentiality enclitics are floating. (Their unmarked location is the predicate.) Their selectivity is low, and they can form a phonological word with proclitics. They cannot form a phonological or a grammatical word on their own.

These six classes of enclitics can be plotted on a continuum[14] between a suffix and a root, with respect to the combination of their properties (see figure 3).

2.4.4 Words with and without clitics in Tariana We have seen that in Tariana, words containing clitics, and clitic-only words, behave differently from phonological words without clitics.

First, Tariana has two phonological processes which are clitic-specific – see F in §1. Aspiration floating is indicative of a clitic boundary within a phonological word which contains enclitics. Regressive vowel assimilation is indicative of the presence of a clitic and of the end of a phonological word which contains enclitics.

Second, when proclitics and aktionsart enclitics appear as independent phonological words, they are unlike any other phonological words in that they are the only instances of phonological words with a short vowel.

Tariana provides evidence in favour of the existence of the following kinds of words containing clitics:

(1) A clitic-containing word consisting of an enclitic and a root (with or without affixes); it coincides with a grammatical word, e.g. *du-hwá=thepì* (3sgf-fall=INTO.WATER) 'she fell into water' from (15).

[14] This continuum is reminiscent of 'clitic cline' mentioned in Woodbury (1996).

(2) A clitic-containing word consisting of a floating enclitic and a focussed word to which it is attached, e.g. *kaní=nihkà* (where=INTER.VIS.PAST) in (17). This sequence does not form a single grammatical word; while *kaní* is a grammatical word, the enclitic forms a grammatical word with the predicate elsewhere in the clause.

(3) A clitic-containing word consisting of a clause-initial proclitic and its host (to which it is procliticised, e.g. *kay=ná-ni* 'thus they did' (lit. 'having done thus'), as in (10). This sequence consists of two grammatical words. Since no clitic-specific phonological processes occur on a proclitic boundary, a clitic-containing word of this type is indistinguishable from a phonological word with no clitic – the only difference being that it is not a grammatical word.

A clitic-only phonological word – which consists of a proclitic and enclitic(s) – is undoubtedly one phonological word (there is just one primary stress). It has additional properties:

• First, when proclitics combine with enclitics, e.g. *né=pidanà* (then=REM.P. REP) in (12), to form a phonological word, the primary stress falls on the proclitic, and each enclitic maintains its secondary stress. That is, such a word has its primary stress on the first syllable.

• Second, a phonological word consisting of a proclitic and enclitic(s) differs from other words in three ways:

(a) It can contain no more than two enclitics.

(b) There is the following restriction on its syllable structure. If a clitic-only word contains two syllables (that is, if a monosyllabic enclitic is hosted by a proclitic), the vowel of the proclitic – which receives the primary stress – is phonetically lengthened, e.g. *né=mhà* 'then=PRES.NON.VIS' is pronounced as [né:=mhà], and *né=nà* (then=REM.P.VIS) as [né:=na]. This does not happen if it contains more than two syllables, e.g. *né=pità* (then=REPETITIVE) or *né=sinà* (then=REM.P.INFR).

(c) No segmentally marked pauses can occur between a proclitic and an enclitic.

Clitic-only words are of two kinds:

(I) A clitic-only word consisting of the proclitic *ne* 'then, there' followed by the enclitic *=nukù* 'topical non-subject', as in (13). It coincides with a grammatical word: since these two morphemes occur together (and thus satisfy the criterion of cohesiveness), in a fixed order, and have a conventionalised coherence and meaning; *=nukù* is used to show that the connective *ne* is topical.[15]

---

[15] An additional piece of evidence in favour of *né=nukù* (then, there=TOP.NON.A/S) as a grammatical word comes from the slightly different variety of Tariana spoken in the village of

Table 5 *Properties of clitic-containing and clitic-only words in Tariana*

type of words	structure	example	one grammatical word
1. Clitic-containing	a root (with or without affixes) and an enclitic	*du-hwá=thepì* (3sgf-fall=INTO.WATER) 'she fell into water' in (15)	yes
2. Clitic-containing	a floating enclitic and a word to which it is attached	*kaní=nihkà* (where=INTER.VIS.PAST) in (17)	no
3. Clitic-containing	a clause-initial proclitic and the following word to which it is procliticised	*kay=ná-ni* 'thus they did' (having done thus)' in (10)	no
I. Clitic only	proclitic *ne* 'then, there' and enclitic *=nukù* 'topical non-subject'	*né=nukù* in (13)	yes
II. Clitic only	a proclitic and one or two floating enclitics	*né=pidanà* (then=REM.P.REP) in (12)	no

(II) A clitic-only word consisting of a proclitic and one or two floating enclitics, e.g. *né=pidanà* (then=REM.P.REP) in (12). It does not coincide with a grammatical word: *né* is one grammatical word, and *=pidanà* forms part of the predicate, which is a different grammatical word.

Table 5 summarises the properties of clitic-containing and clitic-only words in Tariana.

3   Summary: the status of clitics

We have seen that in Tariana each prosodically deficient morpheme occupies a particular place within a multidimensional continuum, from a fully bound to a more independent morpheme. None of these morphemes shares all the prosodic properties of affixes, or of roots.

Proclitics differ from enclitics in most properties; proclitics form a phonologically defined class (the direction in which they attach to the host, plus no phonological boundary process), but not a coherent grammatical class. By their grammatical properties they are closer to independent words than to prefixes.

Periquitos. In this dialect, *né=nukù* can serve as the basis for derivation *ne=nukú-peni* (then, there=TOP.NON.A/S-ANIM.PL) 'those from right there'. This is one phonological word with primary stress on *-nukú,* which then behaves as a suffix.

The two groups of enclitics – nominal and verbal – differ in how similar they are to suffixes and to independent roots. They fall into several subclasses, depending on whether they can occur as a grammatical and as a phonological word, and whether they have nominal grammatical categories of their own.

Predicate enclitics have the predicate as their preferred location. Fixed position aktionsart enclitics are similar to suffixes. Floating tense-evidentiality enclitics are unlike suffixes and unlike aktionsart enclitics in that they are capable of forming a clitic word together with a proclitic.

We have also demonstrated the existence of at least three different kinds of clitic-containing words and of two kinds of clitic-only words in Tariana.

The following properties are criterial for distinguishing words with clitics from phonological words of other types:

- their relationship with stress – parameter D;
- their segmental properties – parameter E;
- their phonological cohesion, that is, phonological processes applying within them or on their boundaries – parameter F;
- their internal structure (whether they contain just clitics, or other elements as well) and their ability to combine with other clitics – parameter H;
- their ordering with respect to one another and to affixes – parameters I and J;
- and their correlation with grammatical words – parameter K.

All this – and especially the existence of clitic-specific phonological processes (see §2.4.4) – provides a rationale for a typology of clitics.

An alternative approach would be to restrict oneself to recognising only words and affixes, as suggested by Joseph in chapter 10. But whether by doing this we gain 'in elegance and precision' remains an open question. As Matthews points out in §4 of chapter 11, 'it may simply be that, in a particular language, a few forms which are either affix-like or word-like nevertheless do not have every property that affixes or words in general do have'. Various parameters suggested above demonstrate 'how much might all "clitics" have in common' (in Matthews' words).

A continuum between words and affixes – advocated in this chapter – covers clitics of different kinds. It is designed to present a clearer view of the 'messy reality' (in Joseph's words) than a simplistic binary division of units into words and affixes.

Appendix Additional issues concerning clitics, and parameters suggested for distinguishing between clitics and affixes

A great amount of literature has appeared on various issues concerning clitics (see, for instance, Nevis et al. 1994, Anderson 1992, 1995, Sadock 1991, 1995, and Halpern 1998). This literature is not quite as vast as that on 'word'; however, I will not attempt a full survey. Here I assume that clitics have to be realised as morphemes; that is, I exclude any discussion of morphological processes which may be functionally reminiscent of clitics (see Anderson 1992, 1995: 22–3, for analysis of stress shift in Tongan, of mutation in Welsh, and of initial consonant mutation in some Algonquian languages; also see Ball and Müller 1992: 178–80, for a similar approach to Welsh).

Sadock (1995: 259) introduces clitics as items that 'appear to be positioned in syntax by ordinary principles, but at the same time show a non-syntactic fondness for attachment to a nearby word'. He exemplifies a typical clitic with the English auxiliary clitic '*ll* realised as a non-syllabic [1] after pronouns; syntactically, 'the linear position of the clitic is exactly the same as the functional equivalent free word *will*, but the enclitic must be suffixed to a particular morphological word type, a pronoun'. However, this is not true of all clitics – as Zwicky (1977) pointed out, some so-called clitics are not positioned by syntactic rules, and some 'depend only phonologically on host words'.

A cross-linguistic definition of clitics appears to be so problematic that Sadock (1995: 260) comes up with the following 'sociological' definition of clitics: 'A clitic is an element whose distribution linguists cannot comfortably consign to a single grammatical component'; thus arguing that there is no 'natural class' of clitics defined in terms of genuine grammatical properties.

The alternation between a bound morpheme and a free word in individual languages depends on various factors – one of them speech style or register (cf. *I'll* and *I will* in English); this is the basis for distinguishing between simple clitics and special clitics (Zwicky 1977, 1985; Anderson 1992: 200ff). A simple clitic is an element of some basic word class which appears in a normal syntactic position where its non-cliticised counterpart would appear, e.g. *give 'em the plate*; while a special clitic is an element whose position is determined by other rules, e.g. second position clitics.

Anderson (1992: 201) assumes that 'a simple clitic is merely a lexical item whose phonologcal form does not include assignment to a prosodic unit at the level of "word" (or some other appropriate unit that constitutes an essential domain of stress assignment)'.

What are loosely grouped under the notion of 'special clitics' are more similar to affixes – for instance, English possessive enclitic '*s* which has exactly the same set of conditioned allomorphs as the plural inflection and third person singular present tense. Clitics appear to be less selective than affixes with respect to their 'host'; there is often no close grammatical link between a clitic and its host, just a phonological 'association of convenience'. For instance, the possessive '*s* in English attaches at the end of any NP no matter how long it is, and 'clitic-like' post-inflectional affixes in Yidiɲ (Dixon 1977: 236) occur on any word. But some clitics are more selective than others – the contracted negator *n't* in English is highly selective (and yet is treated as a clitic by at least some linguists, although as an affix by others – e.g. Zwicky and Pullum 1985). Other clitics display high selectivity: for instance, pronominal clitics in Romance languages have to precede or follow the verb (and can thus be termed 'verbal' clitics: Halpern 1998).

However, the binary division into 'simple' clitics and 'special' clitics appears too simplified (just as the ±clitic parameter – suggested, for instance, in Anderson 1992 – is hardly applicable to language analysis, since deciding what is a clitic and what is not involves a number of parameters, as suggested below). See Klavans (1983, 1985), for an account of clitics operating with just three parameters; and criticism of this in Sadock (1991) and Halpern (1998).

Zwicky and Pullum (1985) and Sadock (1991) provide a number of criteria for distinguishing between affixes and clitics. These are subsumed under the parameters suggested here.

Parameter A in Zwicky and Pullum (1985) states that clitics can exhibit a low degree of selection with respect to their hosts, while affixes exhibit a high degree of selection with respect to their stems: the more complicated the distribution, the likelier the element is to be an affix. This is subsumed under my parameter B (selectivity of clitics). This parameter cannot be defining for a clitic to constitute a prosodic class of morpheme by itself. Some clitics do attach to any word class, or to almost any word class; however, others attach to members of particular word classes (for instance, cliticised auxiliaries tend to be positioned close to the main verb; also see Halpern 1998 on verbal clitics). There are also affixes which are not selective, e.g. person–number–gender cross-referencing, negative *ma-* and relative–attributive *ka-* in Arawak languages (Aikhenvald 1999a). Selectivity – or lack of it – can be one of the scalarly defined parameters in defining a clitic; but it is not a necessary condition for a morpheme to be a clitic.

Zwicky and Pullum's parameter B states that arbitrary gaps in the set of combinations are more characteristic of affixed words than of clitic groups; for instance, derivational affixes often present gaps in paradigms. This is covered by my parameter M (which refers to the possibilities of lexicalisation, and semantic and morphological idiosyncrasies of clitics). However, this is not a definitional parameter by itself since one of the definitional properties of inflection – as opposed to derivation – is also the lack of arbitrary gaps in paradigms. In addition, in polysynthetic languages, gaps in combinations of what qualifies as clitics do occur (for instance, in Tariana, apprehensive modality does not co-occur with tense-evidentiality).

Zwicky and Pullum's parameters C and D state that morphophonological and semantic idiosyncrasies are more characteristic of affixed words than of clitic groups; this is again covered by м. These parameters may provide a set of scalar properties; however, only an analysis based on language-specific characteristics can help in establishing and comparing a given set of morphemes with respect to their affix-hood or clitic-hood; for instance, the emphatic clitic -*e* in Kannada behaves in an idiosyncratic way with verbs and with other constituents (see below). In languages with sequences of clitics, the rules of sequencing may be totally different from the rules that apply to independent words and to affixes (e.g. Hittite; and other examples below). A host and a clitic can get lexicalised, e.g. English modal auxiliaries *gonna, wanna* (e.g. Pullum 1997; also see examples from Piedmontese and Tariana under м in §1).

Zwicky and Pullum's parameter E states that syntactic rules can affect affixed words, but cannot affect clitic groups. This is true for clitics whose position depends on some phonological rule (e.g. second-position clitics, or phrase-final clitics). Once clitics attach to some particular word class (e.g. verbal clitics or cliticised auxiliary), they form a constituent with their host and can be affected by syntactic rules (see below). Clitic-specific rules, as one of the defining parameters for clitics, are covered by my parameter N (referring to clitic-specific syntactic rules).

According to their parameter F, clitics can attach to material already containing clitics, but affixes cannot. This statement is not quite correct since in the recent literature a number of examples have been quoted where clitics appear in between inflectional markers (e.g. Albanian, Platense Spanish and Eskimo discussed in Sadock 1991: 57; Ngiyambaa and Beja discussed by Klavans 1979; the example of Portuguese 'mesoclisis'; and Tariana examples above). The positioning of clitics with respect to each other and with respect to affixes is covered by my parameters I (relative ordering of clitics) and J (the position of clitics with respect to what can be defined as affixes).

Turning to another author, all of the 'commonly mentioned properties of clitics' listed by Sadock (1991: 52) are subsumed under the parameters above – see table 6. Parameters Ia-e are problematic as to their universal validity for all prosodically deficient elements – see discussion above. For instance, though Ia is sometimes true, clitics in many languages are known to alternate with free morphemes depending on various factors, one of them the speech style or register (cf. *I'll* and *I will*). Parameter IIa is problematic; and IIb goes against Id, and is also problematic (see discussion under в in §1 above). Parameter IIIa depends on interpretation of what is meant by semantic function; however, it is clear that clitics hardly form a single semantic class anyway. IIIb is problematic (see discussion of the syntactic scope of clitics under L in §1), and so are IVa–d and Va-b (see dicussion in §1). However frequently some or all of these

Table 6 *The 'commonly mentioned properties of clitics' (Sadock 1991) and the parameters above in § 1*

I. Morphology	a. Clitics are bound morphemes	Parameters D and K
	b. They attach outside inflection	Parameters I and J
	c. They block further morphology	Parameters I and J
	d. They attach without regard to the morphological class of the host	Parameter B
	e. They are completely productive	included in M
II. Syntax	a. Clitics are independent elements of syntax	included in K, N, O
	b. They are syntactically adjacent to their morphological host	included in B
III. Semantics	a. Clitics are semantic functions	depends on
	b. They take the meaning of a phrase as argument	interpretations under L
IV. Phonology	a. Clitics are phonologically dependent	under D
	b. They are agglutinative	under F
	c. They are stressless	under D
	d. They are subject to automatic phonological rules only	under F
V. Lexicon	a. Host + clitic forms are not lexicalised	problematic, discussion under M
	b. Clitics alternate with free words	D and K

properties are quoted, as Sadock (1991: 54) states, 'clear examples of clitics can be found in the world's languages that differ in respect to almost any one of the behaviours listed in I through V'.

References

Aikhenvald, A. Y. 1995. *Bare*. Munich: Lincom Europa.

1996. 'Words, phrases, pauses and boundaries: evidence from South-American languages', *Studies in Language* 20.487–517.

1998. 'Warekena', pp 225–439 of *Handbook of Amazonian languages*, Vol. 4, edited by D. C. Derbyshire and G. K. Pullum. Berlin: Mouton de Gruyter.

1999a. 'The Arawak language family', pp 65–105 of *The Amazonian languages,* edited by R. M .W. Dixon and A. Y. Aikhenvald. Cambridge: Cambridge University Press.

1999b. 'Multiple marking of syntactic function and polysynthetic nouns in Tariana', pp 235–48 of *CLS* 35, Part 2.

1999c. 'Serial verb constructions and verb compounding: evidence from Tariana (North Arawak)', *Studies in Language* 23.479–508.

2000. 'Areal typology and grammaticalisation: the emergence of new verbal morphology in an obsolescent language', pp 1–37 of *Comparative linguistics and grammaticalisation*, edited by Spike Gildea. Amsterdam: John Benjamins.

forthcoming. *A grammar of Tariana, from northwest Amazonia*. Cambridge: Cambridge University Press.

Anderson, S. R. 1985. 'Inflectional morphology', pp 150–201 of *Language typology and syntactic description*, edited by T. Shopen. Cambridge: Cambridge University Press.

1992. *A-morphous morphology*. Cambridge: Cambridge University Press.

1993. 'Wackernagel's revenge: clitics, morphology and the syntax of second position', *Language* 69.68–98.

1995. 'Rules and constraints in describing the morphology of phrases', pp 15–31 of *CLS* 31, Part 2.

Asher, R. and Kumari, T. C. 1997. *Malayalam*. London and New York: Routledge.

Ball, M. J. and Müller, N. 1992. *Mutation in Welsh*. London and New York: Routledge.

Chafe, W. L. 1977. 'The evolution of third person verb agreement in the Iroquoian languages', pp 493–524 of *Mechanisms of syntactic change*, edited by Charles N. Li. Austin: University of Texas Press.

Curnow, T. J. 1997. 'A grammar of Awa Pit'. PhD thesis, Australian National University.

Derbyshire, D. C. 1985. *Hixkaryana and linguistic typology*. Dallas: Summer Institute of Linguistics and the University of Texas at Arlington.

Dimitrova-Vulchanova, M. 1995. 'Clitics in Slavic', *Studia Linguistica* 49.54–92.

Dixon, R. M. W. 1977. *A grammar of Yidiɲ*. Cambridge: Cambridge University Press.

Everett, D. and Kern, B. 1997. *Wari': the Pacaas Novos language of western Brazil*. London: Routledge.

Facundes, S. da Silva. 2000 'The language of the Apurina people of Brazil'. PhD thesis, State University of New York, Buffalo.

Friederich, J. 1974. *Hethitisches Elementarbuch I*. Heidelberg: Carl Winter.

Haas, M. 1977. 'From auxiliary verb phrase to inflectional suffix', pp 525–37 of *Mechanisms of syntactic change*, edited by Charles N. Li. Austin: University of Texas Press.

Haberland, H. and Van der Auwera, J. 1990. 'Topics and clitics in Greek relatives', *Acta Linguistica Hafniensia* 22.128–37.

Haiman, J. 1991. 'From V/2 to subject clitics: evidence from Northern Italian', pp 135–59 of *Approaches to grammaticalisation*, Vol. 2, edited by Elizabeth Closs Traugott and Bernd Heine. Amsterdam: John Benjamins.

Hall, T. A. 1999. 'Phonotactics and the prosodic structure of German function words', pp 99–132 of Hall and Kleinhenz 1999.

Hall, T. A. and Kleinhenz, U. 1999. Editors of *Studies on the phonological word*. Amsterdam: John Benjamins.

Halpern, A. 1998. 'Clitics', pp 101–22 of *The handbook of morphology*, edited by A. Spencer and A. M. Zwicky. Oxford: Blackwell.

Harris, A. and Campbell, L. 1995. *Historical syntax in cross-linguistic perspective*. Cambridge: Cambridge University Press.

Heine, B. 1993. *Auxiliaries: cognitive forces and grammaticalisation*. New York: Oxford University Press.

Joseph, B. D. and Philippaki-Warburton, I. 1987. *Modern Greek*. London: Routledge.

Klavans, J. 1979. 'On clitics and words', pp 68–80 of *The elements: a parasession on linguistic units and levels*, edited by P. R. Clyne, W. F. Hanks and C. L. Hofbauer. Chicago: Chicago Linguistic Society.

　　1983. 'The morphology of cliticisation', pp 103–21 of *CLS* 19, Part 2.

　　1985. 'The independence of syntax and phonology in cliticisation', *Language* 61.95–120.

Matthews, P. H. 1997. *The concise Oxford dictionary of linguistics*. Oxford: Oxford University Press.

Meira, S. 1999. 'A grammar of Tiriyó'. PhD dissertation, Rice University.

Nespor, M. and Vogel, I. 1986. *Prosodic phonology*. Dordrecht: Foris.

Nevis, J. A., Joseph, B. D., Wanner, D. and A. M. Zwicky 1994. *A bibliography of clitics 1892–1991*. Amsterdam: John Benjamins.

Parker, S. 1999. 'On the behaviour of definite articles in Chamicuro', *Language* 75.552–62.

Payne, D. L. and Payne, T. E. 1990. 'Yagua', pp 249–474 of *Handbook of Amazonian languages*, Vol. 2, edited by D. C. Derbyshire and G. K. Pullum. Berlin: Mouton de Gruyter.

Payne, T. E. 1983. 'Yagua object clitics: syntactic and phonological misalignment and another possible source of ergativity', pp 173–84 of *CLS* 19, Part 2.

Peperkamp, S. 1995. 'Enclitic stress in Romance', pp 234–49 of *CLS* 31, Part 2.

Prasse K.-G. 1972. *Manuel de grammaire touarègue*, Vols. I–III. Copenhague: Akademisk Vorlag.

Pullum, G. K. 1997. 'The morpholexical nature of English *to*-contraction', *Language* 73.79–102.

Sadock, J. M. 1991. *Autolexical syntax: a theory of parallel grammatical representations*. Chicago: University of Chicago Press.

　　1995. 'A multi-hierarchy view of clitics', pp 258–79 of *CLS* 31, Part 2.

Sapir, E. 1930. *The Southern Paiute language*, Part 1: *Southern Paiute, a Shoshonean language. Proceedings of the American Academy of Arts and Sciences* 65(1).1–296. Reprinted (1992) in W. Bright, ed. *The collected works of Edward Sapir* 10. Berlin: Mouton de Gruyter.

Schachter, P. and Otanes, Fe. T. 1972. *Tagalog reference grammar*. Berkeley and Los Angeles: University of California Press.

Shaul, D. 1983. 'Clisis and word order in Tepiman', pp 259–70 of *CLS* 19, Part 2.

Smith, I. and Johnson, S. 2000. 'Kugu Nganhcara', pp 357–507 of *The handbook of Australian languages*, Vol. 5, edited by R. M. W. Dixon and B. J. Blake. Melbourne: Oxford University Press.

Sridhar, S. N. 1990. *Kannada*. London: Routledge.

Steele, S. 1977. 'Clisis and diachrony', pp. 539–82 of of *Mechanisms of syntactic change*, edited by Charles N. Li. Austin: University of Texas Press.

Tosco, M. forthcoming. 'When clitics collide: on 'to have' in Piedmontese', *Diachronica*.

Vigário, M. 1999. 'On the prosodic status of stressless function words in European Portuguese', pp 255–94 of Hall and Kleinhenz, 1999.

Waters, B. 1989. *Djinang and Djinba: a grammatical and historical perspective*. Canberra: Pacific Linguistics.

Woodbury, A. C. 1996. 'Clitics in Autolexical Syntax', pp 320–63 of *Autolexical theory: ideas and methods*, edited by E. Schiller, E. Steinberg and B. Need. Berlin: Mouton de Gruyter.

Zec, D. and Inkelas, S. 1990. 'Prosodically constrained syntax', pp 365–78 of *The phonology–syntax connection,* edited by S. Inkelas and D. Zec. Chicago: University of Chicago Press.

Zwicky, A. M. 1977. *On clitics.* Bloomington: Indiana University Linguistics Club.
    1985. 'Clitics and particles', *Language* 61.283–305.

Zwicky, A. M. and Pullum, G. K. 1985. 'Cliticisation vs. inflection: English n't', *Language* 59.502–13.

3   The word in Cup'ik

Anthony C. Woodbury

1   Introduction[1]

Ideally, the word is a transcendent unit of linguistic organisation serving at once as the maximal domain of lexical phonology, the maximal domain of morphology and the atom of syntax. Our everyday notion of 'word', I think it is fair to say, implies just this convergence, as do such scientific theories as the lexicalist hypothesis (of which Lapointe 1980 and DiSciullo and Williams 1987 are among the strongest formulations). This ideal is upheld empirically for a given language when, in the internal organisation of phonology, morphology and syntax, many logically independent processes each refer crucially, in some way, to the same unit or its boundaries, and when that unit is clearly comparable across languages. But to the extent that the ideal may not be upheld in each language, it is important for a general theory to be able to specify the ways in which phonology, morphology, syntax, and perhaps other subsystems may resolve the stream of speech in different, non-convergent ways.

I begin by introducing Cup'ik (§2), its typology (§3), and the word for 'word' in Cup'ik (§4). I then turn to the grammatical word (§5), the question of clitics and their grammatical status (§6), the phonological word (§7). I then summarise the mismatching that occurs between the grammatical and the phonological word (§8) and end with a brief conclusion (§9).

2   The language

Cup'ik is the name of the variety of Central Alaskan Yup'ik that is spoken in Chevak, Alaska, 11 miles inland from the Bering Sea on southwest Alaska's Yukon-Kuskokwim Delta. In Chevak (pop. 800 in 1997) Cup'ik is spoken by

[1] I wish to thank Leo Moses, Mary Moses, Rebecca Kelly, John Pingayak, the late Joe Friday and many others in Chevak who have taught me what I know of Cup'ik over the years. I gratefully acknowledge support for my work in Chevak from the National Science Foundation (grants SBR 9511856, BNS 8618271 and BNS 8217785). Many thanks to Bob Dixon and Sasha Aikhenvald for their work in articulating the problem of the word and bringing together the group represented in this volume, many of whom have contributed comments that have helped me in the preparation of this paper.

practically all native people born before 1970 but by very few born after 1980. Correspondingly, English is spoken to some extent by most people born after 1940. Central Alaskan Yup'ik, encompassing several varieties, is indigenous to the entire Delta area from Unalakleet to Bristol Bay and has about ten thousand speakers. Together with Alutiiq to the south, Central Siberian Yup'ik on Saint Lawrence Island and in the Russian Far East, and Naukanski in the Russian Far East, it is a member of the Yupik branch of Eskimo. The other major branch is Inuit, spoken from North Alaska to Canada to Greenland in a range of varieties (Woodbury 1984).

Almost nothing, except specific morphological and lexical choices and phonological variations distinguishes Cup'ik from other Central Alaskan Yup'ik varieties. There is also remarkably little difference in respect to most major points raised in this paper among any Yup'ik language or Inuit variety, although some minor but interesting differences can be noted.

All data are given in the standard Central Alaskan Yup'ik orthography. Symbols have their IPA phonetic values except: vv = [f]; ll = [ɬ]; ss = [s]; g = [ɣ], gg = [x]; r = [ʁ], rr = [χ]; c = [č]; ng = [ŋ]; y = [j]; e = [ə]; and ' = gemination. Also, voiced continuant symbols represent their voiceless counterparts in clusters with other voiceless sounds, hence *maligtellruanga* 's/he followed me' represents [malixtəɬχuaŋa].

3   A thumbnail typology

Cup'ik is a highly polysynthetic AOV/SV, 'double marking' language (i.e., both head-marking and dependent-marking) with extremely well-developed derivational and inflectional morphology. Despite this, the morphology is formally simple in that it utilises exactly one 'grammatical process', suffixation. There is no compounding, no prefixing, infixing, ablaut, consonant mutation, reduplication, or morphological use of accentual change (except in some expressive contexts). Each suffix combines with a base to create a new base and, in derivation especially, predicates something of the old base. Cup'ik is somewhere between agglutinative and fusional: while there is often a one-to-one relationship between morphological formatives (bases, suffixes) and units of meaning, morphophonological fusion is aggressive, and, in the inflectional morphology especially, there is limited suppletion and considerable form–function mismatching, i.e., multiple marking of one category and portmanteau marking of several categories. Prosodically, Cup'ik has a left-to-right, quantity-sensitive, iambic-foot-forming stress system that robustly defines a hierarchy of syllable, foot, phonological word-minus-enclitics and phonological word-including-enclitics. Despite the high degree of polysynthesis and the moderately agglutinative character of the morphology, phonological words are uninterruptable by pause.

4   The word for 'word' in Cup'ik

I have not systematically studied metalinguistic speech in Cup'ik. In his Yup'ik dictionary, Jacobson (1984: 312) defines *qaneryaraq*, the only word for 'word' that I know of, as 'language, word, saying; Bible', and he gives the following example:

(1)   Kitak cali   apqerru   qanellren   cukaunak,
       please again say   your.words   slowly
          caperrnailngurnek   qaneryaranek   aturluten.
          not.difficult   words   using
       Please repeat what you said slowly, using simple words.

In tracking *qaneryaraq* in Cup'ik natural texts by elder traditional speakers that I have transcribed, I find the sense 'word, sayings, message' to be by far the most common, for example:

(2)   Awa=i   cal',   awna   **qaneryaraq**   tuavesqevkenaku
       there! also   that   message,word   saying.never.panic
          imarpigmi   kanani;   **qaneryara**ullilria.
          at.ocean   down.there   that seems to be the message
       And that message is never to panic down there at the ocean, that
          seems to be the message.

5   Grammatical word

Cup'ik inflectional morphology offers a systematic and pervasive definition of a unit which meets at least our intuitive sense of what a 'word' is. I will begin with a discussion of the morphosyntactic categories and formal mechanisms of Cup'ik noun, verb and particle inflection (§5.1); I then discuss how inflection (§5.2), the notion of a morphological base (§5.3) and the ability to stand alone as an utterance (§5.4) all converge to define a single coherent notion of a grammatical word. In §5.5 I will briefly consider a minor complication whereby a phrase can be embedded morphologically within a word. I end with a summary (§5.6) that relates the specific criteria raised in this section to the general criteria for word raised by Dixon and Aikhenvald in chapter 1.

5.1   The inflectional system

Inflection defines a successful candidate-unit for word in Cup'ik. Cup'ik has a huge inflectional system, with almost 300 possible inflectional endings for ordinary nouns, and about 1,200 possible inflectional endings for ordinary verbs. In Sapir's (1921) terms, Cup'ik is *mixed relational*: its categories of obligatory inflection mix concrete categories such as person and number with purely relational notions such as case and possession. I follow Anderson (1982) in taking inflection to involve those morphological categories whose marking is in any sense relevant at the phrasal level, and, accordingly, wish to take some care in establishing that what I call inflection is, in that sense, really inflection.

5.1.1 Noun inflection Noun inflection categories are categories that are obligatorily marked in the open class of ordinary nouns, as well as in a number of closed noun subclasses such as pronouns, attributive adjectives, quantifiers and demonstratives. Ordinary nouns are marked for the relational category of case (3) and the inherent category of number (4):

(3)   Absolutive: arnaq   woman (S or definite O)
       Ergative:[2]   arna-m   woman (A) or woman's
       Ablative-modalis: arna-meng   woman (indefinite O); from the/a
                                      woman
       Locative: arna-mi   at the/a woman
       Vialis: arna-kun   via the/a woman

(4)   Absolutive singular: arnaq   woman
       Absolutive dual: arna-k   two women
       Absolutive plural: arna-t   three or more women

Beside the locative and vialis, there are several other oblique cases not shown in (3). Nouns are also marked for the person and number of the possessor, if any. This marking is present whether or not the possessor is overt:

(5)   (arna-m)   eni-i
       woman-ERG.sg   house-ABS.sg+3sgP
       (the woman's)/her house

(6)   (wii)   en-ka
       my-ERG   house-ABS.SG+3plP
       my house

This leads to fairly extensive paradigms of inflectional endings, sampled in (7):

(7)   ABS.sg (unpossessed)   qayaq   kayak
       ABS.sg+1sgP   qaya-qa   my kayak
       ABS.pl+3sgP   qaya-i   his kayaks
       ABS.du+3plP   qaya-gkek   those two's two kayaks
       LOC.sg+3REFLEXIVEsgP   qaya-mini   in his own kayak
       VL.du+2sgP   qaya-gpekun   via your two kayaks

---

[2] Or 'relative', as it is known in the literature on the language family.

Of these endings, some show an agglutinative one-to-one matching between categories and formatives (8); some are fully fusional *portmanteaux*, having one formative for several categories (9); and some show *doubling*, the opposite fusional tendency, where there are two formatives for the same category (in (10) there are two markers of the absolutive dual, and in fact all three formatives are contextual variants of the etymological dual -g-).

(8)   VL.du+2sgP   -g-pe-kun
                     -du-2sgP-VL

(9)   ABS.pl+3sgP   -i
                      -ABS.pl+3sgP

(10)   ABS.du+3duP   -g-ke-k
                     -ABS.du-ABS.du-3duP

A similar mix of agglutination and fusion is found in verb inflection.

5.1.2 Verb inflection Verb inflection is obligatory for all verbs. Verbs are inflected for mood, and for person and number of S, O and (except in the Appositional Mood) A. Moods indicate the illocutionary force of a main clause or the syntactico-semantic linkage of a subordinate clause to its matrix clause:

(11)   Indicative   tekit-uq   s/he arrived
       Interrogative tekit-a   s/he arrived
                                     (in WH question)
       Optative   teki-lli   may s/he arrive
       Participle   tekite-lria   (then, surprisingly) s/he
                                     arrived
       Appositional   teki-lluni   then (as in narrative) s/he
                                     arrived; s/he, arriving
       Consequential tekic-an   when s/he arrived
       Concessive   teki-ngraan   when s/he arrived

Beside the consequential and concessive, there is a number of other oblique moods not shown in (3). Inflectional marking for person and number of S, O, and A are obligatory, whether or not the corresponding NPs are overtly present:

(12)   (Arnaq)   qavar-tuq.
       woman.ABS.sg   sleep-IND.3sgS
       (The woman)/She is sleeping.

(13)   (Wangkuta)   qavar-tukut
       we-ABS.pl   sleep-IND.1plS
       We are sleeping.

(14)   (Arna-m)   (kaugpii-t)   tangrr-ai.
      woman-ERG.sg   walrus-ABS.pl   see-IND.3sgA+3plO
      (The woman)/she saw (the walruses)/them.

(15)   (Kaugpii-m)   (wii)   tangrr-aanga.
      walrus-ERG.sg   1sg.ABS   see-IND.3sgA+1sgO
      (The walrus)/it saw me.

5.1.3 Particles Particles are the third word category, defined by the lack of any inflection. Syntactically, most of these words are either adverbs or interjections:

(16)   keyianeng   always
      unuk   last night
      cali   also; more
      tawa   that's enough; now; then
      qa   huh? (forms yes-no question)
      Kiiki!   Hurry up!
      Uuminaqsaga!   Darn!

Enclitics are a subclass of particles. Like other particles they are uninflected; however, they are phonologically dependent on another grammatical word. They will be considered in §6, but for now let us take as the null hypothesis the idea that enclitics are words just like any other particle.

5.2   Inflection as a criterion for wordhood

Suppose we assume the following morphological rules defining the three grammatical word classes:

(17)   noun word   = noun base + noun inflection
      verb word   = verb base + verb inflection
      particle word   = particle base

These rules correspond to criterion (e) for the grammatical word in the introduction ('There will be just one inflectional affix per word') so long as we consider the inflectional affix to be the formative-category bundle that makes up the complete inflection as defined in §5.1. If these rules are correct, then for every noun inflection and for every verb inflection, the unit preceding it should be definable, respectively, as a noun base or a verb base. We now need criteria for this.

5.3   The base as a criterion for wordhood

We will begin by observing the structure of bases and from there we will use characteristics of that structure as our criterion for identifying the base independently.

By (17), noun and verb bases should be identifiable by peeling off the inflection, while particle bases should be identical with particle words. That is
what is shown in each of the example sets below. But these sets also show
that bases are derived recursively from more primitive bases via derivational
suffixation:

(18)   ivruci-t   waterboots (ABS.pl)
        ivruci-li-uq   she is making waterboots
                                                  (IND.3sgS)
        ivruci-li-sta   waterboot maker (ABS.sg)
        ivruci-li-ste-nger-tut   they have someone to make
                                                  (them) waterboots (IND.3sgS)
        ivruci-li-ste-ngqer-sugnait-uq   they definitely don't have anyone
                                                  to make them waterboots
                                                  (IND.3sgS)

(19)   quuyurni-uq   s/he is smiling (IND.3sgS)
        quuyurni-art-uq   s/he is smiling quickly
        quuyurni-arte-llru-uq   s/he suddenly smiled quickly
        quuyurni-arte-llru-yaaq-uq   s/he suddenly smiled quickly,
                                                  but in vain
        quuyurni-arte-llru-yaaqe-llini-uq   evidently s/he suddenly smiled
                                                  quickly, but in vain

(20)   Nakleng!   Poor thing! (Particle)
        Nakl-u'rluq!   Dear poor thing! (Particle)

In (18) the most elementary base is a noun base meaning 'waterboot'; in (19)
it is a verb base meaning 'to smile'; and in (20) it is a particle base meaning
'poor thing'.

   The derivational process can be summarised as in (21), where the suffixes
are designated *postbases* following the practice of most Yup'ik-Inuit specialists:

(21)   base = base (+ postbase)

Because it is recursive, (21) allows for a base to be followed by any number of
postbases, and indeed there are well over 400 postbases, a great many of which
are perfectly productive. Furthermore (21), makes no provision for a postbase
to occur alone with an inflection. This is appropriate, since postbase-inflection
units are always ill-formed in isolation or as syntactic constituents, as in (22).
Indeed to express such ideas, a pleonastic base *pi-* 'thing; do' must be allowed
to serve as the base, as in (23).

(22)   *li-uq   s/he made (something)
        *yugnait-uq   s/he definitely didn't
        *llini-uq Peter-aq   Peter evidently did

(23)	pi-li-uq	s/he made it/one
	pi-yugnait-uq	s/he definitely didn't
	pi-llini-uq Peter-aq	Peter evidently did

Because it essentially says that a base contains a base, there is a semi-circularity to (21) as a *criterion* for identifying a base. This problem disappears, however, if we recognise unanalysable bases as stems, a proper subset of bases. There is a perfect disjunction between the stem and postbase lexicons of Cup'ik: a stem cannot be a postbase, nor a postbase a stem. Thus for every non-inflectional formative, it is possible on the basis of (21) to determine whether it is a stem or postbase. (Even diachronically there is little overlap, that is, postbases almost never have etymologies as 'grammaticalised' bases, or vice versa.) Thus further – because there is no rule allowing the compounding of bases – every word begins with a stem, and every occurrence of a stem marks the beginning of a word. This is a fully independent criterion for identifying both a grammatical word and a base. It works together with (17), which incorporates this notion of base *and* defines the endings of (non-particle) grammatical words.

5.4   *Grammatical word as stand-alone*

Every grammatical word as defined by (17) and (21) can stand alone as a complete utterance (except most enclitics, see §6). This is especially true in actual practice due to a stylistic preference for ellipsis in answers to questions:

(24)	Ca?	What? (noun, ABS.sg)
	Unuk?	Last night? (Particle)
	Qai-ngatnun.	On top of them. (e.g., answering 'Where does this go?' (noun, TERMINALIS.s+3plP)
	Pingremi.	(Yes,) even though he did. (verb, CONCESSIVE.3REFLEXIVEsgS)

Crucially, no piece of a grammatical word as defined in (17) can stand alone as a complete utterance.

Related to this, words as defined by (17) and (21) can all function as minimal phrases in syntax. That is, every noun word so defined can function as the sole noun of an NP; every verb word as the sole verb of a VP; and every particle word as the sole adverb of an adverbial phrase, or as an interjection.

5.5   *Phrase within a word: a complication*

A complication is posed by the construction in (25), particularly when compared to that in (26):

(25)   Ene-m   aki-an-et-ut.
         house-ERG.sg   opposite-LOC.sg.3sgP-be-IND.3plS
         They are at the opposite side of the house.

(26)   Ene-m   aki-ani   et-ut.
         house-ERG.sg   opposite-LOC.sg.3sgP   be-IND.3sgS
         They are at the opposite side of the house.

In (25), the base *aki* 'opposite' is followed by a locative case inflection, giving what should be a complete word according to (17); that word, however, is followed by a postbase -*et*- 'be' and an indicative mood verb inflection, something licensed by neither (17) nor (21), whether or not *aki-an*- 'at the opposite side' is taken to be a word by itself. A further problem with (25) is that an ergative case NP should not appear as an argument in an intransitive clause. By contrast, (26) is well-behaved, dividing into three properly inflected words, with the ergative NP as the possessor argument not of a verb but of an independent locative case noun. In Cup'ik, (25) is the common construction, whereas (26) is somewhat archaic. In most varieties of Yup'ik, (25) appears to the exclusion of (26).

Evidently, (25) is a rare exception to the claim that stems such as *et*- 'be' are never grammaticalised as postbases, for this is indeed what has happened in the case of this verb. It is reasonable to assume that this construction is licensed by a minor rule of grammar, as follows:

(27)   verb base = NP[LOC] + postbase[*et*-]

Some support for this claim is provided by the ungrammaticality of (28) and (29), which are permutations, respectively, of (25) and (26):

(28)   *Akianetut enem.

(29)   *Akiani etut enem.

(29) shows that the entire locative NP *enem akiani* 'on the opposite side of the house' is an inseparable unit in syntax; and (28) shows that that inseparable unit is, apparently, imported wholesale into the morphology in (25), where it seems to function as a base. Thus, (27) introduces a paradox where a phrase is embedded into a word. (The phonology resolves this grammatically introduced paradox in its own way – it treats as separate words the possessor and the possessum-plus-postbase-plus-ending unit.)

There is independent evidence for this same process in another minor construction:

(30)   Maklagaa-m   citug-tur-tuq.
         bearded seal-RLsg   nail-**eat**-IND.3sgS
         S/he is eating fermented bearded seal flipper.

(31)   Maklagaa-m   citu-i.
         bearded seal-RL.sg   nail-ABS.pl+3sgP
         fermented bearded seal flipper (lit. 'bearded seal's, its nails')

Example (30) is like (25) in that it appears that the postbase *-tur-* 'eat' is in construction with a possessed NP that would appear independently as (31); and the order of the words in (30) cannot be reversed (cf. (28)). It is different from (25), however, in three important respects: (a) the postbase *-tur-* 'eat' cannot appear as an independent verb; (b) *-tur-* is added here to the noun base *citug-* 'nail', not the inflected noun *citui* 'its nails'; and (c) *-tur-* only appears to form constructions of this kind when the NP in question is an idiom: note that the literal meaning of (31) is merely 'bearded seal's nails', not 'fermented bearded seal flipper' (a specific food preparation). Normally, *-tur-* only occurs with an unpossessed noun stem. The (minor) rule for (30) can thus be given as:

(32)   verb base = NP[+IDIOM, −INFL] + postbase

−INFL indicates that the whole NP head is uninflected (i.e., *maklagaam citug-* rather than inflected, as in (31)). The important point in common between (27) and (32) is that both license limited embedding of phrases within words.[3]

5.6   Summary

In this section we have given criteria for the grammatical word based on inflection; on the notion of the base; and on the grammatical word as stand-alone in utterances and phrases. I have also discussed minor, but problematic constructions where phrases appear to be embedded into words as bases. It is worth pointing out that our formulations in (17) and (21) ensure the two principal criteria for the grammatical word proposed by Dixon and Aikhenvald in chapter 1: that elements within the word occur together (criterion (a)) and in a fixed order (criterion (b)). (17), as noted already, also ensures that there will be only one inflectional affix per word (criterion (e)), except in those limited cases where phrases are embedded into words. Example (21), because of its recursion, implies a contradiction of criterion (d), that in some languages at least, morphological processes tend to be non-recursive. It has been noted that the grammatical word, so defined, functions as an utterance (criterion (g)). As for the remaining criteria, I found it difficult to say much about conventionalised coherence and meaning (criterion (c)), a notion I found difficult to apply; and I defer discussion of the placement of pauses (criterion (f)) to the discussion of the phonological word in §7.

---

[3] There are different, but related constructions in Cup'ik and all other Yup'ik-Inuit languages in which the grammatical definition of word raised in this section is not violated at all, but where, nevertheless, a base and postbase function as independent syntactic atoms or 'syntactic words'. For extensive discussion, see Sadock 1980, 1985, 1991 and Woodbury 1981, 1996.

In all, the above shows that the grammatical word is an extremely clear and robust concept, clouded only by a (remarkably) limited degree of phrase-in-word embedding. It is likely due, more than anything, to the pervasiveness of the inflectional system and the virtual absence of compounding in the derivational morphology.

6   Enclitics in grammar

In §5.1.3 it was claimed that grammatically speaking, enclitics are particles: they are uninflected, and function as adverbs or interjections. We stated, as our null hypothesis, that like any other particle, they are words. Be that as it may, there are certain ways in which they differ from other grammatical words: they cannot occur alone in an utterance (§5.4), and, as will be seen in §7, they are constituents of the phonological word. In this section, we will first consider the grammar of enclitics and then ask why they should not be considered as part of the grammatical word.

6.1   Enclitic grammar

Following are some principal Cup'ik enclitics (there are about a dozen in all):

(33)   =am   but; emphasis in conversation (can occur as
                        independent word)
         =gguq   it is/was said
         =kiq   I wonder
         =llu   and, also
         =mi   what about?
         =qa   huh? (forms yes-no questions) (can occur as
                        independent word)
         =ga/=wa   well (at least) ...
         =tuq   I wish (used with optative)
         =gga   Voilà! (used with predicating participles and in
                        nominal sentences)
         =i   forms interjection from demonstrative adverb
                        particle

Several enclitics can also occur as independent words; this simply means that they have lexical entries both as enclitics and ordinary particles. =i occurs only with a specific category of particle and is in that sense lexically hosted. Likewise, some of the others are lexically hosted in the sense of forming particle idioms in combination with certain particle words (never inflected nouns or verbs):

(34)   maa=i 'here!' < maa 'here' + =i
         tawa=llu 'well now!' < tawa 'there' + =llu 'and'
         Wa=qa! 'what's up? Hello!' < wa 'here' + =qa 'huh?'

Otherwise, the enclitics have phrasal scope, occurring in phonological construction with the first grammatical word of the phrase; such is the case for *=llu* 'and' in (35), *=am*, a marker of emphasis, in (36); and *=gguq* 'it is said' in both examples:

(35)   Neqiviak=llu=gguq   taun'   imaicuunani
        their.food.cache=and=it.is.said   that   it was never empty
        And, it is said, that food cache of theirs was never empty.

(36)   Tamatum=ggur=am   nalliini   tunucillget   makut,
        of that=it.is.said=emphasis   at its time   loons   these
            qaraliinateng   taw'...
            lacked.coloration   then
        So it is said, at that time these loons lacked coloration then...

Further evidence of enclitics having phrasal scope is provided by those which require that the clause in their scope be of a certain mood. Thus *=tuq* 'I wish' in (37) requires optative, *=gga* 'voilà!' in (38) requires a participle and *=qa* 'huh?' in (39) requires one of the declarative moods (here indicative) in order to form a yes-no question:

(37)   Qalu=tuq   kan'   tagullitgu!
        dipnet=I.wish   that.down.there   may.they.bring.it.up (OPTATIVE)
        I wish they'd bring up that dipnet down there!

(38)   Maqiyuilnguq=gga   taw'   agaani,
        he.who.never.took.firebaths (PARTICIPLE)=voilà   well   across.there
            ukani   tawaam!
            this.side instead
        (It was) he (who) never took his firebaths across there, (but did it) on
            this side instead!

(39)   Aana=qa   an'uq?
        mom=huh?   she.went.out (INDICATIVE)
        Did mom go out?

6.2   *Why not consider enclitics as grammatical suffixes?*

I considered this question as a theoretical matter in Woodbury (1996), arguing they should not be considered as grammatical suffixes, and hence not included in the definition of the grammatical word (see also Halpern 1995). For the Cup'ik enclitics at hand, it should be noted, first, that even if enclitics were to be considered part of the grammatical word, they would not be part of the inflectional ending since they are not category-specific, they can occur on particles, and they do not signal categories within category classes which are obligatory (as, e.g., are case, mood and person-and-number agreement). Thus, they would have to be post-inflectional elements of some kind.

However, as just shown, enclitics grammatically pertain to phrases and not words; and because they are generally hosted by the first word in the phrase, whatever that may be, they need not have any direct grammatical constituency with the host word. Thus a word-plus-enclitic unit is not a grammatical unit independent of the whole phrase in which it occurs.

But what about the so-called particle idioms of (34)? They are phonological words and they are lexical entries, so why not call them grammatical words? I see no reason to do so as long as they show regular enclitic phonology. It is sufficient to consider them as idioms made up of two grammatical entities (word particle plus enclitic particle) bound as one phonological word. To be sure, many bona fide particles have their etymological origin as particle idioms, but in these cases, the phonology is reanalysed to be that of a single particle word (e.g. *tawaam* 'however' is presumably from *tawa* 'then' plus =*am*; but *tawa=am* should be pronounced [tawá:am] whereas what occurs is [táw:a:m] the expected result when footing rules are applied to *tawaam* with no enclitic boundary).

7   Phonological word

We now turn to phonological indicators of domains and boundaries.

7.1   Prosodic criteria

The main prosodic phenomenon of Cup'ik is a set of foot formation rules determining stress and other prosodic features. These rules form quantity-sensitive iambic feet from left to right within a domain which all analysts have taken to be the 'word'. On the analysis assumed here, the final syllable of that domain, as well as certain medial CVC syllables, are left unfooted and hence also unstressed (for more details see Woodbury 1987 and Hayes 1995: 239–360). Phonetically, the foot-final syllable is stressed and, if open, lengthened. In the examples in this section, the first line marks feet with parentheses while the second line gives the morphological segmentation:

(40)   (pi.ssú:.)(tu.llí:.)(ni.lú:.)ni
        pi-ssu-tu-llini-luni
        thing-hunt-always-apparently-APPOSITIONAL.3REFLEXIVEsgS
        s/he is apparently always hunting something

(41)   (ma.llú:.)(ssu.tú:.)(lli.ní:.)lu.ni
        mallu-ssu-tu-llini-luni
        beached.whale-hunt-always-apparently-APPOSITIONAL.3REFLEXIVE.sgS
        s/he is apparently always hunting beached whales

(42)   (áng.)(yar.kág.)ka
        angyar-kag-ka
        boat-future-ABS.du+1sgP
        my two future boats

(43)   (páq.)naq.(sa.qú:.)na.ku
        paqnak-saqu-naku
        check-NEG-APPOSITIONAL.3sO
        Don't check it!

All the items in (40–3) are inflected forms of postbase-derived bases, i.e., grammatical words as we have been defining them. Example (41), in comparison
with (40), shows that the same postbase-and-inflection sequence gets different
footing depending on what is 'upstream' of it in the left-to-right foot assignment
process. Moreover, it is clear that the footing of a word is not affected by the
footing of the prior word, for example, the words in (40–1) keep their footing
when juxtaposed as a phrase, in either direction:

(44)   a. (pi.ssú:.)(tu.llí:.)(ni.lú:.)ni (ma.llú:.)(ssu.tú:.)(lli.ní:.)lu.ni
            s/he is apparently always hunting something, apparently always
                hunting beached whales
        b. (ma.llú:.)(ssu.tú:.)(lli.ní:.)lu.ni (pi.ssú:.)(tu.llí:.)(ni.lú:.)ni
            s/he is apparently always hunting beached whales, apparently
                always hunting something

The entire system places certain conditions on the beginnings and ends of words
which can serve as diagnostics for both word-beginnings and word-endings.
For example, there is a rule that creates a unary foot from a word-initial (C)VC
syllable, as shown in (42–3), which in turn ensures that that syllable is stressed.
Thus no word can begin with an unstressed (C)VC syllable (although not every
stressed CVC syllable is word-initial, cf. (42)). As for word-endings, their
location is often deducible because of the already-mentioned ban on word-final
feet. Thus, no word can end with a stressed syllable. Futhermore, the presence of
two light unstressed syllables next to each other, as in (41) and (43), is always
the result of the failure of word-final iambic footing and is thus a sufficient
condition for the end of a word. There is also a rule which automatically creates
a unary foot from any (C)VV(C) syllable, except word-finally. Hence, any
syllable containing VV that is not stressed is necessarily word-final.

Interestingly, the domain for all these processes, although definable entirely
on prosodic rather than grammatical terms, happens nevertheless to converge
exactly with the grammatical word as it was defined in (17) and (21).

However, this same system, with just a few modifications, extends to include
the phonological word plus enclitics. I will argue that the domain of the extended system is in fact the phonological word proper (PW), while the domain

of the basic system just described is a subdomain of the phonological word which I will symbolise as PW–. Thus PW corresponds, grammatically, to a grammatical word plus its enclitics; whereas PW– corresponds to the grammatical word minus any enclitics. Let us now examine the prosodic similarities and differences between PW and PW–.

In some prosodic contexts PW behaves phonologically, exactly like PW–. Thus, when =*llu* 'and' and =*gguq* 'it is said' are added to the words in (40–1), the domain for binary footing extends just as it would within PW–:

(45)   (pi.ssú:.)(tu.llí:.)(ni.lú:.)(ni.llú:.)gguq

(46)   (ma.llú:.)(ssu.tú:.)(lli.ní:.)(lu.ní:.)llu gguq

These examples show that the ban on final footing is in fact a characteristic of PW, and not PW–, since in each case the PW– final syllable is now footed. It also shows that left-to-right footing is a characteristic of PW. In other contexts, PW shows some differences:

(47)   (míng.)qut.ka.mi
        mingqut-ka-mi
        needle-future-LC.sg
        at the future needle

(48)   (Míng.)(qut.ká:.)mi? *or* (Míng.)(qut.kám.).:i
        mingqut-ka=mi
        needle-ABS.sg+1sgP-what about
        What about my needle?

In this minimal pair (from Miyaoka 1985), (47) shows the PW– pattern, in which a closed–open syllable sequence, here *qut.ka.*, resists iambic footing, and hence there is no stress in the word beyond the initial syllable; cf. also (43), where *naq.sa.* likewise resists footing and hence stress. Example (48), in contrast to the otherwise-identical (47), contains an enclitic boundary and hence shows the PW pattern: here the closed–open sequence *qut.ka.* is footed, the syllable *ka* is stressed, and is further affected in one of two ways: either /a/ is lengthened or the syllable is closed by the gemination of the following /m/.

The pattern in (47–8) is general: a closed–open syllable sequence forms a foot, if and only if it contains, or is adjacent to, an enclitic. Some enclitics, like =mi in (48), permit either lengthening or gemination at the end of the open syllable; some allow only lengthening; and some allow only gemination: cf. Jacobson (1984: 619) and Miyaoka (1985) for the Yup'ik facts. In some sense, those allowing only lengthening are most suffix-like, while those allowing only gemination are uniquely enclitic-like. However, these subclasses seem to be partly determined by the initial segment of the enclitic in question, but partly idiosyncratic; moreover they do not correlate with sequential ordering among the clitics, ruling out the possibility of intermediate 'levels' between PW– and PW.

7.2   *Segmental criteria*

There are a number of respects in which segmental alternations depend on whether the segment occurs word-internally, word-finally before an enclitic, or word-finally with no following enclitic. That is, segmental phonology, like prosodic phonology, respects both PW– and PW as phonological levels and correlates them, respectively, with the grammatical word and the grammatical-word-plus-enclitics.

In one such instance, base-final uvulars (and velars) are continuants before suffixes, but stops before obstruent-initial enclitics and word finally with no following enclitic:

(49)   qayar-kaq   'makings of a kayak'   (base-final uvular before postbase)
        qayar-put   'our kayak'   (base-final uvular before inflection)
        qayaq=kiq   'the kayak, I wonder ...'   (word-final uvular before enclitic)
        qayaq   'kayak'   (absolute word-final uvular)

However, these same uvulars (and velars) are continuants when a following enclitic is sonorant-initial; and they can be either continuants or stops when a sonorant-initial word follows:

(50)   qayar=mi   'indeed, a/the kayak'   (sonorant-initial enclitic follows)
        qayar man'a   'kayak, this one'   (sonorant-initial word follows)
        qayaq man'a   'kayak, this one'   (sonorant-initial word follows;
                                               slow speech variant)

In all, then, base-final uvulars have one behaviour when followed within the grammatical word by postbases or inflectional endings; another behaviour when followed by an enclitic; and a third behaviour when followed by nothing. (The pre-enclitic behaviour is also an option when another word follows in the phrase.)

A second relevant phenomenon is the treatment of /t/+/t/ clusters arising heteromorphemically within words versus the treatment of those arising between a word and an enclitic or another morphsyntactic word:

(51)   mingqut'ten   [míŋquttən]
        mingqut-ten
        needle-ABS.pl+2sg
        your needles

(52)   enait=tuq   [ə́n:aíttuq] *or* [ə́n:aítuq]
        their.houses-I.wish
        I wish their houses ...

(53)   enait   taukut   [ə́n:aíttaúkut] *or* [ə́n:aítaúkut]
        their.houses   those
        those houses of theirs

Grammatical-word-internally, as in (51), each /t/ is pronounced and released separately, whereas across a grammatical word boundary, as in (52) and (53), the two /t/s optionally coalesce as a single /t/. Again, this offers phonological support for the right boundary of PW– and for its coincidence with the right boundary of the grammatical word.

A third relevant phenomenon is the distribution of syllable shapes. Word-initially and enclitic-initially, a syllable may begin with a vowel; elsewhere every syllable must begin with exactly one consonant:

(54)   Words: angyaq 'boat', ii 'eye', una 'this', ena 'house'
        Enclitics: =am 'but', =i (interjectional with demonstrative adverbs)

This offers independent phonological support for the left boundary of the grammatical word. Furthermore, because internal syllables are C-initial and contain no more than two vowel moras, no grammatical word shows a surface sequence of more than two vowel moras. But three-mora surface sequences can arise when a vowel-initial enclitic combines with a grammatical word ending in two vowel moras:

(55)   angyaa=am   'but his boat'
        yaa=i   'there yonder!'

This is another respect in which word plus enclitic units are phonologically unique.

Like the footing rules, the realisation of base-final uvulars, the treatment of /t/+/t/ clusters, and the distribution of syllable types independently refer to the beginning or the end of the grammatical word, as defined in §5. But they also refer to the superordinate domain of word plus enclitic.

7.3   *Grammatical word with enclitics as phonological word domain*

If we consider these processes and constraints as pertaining to a hierarchy of domains, we can summarise our results as in table 1. We have two phonological domains, PW– and PW, corresponding to two morphosyntactically definable domains: the grammatical word, which is subordinate; and the grammatical word plus any enclitics, which is superordinate. I must now justify my treatment of the latter, rather than the former, domain as the PW. In principle, the lexical phonology should yield a set of structures belonging to its maximal domain; and that domain should be qualitatively different from any

Table 1 *Correlation of phonological domains with grammatical units and with phonological processes and constraints*

phonological domain	grammatical unit	process or constraint
PW–	Grammatical word	L–R footing; closed–open syllable pairs are not footed
		Internal uvulars are continuants, final uvulars are stops
		/t/+/t/ sequences may not coalesce
		Initial syllable can be vowel initial
PW	Grammatical word plus enclitics, if any	L–R footing; closed–open syllable pairs footed adjacent to enclitic boundaries
		Ban on final foot
		Pre-enclitic uvulars are continuants if enclitic is continuant-initial, stops otherwise
		/t/+/t/ sequences may coalesce across enclitic boundary
		Trimoraic vowel sequences licit across enclitic boundaries

superordinate, post-lexical phrasal domain in what can now be considered as the usual ways (Kiparsky 1985). That is, it should involve processes that are structure-preserving (rather than structure-creating) and categorical (rather than gradient). It is reasonable, I think, to reserve the term *phonological word* for the maximal domain of the lexical phonology. All of the processes here seem to be of the structure-preserving, categorical type, and thus the two domains we are considering should be deemed a part of the lexical phonology. This should make the grammatical word plus any enclitics the phonological word; and the grammatical word a clearly demarcated subdomain within that.[4] This result is rather unremarkable, since it amounts to the classic treatment of enclitics as phonologically bound, but grammatically independent.

7.4   The pause criterion

Pausing practices in Cup'ik natural speech provide strong independent evidence for our identification of the grammatical word plus any enclitics with the PW. Every such unit may be preceded and followed by a pause; whereas no such unit may be interrupted by a pause. For example, in an experiment designed to test the correlation of pause duration with syntactic boundary strength, speakers were asked to utter the following sentence at various rates:

[4] To conserve space, I have excluded a demonstration that tonological and segmental word-to-word sandhi phenomena earlier analysed as categorical are, in fact, gradient and non-structure-preserving. Argumentation is given along the same lines for related Nunivak Cup'ig, in Woodbury 1999.

(56)   Sekulartek   an'ngamek   angutek   atkukek
       2.teachers   when.they.went.out 2.men   their.2.parkas
          agutakek   amavet
          they.took.them   over.there
       When the two teachers went out, they took the two men's two parkas
       over there.

For each word except the penultimate one, there were tokens in which it
was followed by a pause (and in elicitation, a pause was accepted there as
well).

Furthermore, if a pause or speech error occurs in the midst of a PW, the
speaker will go all the way back to the beginning of the word and start again,
as shown in the following taped instances from natural speech:

(57)   Akulit – Akuliitnun!   To the side!
       Qanemci – Qanemci – Qanemci –   I'm going to tell a story . . .
         Qanemcikqaqataraqa un'
       kenig – kenillermun kanavet   to the firepit down there
       anelrar – anelreraraama   when I was inching out . . .
       Amissaa – Amissaagngama   When I found the door (amik)
       ataucit – ataucitun ayuqngameng   as one, they are all alike

Finally, I find no examples in any text of resumptions that begin with an enclitic.

In summary then, pausing behaviour respects the notion of PW developed
here.

8   Summary of grammatical-word–phonological-word mismatches

Clitics present one typical domain for grammatical-word–phonological-word
mismatches, namely, where the phonological word may consist of more than
one grammatical word. This is the case, strictly speaking, for Cup'ik, as we
have seen. Even so, the phonology *also* has a distinct subdomain, called here
PW–, which does correspond exactly to the grammatical word.

The only other case of grammatical-word–phonological-word mismatching
that we have encountered is that considered in §5.5 under the heading, 'phrase
within a word'. In the case of (25), a phonological word consists of two grammatical words, at least etymologically speaking (cf. (26)). On the synchronic
analysis argued for, however, a phrase behaves as a constituent of a grammatical
word, and thus the construction exemplifies the situation where a grammatical word consists of two phonological words. A similar analysis was given
for (30).

9   Conclusion

In this chapter, we found well-supported independent notions of grammatical word and phonological word, as well as a subdomain of the phonological word that corresponded exactly to the grammatical word. In each case, the support was manifold – many independent grammatical and phonological criteria supported each domain. Ambiguity arose only in the case where word grammar recursively treated possessed-noun phrases as bases, offering ambiguous possibilities for parsing into phonological words. Likewise – although the issue was not explored – the literature indicates serious problems if certain word constituents are taken to be 'invisible' to the syntax.

How well do the grammatical word and the phonological word of Cup'ik compare with the corresponding notions in other languages? That is, have I conceived of them in conventional ways, or have I made them 'work' only by defining them in cross-linguistically unusual ways?

My answer is that the Cup'ik word itself is at a typological extreme, not only for its high level of synthesis and its elaborate inflectional system, but also for its reliance on suffixation to the virtual exclusion of any other technique including compounding. Cup'ik may also be extreme in the high level of salience that the word has, perhaps directly due to its clear, simple base-and-suffix structure. But however extreme may be the Cup'ik word itself, the criteria used to identify it have been the ones used not only in the other chapters of this volume, but extensively elsewhere as well. These include: the distribution of inflection relative to bases and derivation (*cohesiveness*, as formulated by Dixon and Aikhenvald in chapter 1); the tendency of word elements to occur together, in fixed order; the stand-alone potential in an utterance or phrase; the possibility of pausing at word boundaries but not within words; prosodic footing domains; lexical versus post-lexical phonological characteristics. Because of this, I think it is reasonable to assert that what I have been calling 'word' for Cup'ik is essentially the same as what has been called word in most other well-analysed languages. Furthermore, the chapters in this volume as well as such theoretical explorations of mismatching as Sadock (1991) and Halpern (1995) suggest that the level of mismatching found in Cup'ik is not anomalous.

References

Anderson, S. R. 1982. 'Where's morphology?' *Linguistic Inquiry* 13.571–612.
Bloomfield, L. 1933. *Language*. New York: Holt, Reinhart, Winston.
DiSciullo, A. M. and Williams, E. 1987. *On the definition of the word*, Linguistic Inquiry Monographs 14. Cambridge, Mass.: MIT Press.
Halpern, A. 1995. *On the placement and morphology of clitics*. Stanford, Calif.: CSLI.
Hayes, B. 1995. *Metrical stress theory: principles and case studies*. Chicago: University of Chicago Press.

Jacobson, S. A. 1984. *Yup'ik Eskimo dictionary.* Fairbanks: Alaska Native Language Center, University of Alaska.

Kiparsky, P. 1985. 'Some consequences of lexical phonology', *Phonology Yearbook* 2.85–138.

Lapointe, S. 1980. 'A theory of grammatical agreement'. Doctoral dissertation, University of Massachusetts.

Miyaoka, O. 1985. 'Accentuation in Central Alaskan Yupik', pp 51–76 *of Yupik Eskimo prosodic systems: descriptive and comparative studies,* edited by M. Krauss, Alaska Native Language Center research papers 7. Fairbanks: Alaska Native Language Center, Unversity of Alaska.

Sadock, J. 1980. 'Noun incorporation in Greenlandic: a case study of syntactic word formation', *Language* 56.300–319.

　　1985. 'Autolexical syntax: a theory of noun incorporation and similar phenomena', *Natural Language and Linguistic Theory* 3.379–440.

　　1991. *Autolexical syntax: a theory of parallel grammatical representations.* Chicago: University of Chicago Press.

Sapir, E. 1921. *Language: an introduction to the study of speech.* New York: Harcourt, Brace.

Woodbury, A. C. 1981. 'Study of the Chevak dialect of Central Yup'ik Eskimo'. Doctoral dissertation, University of California, Berkeley.

　　1984. 'Eskimo and Aleut languages', pp 49–63 of *Arctic,* edited by D. Damas, Vol. 5, *Handbook of North American Indians,* edited by W. C. Sturtevant. Washington: Smithsonian Institution Press.

　　1987. 'Meaningful phonological processes: a consideration of Central Alaskan Yupik Eskimo prosody', *Language* 63(4). 685–740.

　　1996. 'On restricting the role of morphology in Autolexical Syntax', pp 319–363 of *Autolexical syntax: ideas and methods,* edited by E. Schiller, B. Need and E. Steinberg. Berlin: Mouton.

　　1999. 'Utterance-final phonology and the prosodic hierarchy: a case from Cup'ig (Nunivak Central Alaskan Yup'ik)', pp 47–63 of *Proceedings of the Fourth Linguistics and Phonetics Conference,* edited by O. Fujimura, B. D. Joseph and B. Palek. Prague: Charles University in Prague/Karolinum.

John Henderson

1   Introduction[1]

Eastern/Central Arrernte (ECA) is a mesh of closely related dialects in the area around and to the east of Alice Springs in central Australia. These dialects form part of a larger dialect mesh for which there is no vernacular term. The language which incorporates the ECA dialects has been variously defined and labelled as Upper Aranda (Hale 1962), Eastern Arrernte (Wilkins 1989: 15) and Arrernte (Aranda) (Dixon 2001). ECA and Wilkins' Eastern Arrernte are more or less coextensive terms. Much of the description in this chapter cannot be extended to Arandic varieties beyond ECA.

There are estimated to be between 1,500 and 2,000 speakers of ECA, and probably around 4,500 speakers of Arandic group varieties in total (Henderson and Dobson 1994). ECA is under considerable pressure from English, which dominates local media, education and government. Nearly all ECA speakers also speak at least some English, often a distinctive Aboriginal variety. Many older people believe that younger speakers are not learning or using ECA as well as they should be, particularly in the areas closer to Alice Springs. Some of the phenomena described in the latter part of this chapter have been recorded primarily from middle-aged or older speakers. Principal sources on ECA are Wilkins (1989), Breen (1990), Henderson and Dobson (1994), Henderson (1998) and Breen and Pensalfini (1999).

There is no Arrernte term which exclusively picks out a word-level unit. A nominalised form of *angk+*[2] 'speak', *angkentye*, covers a wide range of linguistic and textual units: language, word, phrase or other piece of language, message, news, story, Aboriginal language, way of talking. Sporadic attempts

---

[1] I am grateful to Bob Dixon and Sasha Aikhenvald for their comments on an earlier version of this chapter; to my Arandist colleagues, especially Gavan Breen, for discussion of these matters over the years; and to the Arrernte speakers who have helped me, especially Veronica Dobson, Margaret Heffernan, Therese Ryder and Margaret Mary Turner.

[2] In citation of a single morpheme/allomorph in the text the '+' symbol indicates (bound) root or suffix status. In morpheme-by-morpheme word glosses it indicates an affix boundary. In glosses, '=' indicates a clitic boundary and '-' indicates the boundary between elements of a compound or contiguous elements of a complex verb. '-' has the same function in the orthography but also marks clitic boundaries.

have been made in the educational context to select a standard term exclusively referring to a word-level unit, without long-term success, e.g. *angkentye akweke* literally 'small unit of language'.

There is recognition of a word unit in the taboo on mentioning the personal names of recently deceased people and people with the same name as the speaker. This is extended to words resembling those names, applying most commonly to nominal lexemes, especially the open class items. Personal names, in particular, are usually replaced with the substitute word *kwementyaye*. Other nominals are often replaced by a descriptive compound or phrase, for example *ake-arrirlpe* 'pointy head' as a substitute for the word for 'crested pigeon'.

With regard to orthographic word status, there is variation both across writers and within the work of individual writers whereby disyllabic or larger clitics and compound elements are written as separate words, hyphenated or as a single word:

(1)   water=COMIT   kwatyakerte   kwatye-akerte   kwatye akerte
        remember+PRES   itelareme   itele-areme   itele areme

In this chapter, I will discuss the basic definitions of phonological word in §3 and grammatical word in §4, give an account of clitics in §5 and discuss the alignment of phonological and grammatical words in §6. The issues of word status in complex predicates are presented in §7. Finally, the discussion is summarised in §8.

2   Brief summary of typology

The verbal system, which contains most of the morphological complexity in the language, is basically agglutinating with tendencies towards both polysynthetic and analytic structures. Reduplication and compounding play important roles. Clause-level constituent order is relatively free but with a preference for AOV and SV, while relatively strict ordering prevails within nominal phrases and between the parts of complex predicates. Grammatical function of NPs is indicated by pronoun form or by case clitics which attach to the final word of the NP. Phonologically, ECA has a number of less common features: prestopped nasal consonants (i.e. stop+nasal), contrastively labialised consonants and, in some dialects, contrastively pre-palatalised consonants. Breen (1990) has claimed that syllable structure is exclusively VC at some level.

3   Phonological word

This section introduces the basic criteria for the phonological word in ECA. More complex issues, including mismatch with grammatical word will be discussed in §§6–7. The phonological word in ECA can only be discussed in

Table 1 *Consonants in ECA orthography*

	labial	lamino-dental	apico-alveolar	apico-post-alveolar	lamino-alveo-palatal	velar	uvular
stop	p	th	t	rt	ty	k	
nasal	m	nh	n	rn	ny	ng	
pre-stopped nasals	pm	thn	tn	rtn	tny	kng	
lateral		lh	l	rl	ly		
approximant	w			r	y		h
tap/trill			rr				

relation to the other elements of the phonological hierarchy. The syllable is introduced in §3.1. The prosodic morphology of verbs, including the suffix allomorphy discussed in §3.1 and stress (§3.5) provide evidence for disyllabic feet, but this foot structure does not always correspond directly to surface patterns of stress. Above the word level, an intonational phrase level can be recognised as the domain of intonational contours. This has been claimed by Breen and Pensalfini (1999) to be the domain of rules relating to certain vowels (§3.2).

The consonant inventory is given in the standard orthographic form in table 1, except that there are also labialised counterparts, written *Cw*, for all apart from /w/ and /h/. All dialects have /a/, /i/ and /e/ (basically [ə]). Less conservative lects also have /u/ in contexts where conservative lects derive the surface vowel rounding from /e/ before a labialised coronal. For simplicity's sake, the description here is of the less conservative lects.

3.1   *Prosodically conditioned allomorphy*

According to Breen's (1990) analysis, the basic syllable structure is exclusively VC(C), at least at the level of prosodic morphology. This, of course, goes against claimed universals whereby onsets are never forbidden and codas never obligatory (Jakobsen 1962). While other analyses are possible, the VC analysis permits a simple statement of prosodic morphological phenomena, and will be assumed here.

Surface syllable structure is not restricted to VC syllables. Phonetically, words may begin with a consonant and end with a vowel. According to Breen and Pensalfini (1999), morpheme-initial /e/ is not realised in initial position in an intonational phrase (and is not represented in the orthography). However, at the beginning of a phonological word in medial position within an intonational phrase, /e/ is usually realised, partly depending on the surrounding consonants. See (3) and (4) below.

Table 2 *Verb number and Reciprocal allomorphy*

number of	Plural			
preceding syllables	Common	Uncommon	Dual	Reciprocal
odd	+errirr	+err	+err	+err
even	+irrer	+irr	+irr	+irr
>1	+ewarr			

Allomorphy of the Reciprocal verb suffix and part of the allomorphy of the Dual and Plural verb suffixes depend on the number of syllables found between the beginning of the phonological word and the suffix, as shown in table 2. There are restrictions on which forms can occur with various classes of stems, and there are also other non-prosodically conditioned allomorphs. Assuming binary footing from the beginning of the word, the prosodic conditioning can alternatively be stated in terms of the position of the first syllable of the suffix within the foot structure: non-head syllable of foot, head syllable of foot, or not in the first or head foot. Note that the first and third conditioning environments overlap: a three-syllable[3] stem can take both the *+errirr* and *+ewarr* Plural allomorphs, as in (2e) below.

Allomorphy of the Plural markers in table 2 is illustrated in (2). The Uncommon forms are in free variation with their Common counterparts but occur less frequently, and mostly in the speech of older speakers. The pseudo-orthographic forms in parentheses indicate the syllabification, showing in (a) and (c) how this takes into account underlying initial /e/, even though this vowel is not realised in surface forms. In what follows, where I refer to syllables this is at the level of the VC analysis unless otherwise indicated.

			Present	Common Plural	Uncommon Plural
(2)	a.	'poke'	th+eme	th+errirr+eme	th+err+eme
			(eth.em)	(eth.err.irr.em)	(eth.err.em)
	b.	'grind'	ath+eme	ath+errirr+eme	ath+err+eme
			(ath.em)	(ath.err.irr.em)	(ath.err.em)
	c.	'swallow'	kwern+eme	kwern+ewarr+eme	kwern+irr+eme
			(ekw.ern.em)	(ekw.ern.ew.arr.em)	(ekw.ern.irr.em)
	d.	'insert'	akwern+eme	akwern+ewarr+eme	akwern+irr+eme
			(akw.ern.em)	(akw.ern.ew.arr.em)	(akw.ern.irr.em)
	e.	'leave for later'	alwarrern+eme	alwarrern+ewarr+eme	alwarrern+err+eme
			(alw.arr.ern.em)	(alw.arr.ern.ew.arr.em)	(alw.arr.ern.err.em)
				alwarrern+errirr+eme	
				(alw.arr.ern.err.irr.em)	

---

[3] Though a five-syllable stem preceding number marking appears to be theoretically possible, none has actually been recorded.

3.2   *Final vowels*

A final vowel, typically central [ə] ~ [ɐ], may be added, at the end of an intonational phrase according to Breen and Pensalfini (1999). This depends on the nature of the final word. If the final phonological word in the phrase is of the underlying form /eC(C)/, then the final vowel is obligatory. See (8e). Leaving aside a few other complications, the final vowel is otherwise generally optional, as shown in (3) where the second line indicates a pronunciation of each word as a separate intonational phrase.

(3)   [ɛ́tnəmə́ŋɐkŋɛ́rɛnə́kə] ~ [ɛ́tnəmə́ŋɐkŋɛ́rɛnə́k]
       [ɛ́tnə   mə́ŋə   ɐkŋɛ́rə   enə́kɐ]
       /itn   emern   akngerr   inek/
       itne   merne   akngerre   in+eke
       3pl:ERG food   big:ACC   get+PAST
       They got a lot of vegetable food.

A word in isolation constitutes an intonational phrase on its own, as in (4). Word-initial /e/ is therefore not realised. A phrase-final vowel will frequently occur on the end of the word, depending on the overall word form, as just noted. It is on this basis that the orthography writes final 'e' on all words.

(4)   kwatye   water   /ekw.aty/   [kwá·ɟə] ~ [kwá·ɟ]

As the basic syllable structure implies, there are no underlying sequences of vowels within words. (Surface diphthongs result from vowel–glide sequences.) The insertion of intonational-phrase-final vowels means that a sequence of such a vowel followed by some other vowel is generally a sufficient criterion for an intonational phrase boundary and therefore for a phonological word boundary. The exception is that in pronunciations directed to second language learners, a prosodic word consisting of three or more syllables (including words comprising a mono-morphemic grammatical word) may sometimes alternatively be pronounced in more than one part, and each of the parts may have a final vowel, as in (5). This is not particularly common. The parts tend towards disyllables (VC) but do not necessarily represent a strict division of the prosodic structure of the word: in some cases a single underlying consonant occurs both as the last consonant of one part and the first consonant of the next.

(5)   utnathete   'mulga blossom'   [utná·ʈətə]   [utnə ɐʈətə]
       tnerurre   'ridge'   [tnéɻo·rə]   [tnéɻə ɻó:rə]

3.3 Initial vowels and other segments

Unstressed word-initial /a/ can optionally be reduced to /e/, depending on the form of the word and the context in which it occurs. This means that many words have an initial [ɐ] ~ Ø variation, as in (6), even in citation form.[4] This is not a boundary signal since it does not result in phonetic elements which occur only at word boundaries, but it does require reference to the phonological word. It is particularly relevant to the discussion of complex verb forms in §7.

(6)   alheme 'go+PRES'   /alh.em/   [ɐḽə́mə] ~ [ḽə́mɐ] ~ [ɐḽə́m] ~ [ḽə́m]

Restrictions on other word-initial segments or sequences of segments do not translate well into boundary signals because of /a/-reduction. While /r/ and /tnh/ do not occur underlyingly after word-initial /e/, their presence cannot be a negative signal because reduction of initial /a/ can result in equivalent sequences, /ar/ and /atnh/ giving rise to initial [#ɾ...] and [#t̪n̪...] and phrase-medial [...əɾ...] and [...ət̪n̪...]. Similarly, there are a number of clusters that cannot occur after initial /e/ but can occur elsewhere: /nng/, /nm/, /rrp/, /rrk/, /rrty/, /rrth/, /rrpm/, /rrkng/, /rrtny/. In these cases, however, reduction of initial /a/ is very infrequent but can result in the same surface forms expected with initial /e/, for example [#ɾp...] and phrase-medial [...ənŋ...]. Again they cannot function categorially as negative boundary signals, though in this case they do have a high probability of being word-internal.

Retroflex consonants are optionally pre-palatalised following /a/ in word-initial position but only prepalatalised after /a/ in non-initial position if they are also immediately followed by a heterorganic consonant. The phonetic result is a diphthong: [ɛ͡ɪt̪ə́pə] artepe 'back'. This means that prepalatisation where a single retroflex consonant or homorganic cluster follows /a/ indicates the beginning of a phonological word, though its occurrence at the beginning of clitics raises questions about their status (see §5). There is one further context in which this type of prepalatisation occurs, idiosyncratically, the Past Habitual verb suffix +etyarte.

3.4 The Rabbit Talk play language

The play language 'Rabbit Talk' (Turner and Breen 1984, Breen 1990) involves a number of processes which obscure the standard form of words. Two of these

[4] Though there are individual and dialect differences with regard to frequency of /a/ reduction. Further, in some cases, a word with initial /a/ may correspond to a word in another ECA dialect with initial /ə/. In surface terms, the word in the first dialect will show [ɐ]~Ø alternation in citation form while the cognate form in the other dialect is phonetically consonant-initial in citation form.

are of interest here. In the case of polysyllabic words, the first syllable of a word is transposed with the remainder of the word, as for example the /amp/ syllable in (7a). This process may thus split a morpheme, as it does with the verb roots in (7a–b). In the case of monosyllabic words, a syllable /ey/ is prefixed, as in (7d–e). Although these two processes are obviously formally distinct, they clearly have a common outcome: the first section of the morphological word becomes the last section of the prosodic word, which is consequently no longer in a linear correspondence with the morphological word.

(7)   ordinary speech   Rabbit Talk
    a. moan+PRES   ampangk+eme   /amp.angk.em/   /angk.em.amp/
    b. smell+PRES   ntyern+eme   /enyty.ern.em/   /ern.em.enyty/
    c. that (mid)   yanhe   /ey.anh /   /anh.ey/
    d. man   artwe   /artw/   /ey.artw /
    e. Let's go!   mpe!   /emp / [mpɐ]   /ey.emp/

The domain of these processes of the Rabbit Talk play language appears to be the phonological word. However, there are complexes of morphemes which Rabbit Talk variably treats as a single domain or as multiple domains: nominal plus disyllabic case clitic and complex verbs. Both are discussed further below. The value of Rabbit Talk evidence is limited by the restricted data available. It is mostly only known by some older speakers, particularly from the northeastern part of the ECA area, and is no longer in common use. It was used, by people of all ages, for secrecy sometimes but mostly for humorous effect, including to downplay the imposition in requests for food.

3.5   Stress

Stress in ECA is not always clear and consistent, particularly but not exclusively in casual and/or extended speech. A thorough analysis still remains to be done but some preliminary statements can be made with a fair degree of validity, or at least optimism. Each phonological word bears a primary stress. Some basic rules can be stated in terms of (VC) syllable structure: in words of two or more syllables, the second syllable bears primary stress, as in (8a–d); in words of four or more syllables secondary stresses *may* occur on alternating syllables after the primary stress, as in (8d). Secondary stresses are more likely in citation forms. A final vowel is not stressed except in Imperative forms of verbs and where it is the only surface vowel of the word, as in (8e). In words of the underlying form VC(C) where V is /a/, /i/ or /u/, there is dialectal variation between placing primary stress on the initial vowel or the predictable final vowel, as in (8f).

(8)   a. merne   'food'   /emern/   [ménə]
      b. atherrke   'green'   /atherrk/   [ɐt̪érkə]
      c. ampetyele   'back(wards)'   /ampetyel/   [ɐmbéɟələ]
      d. atekertneme   'cough+PRES'   /atekertnem/   [ɐtékətnə̀mə]~
                                                            [ɐtékətnəmə]
      e. re   '3sgNOM/ERG'   /er/   [ɹé]
      f. ampe   'child'   /amp/   [ámpə]~[ampé]

Primary stress may be attracted to word-initial /a/, /i/ or /u/ if the following
vowel is [ə]. This is more likely if the consonant(s) of the first syllable are
coronal, especially apicals. The language name Arrernte, for example, can be
stressed [ɐrénd̪ɐ] or [érənd̪ɐ] (Wilkins 1989: 94-5). Stress may also be attracted to the initial /a/, /i/ or /u/ of clitics and compound elements. The question
of whether this is primary or secondary stress is discussed in §5 and §6.

A significant problem in the analysis of stress is that it is difficult to distinguish between secondary stress within a phonological word and the varying
degrees of prominence associated with the primary stresses of words in a phrase.
It is thus difficult to determine in some cases whether two morphemes constitute two phonological words in sequence within a phonological phrase or a
single phonological word in which an affix, clitic or compound element bears
a secondary stress.

3.6   Summary

In this section we have seen that the basic phenomena which characterise the
phonological word in ECA are prosodically conditioned verb suffix allomorphy,
the processes of Rabbit Talk, position and degree of stress, and the realisation of
vowels at word margins. The significance of these criteria varies: the allomorphy
is relevant only to verbs, while stress can be difficult to determine.

4   Criteria for grammatical word

There is no simple definition of grammatical word in ECA. Nominal morphology is limited to compounding, and limited suffixation in the pronoun
system inasmuch as it is analysable.[5] NP case is otherwise marked by case
enclitics. In terms of conventionalised coherence (see chapter 1), speakers
usually speak of nominal plus clitic sequences as single 'words' though

---

[5] Pronouns distinguish person, number, case and optionally kin category. Suffixes marking case
and kin category can be distinguished in some forms; other forms are suppletive. Only a subset
of cases are distinguished in the basic pronominal forms – Ergative, Nominative, Accusative,
Dative and Possessive – with other cases marked by case enclitics attached to the Dative forms.

disyllabic clitics are sometimes spoken of as separate from the nominal they attach to. However, this may reflect phonological word rather than grammatical word.

Verbs and adverbs can bear affixation, always suffixes. For verbs, two classes of morphological elements can be recognised apart from the root, non-obligatory and obligatory morphology, in that order. The non-obligatory class includes markers of aspect, subject number and motion associated with the verb stem action. These markers include simple suffixes, compounded verb roots and combinations of both, and fall into several categories of incompatible elements. The obligatory class marks tense, mood and/or dependent clause relation. Each verb must contain at least one element from this class. The order of morphological elements of both classes within the verb is largely fixed, though there are alternative sites for some markers and very limited multiple marking, such as the Plural in (9).

(9)   unth+ilirr+erl+t-ap+erl-iw+eme
        look.for+PLURAL+CONT.GO$_1$+PLURAL-CONT.GO$_2$+PLURAL+PRES
        They are walking around.

Verb words have conventionalised coherence and meaning: suffixes are not usually spoken of by ECA speakers. The most common citation form for verb lexemes is the present tense form.

All this suggests that a verb word can be defined on the basis of cohesiveness, fixed ordering and conventionalised coherence. However, certain non-verbal morphemes may intervene at specific points within verb structures. For example, in (10a) the verb morphology is interrupted by the particle *akwele* 'supposedly' which can alternatively occur after the entire uninterrupted verb, as in (10b), with apparently the same meaning (though there may be subtle pragmatic differences). The particle can also occur with NPs and in isolation. This raises the possibility that the verb in fact constitutes two grammatical words. This phenomenon is discussed in more detail in §7.

(10)   a. arrerne   akwele   lh+eme
           place   SUPPO   REFL+PRES
           supposedly sit down
        b. arrern+elh+eme   akwele
           place+REFL+PRES   SUPPO

5   Clitics

All clitics in ECA are enclitics. Wilkins (1989: 347–59) categorises them into three groups on the basis of the categories of hosts to which they attach:

(i) clitics which attach only to nominals.

(ii) clitics which attach to either adverbs or nominals

(iii) clitics which attach to either verbs or nominals

To this can be added case clitics, which attach to verbs, nominals, certain adverbs, and certain particles which can occur within an NP (eg. the Intensifier *anthurre*). Case clitics most commonly attach to a nominal or *anthurre*, but if an NP contains a relative clause, and the verb of that clause is the final word of the NP, then the case marker can attach to that verb directly after the obligatory verbal morphology, as in (11).

(11) $_{NP}$[ahelhe   lterrke $_{RC}$[akethe=arle   il+ek]$_{RC}$=eke]$_{NP}$
         ground   hard   clear=RC   TV+PAST=DAT
         arrern+em+ele
         place+PRES+SAMESUBJ
         . . . and putting (them) on the hard ground that they had cleared

NPs are recursive, with case marking indicating relations at each level of embedding within an NP as well as the clause-level function of the overall phrase. The order of case clitics therefore follows from the structure of the NP, as illustrated in (12). Restrictions on the possible sequences result from the applicability of particular cases to particular levels. Core grammatical cases such as Ergative are applicable only to the highest level of the NP since they indicate clause-level relationships (except that a relative clause may contain an Ergative marked argument for the same reasons). A majority of the semantic cases can mark relations within an NP, and therefore can be followed by higher level case clitics. However these principles do not mean that highest level case clitic is final in an NP – some NP-internal non-case clitics may follow, for example =*areye* Plural.

(12)   [akngwelye   [ampe   [town=arenye]$_{NP}$ =kenhe]$_{NP}$ =le]$_{NP}$ uthn+eke
         dog   child   town=ASSOC=POSS=ERG   bite+PAST
         The kid from town's dog bit (someone).

Although clitics and postpositional particles are typically phrase-final, in complex verbs some can occur either after the entire verb or after a first or non-final element of the complex verb, usually with no apparent difference in meaning. For example, the relative clause marker in (11) could alternatively occur after the Past tense marker.

   Non-case clitics occurring with an NP generally have scope only over the preceding phrase, but some may also have scope over the whole clause, for example, =*ekamparre* 'first' in (13). Where they follow verbs, many non-case clitics seem to be ambiguous between scope over the verb and scope over the whole clause. For some clitics, the scope depends on the specific function. In its relative clause marker function, =*arle* may follow the verb or the first constituent or both but marks the status of the whole clause. In its focus marking function, it has scope only over the preceding phrase.

(13)   urreke itnenhenhe merne   awele-awele   ak+etyeke
        later   3pl:ACC   veg.food   bush.tomato:ACC cut+PURP
        akng+etyenh+ele,   kwatye ngenty=ekemparre the
        take+FUT+SAMESUBJ water soakage:ACC=FIRST 1sg:ERG
        tny+em=enge
        dig+PRES=ABL
        We'll take them to gather bush tomatoes later – I'm going to dig a
        soakage first.

The emphatic clitics =*ay*, =*ew* and =*eyew*, and the interrogative clitic =*ey*, always occur last in a clitic sequence (but may be followed by a post-positional particle to which further clitics may be attached). There is some evidence that polysyllabic clitics, such as =*ekamparre* 'first', should be analysed as clitic complexes but there is insufficient space to deal with this here.

Wilkins (1989: 347) observes that it is often not clear whether certain morphemes are to be analysed as clitics or particles. The problematic cases are items which are exclusively post-positional (or at least not clause-initial). Others which are post-positional but can also occur clause-initially and/or in isolation, are more clearly particles. Though any of the problem particles/clitics may clearly occur within the same intonational phrase as the preceding element, it is not always clear whether it constitutes a separate phonological word. This difficulty applies especially with disyllabic and larger forms. Stress typically falls on the second syllable of a disyllabic particle/clitic but, as noted above, it is difficult to decide whether the degree of stress is to be interpreted as secondary stress within a single phonological word, for example *arlwékere-arènye* 'women's camp+ASSOC', or a lesser degree of prominence associated with a primary stress on a separate word within a phrase. In the former case, it is not possible to attribute the location of the secondary stress in forms like *arlwékere-arènye* to the alternating stress rule which otherwise accounts for secondary stresses within phonological words. A separate rule dealing just with disyllabic clitics is required.

However, there is some evidence that disyllabic and larger clitics may constitute separate phonological words. First, as discussed in §3 above, retroflex consonants are optionally prepalatalised following /a/ in word-initial position but only prepalatalised after /a/ in non-initial position if they are also immediately followed by a heterorganic consonant. The clitics =*arteke* Semblative and =*artaye* 'what about?' can be pronounced with prepalatalisation, which suggests the initial /a/ in these forms is word-initial.

Second, Rabbit Talk suggests that disyllabic case clitics, at least, constitute a separate phonological word. In (14a–b), the two elements count as separate domains: the nominal as a monosyllabic word which therefore undergoes /ey/

prefixation while the clitic constitutes a separate word, which being disyllabic, undergoes transposition. There is some inconsistency in the evidence though. One case has been recorded where the nominal and clitic constitute a single domain for Rabbit Talk transposition, (14c), and therefore constitute a single word. Although I do not have any evidence of this type of variation in a single form, it seems likely.

(14)   Rabbit Talk
  a. 'ear=COMIT'[6]   irlpe-akerte   /ey.irlp.ert.ak/
  b. 'night=ASSOC'   ingwe-arenye   /ey.ingw.eny.ar/
  c. 'what=ASSOC'   iwenhe-aperte   /enh.ap.ert.iw/

Monosyllabic clitics are stressed consistent with the primary and alternating stress rules, and are therefore taken to form part of the same phonological word as the host. However, the monosyllabic clitic =*arle* Focus/RC can be pronounced with prepalatalisation, again indicating that the initial /a/ is word-initial and therefore that =*arle* constitutes a separate phonological word. That this is inconsistent with the facts of stress suggests a distinction between prosodic word and phonological word. The available Rabbit Talk evidence shows different behaviour by case and non-case clitics. Monosyllabic case clitics behave as part of the host word, for example *yanh=ele* 'there=LOC' becomes *anheleye*. However, the only monosyllabic non-case clitic recorded behaves in a way that suggests it is a kind of unincorporated appendix to the phonological word. The particle=clitic sequence *kele=arle* 'finished=Focus' is rendered as *lekarle*. The clitic does not count as part of the phonological word as far as transposition is concerned, yet it is not treated as a separate word in that /ey/ is not prefixed.

The only other criterion for phonological word that is applicable to clitics is final vowels. A final vowel cannot occur on the host, which indicates that host and clitic are within the one intonational phrase. Monosyllabic clitics of the underlying form /eC/, such as the Dative case marker /ek/, behave differently to full phonological words of the same form, such as in (8e), since a final vowel is not necessary on the clitic when in intonational-phrase-final position. The behaviour of clitics attached to a monosyllabic word is more complex. This is discussed further in §6.

If, as some of the evidence above suggests, at least disyllabic and larger clitics constitute distinct prosodic/phonological words, this is clearly at odds with the usual notion of a clitic. I propose that such clitics can constitute phonological words but only within a recursive phonological word structure conjoining the phonological words of the host and clitic.

With regard to conventionalised coherence, the sequence of word plus clitic is typically spoken of by ECA speakers as a single word; clitics are not typically spoken of as separate words. Monosyllabic case clitics are typically not written

---

[6] Also lexicalised as the name of a type of boomerang.

as separate from the word they attach to, though monosyllabic non-case clitics and disyllabic case clitics sometimes are.

6   Relationship between phonological and grammatical word

There are a number of situations which diverge from one-to-one alignment of phonological and grammatical words. Some of these reflect a general dispreference in ECA for monosyllabic words.

6.1   *Two grammatical words align with a single phonological word*

This can occur where a monosyllabic nominal is followed by a disyllabic clitic, as in (15a), or a monosyllabic first part of a complex predicate is immediately followed by the second part, as in (15b). Alternatively, but much less commonly in these cases, there can be a separate stress on each part, though it is not clear whether it is a primary or secondary stress on the second element.

(15)   a. fire-COMIT   úre-akérte ~ urákerte
        b. close-IV+PRES   ítwe irréme ~ itwírreme

6.2   *Two phonological words align with a single grammatical word*

Two phonological words can align with a single grammatical word in compound nominals and total reduplications.

In reduplications, both parts bear a stress on their second syllable, with the first being stronger. The position of the stress in the second element cannot be attributed to the alternating stress rule since it is independent of the number of syllables in the first element, as demonstrated by (16a). Initial /a/ before a retroflex consonant can be pre-palatalised, as in (16a), indicating that the second element is a separate phonological word. If the element is greater than three syllables, in addition to the stress on the second syllable of the second element there will also be secondary stress on the second syllable after that, as in (16b). Reduplications of monosyllabic bases typically form a single phonological word.

(16)   a. arlátyeye   'pencil yam (plant)'
            arlátyeye – arlátyeye   'area with lots of pencil yam plants'
        b. arrérnelhétyeke   'to sit down, land' (place+REFL+PURP)
            arrérnelhétyeke-arrérnelhétyeke 'to persistently try to sit down'

The only relevant evidence available from Rabbit Talk involves reduplication of disyllabic elements, in which case it is not possible to distinguish whether the domain of transposition is the entire reduplicated form or each element individually.

However, Wilkins (1984) points out that there is a difference in stress between the reduplication *iperte-iperte* 'rough, holey' and the phrase *iperte iperte* 'deep hole' (*iperte* 'hole' and *iperte* 'deep'). I propose that this behaviour of reduplicated forms be attributed to a recursive phonological word structure in the reduplicated forms, the same as that proposed for host plus disyllabic clitics in §5. Both elements constitute distinct phonological words which are conjoined into a single higher phonological word.

For compound nominals, the details of stress position and degree are as for reduplications, as shown in (17). If the first element is monosyllabic, the compound may consist of either one or two phonological words, as in (17c).

(17) a. southeast   antékerre-ikngérre
      b. bird species (lit. 'stranger coming')   ipénye-apétyeme
      c. back of head (lit. 'head-mound')   aké-tápmwe ~ akértapmwe

The limited evidence from Rabbit Talk shows that at least some nominal compounds can constitute a single domain: *mwerre-akngerre* 'nice' (*mwerre* 'good' *akngerre* 'much') becomes *rrakngerrem*.

6.3   Phonological word is misaligned with two grammatical words

Where a monosyllabic word with underlying initial /e/ precedes another grammatical word with initial /a/, /i/ or /u/ within an intonational phrase, the initial vowel of the second word can combine with the first grammatical word to form a phonological word, with that vowel receiving a primary stress, as shown in (18). Pause between the two prosodic words seems not to be possible. This kind of overlap is optional but very common. It is clearest when the monosyllabic word is in initial position in an intonational phrase and the following word has initial /i/ or /u/. It is less clear where the initial vowel of the second word is /a/ because in that context /a/ can be very similar in quality to the final vowel on a monosyllabic word.

(18)   [ʈɪ́kóʈɐɾə́ŋəkɐ]   ~ [ʈé.ɪkóʈɐɾə́ŋəkɐ]
       [thɪ́l$_{pw}$]   [kwére]$_{pw}$ [arrérneke]$_{pw}$ [thé]$_{pw}$ [ikwére]$_{pw}$[arrérneke]$_{pw}$
       the   ikwere   arrern+eke
       1sg:ERG   3sg:DAT   place+PAST
       I put (something) on it.

(19)   [ʈɛ́nə́ɟekɐ̱ɭə́ɡə]   ~ [ʈé.ɛnə́ɟekɐ̱ɭə́ɡə]
       [rí]$_{PW}$ [nétyeke]$_{pw}$ [alhéke]$_{pw}$ [ré]$_{PW}$ [inétyeke]$_{pw}$ [alhéke]$_{pw}$
       re   in+etyeke   alh+eke
       3sg:NOM   get+PURP   go+PAST
       S/he went to get (it).

This phenomenon can be seen as the result of four things: (i) in words of the underlying form /e(C)C/, the only underlying vowel cannot bear stress, (ii) every phonological word bears a primary stress, (iii) sequences of (non-contrastive) word-final vowel and word-initial vowel are strongly dispreferred if not actually prohibited within an intonational phrase and (iv) core constituents of a clause tend to fall within a single intonational phrase. A similar outcome results from the processes illustrated in (15) and (17c).

7   Complex predicates

The complex predicate constructions present a number of issues for the defininition of phonological and grammatical word in ECA. The basic facts are that these structures appear on some grounds to constitute a single grammatical and phonological word. Wilkins (1989) has described the verb types discussed below in this way, except for the Transitive and Intransitive Verbalisers which he describes as ambiguous between derivational suffixes and free verbs (1989: 216). However, other evidence suggests that all the complex verb predicates discussed below involve multiple grammatical and/or phonological words. Recall the discussion on (10a–b) above.

Six of the complex predicate types are discussed here:
   (i) Suffix+root compounds
  (ii) Lexical Complex Predicates
 (iii) Transitive Verbaliser (TV) complexes
 (iv) Intransitive Verbaliser (IV) complexes
  (v) Attenuative verbs
 (vi) Initial Separation
Each of these involves a division of the predicate into two parts which occur in fixed order and within a single intonational phrase. More than one of the types above can occur in a single complex verb, as demonstrated in (35). Types (i)–(iv) by default involve two phonological words, and when the two elements are contiguous, these phonological words are conjoined under a single higher level phonological word. Their alternative occurrence as a single phonological word can be attributed to the optional flattening of this structure to a single phonological word at a single level.

   The types of evidence which establish the word structure of complex predicates are presented in §7.1. The six complex predicate types are then discussed in these terms in §7.2.

7.1   *Types of evidence for complex word structure*

   7.1.1 Intervening non-verbal morphemes In all complex predicates, non-verbal morphemes can intervene between the two parts. Wilkins, who described this phenomenon as 'particle/clitic insertion' on the basis of more limited data, observed that it is critical to understanding the verb system and the whole issue of 'word' in ECA (1989: 381).

There is considerable variation in the intervening material that can occur with the various types of complex verbs, but it is possible to form a rough scale to indicate which types have been recorded in wider ranges of complex verb types. From most to least widespread, these are:

(i) certain particles and clitics, the most likely being *anthurre* Intensifier, *akwele* 'supposedly', *apeke* 'maybe', =*arle* FOC/RC, =*arlke* 'too', =*ante* 'only'

(ii) *akwete* 'still'

(iii) third person singular pronoun functioning non-referentially as an emphatic (cf. Henderson 2001)

(iv) other pronominal NPs

(v) simple non-pronominal NPs, most likely being a single nominal

(vi) other adverbs, complex NPs

(vii) dependent clauses

Example (10) above exemplifies the least degree of intervening material, the single particle *akwele* 'supposedly' while (20) illustrates an intervening dependent clause with an Intransitive Verbaliser complex verb (the discontinuous elements are shown here in bold face).

(20) **alakenhe** re   ampe akweke   mpwe ulh+etyenh+ele
      thus   3sg:NOM child small:NOM urine excrete+FUT+SAMESUBJ
      irr+entye-akngerre.
      IV+NOMLSR
      Little kids behave that way when they need to have a leak.

The scale above is also roughly implicational. For example, the only complex verb type which permits dependent clauses also permits items from the preceding types. The scale also gives a rough indication of the relative likelihood of occurrence in complex verb types where more than one type of intervening material is possible: even where a broader range of intervening material is possible, items from the particle/clitic end of the scale are more likely. Particles and clitics also appear to be more basic in another way: when any of the other types of intervening material actually occur, it is very likely that that they will be preceded by a particle or clitic.

As might be expected, there tend to be fewer intervening morphemes, rather than more. This suggests a markedness principle favouring the least disruption to a complex verb. It also makes it difficult to precisely determine the range of intervening material permissible for a given complex verb.

In most cases, the intervening material can alternatively occur elsewhere without a difference in meaning. For clitics and particles, the intervening position is typically equivalent to following the entire complex verb, though Wilkins

(1989: 381) reports one combination where there is a meaning difference. Having NPs and higher-ranked items in the intervening position appears to place focus on the verb. If a verb is multiply complex, intervening material is more likely to occur at an earlier boundary rather than a later one.

It will be argued below on the basis of stress placement and prosodically conditioned allomorphy that intervening material, even a monosyllabic clitic, is not phonologically incorporated into the complex verb as a whole.

7.1.2 Stress placement We have seen above that it is difficult to distinguish between secondary stress within a phonological word and the varying degrees of prominence associated with the primary stresses of words in a phrase. This means that degree of stress is not in general a good determinant of phonological word status in complex verbs. It has also been claimed above that secondary stresses appear to be optional even in citation form. Despite these things, arguments can be made for some complex verb types on the basis of the position of stress in the second part.

In all complex verb types discussed here, there can be clear primary stress on the second syllable of the first part of a complex verb. The situation with monosyllabic first parts is slightly more complicated due to the processes discussed in §6. In lexical complex predicates, transitiviser constructions, Attenuative marked verbs and verbs made complex by suffix+root markers, there may also be stress on the second syllable of the second part. In Attenuative forms and some lexical complex predicates, the first part is disyllabic and the position of this stress in the second part is identical with a secondary stress placed by the alternating stress rule within the domain of the entire compound verb. But when the first part is larger than a disyllable, the position of the stress is clearly independent of the number of syllables in the first part and therefore cannot be accounted for by application of the alternating stress rule, as demonstrated in (21). The stress may be optionally attracted to an initial /a/, /i/ or /u/ of the second part but this is also not strictly dependent on the number of syllables in the first part.

(21)   mpwár+ety-alh+érr+eme
       do+PRIOR.MOTION+GO+DUAL+PRES
       two go and then do

The preceding discussion assumes no intervening material, the situation where complex verbs are most likely to be perceived with only the single primary stress. When pronouns, other nominals or dependent clauses intervene, those words typically have their own primary stresses and the stress on the second part of the complex verb is usually relatively clear. If a stress is perceived in the second part, the number of syllables of intervening material has no effect on the position of that stress, regardless of type of intervening material.

All this suggests two possibilities. (i) The second part optionally gets a secondary stress, similar to what appears to happen with disyllabic case clitics discussed above, even though the second part of a complex verb need not commence with a disyllabic morpheme. (ii) The second part constitutes a distinct phonological word, or at least initiates one. The lesser degree of stress could be attributed either to the second part being in non-head position in a phonological phrase or to the separate phonological words of the two parts being united within a higher phonological word (which is optionally reduced to a single flat phonological word). It is not possible to decide this on the basis of stress alone, but the related phonological phenomena of prosodically conditioned allomorphy and the Rabbit Talk processes support the second alternative.

7.1.3 Prosodically conditioned suffix allomorphy The number of syllables in the first part of a complex verb does not count in determining prosodically conditioned allomorphy in the second part, as in (22). Any intervening material is similarly not taken into account. This suggests that the second part is not part of the same phonological word as the first or any intervening material.

(22)   akwáketye-ak+érrirr/*ewarr+eme
         put.arm.around$_1$-put.arm.around$_2$+PLURAL+PRES
         more than two put arms around (someone)

The allomorphy does not vary with any of the apparent variation in stress. Even where there is no secondary stress perceived in the second part, allomorphy in the second part is invariably conditioned only by the preceding content of the second part. The variation in stress is therefore a relatively superficial phenomenon.

There is a small number of cases where allomorphy can alternatively be determined by the entire preceding verb, as in (23), but in that alternative the 'two parts' do not show any other evidence of separate word status and appear to be in the process of being lexicalised. These mostly involve monosyllabic first parts.

(23)   a. aheye+ewarr/*errirr+eme
             breathe$_1$-breathe$_2$+PLURAL+PRES
         b. aheyangk-angk+errirr/*ewarr+eme
             breathe+PLURAL+PRES
             more than two breathing

7.1.4 Rabbit Talk processes For the complex verb types for which there is evidence, Rabbit Talk varies between treating a complex verb type as a single domain, as in (24), and the two parts as separate domains, as in (25–6), though there is no evidence of this type of variation within a specific complex verb.

		Rabbit Talk
(24)	apek+erle-an+eme	kerlanemap
	smash+CONT+PRES	
(25)	arrern+etye-alp+eme	rnetyarre malp
	place+PRIOR.MOTION-RETURN+PRES	
(26)	akeme[7]+lhe-il+eme	melhak mil
	up+TV+PRES	

If the domain of transposition is the phonological word, as suggested above, then this is consistent with the proposal above that the two parts of complex verbs constitute two phonological words unified within a higher phonological word.

7.1.5 Site of Attenuative marker The Attenuative has a disyllabic marker which precedes the root of a simple verb: the first syllable is a reduplication of the first syllable of the base to which the marker attaches; the second syllable is /elp/, as shown in (27). It creates a complex verb type in its own right (see §7.2.5) but is also relevant here because, for nearly all complex verb types, including the lexical complex predicate in (28), the marker can attach to either the first or second part. Again, this makes no obvious difference in meaning but there may be subtle pragmatic effects.

(27)   at+elp-atak+eme
ATTEN(REDUP+elp)-demolish+PRES
start to demolish (something)

(28)   a. akw+elpe-akwaketye-ak+eme
ATTEN(REDUP+elp)-put.arm.around+PRES
b. akwaketye-ak+elpe-ak+eme
put.arm.around$_1$-ATTEN(REDUP+elp)-put.arm.around$_2$+PRES
start to put (your) arm around (someone)

7.1.6 Conventionalised coherence Despite the evidence that the parts of complex verbs constitute separate phonological words, speakers usually speak of them as a single word. This often even happens when there are intervening particles or clitics. In writing, complex verbs are often represented as a single word but are sometimes written as two words or with a hyphen between the parts. However, when intervening material is more extensive or consists of pronouns, other nominals, etc., the two parts of the complex verb will usually be written as separate words. The significance of these practices in writing is not completely clear since they might reflect the way the speakers' Arrernte literacy was acquired or reflect some influence from English.

---

[7] This is a bound morpheme which occurs only with the Transitive and Intransitive Verbalisers.

7.2   Discussion of complex predicate types

7.2.1 *Suffix+root markers* A number of verbal categories, including
Associated Motion and Aspect, have compounding markers which introduce an
additional verb root. Some of these markers also involve a suffix preceding that
root. For example, the Associated Motion form which indicates that the subject
goes somewhere then performs the verb action, consists of a suffix +*ety* which
can be glossed as Prior Motion and the verb root *alh+* 'go', as shown in (21).
The only prosodically conditioned allomorphy following the introduced root in
all types is the Dual, the form of which is as expected if only the introduced root
counts in determining the number of preceding syllables. Intervening material
appears to be limited to certain particles and clitics, pronouns and the adverb
akwete 'still', but this appears to vary with the various suffix+root markers, as
in (29).

(29)   ar+étye=arle   akwéle   alh+érr+eme
        see+PRIOR.MOTION=FOC   SUPPO   GO+DUAL+PRES
        two supposedly go and then see

The Attenuative may precede the entire complex verb, as in (30), but cannot
occur before the second part, as shown in (31). This suggests that the second part
does not constitute a word in the sense that a simple verb does. If it constitutes a
separate phonological word as the discussion above suggests, then the evidence
of the Attenuative suggests that it does not constitute a separate grammatical
word.

(30)   mpwelpe-mpwar+etye-alh+eme
        ATTEN(REDUP+elp)-do+PRIOR.MOTION-go+PRES
        start to {go and then do}

(31)   *mpwar+ety-alhelpe-alh+eme
        do+PRIOR.MOTION-ATTEN(REDUP+elp)+go+PRES

Despite the difficulties in defining grammatical word in ECA, an argument that
root+suffix verbs are single grammatical words can be made in some cases on the
grounds that the root and suffix parts are in general co-dependent. For example,
the marker for continuous action while in motion is the compounding =*erl-ap*,
the two parts of which can be separated by intervening material, as in (32).
While the -*ap* part can be analysed as a verb root, it does not occur productively
as the sole root of a non-compound verb.[8]

(32)   apan+erle=arteke   re   ap+em+ele
        feel+DO.ALONG₁=SEMBL   3sg:ERG   DO.ALONG₂+PRES+SAMESUBJ
        like going along continuously feeling (its way)

[8] The existence of the full verb *ap+* 'go' in Kaytetye suggests that this was once the case in ECA.
It is now restricted to to the compounding +*erl-ap* and combination with +*ety* 'hither'.

7.2.2 Lexical complex predicates These consist of a pre-verb word which cannot occur with any verbal morphology except Attenuative, and an inflected verb. They are distinguished from adverb and verb combinations by their fixed order and lack of productivity. In most cases, it is not possible to ascribe separate meanings to the two parts, though the verb parts are always homophonous with independent verbs. Intervening material can include particles and clitics, pronouns and simple non-pronominal NPs.

(33) ikerrke   anthurre   re   anteme=arle   re   iw+elh+eke
      stick₁   INTENS   3sg:NOM   now=FOC   3sg:NOM   stick₂+REFL+PAST
      He's got himself really stuck now.

(34) itele   ware   ampe   nhenhe   ar+eke
      remember₁   just   child   this:ACC remember₂+PAST
      (S/he) just remembered this kid.

7.2.3 Transitive Verbaliser The Transitive Verbaliser has two forms, +*elhe-il* and -*il*, with overlapping distribution and slightly different behaviour. The +*elhe-il* form is formally a kind of suffix+root marker where the -*il* initiates the second part but is distinct from the others discussed above because the Attenuative may apply to either part, as in (35). Single uninflected nominal and adverb words may generally combine with either +*elhe-il* or -*il*. Purposive and nominalised clauses and NPs with multiple words or bearing a final case clitic only combine with -*il*. Pre-obligatory verb stems combine only with +*elhe-il*. Intervening material appears to be limited to particles and clitics and the third person pronoun with +*elhe-il*, as in (36); adverbs and simple NPs can also intervene with -*il*.

(35) a. ap+elpe-apat+elhe-il+eme
          ATTEN(REDUP+elp)-be.stunned+TV+PRES
      b. apat+elhe-il+elpe-il+eme
          be.stunned+elh-ATTEN(REDUP+elp)-il+PRES
          start to stun someone

(36) mperlk+elhe   anthurre   renhe   *il*+eme
      be.white+elhe   INTENS   3sg:ACC   TV+PRES
      make it go really white

7.2.4 Intransitive Verbaliser Like its transitive counterpart, the Intransitive Verbaliser combines with a single nominal word or phrase, adverbs and certain clause types. It is the freest of all complex verb types with regard to intervening material, permitting all types including dependent clauses, as in (20) where the Intransitive Verbaliser forms a complex predicate with *alakenhe* 'thus' meaning 'behave that way'.

7.2.5 Attenuative As already noted, the partially reduplicative Attenuative marker precedes a verb word, as shown in (37). Pronouns and certain
particles and clitics have been recorded as intervening material, as in (38). An
unusual aspect of this is that the reduplicant is therefore separated from its
source by other morphemes. There is no Rabbit Talk evidence available.

(37)   at+elp-at+errirr/*ewarr +eme
         ATTEN(REDUP+elp)-burst+PLURAL+PRES
         start to burst

(38)   kwatye   uyelpe   aneme=arle   uyerr+erlenge
         water:NOM   ATTEN(REDUP+elp)   THEN=FOC   disappear+DIFFSUBJ
         the water started to go away then

In verbs which are also otherwise complex, there are certain limitations with the
Attenuative. Intervening material between the unit consisting of the Attenuative
plus the first part, and the second part of the verb appears to be limited to particles
and clitics and the third person singular pronoun, as in (39). Both the Intransitive
and Transitive Verbalisers can form complex predicates with a single nominal
or a larger NP. The Attenuative can apply to a nominal in that context but only
to a single nominal (including a compound or a single nominal bearing a case
clitic), not to an NP consisting of more than one nominal, as in (40).

(39)   ingwelpe-ingwe=arle   irr+eme
         ATTEN(REDUP+elp)-night=FOC   IV+PRES
         starting to get dark

(40)   a. antywe   akngerre-apenhe=arteke   ilelpe-il+eme
            nest   big=SEMBL   ATTEN(REDUP+elp)-TV+PRES
            start to make into (something) like a big nest
         b. *antywelpe-antywe   akngerre-apenhe=arteke   il+eme
            ATTEN(REDUP+elp)-nest   big=SEMBL   TV+PRES

Evidence from prosodically conditioned allomorphy and Rabbit Talk suggests
that the combination of a single nominal word with either of the verbalisers
involves separate phonological words. The first nominal in a multiword NP
also constitutes a distinct phonological word. This constraint on the Attenuative
suggests that the combination of a single nominal and verbaliser is structurally
different in a way that can be accounted for by the proposal that the two prosodic
words of a complex verb are unified within a higher prosodic word when they
are contiguous (or when only clitics intervene).

7.2.6 Initial Separation The first two, or rarely three, syllables of a
verb can optionally be separated from the remainder of the verb. Intervening material seems to be limited to particles, clitics, pronouns and simple NPs.

(Cf. (41) and (42).) Separation is subject to the constraint that the first morpheme of the resulting second part is not an element of obligatory morphology or the suffix part of a suffix+root marker. Morphological structure is not otherwise relevant. In particular, separation does not appear to require that specific morphemes initiate the second part. It may even split morphemes, both roots, as in (43), and suffixes, as in (44–5). Note that because the first part consists of a root or stem without obligatory morphology, it is homophonous with a Ø-marked Imperative form.

Initial separation is distinct from other complex verbs because the evidence of prosodically conditioned allomorphy indicates that the unseparated verb constitutes a single prosodic word, as in (46). Initial separation does not appear to be possible where the allomorphy unambiguously takes into account the entire preceding stem, the *+ewarr* form of Plural, but it is possible with the *+errirr* form which simply requires that an odd number of syllables precedes it in the stem and which therefore does not indicate whether the first part is taken into account.

(41)   artnerr+enh+eke
       crawl+PASSING+PAST
       (He) crawled off.

(42)   artnerre   aneme   akwele   re   nheke
       crawl   then   SUPPO   3sg:NOM   PASSING+PAST
       Then he supposedly crawled off.

(43)   ateke   akwele   tn-eme
       cough$_1$ SUPPO   cough$_2$-PRES
       (She's) supposedly coughing.

(44)   unth+err=arle-irr+etyarte
       walk.around+PLURAL$_1$=FOCUS-PLURAL$_2$+PASTHAB
       They used to walk around.

(45)   arrerlk+ew=arle-arr+eme
       look.white+PLURAL$_1$=FOC-PLURAL$_2$+PRES
       They look white.

(46)   apern+elh+ewarr/errirr+eme
       paint+REFL+PLURAL+PRES
       They are painting themselves.

Initial separation is related to two other phenomena. First, all verbs which can undergo initial separation also permit reduplication of the first two syllables, though not simultaneously, as in (47). Second, in some verbs which permit disyllabic initial separation, the Attenuative can alternatively occur immediately before what would be the beginning of the second part under separation, as in (48). The range of verbs where this applies is not yet clear.

(47) aperne-apern+elh+eme
      ITER(REDUP)-paint+REFL+PRES
      (She's) quickly painting (her)self.

(48) aperne-lh+elpe-lh+eme
      paint-ATTEN(REDUP+elp)-REFL+PRES
      (She's) starting to paint (her)self.

7.3   Summary

In this section we have seen that while complex predicates may show some evidence that they are single grammatical and phonological words, there is a range of evidence that they constitute more than one grammatical and phonological word. The process of Initial Separation takes an underlyingly simple verb word and renders it into two grammatical and phonological words. The other complex predicate types are underlyingly complex, involving two grammatical and phonological words.

8   Conclusion

As in many languages, it is difficult to precisely define phonological and grammatical word in ECA. A range of criteria have been proposed for both in this paper. With regard to phonological word, the criteria give fairly consistent results though there are difficulties in the description of stress level and position and some conflicting evidence in the prepalatalisation of single consonants in monosyllabic clitics. There is no simple definition of grammatical word in ECA. Phonological and grammatical word coincide in most cases but there are significant exceptions. Some phenomena are attributed to the conjunction of phonological words under a single higher level phonological word. Complex predicates are complex in phonological and grammatical word structure and in the relationship between them.

References

Breen, G. 1990. 'The syllable in Arrernte phonology', ms.

Breen, G. and Pensalfini, R. 1999. 'Arrernte: a language with no syllable onsets', *Linguistic Inquiry* 30 (1).1–16.

Dixon, R. M. W. 2001. 'The Australian linguistic area', pp 64–104 of *Areal diffusion and genetic inheritance: problems in comparative linguistics*, edited by A. Y. Aikhenvald and R. M. W. Dixon. Oxford: Oxford University Press.

Hale, K. L. 1962. 'Internal relationships in Arandic of Central Australia', pp 171–83 of *Some linguistic types in Australia*, edited by A. Capell. Sydney: Oceania Linguistic Monographs.

Henderson, J. 1998. 'Topics in eastern and central Arrernte grammar', PhD thesis, University of Western Australia.

　　2001. 'Non-referential third person singular pronouns in adverbial phrases in eastern and central Arrernte', in *Proceedings of ALS2k, the 2000 Conference of the Australian Linguistic Society*, edited by K. Allan and J. Henderson, http://www.arts.monash.edu.au/ling/als/als2kproceedings. shtml.

Henderson, J. and Dobson, V. 1994. Compilers of *Eastern and central Arrernte to English dictionary*. Alice Springs: IAD.

Jakobsen, R. 1962. *Selected writings*, Vol. 1: *Phonological studies*. The Hague: Mouton.

Turner, M. M. and Breen, G. 1984. 'Akarre Rabbit Talk', *Language in Central Australia* 1.10–13.

Wilkins, D. P. 1984. 'Nominal reduplication in Mparntwe Arrernte', *Language in Central Australia* 1.16–22.

　　1989. 'Mparntwe Arrernte (Aranda): studies in the structure and semantics of grammar', PhD thesis, Australian National University.

5   The eclectic morphology of Jarawara, and the status of word

R. M. W. Dixon

Jarawara has an eclectic verbal morphology in which some suffixes cannot have other suffixes added directly to them, and some suffixes cannot be directly added to what precedes. However, phonological word and grammatical word can be straightforwardly defined, and almost always coincide. There are just four circumstances in which one type of word involves two instances of the other. In providing a grammatical description for Jarawara – as for other languages – it is important to distinguish between the structure of a predicate and the structure of a verbal word.

1   Introduction

The small Arawá family of southern Amazonia (quite distinct from Arawak) consists of five extant languages – Dení, Kulina, Sorowahá, Paumarí and Madi (see Dixon 1999). The Madi language consists of three closely related dialects: Jamamadí (with about 190 speakers), Banawá (about 80 speakers) and Jarawara (about 150 speakers, spread over eight jungle villages). The description of Jarawara given here is based on materials gathered during six field trips, during 1991–99.[1]

Jarawara is a highly synthetic language, basically agglutinative but with developing fusion (particularly in the gender-marking forms of inalienably possessed nouns – see Dixon 1995). There is a closed class of about fourteen adjectives, which only function as modifiers within an NP or as copula

---

[1] My major debt is to the Jarawara people who have welcomed me as a temporary member of their community, worked at teaching me their language, and answered all of my questions – Okomobi, Mioto, Soki, Kamo, Botenawaa, Kakai, Wero and others. Alan Vogel is collaborating with me on a grammar of Jarawara and we have discussed many of the points in this paper. Example (26) comes from a Dyirbal text told by Chloe Grant. Example (29) is from a Fijian story told by Falavia Matavesi and explicated by Josefa Cokanacagi and Inoke Soqooviti.

The details of Jarawara have been slightly simplified below, for pedagogic purposes. None of the extra complications which have been left unstated (or else just referred to in a note) would affect the points being made.

':' indicates a phonological word boundary within a grammatical word; '+' indicates a grammatical word boundary within a phonological word; '[...]' enclose a predicate or NP consisting or two or more words, except when a predicate makes up a complete clause.

complements (other adjectival-type concepts are coded as verbs). Jarawara is head-marking, with the predicate including obligatory markers for S or A, and for O in a transitive clause. The verb has six possible prefixes, in three prefix slots, and at least eighty suffixes (almost all existing in feminine and masculine forms) organised into about twenty-four suffix slots. All suffixes are optional.

There are two transitive construction types for main clauses – one with the A argument identified as pivot (called the A-construction) and the other with the O argument as pivot (the O-construction). These have a similar functional role to active/passive and antipassive/active in other languages, but in Jarawara the A-construction and the O-construction are both fully transitive and it is not profitable to try to derive one from the other. Their use is motivated by discourse structure. If the pivot (grammaticalised topic) for a stretch of discourse is in A function in a transitive clause within the stretch then an A-construction must be used; if it is in O function then an O-construction must be used. If both A and O are third person in an O-construction, this is marked by *hi-* as first order prefix to the verb. (Full details are in Dixon 2000.)

Nouns divide into (i) free nouns, an open class; and (ii) inalienably possessed nouns, a semi-closed class (with about 150 members known) referring to body parts, orientation ('top of'), 'smell', 'home', etc. Each free noun is assigned to one of the two genders, feminine (f) or masculine (m); gender is not marked within the form of the noun itself, but by agreement with possessed nouns, some adjectives and demonstratives within its NP, and in gender agreement on the verb.

In an intransitive clause, verbal suffixes agree with the S argument. In a transitive A-construction, agreement is always with the A argument. A transitive O-construction provides a more complex picture; here mood suffixes always agree in gender with the O argument, while tense–modal suffixes agree sometimes with O and sometimes with A (full details of the factors conditioning this are provided in Dixon 2000).

Feminine is the functionally unmarked gender. For example, all (non-zero) pronouns are cross-referenced as f, irrespective of the sex of their referent(s). And the interrogative *himata* 'what' is, in unmarked circumstances, cross-referenced as f. Gender marked forms will always be quoted f/m. Thus, the declarative mood suffix is *-ke/-ka*, indicating that *-ke* is the form for f and *-ka* the form for m agreement. Similarly the immediate past eyewitness (IPe) tense–modal suffix is *-hara/-hare*, with *-hara* for f and *-hare* for m agreement.

The verb in Jarawara takes both prefixes and suffixes. The noun takes no prefixes and no distinctive suffixes (save for the m suffix *-ne* on some possessed nouns); however a noun can accept a subset of what are primarily verbal suffixes. Non-singular (nsg) pronouns can take the accusative suffix *-ra*. There are no grammatical elements in Jarawara which should be identified as clitics.

The predicate has complex structure, with a mingling of free (phonological and grammatical) words, roots and affixes. In addition, verbal suffixes vary with respect to what they can be added to and/or what can be added to them.

We find that, as grammatical word is defined here, it almost always coincides with the unit phonological word. There are three circumstances in which a grammatical word can consist of two phonological words and one in which a phonological word can be made up of two grammatical words.

§2 discusses the criteria for phonological word. After preliminary discussion, in §3, of clause structure and verb classes, the structure of the predicate is presented in §4, with particular attention to the varying grammatical properties of verbal suffixes. §5 is a general discussion of grammatical word, and the need to distinguish between verb and predicate. Criteria for grammatical word in Jarawara are stated in §6; then §6.1 examines and rejects the idea of taking the entire predicate to be one grammatical word. Finally, §7 recapitulates the instances of non-correspondence between grammatical and phonological word in this language. An appendix lists miscellaneous, tense–modal and mood suffixes.

2   Phonological word

Jarawara has just four vowels (*i*, *e*, *a* and *o*) with contrastive length, and eleven consonants: bilabial *b*, *φ* (written as *f*) and *m*; apico-dental *t* and *n*; apico-alveolar *s* and *r* (with allophones [ɾ] and [l]), lamino-palatal stop *ɟ* (written as *j*, with allophone [y]), dorso-velar *k* and *w*, and a nasalised glottal fricative written as *h*. There is also a glottal stop, *ʔ* (written as *'*) which only appears at certain boundaries, particularly at a phonological word boundary within a grammatical word (see below). Syllable structure is (C)V.

The stress rule operates in terms of moras, with a short vowel counting as one mora and a long vowel as two moras. Now in the related Banawá dialect, stress goes on syllables including the first, third, etc. moras from the beginning of the word, ignoring a word-initial V in a word with three or more moras (see Buller, Buller and Everett 1993); the Jamamadí dialect has a similar rule. It is likely that this was the stress rule at an earlier stage of Jarawara. However, Jarawara now has penultimate assignment – stress goes on syllables including the second, fourth, etc. moras from the end of the word. It will be seen that in a word with an even number of moras the stress rule is the same in all dialects, e.g. *hósi* 'sweet potato'. However, in a word with an odd-number of moras, stress goes on odd-numbered moras in Banawá and Jamamadí, e.g. *kóbajá* 'white-collared peccary', but on even-numbered moras in Jarawara – *kobája*.

Jarawara has a rich set of ordered phonological rules (all applying just within verbs) for various types of assimilation, blending and elision, and for morphophoneme realisation. A number of rules relate to the position of a syllable in a phonological word, counting from the left; we will here exemplify with just one (retaining the rule number from Dixon and Vogel ms.). It will be seen from the list in the appendix that all tense–modal suffixes begin with a syllable -*hV-*. We then have:

> **Rule 8a**: the initial -*hV-* is omitted from a tense–modal suffix when (a) it is an even-numbered mora within a word,[2] and (b) the preceding vowel is *a*.

For example, the feminine form of the immediate past eyewitness tense–modal suffix is -*hara*. With three-mora and two-mora inflecting verb roots we get:

	(1)	be finished-IPef	(2)	eat-IPef
		ahaba-hara		tafa-hara
rule 8a applies:		ahaba-ra		–

The criteria for phonological word in Jarawara are:
(a) A phonological word must include at least two moras. Thus, if it is mono-syllabic the vowel must be long.
(b) The stress rule operates within a phonological word.
(c) Phonological rules which relate to position in a word all apply within a phonological word.
Note that in Jarawara one can pause at a position which is both a phonological word boundary and a grammatical word boundary.

We can now mention two of the three instances in which phonological word does not coincide with grammatical word (the other will be discussed in §4.4). Firstly, a compound noun is one grammatical word (the parts occur together, in fixed order, and have a conventionalised meaning), but each part is a separate phonological word. For example (using ':' for a phonological word boundary within a grammatical word) *báni:kasáko* 'wild dog species', where stress goes on the penultimate mora within each of the two phonological words; if this were one phonological word, stress would go on the second and fourth moras from the end, i.e. **baníkasáko*.

Secondly, one type of verbal reduplication involves repeating the initial CVCV. The reduplication boundary is here a phonological word boundary within a grammatical word, e.g. *kéte:ketébe* 'run a lot' from *ketébe* 'run, follow', where stress goes on the penultimate mora within each phonological word (if this had been one phonological word, the stress would have been **ketéketébe*).

Every word ends in a vowel and many begin with a vowel. A vowel sequence is unremarkable when it spans a boundary between phonological words which

---

[2] It is interesting to note that the syllable which is elided would be unstressed on the counting-from-the-left stress rule which applies in Banawá and Jamamadí and is likely to have applied at an earlier stage in Jarawara. I refer to this as the 'underlying stress cycle'; it conditions many phonological processes in Jarawara. However, as just stated, the actual stress assignment in modern-day Jarawara is on a penultimate counting-from-the right principle.

is also a boundary between grammatical words. However, if two vowels come together at a phonological boundary within a grammatical word, then a glottal stop is likely to be inserted between them, as in the compound noun *mówe:'éte* 'fish species' (from *mowe* and *ete*) and the reduplicated verb *áta:'atábo* 'be very muddy' (from *atábo* 'be muddy').

Examples of the application of phonological rules within a phonological word will be given below – see examples (3), (7), (10), (14), (16), and (22–3).

3   Clause structure and verbal clauses

The basic elements of clause structure are (note that all elements are optional except for the predicate):

(1) Clause-initial peripheral elements (discourse markers, peripheral NPs, subordinate clauses, etc.).

(2) Core NPs: S in an intransitive, A and/or O in a transitive clause (there are ordering preferences but no ordering constraints; nothing concerning the functions of NPs can be inferred from their ordering).

(3) Predicate, including obligatory pronominal reference to core arguments.

(4) Clause-final peripheral elements (peripheral NPs, subordinate clauses, etc.).

Verbs are classified according to two independent parameters.

TRANSITIVITY. Leaving aside copulas, each verb is one of:

(a) intransitive, e.g. *-tafa-* 'eat'; *haa:haa -na-* 'laugh';

(b) transitive, e.g. *-iti-* 'take off, pick up, marry'; *tama -na-* 'hold in the hand';

(c) ambitransitive of type S=O, e.g. *-mato-* 'tie (tr); be tied (intr)'; *baka -na-* 'break off (tr); be broken (intr)';

(d) ambitransitive of type S=A, e.g. *-awa-* 'see, feel'; *kobo -na-* 'meet (tr); arrive (intr)'.

INFLECTING/NON-INFLECTING. Verbs divide into:

(i) inflecting verbs, which themselves accept prefixes and suffixes, e.g. *-tafa-*;

(ii) non-inflecting verbs, which do not themselves take affixes but must be followed by an auxiliary verb (called AUXa, to distinguish it from other kinds of auxiliary, which will be discussed below) which does, e.g. *kobo -na-*. There are two auxiliaries – about a dozen non-inflecting verbs take *-ha-* while the remainder (several hundred) take *-na-*.

Compare:

(3)   *o-tafa-ra*   (4)   *kobo   o-na-hara*
        1sgS-eat-IPef   arrive   1sgS-AUXa-IPef
        I've just eaten   I've just arrived

In (3) 1sg prefix *o-* and immediate past eyewitness feminine suffix *-hara* (reduced to *-ra* by rule 8a, since the *-ha-* is the fouth mora of the word and is preceded by *a*) attach to the inflecting verb root, *-tafa-*, whereas in (4) they attach to the auxiliary *-na-* of the non-inflecting verb *kobo*.

A non-inflecting verb and its auxiliary constituent are separate grammatical words and also separate phonological words. Consider:

(5)   níki   ka-ná-ke
       squeeze   APPLICATIVE-AUXa-DECf
       (she) squeezes (it)

(6)   hatísa   ti-ná-hi
       sneeze   2sgS-AUXa-ImmPosImpf
       you sneeze!

(7)   underlying   jowaba   na-haro
       surface   jowába   ná-ro
                     walk.in.single.file   AUXa-RPef
                     (they) walked in single file

If each of (5) and (6) were one phonological word then stress would go on the last mora of *niki* and on the last and first moras of *hatisa*, since these are even-numbered moras counting from the right of the word; the actual stress patterns are *níki* and *hatísa*, i.e. on the penultimate moras of the non-inflecting verb roots, showing that these are distinct phonological words. If (7) were one phonological word then the *-ha-* of *-haro* would be the fifth mora, counting from the left, and rule 8a would not apply to omit it. But the *-ha-* is omitted showing that it must be in an even-numbered mora counting from the left within its phonological word; it is in the second mora *na-haro*, which must be a separate phonological word from *jowaba*.

4   Predicate structure

This is the most complex part of the grammar of Jarawara. We can recognise eleven types of elements. They are, in order:

A First pronominal slot; obligatory in all transitive clauses – marks O;

B Second pronominal slot; obligatory – marks S or A;

C Prefixes:

    C1 First prefix position: one of 1sg S/A *o-*, second S/A *ti-* (both transferred from slot B); marker of Oc *hi-*, as in (13); or *to-* 'away', as in (8) and (32);

    C2 Second prefix position: applicative *ka-*, as in (5) and (16);

    C3 Third prefix position: causative *na-* (on verb), *niha-* (on auxiliary);

D Verb root, inflecting or non-inflecting (predicate head) – obligatory;

Table 1 *Pronoun paradigm*

	slot A, pronoun in O function	slot B, pronoun in S/A function; and also slot H
1sg	*owa*	*o-*
2sg	*tiwa*	*ti-*
3sg animate	*ø*	*ø*
3 inanimate	*ø*	*ø*
1nsg.inclusive	*e-ra*	*ee*
1nsg.exclusive	*ota-ra*	*otaa*
2nsg	*te-ra*	*tee*
3nsg animate	*mee* or *me-ra*	*mee*

E Auxiliary – obligatory if verb is non-inflecting;

F Miscellaneous suffixes: about fifty-five organised into six echelons, or macro-slots (with one to five ordered slots within each echelon, see §4.5) – all optional;

G Tense–modal suffixes: three past tenses (immediate past (IP), recent past (RP) and far past (FP), each portmanteau with an evidentiality specification, eyewitness (e) or non-eyewitness (n)); and five modalities (future, intentional, hypothetical, irrealis, reported) – all optional (generally only one is chosen, but there can be more than one[3]);

H Third pronominal slot, filled according to certain rules;

I Secondary verb: *ama/ama* 'extended in time' or *awine/awa* 'seems, in my opinion' – optional;

J Mood: declarative, backgrounding, four imperatives, two interrogatives, etc. – optional;

K Post-mood suffixes: a number of tense–modal forms (from slot G) and negation (from slot F) can follow mood, under particular circumstances.

A full list of miscellaneous, tense–modal and mood suffixes (slots F, G, J and K) is given in the appendix.

Note that all suffixes are optional. The distinction between inflectional and derivational morphological processes, while useful for languages from other parts of the world, has no useful role in the description of Jarawara (as of many other South American languages).

We can now comment on some of these slots. Firstly, fillers of pronominal slots A, B and H are given in table 1. It will be seen that 3sg animate and 3 inanimate are always zero. The 3nsg O form is *mee* in an O-construction; in an

---

[3] The attested combinations are: far past non-eyewitness followed by reported; future followed by immediate past non-eyewitness; irrealis followed by far past non-eyewitness, by immediate past non-eyewitness or by recent past eyewitness.

A-construction it is *mee* if A is first or second person and either *mee* or *me-ra* (in free variation) if A is third person.

All the (non-zero) forms in slot A are separate phonological and grammatical words, as are the nsg forms in slot B. However, the sg subject forms from slot B (1sg *o-* and 2sg *ti-*) are prefixes and are transferred to the following first prefix slot, C1, where they are mutually exclusive with *hi-*, the marker of an O-construction in which both A and O are third person, and *to-* which just has semantic effect 'away' (away from a place or from a state, e.g. 'become cold'). There can be no conflict between *o-* and *ti-*, referring to non-third persons, and *hi-*, used just if both core arguments are third person. The prefix *to-* can compete with *o-*, *ti-* or *hi-* and always loses out to them; however, an underlying but suppressed *to-* will surface if the verb is reduplicated, when an *o-*, *ti-* or *hi-* prefix is transferred to a special reduplication auxiliary (see §4.1).

It might be thought that slots B and C1 could be merged. That this is not possible is shown by predicates beginning with, say, *mera* (3nsgO, slot A) followed by *mee* (3nsgA, slot B) followed by *hi-* (O-construction marker, slot C1). These slots have to be treated as distinct, with the stipulation that *o-* and *ti-* from slot B move across into slot C1.

Almost all tense–modal and mood suffixes (in slots G and J) have distinct gender forms which apply wherever in a word they occur (medially or finally). Inflecting verb roots (slot D), auxiliaries (E) and miscellaneous suffixes (F) which end in *a* also show gender, but only when in word-final position; the underlying *a* stays as it is for f agreement and is raised to *e* for m agreement.

Slot H, the third pronominal position, is obligatorily filled when certain grammatical conditions are fulfilled. It always has the same form as slot B, and refers to the S argument in an intransitive clause, to the A argument in a transitive A-construction, and sometimes to the O argument, sometimes to the A argument in a transitive O-construction (the conditioning is set out in Dixon 2000).

An example of a predicate with a fair number of its slots filled is:

(8)   B   C1-D-F1b-F2b-G   H-J

       ee   to-ka-tima-mina-haba   ee-ke

       1nsg.incS AWAY-in.motion-UPSTREAM-MORNING-FUTf 1nsg.inc-DECf

       (We'll sleep here tonight and) we'll travel upstream in the morning

Slot I involves one of two secondary verbs, neither of which may take prefixes. If pronominal prefix 1sg *o-* or 2sg *ti-* is included in slot H before a secondary verb, then the pronominal form jumps over the secondary verb and attaches to the mood suffix in slot J. Example (9) has the 1nsg.exc form, *otaa*, in slots B and H; this is a separate word and retains its place before the secondary verb *ama*, in slot I. In contrast, (10) has pronominal prefix 1sg *o-* in slots B and H; this jumps over *ama* in slot I and attaches itself to the declarative mood marker, *-ke*, from slot J. We now get a (grammatical and phonological) word *o-ke*, consisting just of a pronominal prefix *o-* and a mood suffix *-ke*, with no intervening root.

(9) B   D-G   H   I-J
     otaa   jana-hamaro   otaa   ama-ke
     1nsg.excS   grow.up-FPef   1nsg.exc EXTENT-DECf
         [wara jaa]
         lake   PERIPHERAL POSTPOSITION
     We grew up at the lake

(10) B/C1-D-G   I   H-J
     o-jana-maro   ama   o-ke   [wara jaa]
     1sgS-grow.up-FPef   EXTENT   1sg-DECf   lake   PERI
     I grew up at the lake

4.1   Verbal reduplication

Verbs can be reduplicated in three ways: (i) by initial CV-, indicating 'do a bit'; (ii) by initial CVCV-, indicating 'do with force'; (iii) by final -CV, with a distributive sense. We can also get a combination of (i) with (iii), or (ii) with (iii). See Dixon and Vogel (1996).

Every type of verb – both inflecting and non-inflecting – can be reduplicated. Reduplication brings with it an auxiliary (AUXb; again either *-na-* or *-ha-*) to which verb affixes are transferred. Example (11) shows the inflecting verb *-mita-* 'hear, listen to' with 2sg subject prefix *ti-* and immediate positive imperative suffix (in f gender to agree with the pronoun) *-hi*. When the verb is reduplicated, in (12), both *ti-* and *-hi* are transferred to the reduplication auxiliary *-na-*. (If a clause does not consist of just a predicate, the predicate is enclosed in square brackets. Square brackets are also used to enclose an NP which consists of more than a single word, as in (21) and (26).)

(11) ati_O   [ti-mita-hi]
     language   2sgA-listen.to-ImmPosImpf
     you listen to the talking!

(12) ati_O   [mi.mita   ti-na-hi]
     language   REDUP.listen.to   2sgA-AUXb-ImmPosImpf
     you listen a bit to the talking!

Note that the reduplication auxiliary (AUXb) is distinct from the auxiliary of a non-inflecting verb (AUXa). In fact, *-na-* as the auxiliary of a non-inflecting verb will normally be omitted once its affixes have been transferred to a reduplication auxiliary, although there are circumstances under which it is retained.

Table 2 *Types of miscellaneous suffixes*

		what follows	
		A following suffix can be added directly to X	A following suffix must be added to a special auxiliary (AUXc) following X
what precedes	X is added to a preceding inflecting verb or to the auxiliary (AUXa) of a non-inflecting verb	(I) normal suffixes (twenty-eight)	(II) auxiliary-taking suffixes (twenty-one)
	X must be added to a special preceding auxiliary (AUXd)	(III) auxiliary-bound suffixes (seven)	(IV) suffix which is both auxiliary-taking and auxiliary-bound (just one known)

4.2   Types of suffix

A 'normal' verb suffix is something which is simply added to what precedes it in the verb (the root, or a preceding suffix) and has following suffixes simply added to it. In Jarawara, all tense–modal and all but one mood suffixes (the exception is the immediate negative imperative[4]) are normal suffixes, as are about half the miscellaneous suffixes. The remaining miscellaneous suffixes have unusual properties. One set may not have further suffixes added directly to them, but only to a special following auxiliary (AUXc); I call these 'auxiliary-taking' suffixes. Another set may not be added directly to earlier suffixes (or a verb or AUXa root) but only to a special preceding auxiliary (AUXd); I call these 'auxiliary-bound' suffixes. And there is one suffix which is both auxiliary-taking and auxiliary-bound.

We can usefully summarise the parameters of variation in table 2 (where X represents a miscellaneous suffix). The four types are illustrated in (13–16).

(I) A normal suffix, for example *-tasa* 'again', is added directly to an inflecting verb (as here) or to the auxiliary of a non-inflecting verb; further suffixes are added directly to it (a phonological rule raises the final *a* of *-tasa* to *e* when followed by tense–modal suffix *-himata*).

(13)   fanako$_O$ jimo$_A$ [hi-ta-tase-himari-ka]
         thigh(m)   ant(m)   Oc-bite-AGAIN-FPem-DECm
         then the ant bit him again (this time) on the thigh

---

[4] This is an auxiliary-taking suffix, *-rima -na-hi/-rama -na-ho*, plainly involving the immediate positive imperative suffix *-hi/-ho* as final element.

(II) An auxiliary-taking suffix, for example *-kanikima* 'scattered about', is added directly to an inflecting verb (as here) or to the auxiliary of a non-inflecting verb. However, further suffixes may not be added directly to *-kanikima* but must be attached to a special suffix-determined auxiliary (AUXc) which follows *-kanikima*. It is like a normal suffix with respect to what goes to its left, but it is unusual with respect to what happens on its right. For example:

(14)   mee   tafa-kanikima   na-ra-ke
        3nsgS   eat-SCATTERED   AUXc-IPef-DECf
        they (arrived and spread out) and each ate in a different house

(III) An auxiliary-bound suffix, for example *-wahare/-wahari*[5] 'do many times, in many places', cannot be added to an inflecting verb or to the auxiliary (AUXa) of a non-inflecting verb; it must instead be added to its own suffix-determined auxiliary (AUXd). However, a following suffix may be added directly to *-wahare*. In (15) *-tafa-* 'eat' is an inflecting verb; suffixes such as *-tasa* and *-kanikima* would be added directly to it but *-wahare* requires its own auxiliary to which it attaches. This suffix is normal with respect to what goes to its right, but unusual with respect to what happens on its left.

(15)   Okomobi$_S$ [tafa   na-wahare-hare-ka]
        name   eat   AUXd-MULTIPLE-IPem-DECm
        Okomobi ate in many houses

(IV) The auxiliary-taking and auxiliary-bound suffix *-wi* 'do continuously' combines the unusual properties of *-kanikima* (with respect to what follows) and of *-wahare* (with respect to what precedes). Consider

(16)   jara$_A$ [owa   haa:haa   ka-na   na-wi   na-re-ka]
        branco   1sgO   laugh   APPLIC-AUXa AUXd-CONT   AUXc-IPem-DECm
        the branco laughed at me for a considerable time

Here we have a non-inflecting verb *haa:haa -na-* 'laugh', whose auxiliary (AUXa) bears the applicative prefix *ka-* (this derives a transitive verb 'laugh at'). Note that *-wi* is not added to the verbal auxiliary (the one with *ka-*) but instead requires its own auxiliary (AUXd) to which it is attached. In addition, it does not permit a following suffix to be added to it but instead requires a following auxiliary (AUXc), to which tense–modal suffix (*-re*, a reduced form

---

[5] The final segment of this suffix is most appropriately represented as a morphophoneme *I*, i.e. *-waharI*. The *I* is realised as *i* in an odd-numbered and as *e* in an even-numbered mora counting from the left of the phonological word This provides a further example of a phonological rule applying on the 'underlying stress cycle' (see note 2), counting from the beginning of a phonological word. Other suffixes ending in the morphophoneme include *-hatI* 'do all day', in (24); *-hitI* 'do all along the way', in (32); and *-kI* 'coming' and *-rI* 'on a raised surface', mentioned in §6.

of -*hare*, by rule 8a) and declarative mood suffix (-*ka*) are attached. This suffix is unusual with respect to what happens on its left and also with respect to what happens on its right.

In addition, one of the auxiliary-bound suffixes and ten of the auxiliary-taking suffixes either require or generally take reduplication of the lexical verb. (More detailed information is in the appendix.)

It might be suggested that forms like -*kanikima*, -*wahare* and -*wi* should not really be called suffixes at all. However, there seems to be no other suitable label for them. There is some similarity with the two varieties of verbs. Normal suffixes are like inflecting verbs in allowing affixes to both precede and follow them. Whereas non-inflecting verbs allow no affixes before or after (but require an auxiliary for affixes to be added to), auxiliary-taking suffixes allow no further suffixes to follow (but require an auxiliary for them to be attached to) and auxiliary-bound suffixes cannot have other suffixes immediately preceding them (but must be added to their own auxiliary).[6]

It will be seen that there are four possible types of auxiliary within a predicate: AUXa, the auxiliary of a non-inflecting verb; AUXb, the auxiliary associated with reduplication; AUXc, the auxiliary required to follow an auxiliary-taking miscellaneous suffix, of type II, to which further suffixes are attached; and AUXd, the auxiliary to which an auxiliary-bound suffix, of type III, must be attached. (The first three types of auxiliary can be either -*na*- or -*ha*-; for AUXd only -*na*- is attested.) A predicate can include two or even three instances of -*na*-, as in (16).[7]

The auxiliary -*ha*- is never omitted, but the auxiliary -*na*- may be omitted under certain grammatical conditions. One is the nature of the following suffix. There are some suffixes which always omit an immediately preceding auxiliary -*na*- (these include -*tasa* 'again' and -*ra* 'negative'). There are some which always retain an immediately preceding auxiliary -*na*- (these include -*mina* 'in the morning, tomorrow'). And there are some that omit an immediately preceding -*na*- when it carries a prefix, but retain it when there is no prefix. The miscellaneous suffix -*bisa* 'also' is of this type, as illustrated in:

---

[6] The diachronic origin of non-normal suffixes is an interesting topic for speculation. One possibility is that some or all auxiliary-taking suffixes might at an earlier stage of the language have been non-inflecting verbs, which were then grammaticalised as part of the predicate. To support this hypothesis, we would expect to find lexical verbs in other Arawá languages that are cognate with auxiliary-taking suffixes in Jarawara. I have not been able to uncover any. The hypothesis thus remains speculative.

[7] Note that we do not get all four types of auxiliary in one predicate since there is no suffix that is both auxiliary-taking and auxiliary-bound and requires reduplication. (The one suffix that has been identified as both auxiliary-taking and auxiliary-bound is not common, and I have not tried to elicit it with a verb that is productively reduplicated.)

(17)   otaa   kobo   na-bisa
       1nsg.excS   arrive   AUXa-ALSOf
       we also arrived

(18)   kobo   o-bisa
       arrive   1sgS-ALSOf
       I also arrived

In (17) the subject pronoun, 1nsg.exc *otaa*, is a separate word and precedes the non-inflecting verb root. In (18) the subject pronoun is a prefix, 1sg *o-*, and attaches to the auxiliary *-na-*, causing this to drop when followed by *-bisa*. Thus in (18) we have an auxiliary constituent consisting just of prefix and suffix, without any overt auxiliary root. (This is similar to *o-ke* in (10), another kind of word consisting of just prefix and suffix.)

There are a number of subtypes within the affix sets. We will briefly comment on just two.

4.3   Subtypes of auxiliary-taking suffixes

Here we find the following subtypes:
(a) PREFIX-RETAINING SUFFIXES , those that maintain a pronominal prefix (1sg *o-* or 2sg *ti-*, or Oc prefix *hi-*) on a preceding inflecting verb or auxiliary, and also repeat it on their own auxiliary (and in slot H).
(b) PREFIX-POACHING SUFFIXES, those that omit a pronominal prefix from all preceding positions in the predicate but include it on their own auxiliary (and in slot H).

The different grammatical behaviours can be compared by examining two affixes that have very similar meanings 'soon, immediately': prefix-retaining *-ibote -na-* and prefix-poaching *-kabote -na-*. With the inflecting verb *-sawi-* 'join in' we get:

(19)   o-sawi-bote   o-na-habana   o-ke
       1sgS-join. in-SOON   1sg-AUXc-FUTf   1sg-DECf
       I'll soon join in

(20)   sawi-kabote   o-na-habana   o-ke
       join. in-SOON   1sgS-AUXc-FUTf   1sg-DECf
       I'll soon join in

In (19) the 1sg prefix *o-* is retained on the verb *-sawi-* and repeated on the auxiliary demanded by suffix *-ibote*; in (20) it only occurs on the auxiliary of the suffix *-kabote*. In each sentence it also occurs in slot H.

4.4   Subtypes of normal suffixes

Most normal suffixes form one phonological word with what precedes and follows in the same grammatical word. But there are just a few normal suffixes[8] which behave differently. If one of these is preceded by more than a single mora in the grammatical word to which it belongs, then it begins a new phonological word within that grammatical word (we again use ':' for a phonological word boundary within a grammatical word). This is the third type of situation where one grammatical word may consist of two phonological words, mentioned in §2.

Compare *-tasa* 'again' – in (21) – which has the property of beginning a new phonological word, with *-bisa* 'also' – in (22) – which occurs in the same sixth echelon slot as *-tasa* but continues the same phonological word.

(21)   [Okomobi   ati]o   [o-mita:tasa-habone   o-ke]
        name   speech   1sgA-listen.to:AGAIN-INTf   1sg-DECf
        I'll listen again to what Okomobi says (lit. to Okomobi's speech)

Now if *o-mita-tasa-habone* were one phonological word, the *-ha-* of *-habone* would fall in the sixth mora and be omitted by rule 8a in §2. But it is retained. This is because a new phonological word commences with *-tasa* and the *-ha-* is in the third mora, thus not being available for omission.

(22)   okati   [kamina-bisa-ra-ke]
        1sgPOSS+grandmother   speak-ALSO-IPef-DECf
        (My grandfather spoke and then) my grandmother also spoke

Here the underlying verb form is *kamina-bisa-hara-ke*. The *-ha-* of IPef suffix *-hara* is in the sixth mora and is omitted by rule 8a. If *-bisa* had commenced a new phonological word the *-ha-* would have been in the third mora of *bisa-hara-ke* and would not have been omitted.

We can also contrast (21), in which *-tasa* is preceded by three moras within its grammatical word and commences a new phonological word, with (23), in which *-tasa* is preceded by just one mora in its grammatical word and continues an existing phonological word.

---

[8] There are two suffixes (*-tasa* 'again' and *-ikima* 'two participants, a pair') which always start a new phonological word under the conditions stated. And there is a third suffix, *-mata-* 'short time', whose behaviour varies. It generally continues an existing phonological word but I have a fair number of instances (from both texts and elicitation) where it behaves like *-tasa-* and *-ikima-* in beginning a new phonological word if it is preceded by more than a single mora in the grammatical word to which it belongs. This suffix may be well be in the process of shifting its morphological profile.

There are different conditions under which the suffix-*hite/-hiti* 'do all along the way' may commence a new phonological word; details are in Dixon and Vogel (ms.).

(23)   oko-jibotee$_0$ [jori   o-tasa-ra   o-ke]
         1sgPOSS-spouse   copulate.with   1sgA-AGAIN-IPef   1sg-DECf
         I copulated with my spouse again

The underlying form of the auxiliary constituent is *o-na-tasa-hara* (1sgA-AUXa-AGAIN-IPef). As mentioned above, the auxiliary *-na-* always drops when immediately followed by *-tasa*, giving *o-tasa-hara* which is both one grammatical word and one phonological word. Since the *-ha-* of *-hara* is the fourth mora it is omitted, by rule 8a. Now if *-tasa* began a new phonological word here, then *-ha-* would be in the third mora of *tasa-hara* and would not be omitted. (It would in any case be impossible for *tasa-hara* within *o-tasa-hara* to be a separate phonological word, since that would leave just *o-*; this only has one mora and so could not by itself constitute a separate phonological word.)

4.5   The six echelons of morphological suffixes

The fifty-five or so miscellaneous suffixes fall naturally into six ordered sets which can be called 'echelons'. There are a number of ordered slots within most echelons. In outline (a full list is in the appendix):
- echelon 1, normal suffixes: sixteen in three ordered slots;
- echelon 2, normal suffixes: three in three ordered slots (one suffix may commence a new phonological word);
- echelon 3, auxiliary-taking, prefix-retaining: two (mutually incompatible);
- echelon 4, auxiliary-taking, prefix-poaching (one is also auxiliary bound): twenty, fourteen of which fall into five ordered slots, with six not having been obtained in combination with another suffix from this echelon;
- echelon 5, auxiliary-bound: six, four in two ordered slots (one may commence a new phonological word);
- echelon 6, normal suffixes: seven in five ordered slots (two may commence a new phonological word).

There are two further miscellaneous suffixes which appear to have considerable freedom both of positioning and of morphological type: (a) *-waha* can be a normal suffix 'now, the next thing, then' while *-waha -na-* can be an auxiliary-taking suffix 'second time'; (b) *-tee* can be a normal suffix 'habitual, customary' or an auxiliary-bound suffix 'remembering something from the past'.

In most languages which have pronominal elements referring to core arguments, these are only marked once within the predicate. Jarawara is unusual in that a predicate typically includes two occurrences of a prefixal or non-prefixal subject pronoun, in slots B and H (or, two occurrences of an object pronoun in some transitive O-constructions, in slots A and H); this is seen in (8–10), (19–21) and (23).

There are also predicates including three occurrences of a pronominal prefix. In (19), for instance, 1sg *o-* is added to the inflecting verb, which is followed by the auxiliary-taking suffix *-ibote*; it is on the auxiliary required by *-ibote*; and it is also in slot H. A different way of achieving three occurrences of a pronominal prefix within one predicate is shown in (24), where *o-* is attached to the inflecting verb *-ka-* 'be in motion' which takes first echelon miscellaneous suffix *-tima* 'upstream'. The verb also takes fifth echelon suffix *-hate/-hati* 'do all day', but this is auxiliary-bound and is added to its own AUXd, which also takes the *o-* prefix. The third occurrence of *o-* is in slot H.

(24)   o-ka-tima   o-na-hate-hara   o-ke
        1sgS-in.motion-UPSTREAM   1sgS-AUXd-ALL.DAY-IPef   1sg-DECf
        I just went upstream all day

It is possible to get a sequence of two auxiliary-bound suffixes, each with its own AUXd, on which a pronominal prefix is copied. We thus get a total of four occurrences of 1sg *o-* within a single predicate; as in (25), with *-wahare/-wahari* 'do many times, in many places' plus *-hate/-hati* 'do all day'. (Note that *-wahare/wahari* omits its immediately preceding AUXd, *-na-*.)

(25)   o-tafa   o-wahare   o-na-hate-hara   o-ke
        1sgS-eat   1sgS-MULTIPLE   1sgS-AUXd-ALL.DAY-IPef   1sg-DECf
        I ate, in different houses, all day

In every example given thus far, each space represents both a phonological word boundary and a grammatical word boundary. That is, every orthographic word is a grammatical word. Every orthographic word is also one phonological word, except where there is a ':', indicating a phonological word boundary within a grammatical word, as in (21).

Before turning to a discussion of grammatical word in Jarawara it will be useful to examine, in a more general way, the distinction between predicate and grammatical word.

5   Grammatical word and predicate – general discussion

A grammatical word is a unit bigger than the morpheme. But how much bigger? As mentioned in §2 of the introduction, some early writers denied that polysynthetic languages had any unit 'word', since the grammatical unit next up from the morpheme seemed to them too big to justify the label 'word' (Milewski refers to it as 'syntactic group').

It is now accepted that the size of a grammatical word varies with the morphological type of a language. In an analytic language a word will most often consist of just one morpheme, occasionally of two or more. In a polysynthetic language a verbal word may typically include from six to ten morphemes (and, perhaps, always at least three).

In most languages the areas of greatest structural complexity include the verb and/or the predicate[9] (or verb complex or verb phrase). It is, in fact, important to distinguish between predicate and verb, and not to muddle up their respective structures.

Some languages have a fairly synthetic verb structure but a rather simple predicate structure. In Dyirbal, for instance, a verb can consist of root plus five or six suffixes, whereas the great majority of predicates consist of just one verb. The most complex predicate involves two verbs – one of them generally having an adverbal-type meaning – which agree in transitivity and in final inflection. For example, both *bura-* 'see, look at', and *ŋuyma-* 'do properly to' take the antipassive derivational suffix *-lay-* and the purposive inflection *-gu* in (Dixon 1972: 386):

(26) ŋadja [bura-lay-gu   ŋuyma-lay-gu]
      1sgS   look.at-ANTIPASS-PURP   do.properly.to-ANTIPASS-PURP
         [gayga-gu   ba-gu-n]
         eye-DAT   THERE-DAT-f
      I really looked at her eyes

English has a relatively simple verb structure. Leaving aside derivational affixes like *-ify* which yield a verb stem, we just have stem plus suffix *-ed* or *-ing*. However, predicate structure can be quite complex as in:

(27)   will have been killing

(28)   was having to be filtered

Now, putting aside our ingrained ideas about word, based on the traditional way of writing word spaces (which can be an historical relic, out of accord with the structure of the present-day language, as in the case of French, mentioned in §4.2 of chapter 1), why do we not regard each of (27) and (28) as a single grammatical word?

There are several reasons why not. One is that it is possible to pause at the word boundaries written in (27) and (28). A second is that an adverb can be inserted into a predicate, prototypically after the first word (*will probably have been killing*) but potentially after any word (for example, *will have probably been killing*). And if each of (27) and (28) was taken to be one grammatical word the roots would presumably be the lexical forms *kill* and *filter*; but then *-ing* would be a suffix in some occurrences and some kind of prefix (or component of a proclitic?) in others. It is clear that the only feasible treatment of English is to take each orthographic word in (27) and (28) to be a grammatical word.

---

[9] Here I use the term predicate (or verb complex, or verb phrase) for a unit that does not include any NPs (an O NP in the case of an accusative, or an A NP in the case of an ergative syntax) but just the verb and its modifiers and bound pronominal attachments.

This is simply a language with rather simple verb structure and fairly complex predicate structure.

Let us now look briefly at Fijian. As described in chapter 1, a grammatical word is centred on a root (or compound stem) and may have prefixes and/or suffixes added to it. Function items – such as prepositions, articles, tense–aspect markers and verb modifiers – are also each regarded as a grammatical word. Those grammatical words that have two moras are also distinct phonological words. Those that have a single mora either attach to another single-mora function item to jointly create a phonological word (e.g. *o=na* '2sg.subject.pronoun=future.tense'), or function as proclitic to a following phonological word.

Now Fijian is a typical Oceanic language with a fairly analytic verb but a richly structured predicate. Most verbs consist just of a root, although there can be one or even two prefixes, and either an incorporated noun or a transitive suffix. However, it does have a complex predicate structure. A predicate (making up a complete clause) along the lines of (29) is fairly typical (Dixon 1988: 310):

(29)   rau   saa   la'i   dabe   vata   sara   to'a
        3duS   ASPECT   GO.AND   sit   TOGETHER   AT.ONCE   TEMPORARILY
        the two of them went and right away sat together for a while

It might be asked why we could not take (29) as a single polysynthetic verb, consisting of seven small phonological words. After all, the elements in (29) must occur in fixed order and do make up a grammatical unit. The head is the lexical verb *dabe* 'sit'. The first element (the only other obligatory element) is a subject pronoun. There is then one element chosen from a set of six tense–aspect markers (more than one could have been chosen), here *saa*, which contrasts this moment with a previous one. This is followed by one chosen from a set of eleven pre-verbal modifiers, *la'i* 'go and do'. Following the verb (which could bear affixes although it does not here) there can be choices from a set of about twenty-four post-verbal modifiers (arranged in about eleven structural slots); here we find *vata* 'together', *sara* 'immediately, at once' and *to'a* 'done on an interim basis, temporarily'.[10] This is all rather reminiscent of the complex structure of a verb in a polysynthetic language. Could we not treat (29) as one complex verb and then add Fijian (about perhaps most of the five hundred or so other Oceanic languages, which have similar structures) to the inventory of polysynthetic languages?

This is not in fact a feasible line of analysis. Firstly, similarly to the situation in English, an adverb (e.g. *va'a-totolo* 'quickly') can be included within a

---

[10] The account of Fijian given here has been slightly simplified, by omitting mention of some elements; this simplification does not affect the points being made. Full details are in Dixon (1988).

predicate. It may come either immediately after the verb – that is, between *dabe* and *vata* in (29) – or at the very end of the predicate – after *to'a*. Secondly, one can pause at every orthographic boundary in (29).

Another point is that some of the predicate modifiers also occur as full lexemes and then have grammatical word status. There is one example of this in (29) – *to'a* can be a verb meaning 'sit on one's heels, squat' and also a postverbal modifier 'done on an interim basis, temporarily'. (Others of this type include *ti'o* which means 'reside, remain, sit' as a lexical verb and 'happening continuously now but not before or afterwards' as a modifier, and *tuu* which means 'stand' as a lexical verb and 'permanently, or happened over an extended period and now finished' as a modifier.) Note that it could not be suggested that in (29) *to'a* is somehow incorporated into the verb; Fijian does have a process of incorporation, involving a noun that is attached directly to the verb root, e.g. *ta'i:wai* 'fetch:water'.

The putative analysis of (29) as one grammatical word must be discarded. This is a complex predicate consisting of seven words (each being both a phonological word and a grammatical word). What we have is a language with complex predicate structure and rather simple verb structure.

In some languages the units grammatical word and phonological word always coincide. In others there are some instances where the two units do not coincide, but these are greatly outnumbered by instances where they are the same (and note that this applies in analytic, synthetic and also polysynthetic languages). Indeed, this is the basis on which the label 'word' is used in naming the two units.

In some highly polysynthetic languages it is necessary to recognise as grammatical word a long and complex unit (these languages tend to have a simple predicate structure). Other languages can have a complex predicate structure, which must be recognised as a quite different phenomenon. In summary, there is no basis on which Fijian (and the many other Oceanic languages, with similar profiles) should be added to the inventory of languages with polysynthetic verb structure.

6   The grammatical word in Jarawara

The definition of grammatical word in Jarawara is straightforward.

(a) Each lexical root, and each auxiliary and secondary verb root, forms the core of a grammatical word; prefixes and suffixes to a root are part of the same grammatical word. When a root undergoes reduplication it remains one grammatical word. Two roots combined to form a compound stem make up one grammatical word. In each of these instances the elements of a grammatical

word occur together, in fixed order, with the whole having a conventionalised coherence and meaning.

As shown by *o-bisa* in (18), the auxiliary root *-na-* can be dropped in specified grammatical circumstances, so that we get an auxiliary constituent which actually lacks an auxiliary root and just consists of prefix plus suffix. In similar fashion we can have a pronominal prefix plus a mood suffix, such as *o-ke* in (10). Each of these is one grammatical word and one phonological word.

(b) Free pronouns (that is, every pronoun other than prefixes 1sg *o-* and 2sg *ti-*), deictics, interrogatives, discourse markers, postpositions and interjections also constitute grammatical words. Each of these has at least two moras and is also a phonological word.

For instance, the all-purpose preposition (corresponding to *to, from, at, on, in, with*, etc. in English) has the form *jaa* in Jarawara and is here a distinct grammatical word, as in (9–10). (A full analysis has not been undertaken of the other dialects of Madi, but my preliminary impression is that the preposition may here be *=ja*, with a single mora, functioning as enclitic to the preceding word.)

Every noun and adjective (which most often occur without suffixes) and every non-inflecting verb (which cannot take suffixes)[11] has at least two moras; each of them is thus both a grammatical word and a phonological word. Thus, if one of these items is monosyllabic, its vowel must be long; for example 2nsg pronoun *tee* (in table 1) and non-inflecting verb *hoo -na-* 'snore, (dog) growls'.

There are some inflecting verbs which do have monosyllabic form with a short vowel. The most common verb of all is *-ka-* 'be in motion'. This verb never occurs without a directional affix, at the least it must take one of prefix *to-* 'away', suffix *-ke/-ki* 'coming' or suffix *-ma* 'back'. Thus a word including *-ka-* always has at least two moras. (Note that *to-* can be replaced by a pronominal suffix, but there are then still at least two moras in the word.)

A few other monosyllabic verbs have one allomorph with a short vowel and another with a long vowel. For example 'stand' is *-wa-* if there is a prefix or if it takes the miscellaneous suffix *-re/-ri* 'on a raised surface', and *-waa-* otherwise, again ensuring that each verbal word has at least two moras. Evidence can be provided that the underlying form here is *-waa-* with the vowel being shortened in certain circumstances. In contrast, the underlying form of the verb 'exist' is *-na-*, with a short vowel. This almost always takes some affix(es) but it can be used without any; when this happens the vowel is lengthened, giving *naa*, and ensuring that this grammatical word is also a full phonological word.

---

[11] Nothing in the grammar of Jarawara is simple. There is in fact a 'distributive' suffix *-ri*, which is unique in that it is added to the root (not the auxiliary) of a non-inflecting verb (it is only attested with a handful of verbs) e.g. *weje -na-* 'carry', *weje-ri -na-* 'each carries their own'.

The vowel of auxiliary *-na-* is never lengthened. This auxiliary generally takes some kind of prefix and/or suffix; an example is in (30). But sometimes it does not, as in (31). What happens then is that *na* forms part of a phonological word with the preceding non-inflecting verb root. Note that it is a full part of this phonological word, for application of the stress rule: stress goes on the penultimate mora of *amó+na* (here using '+' to indicate a grammatical word boundary within a phonological word).

(30) ámo   o-ná-habóne
      sleep   1sgS-AUXa-INTENTIONf
      I'm going to sleep

(31) amó+na
      sleep+AUXaf
      she sleeps

This is the only instance I know of one phonological word consisting of two grammatical words.

6.1   Rejecting an alternative analysis

The basis for sound linguistics lies in investigating a number of possible analyses for a given set of data, and examining the pros and cons of each before deciding on the most appropriate analysis.

In this spirit, let us consider a typical Jarawara predicate (here making up a complete clause), in (32), and examine whether it could be regarded as a single complex grammatical word.

(32) A   B   D   C1-E-F1C-F5-G   H
      otara   mee   haa   to-na-ma-iti-haro[12]   mee
      1nsg.excO   3nsgA   call.to   AWAY-AUXa-BACK-ALONG.WAY-RPef   3nsg
        I-J
      ama-ke
      EXTENT-DECf
      they were calling out to us all along the way back

These predicate elements must occur in a fixed order. Why should we not say that they make up one grammatical word? Note that, unlike in English and Fijian, no adverbs can be inserted into a predicate in Jarawara (adverbal constituents are peripheral NPs which must be placed in the first or last slot of clause structure – see §3). Note that if (32) were analysed as one grammatical word, then so should every other predicate be.

---

[12] The intial *-h-* of *-hite/-hiti* 'all along the way' may – as here – be omitted when preceded by *a* and in an even-numbered mora from the beginning of its phonological word.

We can outline four arguments against this analysis.

(a) It is possible to pause at every orthographic boundary written in (32), or in any other predicate.

(b) Some of the elements written as separate words in (32) may also be used outside a predicate and always then make up one grammatical word. For instance, all of the non-prefixal pronouns can be used as copula complement within a copula clause. The secondary verb *ama* 'extended in time' is homophonous with (and pretty certainly developed from) the copula *ama* 'be'. The other secondary verb, *awine/awa* 'seems, in my opinion' is historically derived from the lexical verb *-awa-* 'see, feel' plus miscellaneous suffix *-ine/ø* 'continuous'. Thus, just as one reason for recognising the auxiliary element *have* (or *had* or *having*) as a grammatical word in English is that it is homophonous with the lexical verb *have* (with inflected forms *had* and *having*) – and similarly for *to'a* in Fijian – so the occurrence of *ama* and *awine/awa* in Jarawara both as modifying elements within the predicate and as independent verbal words is one reason for regarding them to be full grammatical words in each occurrence.

(c) A number of alternations within the grammar of Jarawara depend for their explanation on the definition of grammatical word given in §6. Recall the rule stated in §4.4 that *-tasa* (and some other miscellaneous suffixes) commences a new phonological word if preceded by more than a single mora in the grammatical word to which they belong, but continue an existing phonological word if preceded by a single mora. If the predicate in (23) were treated as one grammatical word, *-tasa* would be preceded by three moras within it (*jori* and *o-*) and should commence a new phonological word, as it did in (21). It does not, showing that *jori* and *o-tasa-ra* in (23) must be regarded as distinct grammatical words.

(d) Consider the predicate in (16), repeated here for convenience:

(16′)   owa   haa:haa   ka-na   na-wi   na-re-ka
          1sgO   laugh   APPLIC-AUXa   AUXd-CONT   AUXc-IPem-DECm
          he laughed at me for a considerable time

If this were one grammatical word we should have three occurrences of the auxiliary *-na-* as suffixes to the lexical verb root *haa:haa* (and two of them would be sequential). The situation becomes even more complex when we consider (25), also repeated here for convenience.

(25)   o-tafa   o-wahare   o-na-hate-hara   o-ke
         1sgS-eat   1sgS-MULTIPLE   1sgS-AUXd-ALL.DAY-IPef   1sg-DECf
         I ate, in different houses, all day

If this were a single grammatical word, with - *tafa-* as head, we would have 1sg *o-* as prefix once and as suffix three times.

Such an analysis would be unbearably complex and would lack explanatory power. In contrast, the statement of grammatical word presented in §6 is maximally clear: auxiliary *-na-* is always the basis for a distinct grammatical word; 1sg *o-* is always a prefix – to an inflecting verb, or to an auxiliary, or to a mood suffix as in (10).[13]

In the approach followed here, grammatical and phonological words in Jarawara fall together almost all of the time. There are just four exceptions, which will be recapitulated in §7.

We pointed out in §5 that both English and Fijian have a relatively simple verb word but rather complex predicate structure, in contrast with polysynthetic languages which tend to have a complex verb word but simple predicate structure. It is important to distinguish between predicate and verb.

Jarawara has a fairly complex verb structure. There can be up to three prefixes and we frequently get three miscellaneous suffixes plus one (or two) tense–modal markers and a mood suffix; a verb with six morphemes is common. It also has a fairly complex predicate structure, with pronominal words in slots A, B and H, a secondary verb in slot I, and a number of miscellaneous suffixes that require their own auxiliary (making up a separate grammatical/phonological word), either to which they must be attached or to which following suffixes must be attached.

7   Summary of instances where the two kinds of word do not correspond

As already stated, the units phonological word and grammatical word correspond for the great majority of cases. We find only four types of disparity.

One grammatical word consisting of two phonological words:
  (i) In a compound, e.g. *báni:kasáko*, described in §2.
  (ii) In reduplication, e.g. *kéte:ketébe* and *áta:'atábo*, also described in §2.

---

[13] In considering and rejecting an analysis where all of, say (30), is one grammatical word, I am not tilting at a straw man. This approach is taken in all the publications of the Summer Institute of Linguistics missionary linguists Robert and Barbara Campbell on the related dialect Jamamadí, on which they have been working since 1962. That is, in (30) *amo o-na-habone*, they would take the 1sg bound pronoun *o* to be a suffix to the (what is, for me, a non-inflecting) verb *amo*, with the auxiliary root *na* a further suffix after this, i.e. *amo-o-na-habone*. See, for example. B. Campbell (1986) and R. Campbell (1988).
  Under this analysis it would not be possible to provide any explanatory statement of the phonological rules; it appears that the Campbells have not considered the matter of phonological rules.

(iii) When one of a small number of miscellaneous suffixes is preceded by more than a single mora within its grammatical word, it commences a new phonological word, described in §4.4.

One phonological word consisting of two grammatical words:

(iv) A non-inflecting verb root plus a following auxiliary *-na-* which bears no affix, described in §6.

Appendix List of miscellaneous, tense-modal and mood suffixes

Slot F Miscellaneous suffixes

The following abbreviations code the various properties of miscellaneous suffixes:

A	when the suffix immediately follows auxiliary *-na-*, the auxiliary is retained
*	auxiliary *-na-* drops when immediately followed by this suffix
**	auxiliary *-na-* drops when immediately followed by this suffix if there is also a prefix
***	always takes prefix *to-* (for semantic reasons) and omits an immediately preceding auxiliary *-na-*
@	auxiliary *-na-* drops when immediately followed by this suffix unless the auxiliary has prefix *to-* or *ka-* or a first or second echelon suffix
n.d.	not determinable – used of a suffix whose occurrence is so restricted that it is not possible to categorise it as A, *, **, *** or @
R	suffix requires initial CV- reduplication of lexical verb (just for *-ba -na-* the reduplication can be initial CV- or initial CVCV-; just for *-kawa(ha)* the reduplication can be initial CV- or final -CV)
(R)	suffix often takes initial CV- reduplication of lexical verb
NPW	the suffix begins a new phonological word within its grammatical word, under specified conditions

First echelon, F1 – all are normal suffixes
slot F1a (1) ** *-ife/-ifi* 'relating to water'
        (2) ** *-re/-ri* 'raised surface (i.e. off ground), edge'
slot F1b (3) ** *-tima* 'upstream', as in (8), (24)
        (4) ** *-imisa* 'up (other than upstream)'
        (5) A   *-risa* 'down; done anyhow; etc.'
        (6) ** *-riwa(ha)* 'across'

(7)	**		*-basa* 'to/on the edge'
(8)	**		*-fara* 'clear space'
(9)	A		*-ijoma* 'through gap'
(10)	A		*-kosa₁* 'between two extremes'
(11)	**		*-kosa₂ ∼ -sa* 'do once, do a bit, something happens cleanly and clearly'
(12)	*		*-kasa* 'a lot at once'
slot F1c (13)	A		*-ke/-ki* 'coming'
(14)	A		*-ma* 'back, return', as in (32)
(15)	A		*-make/-maki* 'following'
(16)	***		*-wite/-witi* 'from a place, outward from centre'

Second echelon, F2 – all are normal suffixes
slot F2a (1)   A   *-ikima* 'two participants, a pair' (NPW)
slot F2b (2)   A   *-mina* 'in the morning', as in (8)
 slot F2 (3)   A   *-iba(ha)* 'do first'

Third echelon, F3 – both are auxiliary-taking, prefix-retaining suffixes
(1)   **   *-saa -na-* 'still'
(2)   A   *-ibote -na-* 'soon', as in (19)

Fourth echelon, F4 – all are auxiliary-taking, prefix-poaching (and one is, in addition, auxiliary-bound).

We first recognise five slots where the suffixes in each slot cannot co-occur, and the slots occur in order. Then follow a number of suffixes which could not be placed in slots.

slot F4a (1)	@		*-nati -ha-* 'be the only person doing something'
(2)	A	R	*-mii -na-* 'walking around'
slot F4b (3)	@		*-inima -na-* 'want to, need to, about to'
(4)	@		*-ihina -na-* 'can do, it is possible to do'
(5)	*		*-rima -na-* 'intermittently, at intervals'
(6)	*	R	*-baa -na-* 'do at/from a distance'
(7)	*		*-kanikima -na-* 'scattered, spread out in lots of different places', as in (14)
(8)	@	R	*-karahama -na-* 'continue doing, do without stopping, only do'
slot F4c (9)	*	(R)	*-raba -na-* 'do a bit'
(10)	@	(R)	*-rama -na-* 'unusual, unexpected'
(11)	@	R	*-biti -ra-*, 'not even a little bit, not even one' (takes negator *-ra-*, from before which auxiliary *-na-* is omitted)

slot f4d (12)	@		-*kabote -na-* 'soon', as in (20)
(13)	@		-*kaba -na-* 'do without stopping'
slot f4e (14)	A		-*ihiti -ha-* 'do quickly'
others (15)	*	R	-*ba -na-* 'hasn't been done but should be done, or should be done more; do what you don't want to do'
(16)	A		-*hama -na-* 'pretending, unexpected result or unfulfilled expectation'
(17)	n.d.	R	-*kii -na-* 'be just [one or two]'
(18)	n.d.	R	-*nama -na-* 'a lot, the most'
(19)	***	R	*(to-)-sii -na-* 'going along a path'

There is one suffix which is prefix-poaching auxiliary-taking and also auxiliary-bound:

(20)   AUXa: **; AUXd: A -*wi -na-* 'continuously', as in (16)

Fifth echelon, F5 – all are auxiliary-bound suffixes
As with -*wi-* above, we need to specify the possibilities for omission of both the verbal auxiliary (AUXa) and the suffix-bound auxiliary (AUXd)

	AUXa	AUXd		
slot f5a (1)	@	**		-*wahare/-wahari* 'do many times, in many places', as in (15), (25)
slot f5b (2)	@	*		-*inofa* 'happened continuously over recent time'
(3)	@	A		-*(ha)ba* 'do/happen all night, or for a good portion of the night'
(4)	@	A		-*(ha)te/-(ha)ti* 'do/happen all day, or for a good portion of the day', as in (24–5)
others (5)	@	*	R	-*kawa(ha)* 'do for a while'
(6)	A	A		-*((h)i)te/-((h)iti* 'all along the way') NPW, as in (32)

Sixth echelon, F6 – all are normal suffixes

slot f6a (1)	*	-*tasa* 'again' (NPW), as in (13), (21), (23)
(2)	**	-*bisa* 'also', as in (17–18), (22)
(3)	**	-*ifako* 'do a lot'
slot f6b (4)	**	-*rawa*, at least one core argument is f nsg
slot f6c (5)	**	-*mata* 'short time' (NPW)
slot f6d (6)	*	-*ra* negator
slot f6e (7)	**	-*ine/ø* 'continuous'

Extra-echelon suffixes
(1)   ** -*wa(ha)* 'now, the next thing, then', a normal suffix; and auxiliary-taking -*waha -na-* 'second time'

(2)   *   *-tee* 'habitual, customary', a normal suffix; and auxiliary-bound
          -tee 'remembering something from the past'

Slot G Tense–modal suffixes (given as f/m)

Past tense
A *-(ha)ra/-(ha)re*   immediate past eyewitness, IPe, as in (1–4),
                             (14–16), (22–5)
A *-(ha)ro/-(hi)ri*   recent past eyewitness, RPe, as in (7), (32)
A *-(ha)maro/-(hi)mari*   far past eyewitness, FPe, as in (9–10), (13)
A *-(ha)ni/-(hi)no*   immediate past non-eyewitness
A *-(he)te/-(hi)ta*   recent past non-eyewitness
A *-(he)mete/-(hi)mata*   far past non-eyewitness

Modalities
A *-(ha)ba(na)/-(hi)ba(na)* future, FUT, as in (8), (19–20)
A *-(ha)bone/-(hi)bona*   intentional, INT, as in (21), (30)
A *-(he)ne/-(hi)na*   irrealis
A *-(he)mene/-(hi)mana*   hypothetical
A *-(ha)mone/-(hi)mona*   reported

Slot J Mood suffixes (given as f/m)

Indicative
A *-ke/-ka*   declarative, DEC, as in many of the examples quoted
A *-ini/ne*   backgrounding

Imperative
A   *-hi/-ho*   immediate positive imperative, ImmPosImp,
                             as in (6), (11–12)
**   *-ija-hi/ja-ho*   distant positive imperative
*   *-rima -na-hi/-rama*   immediate negative imperative (auxiliary-
     -na-ho   taking suffix, with pronominal prefixes
                             attached to *-na*).
*   *-ri-ja-hi/-ra-ja-ho*   distant negative imperative

Interrogative
A *-ra/-ra*   content interrogative
A *-ini/-ø*   polar interrogative
** *-ibana/-bana* polar future interrogative

Others
**   *-rihi/-rihi*   contrastive negator
**   *-ibe(ja)/-ba(ja)*   immediate

**	*-ikani/-kani*	counterfactual
?	*-inihi/-noho*	climax
**	*-imakoni/-mako*	unusual, unexpected

Slot κ Post-mood suffixes

from slot F
| *-re/-ra* | negator |

from slot G
-ni/-no	immediate past non-eyewitness
-bone/-bona	intentional
-ne/-na	irrealis
-mone/-mona	reported

References

Buller, E., Buller, B. and Everett, D. 1993. 'Stress placement, syllable structure and minimality in Banawá', *International Journal of American Linguistics* 59.280–93.

Campbell, B. 1986. 'Repetition in Jamamadí discourse', pp 171–85 of *Sentence initial devices*, edited by J. E. Grimes. Dallas: Summer Institute of Linguistics and University of Texas at Arlington.

Campbell, R. 1988. 'Avaliação dentro das citações na língua Jamamadí', *Série Lingüística* [Summer Institute of Linguistics, Brazil] 9(2).9–30.

Dixon, R. M. W. 1972. *The Dyirbal language of North Queensland.* Cambridge: Cambridge University Press.

1988. *A grammar of Boumaa Fijian.* Chicago: University of Chicago Press.

1995. 'Fusional development of gender marking in Jarawara possessed nouns', *International Journal of American Linguistics* 61.263–94.

1999. 'Arawá', pp 293–306 of *The Amazonian Languages*, edited by R. M. W. Dixon and A.Y. Aikhenvald. Cambridge: Cambridge University Press.

2000. 'A-constructions and O-constructions in Jarawara', *International Journal of American Linguistics* 66.22–56.

Dixon, R. M. W. and Vogel, A. R. 1996. 'Reduplication in Jarawara', *Languages of the World* 10.24–31.

Ms. *A grammar of Jarawara, from southern Amazonia.*

6   Towards a notion of 'word' in sign languages

Ulrike Zeshan

1   Words and signs: on psychological and cultural validity

The question whether all languages have words may look like a nonsense question to many people, the universal existence of words being regarded as a truism in itself. Even though it is widely acknowledged that finding a strictly satisfying definition of 'word' is as difficult as defining similarly universal terms such as 'sentence' or 'language', the existence of words in all languages is not usually questioned.

As with all putative language universals, probing the validity of the claim depends crucially on looking at languages that are as 'different' as possible. If many otherwise very 'different' languages share a certain feature, it is more likely that this feature is a true universal than if only 'similar' languages are considered. The motivation for looking at the concept of 'word' in sign languages lies exactly here: for what could be more 'different' than a sign language? As Anderson (1982: 91) puts it: 'Comparison of spoken and signed languages can be especially valuable because the parallels are so surprising at first, and seem so automatic and natural after we have worked with them. The challenge of finding these parallels produces important insights into the nature of human language in general. So we can often learn more by studying a sign language than by studying one more spoken language.' This is of course not to ignore that modality-related *differences* between signed and spoken language can be just as revealing as the parallels between the two. Sign languages are of great typological importance by virtue of their visual–gestural modality, which makes them stand out as a distinct language type in opposition to the entirety of spoken languages. Certainly, using the hands and body to produce a linguistic signal and the eyes to perceive it should have consequences that mark sign languages as different from languages that use the vocal tract for producing speech signals and the ears for perceiving them. Some possible modality-related differences at the phonological level have been discussed by Gee (1993) and Anderson (1993).[1]

---

[1] Sign language research uses the terms 'phonology', 'phoneme' and so on, although their literal meaning obviously does not apply. The terms are used to refer to sublexical units in signs at an equivalent level of linguistic organisation as phonemes in spoken languages.

This issue will be explored in more detail in §4 of this chapter. At this point, it is sufficient to say that the more universal a feature of language organisation is claimed to be, the more imperative it is to consider its validity with respect to sign languages. This is especially true in the light of the fact that claims about universals of human language have always been based on evidence from spoken languages alone. Sign language research is only just beginning to enter the stage of linguistic typology, and considering the word unit is certainly not the worst parameter to begin with on the way towards integrating the findings of sign language linguistics with spoken language typology.

It is quite striking that sign language linguists do not usually talk about 'words'. Instead, it is the 'sign' that takes the place of the word unit in spoken languages. The question is, of course, whether this is just a terminological convention or whether there is some reason for referring to units at an equivalent level of linguistic organisation as 'words' on the one hand but 'signs' on the other hand. As in most cases of linguistic meta-talk, this issue has, to the best of my knowledge, never been addressed explicitly. So in what way exactly does a sign language sign compare to a spoken language word? Are they completely equivalent, or are signs and words different in character, either essentially or by degree? This chapter is an initial contribution to addressing this issue.

The initial justification for saying that the word and the sign are situated at an equivalent level of linguistic organisation comes from the way sign language users evidently perceive the signs of their sign language. In fact, they talk about signs in very much the same way that spoken language users talk about words, and there can be no doubt that signs as a unit have psychological and cultural validity in deaf communities. A cluster of observations confirms this point.

First of all, it is very revealing to look at meta-linguistic vocabulary in sign languages, and there are some striking generalisations that appear across different sign languages. The central meta-linguistic term in all sign languages appears to be the sign glossed SIGN, which may refer to individual signs as well as the sign language and the signing modality in general. This sign is typically two-handed, with circular, alternating movements of the hands. A form found in a number of sign languages is the one represented in figure 1. By contrast, terms for 'word', 'sentence' and 'language' may arise via influence from the surrounding spoken language, may be used with reference to written language only, or may be lacking altogether.

A number of sign languages, including Indo-Pakistani and German Sign Language, have no word for 'language', in the sense of either French 'langue' or 'langage'. British Sign Language originally lacked signs meaning 'language' and 'culture' (Kyle et al. 1985). The present signs used to represent these meanings have come into existence via the influence of spoken English. Similarly, American Sign Language does have original signs for 'word' and 'sentence'.

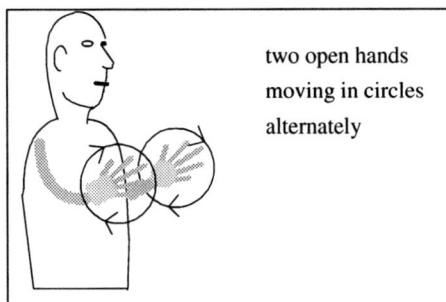

two open hands
moving in circles
alternately

Figure 1 SIGN

Their visual representational character, 'word' being conceived of as a 'small piece' in a sentence, and 'sentence' being conceived of as a 'chain' of words, suggests that they are truly native signs. The current sign for 'language', on the other hand, is a so-called 'initialised' sign. The process of 'initialisation' is a common way for some sign languages to 'borrow' a term from a surrounding spoken language. It relies on the existence of a manual alphabet, where each letter of the alphabet can be represented by a particular shape of the hand. In American Sign Language, a word can be 'borrowed' from English by taking a semantically similar sign and changing its handshape. For the original hand- shape, one substitutes the handshape that corresponds to the initial letter of the target English word. So the sign LANGUAGE is made with the handshape that represents the letter 'L' in the manual alphabet, a handshape with extended index finger and thumb.[2]

In Indo-Pakistani Sign Language, the meta-linguistic vocabulary includes signs for 'word' and '(written) line/sentence/subtitle etc.', but these are pre- dominantly used when talking about the written representation of a spoken lan- guage, for example English or Hindi, rather than with reference to the signed language. For the latter, SIGN is the usual term. Instead of a general term for 'language', two different terms are used to refer to either the 'speaking' or 'signing' modality. Terms for individual spoken languages are either the same as signs for the country and its people, such as 'German/Germany', or the same as the signs for writing the language, such as '(write) English', '(write) Urdu' (see Zeshan 2000b: 21f).

When deaf individuals talk about linguistic issues, they do so largely in terms of 'words', using the term SIGN. For example, deaf signers in India and Pakistan may state that the signs in different parts of the Indian subcontinent are similar

---

[2] According to a common convention in sign language research, signs are represented by English words in capital letters in this chapter. The word stands for the sign whose meaning comes closest to the meaning of the English word. When the form of a sign is important, graphic representations are used.

or different, but they do not comment on grammatical differences. Hearing and deaf people alike conceive – erroneously – of sign language as essentially lacking grammar, so that once you have learned the vocabulary of signs, you basically know the language (for more details on sociolinguistic attitudes, see Zeshan 2000b: 19ff). A similar attitude can be sensed in the efforts of deaf communities in various parts of the world to document their sign languages. Inevitably, their first objective will be to produce a sign language dictionary, listing the sign inventory and corresponding meanings in the surrounding spoken language. Efforts in this direction, made independently of each other, have led to sign language dictionaries produced by deaf associations in countries such as Uganda (UNAD 1998), Tanzania (Tanzania Association of the Deaf 1993), Pakistan (Sir Syed Deaf Association 1989) and Thailand (Wrigley et al. 1990). This is evidence for the strong relevance of the sign unit in deaf communities and is not unlike attitudes of spoken language minority groups speaking languages that have no writing system, no literary tradition and no written grammars.

2   Grammatical and phonological words in sign languages

The issue of delimiting words and differentiating between grammatical and phonological words, as pursued in this volume, has not been widely discussed in the sign language literature. Part of the reason for this is probably the fact that complex grammatical entities consisting of a sequence of elements are rather rare in sign languages. I will briefly discuss examples of two such cases, compounds and host–clitic combinations, in §3.

The lack of complex *sequential* structure does however not imply that sign languages are of a predominantly isolating type. On the contrary, signs show considerable morphological complexity. However, morphological complexity is almost exclusively *simultaneous* rather than sequential. That is, morphological modifications typically take the form of internal modifications to the form of the sign. For example, various modifications to the movement pattern of a basic sign can convey a whole range of aspectual and aktionsart distinctions. The examples in figure 2 are from Indo-Pakistani Sign Language (Zeshan 2000a: 66ff). Another well-known type of simultaneous morphology that is found across sign languages is the mechanism known as directionality. This process can be used to convey the relationship between two arguments by moving the hand from one location in space to another. The starting point usually corresponds to the subject or source of the action, the end point to the object or goal of the action. In fact, there is a continuing controversy in the sign language linguistics literature about what kind of relationship directional predicates convey, a grammatical relationship (subject–object) or a semantic relationship (agent–patient, source–goal). However, I will not go into the details of this controversy here.

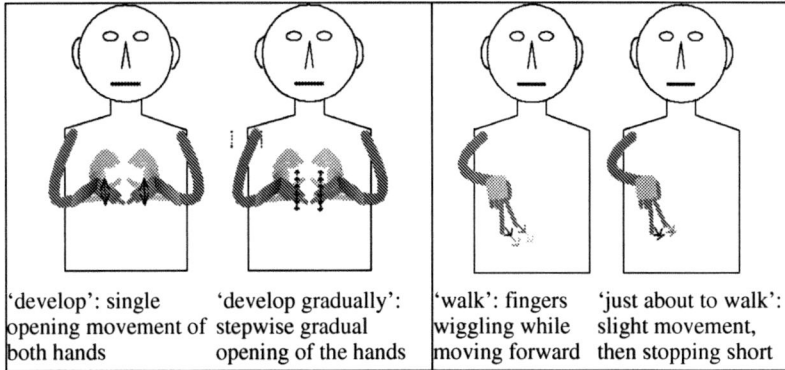

| 'develop': single opening movement of both hands | 'develop gradually': stepwise gradual opening of the hands | 'walk': fingers wiggling while moving forward | 'just about to walk': slight movement, then stopping short |

Figure 2 Aspectual/aktionsart distinctions

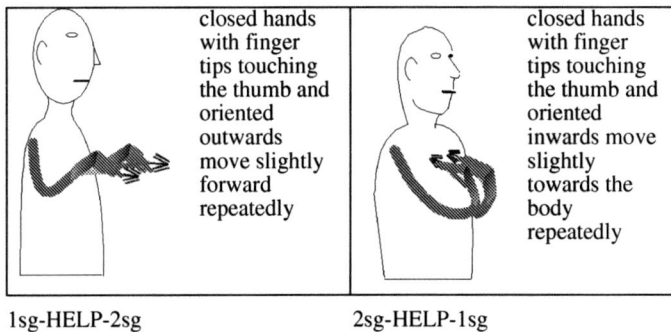

closed hands with finger tips touching the thumb and oriented outwards move slightly forward repeatedly

closed hands with finger tips touching the thumb and oriented inwards move slightly towards the body repeatedly

1sg-HELP-2sg   2sg-HELP-1sg

Figure 3 Directional predicates

The mechanism of directionality (see example (2)) is similar to multiple person marking on verbs in spoken languages, that is, the use of subject and object affixes on a verb stem to express grammatical relations (example (1) from Arabic):

(1)   tu-saa'idu-nii
        2sg:SUBJ-help:IMPERF-1sg:OBJ
        You help me.

(2)   2sg-HELP-1sg (see figure 3)
        You help me.

Modifications to the handshape can also convey morphological distinctions. One type of morphologically complex construction involves handshapes in a 'classificatory' function and will be discussed in more detail in the final section. In another productive process known as numeral incorporation, a handshape

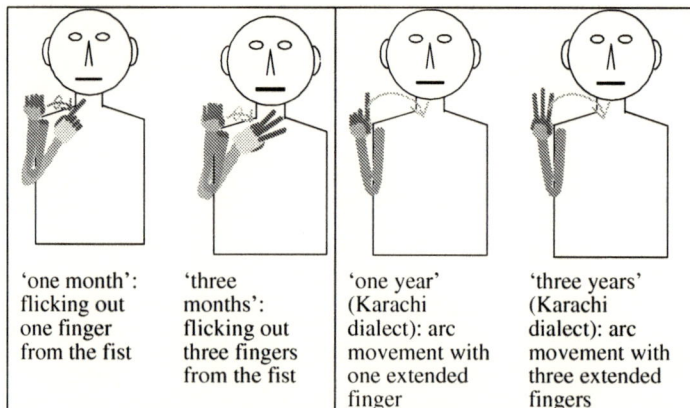

| 'one month': flicking out one finger from the fist | 'three months': flicking out three fingers from the fist | 'one year' (Karachi dialect): arc movement with one extended finger | 'three years' (Karachi dialect): arc movement with three extended fingers |

Figure 4 Numeral incorporation in Indo-Pakistani Sign Language

conveys a numerical value and is superimposed on a basic sign denoting the unit (see figure 4, from Zeshan 2000a: 74).

Moreover, many grammatical functions are marked by facial expressions that co-occur with the manually produced signs. In particular, clause types such as interrogative, negative, conditional and so on, are typically marked simultaneously on the face in various sign languages (see Baker and Padden 1978, Liddell 1980 for American Sign Language, Coerts 1992 for Sign Language of the Netherlands, Zeshan 2000b for Indo-Pakistani Sign Language). A facial expression may be the only way to mark a particular clause type, for example yes/no-questions and subordinate clauses in IPSL.

The type of simultaneous morphology discussed here is quite different in nature from what we typically find in spoken language morphology, which is predominantly realised as sequential affixing. Rather, it is comparable to the grammatical use of tone, ablaut and intonation in some spoken languages. Possible equivalents in spoken languages include mechanisms such as vowel alternations in English or German verbal paradigms of the type 'sing–sang–sung', the use of intonation alone to mark questions in many languages, or the systematic use of tone alone to mark morphological categories in tonal languages. The closest spoken language equivalent, in terms of the extent of simultaneous morphological derivations, might be the Semitic type of morphology, with an underlying root and various superimposed morphological patterns, as in Arabic:

(3)   underlying root: *k-t-b*
       derived forms: *kataba* 'he wrote', *kitaab* 'book', *kaatib* 'writer',
                        maktab 'office', *maktaba* 'library', *aktubu* 'I write'

This type of morphological organisation has consequences for the applicability of the criteria for wordhood status as discussed in the other chapters of this volume with reference to various spoken languages. As far as phonological criteria are concerned, the question is largely one of transferring comparable phenomena to the signed modality. Of course, the term 'phonological' cannot be taken literally when applied to sign languages, since there are no sounds involved. Rather, the term has to be understood abstractly as referring to the lowest sublexical level of linguistic organisation below the morphemic level (see also §4.2.4 on sign language 'phonemes' and 'morphemes'). In this sense, concepts such as 'syllable', 'intonation unit', 'phonological word' etc. have been applied to the signed modality, chiefly with evidence from American Sign Language. It would be beyond the scope of this chapter to discuss the various approaches to sign language phonology. An overview of current theories can be found in Brentari (1996). With respect to the phonological word that concerns us here, the most elaborated recent approach is probably the one in Sandler (1999 and 2000). On the basis of evidence mainly from Israeli Sign Language, issues such as proposed characteristics of the 'canonical prosodic word' (or phonological word in our terms), the marking of phonological phrases and intonation units, and phonological rules operating within and across phonological words are discussed. According to Sandler (1999), the typical phonological word/sign adheres to the following constraints:

(a) it is monosyllabic (Monosyllabicity Constraint);
(b) it uses only one set of fingers for its handshapes (Selected Finger Constraint);
(c) is uses only one major body area (Place Constraint);
(d) it obeys constraints on two-handed combinations, such as the constraint that two moving hands must be symmetrical to each other (Symmetry Constraint).

Sandler (2000) discusses evidence for an entire phonological hierarchy in a sign language, including phonological words, phonological phrases and intonation units. The constraints on the form of a prototypical phonological word/sign all seem to work together to reduce the amount of formational complexity within a sign. When two signs come together to form a single phonological word, assimilation processes are at work to bring the resulting form closer to the form of a prototypical sign. We will see examples of this in §3 on compounds and clitics.

The evidence for the existence of phonological hierarchies in sign languages, including the level of organisation equivalent to a phonological word, seems compelling enough, although the details of their characteristics have yet to be worked out. After all, signing has a temporal as well as a spatial dimension and thus needs to have some rhythmical structure. The problem is mainly one of working out how to adequately identify and characterise each unit in the signed modality.

On the other hand, there seem to be more fundamental problems with respect to the applicability of criteria for the grammatical word as used in the other chapters of this volume. I will briefly discuss three criteria here: cohesiveness, order and conventionalised coherence and meaning.

Grammatical elements in a sign, in the prototypical case a basic form and superimposed morphological derivations, always occur together in the sign unit. However, it is not clear whether this can be taken as evidence for a particular grammatical status of these elements. This has to do with the largely simultaneous nature of the sign. The fact that elements occur together in a sign is due to purely articulatory reasons as much as to a putative grammatical status of the unit. For instance, the numeral handshape morpheme in numeral incorporation (see §2, figure 4) is necessarily coexistent with the movement pattern that stands for the unit. It would be physically impossible to produce a sign or a movement pattern that lacks any handshape. Similarly, it would be impossible for a morphological derivation such as the gradual aktionsart derivation (see §2, figure 2) to occur on its own, for example in a sequence where the basic form of a sign would occur first and the abstract movement derivation would occur separately in a sequence. Therefore, the criterion of cohesiveness is considerably weakened if taken as indicative of grammatical word status.

The criterion of order, with elements within a grammatical word always occurring in a fixed order, is even more difficult to apply to a typical sign. Again due to the sign's simultaneous nature, it is mostly impossible to argue for any order of grammatical elements within a sign, with the possible exception of directionality (cf. the sequential transcription in example (2) above; but even this interpretation can be disputed). To take the same examples as in the previous paragraph, it is impossible to argue that the numerical handshape for THREE and the sign for MONTH in a complex sign such as THREE-MONTHS (see §2, figure 4) occur in any order. They are coextensive over the whole duration of the sign. Similarly, in a complex sign such as DEVELOP-gradual (see §2, figure 2), there is no sequential order of the sign DEVELOP and the superimposed movement pattern that conveys the gradual aktionsart derivation. It would therefore seem that the criterion of order is only marginally applicable to signed languages. Its applicability is confined to particular cases of complex signs, in particular compounds (see §3.1).

The remaining criterion, conventionalised coherence and meaning of a grammatical word, fully applies to sign languages and is particularly important in the comparatively rare cases of sequential combinations of grammatical elements, as the discussion of compounds and clitics in §3 demonstrates. In-between cases of semi-lexicalisation do occur (see Zeshan forthcoming), but they do not in principle challenge the validity of the criterion. I will discuss semi-lexicalisation in more detail in §4.

In a way, the largely simultaneous nature of signs results in enhanced coherence. Indeed, another consequence of this type of morphological organisation is that despite considerable structural complexity, the question of word boundaries hardly ever arises because each sign, simple or complex, is a self-contained unit. Most signs, even when they are morphologically complex, are still 'monosyllabic', consisting of one movement or timing unit. Complex 'polysyllabic' signs, such as iterative aktionsart forms ('do something repeatedly') with repeated movement, mostly involve simple repetition of one and the same movement unit. It seems that the grammatical unit (the sign with its various superimposed morphological patterns) and the phonological unit (the unit of manual sign production) almost always coincide, and there is usually no problem in intuitively identifying words and word boundaries. However, I will argue in §4 of this chapter that the linguistic problems associated with the sign unit in sign languages lie elsewhere. They do not have to do with identifying the unit, but with the nature and characteristics of the sign in comparison to the word. But before we turn to this topic, we will first take a closer look at compounds and clitics in sign languages and discuss how the various criteria for word status, phonological and grammatical, apply to these cases.

3   Compounds and clitics in sign languages

3.1   Compounds in sign languages

One environment where it can be difficult to determine the boundaries between signs is compound formation. When two signs appear next to each other in a signed utterance, they can be more or less closely tied to each other. They may be articulated clearly separate from each other, or there may be certain formational processes of assimilation between them, especially in the case of fast or casual signing, or they may form one sign unit together and be regarded as a compound.

Sign language researchers working on various sign languages have worked out criteria for determining when two adjacent signs should be regarded as one compound sign. The following list of criteria is taken from Zeshan (2000a: 82). Some of the criteria apply to several sign languages (b, c and d) and some may be universal (most likely, a and e).

(a) There is temporal compression, with the first sign being shortened and losing stress, so that the compound has about the same duration as a simple sign (Klima and Bellugi 1979, Lucas and Valli 1995 for American Sign Language; Glück and Pfau 1997 for German Sign Language).

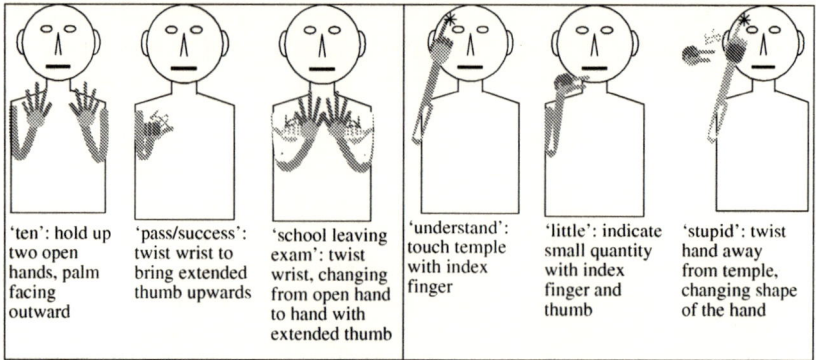

| 'ten': hold up two open hands, palm facing outward | 'pass/success': twist wrist to bring extended thumb upwards | 'school leaving exam': twist wrist, changing from open hand to hand with extended thumb | 'understand': touch temple with index finger | 'little': indicate small quantity with index finger and thumb | 'stupid': twist hand away from temple, changing shape of the hand |

Figure 5 Compounds in Indo-Pakistani Sign Language

(b) Repetition of movement and internal movement are eliminated in the compound (Klima and Bellugi 1979, Lucas and Valli: 1995 for American Sign Language).[3]

(c) There are various assimilation processes such as recessive handshape assimilation (Collins-Ahlgren 1990 for New Zealand Sign Language) and location assimilation (Glück and Pfau 1997 for German Sign Language; Lucas and Valli 1995 for American Sign Language).

(d) A passive hand serving as the place of articulation for one part of the compound is retained in the other part as well (Klima and Bellugi 1979, Lucas and Valli 1995 for American Sign Language; Glück and Pfau 1997 for German Sign Language).

(e) The meaning of the compound may not be predictable from the meaning of the two simple signs (Lucas and Valli 1995 for American Sign Language).

Obviously, the formational criteria mentioned above do not apply to all cases of compound formation, with (a) being the likely exception. Deletion of repeated movement and internal movement only applies if there was any such movement pattern in the original signs in the first place. Similarly, spreading of a passive hand, i.e. the hand that is used as the place of articulation on or at which the other hand articulates, does not apply to signs where only one hand is used anyway. Handshape assimilation or location assimilation does not apply to compounds where handshape or place of articulation is the same in both parts of the compound to begin with. Figure 5 shows two compound signs from Indo-Pakistani Sign Language together with the individual signs to illustrate some possible combinations of formational changes – temporal compression and assimilation of handedness (one- versus two-handed) in the first example,

---

[3] 'Internal movement' refers to movement within a stationary hand, such as finger wiggling and wrist bending.

temporal compression and location assimilation in the second example. Also note that the meaning of the compounds goes beyond the meaning of the individual signs.

The semantic criterion (e) is particularly important because it relates to our criterion of conventionalised coherence and meaning, indicating grammatical word status. Moreover, the two parts of a sign language compound always have to occur together and in the same order. It is not possible, for example, to put the sign PASS before the sign TEN and still obtain a compound with the same meaning. Therefore, a compound is clearly one grammatical word.

Whether compounds involve one or two phonological words is less clear. The various processes of formational reduction and assimilation seem to indicate that the sign is 'trying' to behave like a single phonological word, in particular with respect to monosyllabicity. On the other hand, Liddell and Johnson (1986) present evidence for a phonological break in between the two parts of some American Sign Language compounds. The evidence is based on a particular morphological inflection, the movement pattern of the unrealised–inceptive form. This form is found with certain volitional, process verbs and conveys the meaning of 'just about to do something when . . . ' The morphological process usually operates on the whole sign, but in the case of a compound such as THINK-MARRY 'believe', it operates on the second part of the compound only. Thus the authors conclude that compounds have 'two phonological parts' (Liddell and Johnson 1986: 95). It may be noted that the authors also argue, mainly on semantic grounds, that the 'lexical compounds' under discussion are monomorphemic. However, since the argument here concerns the phonological level, I will not discuss this aspect of their contribution at this point.

While American Sign Language is a very compound-friendly language, Indo-Pakistani Sign Language has very few compounds. Moreover, Indo-Pakistani Sign Language compounds do not lend themselves easily to arguments of the kind discussed here for American Sign Language compounds, that is, arguments about the phonological status of their parts. It seems that while arguments for the status of compounds as grammatical words can be generalised across different sign languages, the question of phonological word status may be language-specific and must be determined on language-internal grounds for each sign language.

3.2   Pronoun clitics in sign languages

Many known sign languages use pointing signs to establish locations in the sign space for referents and to refer back to these locations in what is equivalent to pronominal reference in spoken languages. The following mini-discourse illustrates the principle:

SHOP   SHOP-THERE

Figure 6 Host–clitic combination in Israeli Sign Language (from Sandler 1999: 241; 2000)

(4)   a. MAN pointing-right WAIT
            The man was waiting.
        b. pointing-right IMPATIENT
            He was impatient.

The most common pointing sign, also called index point or simply index, consists of an extended index finger pointing at a location in space (or at the signer and the addressee for first person and second person reference). The index point has many characteristics that are akin to pronouns in spoken languages, and so the index is indeed often called a pronoun in the sign language literature.

One feature that the index has in common with pronouns in spoken languages is that it tends to cliticise. Interestingly, there seems to be evidence for index cliticisation in various unrelated sign languages, although the phenomena reported are often not described in these terms. I will review some of the available evidence in this section.

Sandler (1999) describes two processes of index cliticisation, of which only the first one, 'coalescence', will be discussed here because it is more straightforward. In 'coalescence', a deictic index is encliticised to a two-handed host sign. The example in figure 6 shows the enclitic index point with the host sign SHOP. Both hands first start to articulate SHOP, then midway through the downward movement, the index clitic appears on the right hand while the left hand continues to finish the articulation of SHOP. The cliticised index loses its syllabicity, the whole host–clitic combination being monosyllabic, consisting of a single movement unit in the rhythm of the signed sentence. Thus the host–clitic combination forms a single *phonological* word. On the other hand, the index point is still a complete *grammatical* word, as indicated by the transcription of the combination as SHOP-THERE.

In addition to detailed formational analyses of the kind cited here, further evidence for index cliticisation can be found in the domain of grammatical rules as well. In Japanese Sign Language, questions are marked suprasegmentally by a particular facial expression, in the same way that questions may be marked by intonation, mostly rising intonation, in spoken languages. In polar questions, the facial expression typically includes raised eyebrows and a slight head nod or chin tuck on the last word in the clause (example (5), adapted from Morgan 2000). Syntactically, the word order in polar questions is often rearranged, so that the question ends with an index point, or an earlier index point is repeated in final position. In this case the rule for the assignment of the head nod is slightly different: if there is a clause-final index point, the head nod co-occurs not with the index point alone, but with *both the index point and the preceding sign* (examples (6–8), adapted from Morgan 2000).

(5)   --eyebrow raise
                 ---nod
       ASK-2sg OKAY
       Is it okay if I ask you (a question)?

(6)   INDEX-2sg BUY BOOK
       You bought a book.

(7)   ---------eyebrow raise
            -------------nod
       BOOK BUY INDEX-2sg
       Did you buy the book?

(8)   ---eyebrow raise
                  ---------------nod
       INDEX-2sg SATO INDEX-2sg
       Are you Mr/s Sato?

It seems obvious that for the purpose of head nod assignment, the index point and the preceding sign count as a single phonological word. Although no details of the precise formation of the index point are provided in the source and there is thus no information about factors such as assimilation, shortening and so on, it seems reasonable to interpret the data as evidence for encliticisation of the index point to the preceding host sign.

A parallel case is the spread of mouth patterns in those sign languages where they play a significant role, such as, for example, German Sign Language. A mouth pattern is an imitation of the visible mouth movement that corresponds to a spoken language word, and it occurs simultaneously with manual signs (see Boyes Braem and Sutton-Spence 2000). Usually, each mouth pattern co-occurs with exactly one sign of corresponding meaning. However, sometimes a single mouth pattern may spread over more than one sign, similarly to the spread of the suprasegmental head nod in Japanese Sign Language. This indicates that the two signs are closely connected and can be taken as evidence for host–clitic status of a two-sign sequence. Compare these two utterances in German Sign Language (with mouth patterns in double quotes):

(9)   a. "Mann da" (man there)
        MAN INDEX
        b. –"M a n n"– (man)
        MAN-INDEX

In (9a), each sign is accompanied by one mouth pattern of equivalent meaning, the usual pattern. In (9b), however, only the head word of the host–clitic
combination has a mouth pattern, which spreads over the entire host–clitic combination. So for the purpose of mouth pattern assignment, the two signs seem
to count as one phonological word. Sandler (2000) draws the same conclusion
with respect to the combination SHOP-THERE, which receives a single Hebrew
mouth pattern *xanut* 'shop'.

American Sign Language also has index points that behave quite similarly to
the encliticised forms in Israeli Sign Language. These have been described as
'determiners' in Zimmer and Patschke (1990). Formationally, these signs are
shortened, lacking a movement component of their own, and they often occur
simultaneously with another sign. In addition, the American Sign Language
index signs are peculiar in that the direction of the pointing is insignificant and
arbitrary rather than operating along the lines of localisation and subsequent
anaphoric pronominal reference that I have described above: 'In most cases,
the determiners used with many different characters [i.e. characters in a story]
point to the same location. In fact, the data indicate that signers tend to have a
preferred location that they use consistently for their determiners... Also the
determiners used with one character are not consistently directed toward one
location' (Zimmer and Patschke 1990: 205). I will not address the issue of how
appropriate the characterisation of these index points as 'determiners' is here.
In the context of the present discussion, it should only be noted that the index
points have lost phonological and grammatical weight and might be regarded
as clitics by (a) losing a movement component of their own (b) co-occurring
simultaneously with a host sign and (c) losing a meaningful specification for
location and orientation.

In summary, the following characteristics have been found to occur with
documented cases or likely candidates of cliticised index points:
(a) 'phonological' evidence: loss of syllabicity, loss of movement, loss of spec-
    ification for location;
(b) syntactic evidence: clitic + host behaving as a single sign for the purpose of
    assignment of suprasegmentals (head movements, mouth patterns), clitic +
    host sign occurring simultaneously;
(c) 'functional' evidence: cliticisation occurs with elements that function as
    deictics, pronouns and determiners.

A host–clitic combination represents one phonological word, but two grammatical words. The 'functional' evidence is significant insofar as similar functional classes have been found to be prone to cliticisation in spoken languages,

in particular pronouns. In fact, one of the main differences between compounds and host–clitic combinations is that the former are made up of two items with lexical meaning whereas the latter consist of one lexical sign and one sign with grammatical–functional meaning. Accordingly, compounds are characterised by semantic shifts of various kinds whereas meanings remain unchanged in host–clitic combinations.

4   Words and signs revisited

The fact that it is possible to come up with formational, semantic and grammatical criteria for compounds and clitics that are comparable to criteria used in spoken languages means that there is much common ground between signed and spoken languages at the level of the word. However, although the word/sign unit can be determined in sign languages rather straightforwardly in most cases, and coherent arguments can be advanced for more complicated cases of complex words as well, this is not the whole story. Independently of *identifying* signs, it is important to consider some *properties* of signs that go beyond mere identification of sign boundaries. For example, how many morphemes does a sign typically or maximally consist of? What can be said about the internal structure of a sign? How much semantic information is transmitted in a sign, and how is this information structured? What are the effects of having two articulators (the two hands) in sign languages compared to a single articulatory tract in spoken languages? Issues such as these are addressed in this section, and we will see that signs do differ in important and very interesting ways from the words of spoken languages.

4.1   *Simultaneous words*

One difference between signing and speaking that is immediately evident even to a layman is the fact that people use two hands for signing, while speaking uses only a single articulatory tract. With signs that are one-handed, it is in principle possible to produce two words simultaneously, one with the right hand and one with the left hand. By contrast, speaking does not allow the simultaneous production of two words, so that, in the spoken language medium, there is nothing comparable to simultaneous words.

The simultaneous production of two words does indeed occur in sign languages, although this phenomenon has not been widely documented yet. However, it is clear from the available evidence that there are very specific constraints on the use of simultaneous words. It is not at all the case that one may produce a different word on each hand at any time, so that signed communication would transmit information at a double rate. In fact, as we will see presently, the term 'simultaneous words' is somewhat misleading.

Synchronisation of the two hands in simultaneous words follows one of two patterns. An example of the first pattern is the following, from Indo-Pakistani Sign Language (based on Zeshan 2000a: 124):

(10)   right: PUNJAB   SINDH   PESHAWAR   BALOCHISTAN
         left: ONE----------TWO---------------THREE-------------FOUR
         There are four (provinces): the Punjab, Sindh, the Peshawar (region)
         and Balochistan.

This pattern is quite common in enumerations. One hand signs the items in the list, the other hand signs the numbers. The numeral signs are held during the articulation of the next list item, as indicated by the lines after each numeral sign. Note that at no time do both hands move at the same time, so that a pattern such as in (11) is not allowed:

(11)   *right: PUNJAB   SINDH   PESHAWAR   BALOCHISTAN
         left: ONE   TWO   THREE   FOUR

Although such a pattern would actually fit the term 'simultaneous words' best, it does not occur, presumably because the processing load on both signer and addressee would be too high.

The other type of two-hand sign synchronisation also has to do with discourse organisation. After a two-handed sign, one hand remains in place while the other hand articulates further signs, as in this example (based on Zeshan 2000b: 110; the line again stands for the duration of the held sign):

(12)   right: UNDERSTAND   SQUARE COLOUR REMOVE, ME SELF LITTLE-BIT DESIGN
         left: SQUARE ---
         You know, I change the colour of the picture and add some design myself.

In this example, 'picture' is expressed by the thumb and index finger of both hands presenting a square outline. As long as the signer is talking about the picture, the left hand remains in place, while the right hand goes on signing (see figure 7, with the sign LITTLE-BIT on the right hand, and the sign SQUARE on the left hand). A similar example is reported in Bergman and Wallin (forthcoming) for Swedish Sign Language. In each case, the held left hand indicates current discourse relevance of its referent. When the signer shifts to a new topic, the left hand disappears.

This intricate interplay of the two hands is a mechanism for which nothing comparable can be found in spoken languages. It is one of the fundamental modality-based differences between signed and spoken languages and a small, yet important part of what constitutes the linguistic 'type' of signed languages. Therefore, it should not be surprising that it may be difficult to talk about the relationship between grammatical and phonological words in these signed constructions. The formulation of these concepts, based on linear sequential

'. . . add a little bit to the picture . . .':
right hand: LITTLE-BIT (pinching motion of thumb and index finger)
left hand: SQUARE (thumb and index finger extended forming a right angle)

Figure 7 Simultaneous words in Indo-Pakistani Sign Language (from Zeshan 2000b: 110)

strings of elements, has simply not provided for cases such as these ones. To say, for instance, that the sign SQUARE in example (12) is one grammatical word that consists of two phonological half-words (the two hands), and that one of these half-words can remain on its own and can by itself carry the full meaning in the absence of the other phonological half-word, does not make much sense. The parameters of description used in the other chapters of this volume are of limited use here.

4.2   The semiotics of signs

4.2.1 Iconicity in signs Rather early in the development of sign language linguistics, people started addressing issues related to the effects of the visual–gestural modality on language structure. Two recurrent themes appear in the literature that seem to be of fundamental importance: simultaneity and iconicity (see DeMatteo 1977, Mandel 1977, Armstrong 1983 for examples of earlier discussions of iconicity in sign). While simultaneity has been discussed in §2 and further exemplified in §4.1, this section deals with the effects of iconicity on the character of the word unit in sign languages. Of all topics discussed in this chapter, this issue is of the greatest typological significance and at the same time presents the greatest challenge to linguistic theory.

The iconicity of many signs is one of the first points noticed by people who encounter a sign language for the first time. Iconicity is a non-arbitrary relationship between a symbol and its referent. There are various types and degrees of iconicity, but these will not be discussed in detail here. A classification with respect to sign languages can be found in Mandel (1977). In this section, I will first start with some preliminary considerations about the nature of iconicity in sign and then limit the discussion to aspects of iconicity that are relevant to our notion of the sign language word.

Ever since the Saussurean postulate of 'l'arbitraire du signe', the linguistic symbol has been conceived of as an *arbitrary* association between form and meaning. In fact, this is part of the idea of double articulation, itself thought to be a design feature of language. Double articulation involves two fundamental and distinct levels of linguistic organisation, whereby phonemes that are themselves meaningless make up the minimal meaningful units of language (morphemes), which in turn combine to create all the larger units of language (words, sentences). This organisation allows for a virtually infinite number of ever new utterances to be created on the basis of a very small inventory of phonemic units, a feature unique to human language. The evident and undeniable iconicity of many signs in sign languages represents a serious challenge to this concept. Unlike onomatopoetic and phonaesthetic words and sounds in spoken language, equivalent iconic characteristics in sign languages are not at all marginal, but represent a substantial part of the vocabulary. Boyes Braem (1986) estimated the percentage of iconic signs in Swiss-German Sign Language to be about one third of the total sign vocabulary. However, it seems that this percentage may be much higher in other sign languages. In Zeshan (2000a) I estimated that at least half of the vocabulary of Indo-Pakistani Sign Language, and maybe more than that, is iconic in some way.

In iconic signs, sublexical parts of the sign (chiefly the handshape, the movement and the place of articulation) are meaningful in that they stand for aspects of the meaning of the sign (cf. examples given in §4.2.4). This form–meaning relationship can be much more complex than the simple imitative character of onomatopoetic word such as *cuckoo*. Both concrete and abstract meanings can be represented iconically in signed languages, the latter via metaphors (which are, by the way, often similar to metaphors expressed in spoken languages; note the examples of sign families below).

It is not at all necessary that signers should be aware of the iconicity all the time or even most of the time when they use an iconic sign. The signs that will be discussed in this section are conventional units of the language and are quite different from signs and sign combinations that are created on the fly in order to express a new concept. The latter possibility also exists and can be used with great productivity, but the kind of iconicity I am discussing here is entirely compatible with conventional words. It is not necessary either that all components of a sign should be iconic. There is no strict compositionality of meaning in the kind of iconicity discussed here, so it is entirely viable for signs to have partly iconic and partly arbitrary components. Iconicity of course does not mean either that a sign can only be used when the user understands its iconic basis. Use of the sign is completely independent of its iconicity most of the time. However, there are some situations where the latent iconic potential can suddenly surface. Many sign puns and instances of word play and creative use of signs in poetry are dependent on a sign's iconicity and are evidence for people's underlying awareness of the iconic basis of a sign. Moreover, deaf people will often 'explain' the meaning of a sign in terms of its iconicity.

	tips of thumb and index finger touching the throat		right flat hand taps left fist twice on the back side of the fingers		fist makes contact with cheek while the wrist is twisted outwards
CLEVER		THURSDAY (Delhi dialect)		PUNJAB (Karachi dialect)	

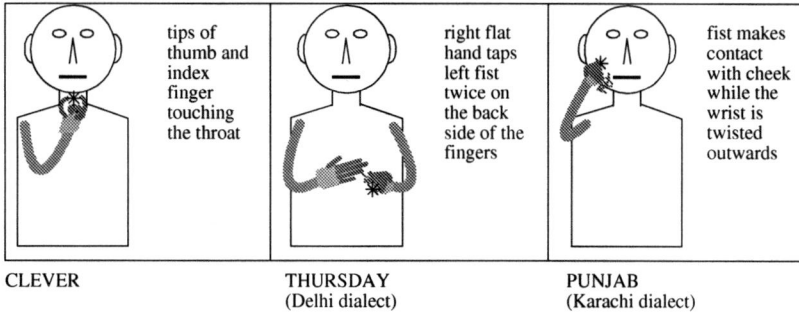

Figure 8 Arbitrary signs in Indo-Pakistani Sign Language

In the remainder of this section, I will discuss three types of form–meaning relationships in signs, of which only the third type presents a serious challenge to current linguistic theory. For each case, we will examine the semantic compositionality and the semiotic type of the signs.

4.2.2 Arbitrary signs Not all signs in sign languages are entirely or partially iconic. Each sign language also has many signs whose form–meaning relationship is entirely arbitrary. For example, the signs in figure 8 do not involve any iconicity and are entirely comparable to the usual spoken language word. This category of signs presents no problem to conventional linguistic analysis. The sublexical units, whichever way one wants to delimit and identify them, are non-morphemic, meaningless building blocks of the sign and are entirely comparable to spoken language phonemes.

4.2.3 Lexicalisation of 'classificatory' constructions Another type of sign has been discussed in detail in Zeshan (forthcoming), so it will be enough to give a brief summary here with respect to the word unit. The structure of signs can be highly complex, bordering on the polysynthetic type of morphology, and this especially happens in a number of constructions known as 'classifier' constructions.[4] In these constructions, the handshape of one or both hands represents a particular type of referent, while the location, arrangement and movement of the hand express something about the referent. Apart from the handshape, sign components such as the movement path, the relationship between two hands, the orientation of the hand in space, and movement of the fingers can all be morphemic. As is typical of the majority of sign language morphology, all morphemes are combined simultaneously.

---

[4] I will not discuss the appropriateness of the term 'classifier' at this point. For a detailed discussion, see Zeshan (forthcoming), where I have argued that the term 'classifier' is not really appropriate for all the constructions. However, this aspect is not immediately relevant to the discussion here.

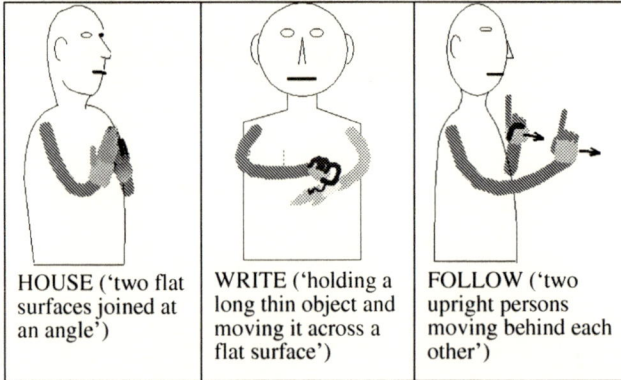

| HOUSE ('two flat surfaces joined at an angle') | WRITE ('holding a long thin object and moving it across a flat surface') | FOLLOW ('two upright persons moving behind each other') |

Figure 9 Lexicalised 'classifier' constructions in Indo-Pakistani Sign Language

Three types of constructions have been associated with the term 'classifier', referring to either the geometrical shape of objects, or the movement and location of a referent, or the handling of an object. All three constructions are highly productive in the sign languages studied so far, and they are a major source of lexical enrichment. Originally productive multimorphemic constructions tend to lexicalise, and the sign gradually loses its semantic compositionality. Therefore, many of these signs have a semantic structure on two levels: on the one hand, the sign is a fully conventional lexical unit whose meaning is non-compositional; yet on the other hand, the original compositional meaning is still underlyingly present and may surface in particular situations, such as linguistic elicitation or poetic use of the language. Figure 9 shows some examples, one from each construction type, with both the original compositional and the lexicalized non-compositional meaning noted (examples are from IPSL, but identical or very similar forms can also be found in a number of other sign languages).

Since the lexicalisation process is gradual, it is not surprising that there are many cases of semi-lexicalisation where a sign is in-between a productive multimorphemic construction and a fully lexicalised sign whose original compositional meaning is not synchronically accessible to signers. The classification of such signs is a major problem for lexicologists: when should a sign be included into a dictionary as a lexical entry and when should it be handled by the grammatical part of linguistic description? A detailed discussion of this problem can be found in Johnston and Schembri (1999), with reference to Australian Sign Language.

Although these constructions present a challenge to the practically oriented linguist, they do not in principle involve fundamental theoretical problems.

In fact, the phenomenon is entirely comparable to a spoken language situation where, for example, productive compounding leads to more or less complete lexicalisation of compounds. Liddell and Johnson (1986) discuss the semantics of compounds in English and American Sign Language and give examples of lexicalised compounds with non-compositional meaning from both languages (e.g. *blackboard* and *breakfast* in English, THINK-MARRY 'believe' in American Sign Language). Once one recognises the diachronic process of gradual lexicalisation, semi-lexicalised forms with partly meaningful components seem natural.

However, there does seem to be a difference between 'classifier' constructions in sign languages and comparable phenomena in spoken languages as far as the character of the sublexical units is concerned. While the parts of lexicalised compounds in spoken languages are 'ex-morphemic' and therefore not synchronically meaningful, the parts of sign language 'classifier' constructions are also 'ex-morphemic', but still partially 'meaningful' because they still carry their original iconic value. The issue is further complicated by the fact that in sign languages, semantic compositionality does not necessarily entail a morphemic status of sublexical units. That is, a sign may consist of sublexical components that are meaningful due to their iconicity, but, as the discussion in the next section will show, this does not automatically mean that they are or have ever been morphemes. As McNeill (1992) notes, even gesture is semantically compositional (the 'synthetic nature' of gesture), yet the components are not morphemes in the linguistic sense of the term. In Zeshan (forthcoming) I have argued that 'classifier' constructions describing the handling of entities are only weakly grammaticalised in Indo-Pakistani Sign Language, yet there is a large number of fully lexicalised signs based on 'handling' constructions. It therefore seems possible in sign language to have semantic compositionality directly carried over from a gestural origin, without first going through a 'morphological' stage. This is a type of lexicalisation channel not found in spoken languages. Also note that even for the more grammaticalised 'classificatory' constructions it is not entirely clear that a description of the sublexical components in terms of 'morphemes' in the usual sense is adequate. However, since it would be beyond the scope of this paper to pursue this issue further, I have gone along with the traditional 'morphemic' analysis in this section.

4.2.4 'Phonosymbolism' in signs Both arbitrary signs with non-morphemic, meaningless components and lexicalised 'classifier' signs with ex-morphemic, partially meaningful components constitute a substantial part of the vocabulary in signed languages. From a semiotic point of view, there is yet a third type of sign which is also commonly found in sign languages and also constitutes a sizeable part of the lexicon. In this type of sign, the sublexical units are not morphemes and, unlike lexicalised 'classifier' signs, have never been morphemes in their history. Yet they are meaningful due to their iconicity. The existence of non-morphemic, yet meaningful sublexical units seriously challenges the traditional concepts of phoneme and morpheme.

The situation in sign languages resembles the case of phonosymbolism in spoken languages. Malkiel (1990) describes phonosymbolism and the theoretical questions that arise when one takes the phenomenon seriously: 'An appeal to phonosymbolism simply means that the analyst endows the sound at issue with the ability to convey, in conjunction with other elements, a certain message of its own, with being, for once, the carrier of a minor, if not necessarily minimal, semantic content. This appeal presupposes the suspension of a very widely held, almost axiomatic assumption, namely that morphemes rather than phonemes are the smallest units of speech that are equipped with this power to transmit ingredients of meaning' (Malkiel 1990: 158). In cases of phonosymbolism, individual sounds or sound combinations convey a certain 'sound-image' that goes with a particular semantic field, such as the initial sounds in English *splash* and *splatter*, or combinations such as *helter-skelter*, *flim-flam*, and the like. These sounds and patterns do not, however, behave as morphemes. Examples of phonosymbolism given in Malkiel (1990) include: the vowels *o* and *i*, cross-linguistically associated with the concepts of 'roundness' and 'smallness' respectively; onomatopoetic words such as Russian *xóxot* 'outburst of laughter', German *krächzen* 'to caw, croak', or French *cliquetis* 'clanking, clatter, jingle'; and English verbs ending in 'consonant+l', such as *wobble*, *wriggle*, *straddle*, *giggle*, *ogle*, *prattle* etc., correlating with situations that are somehow 'non-neutral' as compared to near synonyms such as *laugh* (~*giggle*), *talk* (~*prattle*), *glance* (~*ogle*) etc. Signs and their components are often of a 'phonosymbolic' character in sign languages.

To explore this issue in all detail, one would need to write a whole paper of its own. Therefore, I will just illustrate the nature of 'phonosymbolic' signs with a few examples at this point. The easiest case of an iconically motivated sign is an indexical sign, with the hand or fingers pointing at the referent. The Indo-Pakistani Sign Language sign for 'body' consists of the two index fingers, finger tips towards the body, running downwards along the torso. Although the sign components are clearly meaningful, with the location of the sign corresponding to the referent and the hands in the prototypical 'pointing' handshape, it seems to make no sense to think of them as morphemes. Note that, by contrast with the lexicalised 'classifier' signs, there is no literal reading 'two parallel lines on the torso' or 'fingers drawing lines on the torso' that would make much sense. Rather, the pointing act itself is the iconic motivation for the sign.

The form of many signs in sign languages is motivated by metaphorical links between the form and the meaning of the sign. Often there are a number of signs sharing the same metaphorical basis. Signs that share an aspect of their

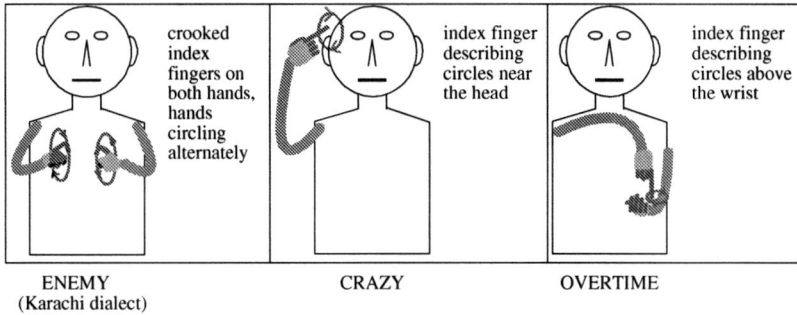

ENEMY   CRAZY   OVERTIME
(Karachi dialect)

Figure 10 'Phonosymbolic' signs in Indo-Pakistani Sign Language

meaning and an aspect of their form are known as 'sign families' (Klima and Bellugi 1979: 81). In Indo-Pakistani Sign Language and other sign languages, a number of signs from the semantic field of cognition have a location at the temple, the metaphorical 'seat of cognition'. Signs that have to do with time are often made at the wrist location. Yet these locations do not function as morphemes in the way that, for instance, the beginning and ending locations of directional predicates do. Another common metaphor is the equation of upwards movement with 'positive' and downwards movement with 'negative', a metaphor occurring in a great many spoken languages as well. This is similar to cross-linguistic phonosymbolism of the type 'i = smallness'. In individual sign languages, particular handshapes may also carry semantic content. In Indo-Pakistani Sign Language, for example, a handshape with only the index finger extended and crooked, originally based on pulling the trigger of a gun, is associated with meanings involving some sort of violent conflict, such as the signs for 'army', 'war' and 'enemy'. This is similar to the examples of language-specific phonosymbolism mentioned above. Note that the term 'sign families' indicates there is a meaningful connection between the members, yet they are not described as being morphologically derived from each other, nor is there any morphological process that would derive these signs from each other or from any underlying form.

Finally, consider the form and meaning of the signs represented in figure 10, all of which are partially motivated. ENEMY uses the crooked index finger handshape symbolising violent conflict, CRAZY uses the temple location symbolising cognition, and OVERTIME uses the wrist location symbolising time. All of these signs have circular movement patterns, yet it does not make much sense to regard this movement pattern as morphemic in the same way that, for example, movement patterns for aspect and aktionsart derivations are morphemic. Rather, the movement in ENEMY is (arguably) meaningless, the movement in CRAZY is based on another metaphor (the internal workings of the brain), and the movement in OVERTIME has yet another motivation, symbolising duration. Note, once again, that literal readings based on a compositional organisation of putative morphemes do not make much sense. While 'holding a long thin object and moving it across a flat surface' is an acceptable literal reading of 'write', a circumlocution such as 'repeated circles next to the head', or even 'a time duration with reference to the head' are not viable morphemic analyses of the sign CRAZY.

For sign language iconicity, the analytical problems are the same as for phonosymbolism, except that in spoken languages, the relatively rare occurrence of phonosymbolism makes it easier for the linguist to ignore it. Note that it is entirely possible that there are languages that make much greater use of phonosymbolism than the 'Standard Average European' languages, but that their true character has not been recognised because the descriptive apparatus used by linguists is inadequate to deal with such phenomena. Results from sign language research could throw new light on such situations. For the sheer number of iconically motivated signs makes it impossible to discount iconicity as some obscure 'exception', as has been the (often unacknowledged and unjustified) tradition in spoken language linguistics. Moreover, the semantic content carried by 'phonosymbolic' elements in signs is not at all minor or minimal, but quite substantial.

Therefore, a reasonable conclusion from sign language data such as those presented in this section is that total arbitrariness of the linguistic symbol is not a necessary feature of human language. Rather, sign languages allow for a type of linguistic symbol that is of a different semiotic status than the usual spoken language word. The 'meaning-bearing' structure of these words is different, allowing for sublexical units that are non-morphemic, yet meaningful. Moreover, this type of word is not at all marginal in sign languages but represents a substantial part of the vocabulary. This argument is of great typological and theoretical importance, given the fact that the arbitrary nature of the linguistic symbol is so deeply entrenched in contemporary linguistics as to be seemingly self-evident. The very nature of the concepts of 'phoneme' and 'morpheme' is necessarily challenged when sign languages are considered seriously and described in their own terms.

Our discussion of data from various sign languages has shown that the concepts of phonological word and grammatical word can be meaningfully applied to sign languages, although the definition of the grammatical word is weakened due to the unusual simultaneous character of sign language morphology. While the two units are almost always coextensive in the sign languages known so far, there are instances of mismatches that parallel the mismatches found in spoken languages. Thus, one phonological word may consist of two grammatical words in host–clitic combinations and one grammatical word may consist of two phonological words in compounds, at least in some sign languages. However, it seems that, from a language typological point of view, the relationship between grammatical and phonological word is not the most interesting aspect of the sign unit. The discussions of simultaneous words and the semiotics of signs have shown how the signs of sign languages may go beyond the horizons of what is known about spoken language words. The typological and theoretical importance of sign languages is all the more evident in cases where linguistic universals - or rather, what had been taken to be linguistic universals – suddenly appear in a new light altogether.

References

Anderson, L. B. 1982. 'Universals of aspect and parts of speech: parallels between signed and spoken languages', pp 91–114 of *Tense–Aspect: between semantics and pragmatics,* edited by P. J. Hopper. Amsterdam: John Benjamins.

Anderson, S. R. 1993. 'Linguistic expression and its relation to modality', pp 273–290 of Coulter, 1993.

Armstrong, D. F. 1983. 'Iconicity, arbitrariness, and duality of patterning in signed and spoken language: perspectives on language evolution', *Sign Language Studies* 3.51–69.

Baker, C. and Padden, C. A. 1978. 'Focusing on the nonmanual components of American Sign Language', pp 27–58 of *Understanding language through sign language re-search.* Perspectives in Neurolinguistics and Psycholinguistics, edited by P. Siple. New York: Academic Press.

Bergman, B. and Wallin, L. Forthcoming. 'Noun and verb classifiers in Swedish Sign Language'. In *Perspectives on classifier constructions in sign languages,* edited by K. Emmorey. Mahwah, N.J.: Lawrence Erlbaum.

Boyes Braem, P. 1986. 'Two aspects of psycholinguistic research: iconicity and temporal structure', pp 65–74 of *Signs of life: proceedings of the Second European Congress on Sign Language Research,* edited by B.Th. Tervoort, Publication of the Institute for General Linguistics Amsterdam: University of Amsterdam 50.

Boyes Braem, P. and Sutton-Spence, R. 2000. Editors of *The hand is the head of the mouth: the mouth as articulator in sign languages.* Hamburg: Signum.

Brentari, D. 1996. 'Sign language phonology: ASL', pp 615–39 of *The handbook of phonological theory,* edited by J. A. Goldsmith. Cambridge, Mass.: Blackwell.

Coerts, J. A. 1992. Nonmanual grammatical markers; an analysis of interrogatives, nega-tions and topicalisations in Sign Language of the Netherlands. PhD dissertation, University of Amsterdam.

Collins-Ahlgren, M. 1990. 'Word formation processes in New Zealand Sign Language', pp 279–312 of *Theoretical issues in sign language research,* Vol. 1, edited by S. D. Fischer and P. Siple. Chicago: Chicago University Press.

Coulter, G. R. 1993. Editor of *Phonetics and phonology,* Vol. 3: *Current issues in ASL phonology.* San Diego: Academic Press.

DeMatteo, A. 1977. 'Visual Imagery and visual analogues in American Sign Language', pp 109–36 of Friedman, 1977.

Friedman, L. A. 1977. Editor of *On the other hand: new perspectives on American Sign Language.* New York: Academic Press.

Gee, J. P. 1993. 'Reflections on the nature of ASL and the development of ASL linguistics: comments on Corina's article', pp 97–101 of Coulter, 1993.

Glück, S. and Pfau, R. 1997. 'Einige Aspekte der Morphologie und Morphosyntax in Deutscher Gebärdensprache' *Frankfurter Linguistische Forschungen* 20.30–48.

Johnston, T. and Schembri, A. 1999. 'On defining lexeme in a signed language'. *Sign Language and Linguistics* 2 (2).115–85.

Klima, E. S. and Bellugi, U. 1979. *The signs of language*. Cambridge, Mass. Harvard University Press.

Kyle, J., Pullen, G., Allsop, L. and Wood, P. 1985. 'British Sign Language in the British deaf community', pp 315–23 of *SLR '83: Proceedings of the Third International Symposium on Sign Language Research, Rome June 22–26, 1983*, edited by W. Stokoe and V. Volterra. Silver Spring, Md.: Linstok and Rome: Istituto di psicologia CNR.

Liddell, S. K. 1980. *American Sign Language syntax*. The Hague: Mouton.

Liddell, S. K. and Johnson, R. E. 1986. 'American Sign Language compounds: implications for the structure of the lexicon', pp 87–97 of *Georgetown University Round Table on Languages and linguistics 1985 – Languages and linguistics: the interdependence of theory, data, and application*, edited by D. Tannen and J. E. Alatis. Washington, D.C.: Georgetown University Press.

Lucas, C. and Valli, C. 1995. *Linguistics of American Sign Language: an introduction*. Washington, D.C.: Gallaudet University Press.

Malkiel, Y. 1990. *Diachronic problems in phonosymbolism: edita and inedita, 1979–1988*, Vol. 1. Amsterdam: John Benjamins.

Mandel, M. 1977. 'Iconic devices in American Sign Language', pp 57–107 of Friedman, 1977.

Morgan, M. 2000. 'Negatives and interrogatives in Japanese Sign Language', Questionnaire for the typological project on negatives and interrogatives in signed and spoken languages, Ms., Melbourne, La Trobe University, Research Centre for Linguistic Typology.

McNeill, D. 1992. *Hand and mind*. Chicago, Ill.: Chicago University Press.

Sandler, W. 1999. 'Cliticization and prosodic words in a sign language', pp 223–54 of *Studies on the phonological word*, edited by A. T. Hall and U. Kleinherz. Amsterdam: John Benjamins.

    2000. 'The medium and the message: prosodic interpretation of linguistic content in Israeli Sign Language', *Sign Language and Linguistics* 2 (2).187–215.

Sir Syed Deaf Association 1989. *Pakistan Sign Language*, edited by Syed Iftikhar Ahmed. Rawalpindi.

Tanzania Association of the Deaf (Chama cha Viziwi Tanzania, Chavita) 1993. *The Tanzania Sign Language dictionary (Kamusi ya Lugha ya Alama Tanzania)*. Dar es Salaam.

UNAD (Uganda National Association of the Deaf) 1998. *Manual of Ugandan signs*. Kampala.

Wrigley, O. et al. 1990. Editors of *The Thai Sign Language dictionary, revised and expanded edition*. Bangkok: National Association of the Deaf in Thailand.

Zeshan, U. 2000a. *Sign language in Indopakistan: a description of a signed language*. Amsterdam: John Benjamins

    2000b. *Gebärdensprachen des indischen Subkontinents*. Munich: LINCOM Europa.

Forthcoming. '"Classificatory" constructions in Indo-Pakistani Sign Language: grammaticalization and lexicalisation processes', in *Perspectives on classifier constructions in sign languages*, edited by K. Emmorey. Mahwah, N.J.: Lawrence Erlbaum.

Zimmer, J. and Patschke, C. 1990. 'A class of determiners in ASL', pp 201–10 of *Sign language research: theoretical issues*, edited by C. Lucas. Washington, D.C.: Gallaudet University Press.

7   A synchronic and diachronic perspective on 'word' in Siouan

Robert Rankin, John Boyle, Randolph Graczyk and John Koontz[1]

Siouan languages were spoken in aboriginal North America in a broad belt stretching from what is now Arkansas northward and westward across the western prairies and eastern great plains to Alberta. In addition there were Siouan languages scattered in the East in what is now Virginia, Alabama and Mississippi. The languages we will be discussing in this chapter are primarily Crow and Hidatsa, of the Missouri River subgroup, and Dakotan (including Dakota and Lakota dialects) and Dhegihan (including Omaha, Ponca, Kansa, Osage and Quapaw) of the Mississippi Valley subgroup. Data from other languages will be introduced as necessary.

1   Typology

Typologically, Siouan languages are primarily head-marking, active–stative, AOV, SV languages of moderate morphological complexity. Verbs are the most highly inflected category, and they may optionally include numerous and productive instances of noun incorporation. There are also many lexicalised noun–verb compounds. Sapir (1921: 142) characterised Dakota Sioux as 'complex pure-relational' in basic type with derivational concepts signalled by agglutinating elements and pure relational (mostly inflectional) concepts somewhat fused. Dakota's overall morphological technique he characterised as 'agglutinative-fusional' and degree of synthesis he characterised as 'synthetic (mildly polysynthetic)'.

1.1   Incorporation

Compared with languages like Inuit or Iroquoian we would probably not want to characterise Dakotan, or the rest of Mississippi Valley Siouan, as productively

---

[1] Rankin is responsible for the organisation and most of the writing in this chapter. Boyle provided discussion of Hidatsa and the interpretation of enclitics in linguistic theory. Graczyk provided examples and discussion of the Crow language. Koontz provided discussion of some of the Dhegiha and Dakotan data, commented on empirical versus formal analyses and did a portion of the writing.

incorporating, but Siouan verbs do incorporate a number of notions that speakers of most European languages would convey with separate words. And these include pronominal, instrumental, locative and directional concepts.[2] They allow incorporation of lexical noun roots that function in a number of different semantic roles vis-à-vis the verb root.

(1)   hiíwapašpukteyelo (adapted from Buechel 1970)
        hi- í-   wa- pa-   špu=kta=   yelo
        tooth-INSTRUMENT-1ACTR-BY.PUSHING-pick=POTENTIAL=MALE.DEC
        I will pick (my) teeth. (I will 'toothpick'.)

In (1), a Lakota verb (and sentence), a single phonological word with a single primary accent, incorporates a body part noun, *hi* 'tooth', a locative–instrumentive prefix, *í-*, that fits into a locative slot in the verb, an actor/agent pronominal, *wa-*, one of a selection of about nine prefixes indicating particular instrumentals, in this instance *pa-* 'by pushing', and the verb root itself. Enclitic to the verb are the potential mode marker, *=kta*, and the male declarative marker, *=yelo*, which, although perhaps best considered an enclitic, often bears accent. The semantics of the verb are fairly transparent in this example, typical of syntactic incorporation in Lakota.

(2)   blučháǀwaxtešni   (de Reuse 1994: 214)
        ø- b-   yu-   chą́t-waxte=šni[3]
        3OBJ-1ACTR-BY.HAND-heart- be.good=NEG
        I made him/her angry.

In (2), the pronominal allomorph, *b-*, which must precede the instrumental prefix *yu-* 'by hand/pulling', comes first, followed by the instrumental and an incorporated noun, *čhąté* 'heart', the verb stem and the negative enclitic *=šni*.[4] Here the meaning 'make angry' is not equivalent to the sum of the meanings of

---

[2] Writing for an audience of non-Siouanists, we have adopted the abbreviations and terms INSTR 'instrumental' and INST 'instrumentive' or 'locative-instrumental' in this chapter to describe two different kinds of instrumental prefixes commonly found in Siouan languages. The *i-* instrumentive used in example (1) is a general agreement prefix for nearly any noun instrument, and it falls into a morphotactic class with the locatives. The other instrumental prefixes form a closed set of about nine with more or less specific meanings such as 'by pulling, by pushing, by heat, by foot, by mouth', etc. (see table 1, columns 4 and 7). Siouanists all too frequently tend to use the term *instrumental* for both kinds, leaving the distinction to context or example.

[3] *čhąté* 'heart' takes the form *čhąǀ-* when fully incorporated because Dakotan only permits sonorants in syllable codas of this kind. Thus, *p, t, č, k → b/m, d/l/n, d/l/n, g/ŋ* respectively in codas. Voiced stops function as sonorants in this context, with nasality conditioned by the preceding (oral versus nasal) vowel. Truncation of incorporanda signals that the overall construct is a single grammatical word.

[4] De Reuse's translation gives 'bad' as the meaning for the stem, *waxté*. If this were the case, the verb would not require the negative enclitic. *Waxté* must be related via fricative symbolism, common in Siouan, to the verb *wašté* 'good' rather than 'bad'.

the individual derivational morphemes and roots that make up the verb. Note also that, comparing (1) and (2), the order of incorporated nouns, pronominals and instrumentals may differ from verb to verb. This is typical of what de Reuse (1994), in his extensive treatment of lexical and syntactic incorporation in Siouan, calls lexical compounding in Lakota.

1.2   Agglutination and fusion

In using the agglutination–fusion scale we must distinguish between derivational and inflectional morphology. As Sapir mentioned, Siouan derivational morphology is quite generally agglutinative, but inflectional morphology has a definite fusional tinge. Consider the allomorphy of the agentive pronominal prefix set in the Kansa language (other Dhegiha dialects are quite similar, and Dakotan also shares reflexes of types (a–d)). Each example represents a conjugation class. Types (a), (b) and (e) are extremely productive; the other classes have relatively few members each, but their members enjoy a high frequency of occurrence. Third person has zero marking and shows the underlying form of the verb.

		1sg	2sg	3sg
(a)	carry	a-kʔį	ya-kʔį	kʔį
(b)	go	b-le	h-ne	yé
(c)	come	p-hü	š-ü	hü
(d)	do	m-ǫ	ž-ǫ	ʔǫ́
(e)	break	p-páxi	š-páxi	baxí
(f)	see	t-tǫ́be	š-tǫ́be	dǫ́be
(g)	make	p-pá·ye	š-ká·ye	gá·ye
(h)	want	k-kǫ́-b-la	š-kǫ́-h-na	gǫ́-ya

The first person singular pronominal affix, historically *wa-, shows a complex alternation pattern that is partly phonologically conditioned and partly lexically conditioned. The first person singular allomorphs are a-/b-/m-/p-/t-/k-. Originally the conditioning factors were phonological and assimilatory in character. The rather involved rule that has developed is virtually identical in every Dhegiha dialect; it generally involved obstruentisation of the original *w-.

Second person pronominals show an even greater degree of fusion, often replacing the initial consonant of the verb stem. Allomorphs are ya-/š-/ž-/h-, from *ya-. Again, prefix vowel syncope and obstruentisation, this time of y, account for the palatal contoid allomorphs. Certain other prefixes, mostly inflectional, also show partially fused allomorphs. Splitting the notion of agglutination from the notion of invariance of form as suggested by Comrie (1989: 45ff), we verify Sapir's judgement that Siouan languages are generally agglutinative with relatively invariant morphemes in their derivational morphology but somewhat fusional and less invariant in their inflectional morphology, which is generally more archaic.

1.3   Polysynthesis

Adopting Comrie's additional distinction between polysynthesis and incorporation, most Siouan languages fall somewhere between synthetic and polysynthetic on the polysynthesis scale but actively incorporate independent lexemes only to a relatively reduced degree. For example, Dakota speakers do not usually incorporate generic noun direct objects. De Reuse (1994) argues that incorporated nouns are pragmatically backgrounded and, in fact, are not arguments of the verb. Siouan, with its optional, pragmatically marked incorporation, is not like Eskimo or Iroquoian in which certain kinds of object incorporation are obligatory (see chapter 3).

Crow and Hidatsa are typologically rather different from Dakotan, tending much more strongly toward both polysynthesis and incorporation. Not only is noun incorporation more common; incorporation of entire relative clauses is possible. Example (3) is a single phonological verb containing a single accent. Pauses within such constructs are not generally possible.

(3)   akdiiammalapáshkuuassaaleewaachiinmook
      ak- dii-ammalapáškuua-ss- aa- lee-waa- čiin- m- oo- k
      REL-2OBJ-Billings-   GOAL-PORT-go- 1ACTR-look.for-one-MODE-DEC
      We'll look for someone who [will] take you to Billings.

Ammalapáškuua 'Billings' (Montana) is itself an incorporated clause meaning 'the place where they cut lumber', Billings having been originally a sawmill town. So there are essentially two relative clauses incorporated here, one syntactic and the other fossilised. Within the Siouan language family, then, we find greater and lesser degrees of polysynthesis.

2   Grammatical words

The Siouan languages are traditionally regarded as having a fairly consistent match between grammatical and phonological words. However, grammatical words in Crow and Hidatsa are potentially rather larger and more complex than in the better-known Mississippi Valley Siouan languages.

Table 1 *Quapaw verb prefixes.*

absolutive	dual inclusive	outer locatives	outer instrumentals	first and second person actor and patient pronominal		dative vertitive reflexive reciprocal suus	inner instrumentals	verb root
1	2	3	4	5	6	7	8	
wa -	ąk-	í-	pá-	ą-	a-	ki-	ba-	
	wa-	á-	tá·-	di-	da-	ki-	di-	
		ó-	pó-	ø	ø	kkik-	na-	
		i-				kkik-	da-	
						kik-	ka-	
							bi-	
something	we	with	cut	me	I	to/for	pushing	
	us	at/on	heat	you	you	back	hand	
		inside	shoot	him/her	s/he	self	foot	
		toward				each/ other	mouth	
						ones/ own	striking	
							pressure	

2.1   Words and prefixes in Dakotan and Dhegihan

To illustrate word structure in Mississippi Valley Siouan languages, consider the Quapaw verb prefixes. Recall that verbs are the most highly derived and inflected category. The order illustrated here is typical of what is found in the rest of the Dhegiha subgroup, and Dakotan is quite comparable. It is presented here as a simplified, combined template for purposes of initial discussion. The actual situation is much more complex. All of the elements that precede the verb root are affixal.

2.1.1 Initial problems with prefix order It is not the case in Siouan that derivation occupies the inner affix orders and inflection the outer ones. Sets 1, 3, 4 and 8 are clearly derivational, while 2, 5, 6 and at least some of 7 are inflectional. The locative and instrumental prefix sets (3, 4 and 8) give Siouan languages some of their polysynthetic 'feel', while noun incorporation and compounding provide the rest. Note that there is no fixed slot for incorporated nouns in this schema. This issue is taken up in the next section.

The bound locatives, pronominals and instrumental affixes yield Quapaw verb forms of the following sort (Rankin 1986) (other Mississippi Valley languages are similar).

(4)   pá- da- baɣe
        INSTR-2ACTR-part.in.two
        you cut it in two (with bladed instrument)

(5)   á- pa- da- baɣe
        LOC-INSTR-2ACTR-part.in.two
        you cut it in two on something

(6)   wa-   tá-- įži
        1du.PAT-INSTR-fail
        we two fail(ed) in cooking (with heat)[5]

(7)   wa-   ó- ta-- įži=we
        1DU.PAT-LOC-INSTR-fail= PL
        we fail(ed) in cooking (with heat) inside something

2.1.2 Order of incorporanda This basic picture becomes more complicated when we consider noun–verb compounding and incorporation. According to most authors (e.g., Boas and Deloria 1941, Mithun 1984), noun incorporation is relatively poorly developed in Siouan, amounting to little more than transparent compounding of a noun root with a verb stem (see de Reuse 1994 for a more detailed view of Dakotan incorporation). Nevertheless, in numerous instances incorporation has a meaning distinct from the sum of its semantic parts – i.e. it has become lexicalised. Much but not all such incorporation involves body parts: Lakota (Buechel 1970), e.g. with *phá* 'head', *i-phá-hį* 'INST-head-lean' = 'lean the head against', *a-ph-ó-mnamna* 'LOC-head-LOC-shake-shake' = 'shake the head about', *i-phá-šloka* 'INST-head-slide' = 'pull off over the head', *phá-šla-ye-la* 'head-bare-CAUS-DIM' = 'making bare the head'; with *hí* 'tooth', *hi-í-pa-špu* 'tooth-INST-INSTR-pluck' = 'pick the teeth'; with *sí* 'foot', *si-yu-thípa* 'foot-INST-INSTR-cramp' = 'have a foot cramp'; with *čhąté* 'heart', *yu-čhą́l-waxte-šni* 'INSTR-heart-good-NEG' = 'make someone angry'; with *thezi* 'stomach', *thezi-yu-thipa* 'stomach-INSTR-cramp' = 'have a stomach cramp'; with *thahu* 'neck', *thahu-yu-thipa* 'neck.bone-INSTR-cramp' = 'have a cramp in the neck'.

Examples from other Siouan languages include, in Kansa (Rankin 1987), with *ną́je* 'heart', *ną́je*-łąye 'heart-great' = 'be brave'; *ną́je-wahehe* 'heart-tremble' = 'be cowardly'; *nąǰ-i-ǫ* 'heart-INST-do' = 'love someone very much'; with *ho* 'voice', *hó-xpe* 'voice-weaken' = 'cough'; in Biloxi (Dorsey and Swanton 1912), with *yądi* 'heart', *{PRN}-yądi-hį* 'heart-think(?)' = 'think of someone constantly'; *{PRN}-yądi-niki* 'heart-lack/be.none' = 'be without any sense';

---

[5] The instrumental prefix *ta·-* 'by extreme of temperature' requires subject pronominals from the patient (stative) set.

{PRN}-yǫd-oye 'heart-be.open' = 'be sad'; and in Tutelo (Oliverio 1996), with *yǫ́·te* 'heart', *{PRN}-yǫ́·t-o-ste·ka* 'heart-LOC-good' = 'to love'. In Biloxi and Tutelo incorporation of nouns within the verb word seems more complete, since the pronominal prefixes typically occur outside the incorporated noun.

Note that these examples of compounding reveal that the verb prefix order we presented above was oversimplified. While it conveys an idea of the relative locations of Siouan prefix classes, Siouan languages really do not lend themselves to description in terms of templatic morphology for reasons that should now become clear. In Lakota 'lean the head against' and 'pull off over the head' the incorporated noun, 'head', follows the locative prefix and precedes the verb root. In 'pick the teeth' the noun precedes both the locative prefix and verb root, while in 'shake the head about' one locative prefix precedes the incorporated noun and another follows it. In 'to have a cramp' the affected body part noun is inserted before the instrumental prefix, while in 'to make angry' the body part, 'heart', follows the same instrumental. So the location of the incorporated noun is rather variable, especially with regard to the locative and instrumental prefix sets. Semantic role of the incorporated noun is not a determining factor.

A more complicated case involves verbs like 'cough'. Historically, it incorporates *ho* 'voice', but comparing Mississippi Valley Siouan languages, we find two distinct conjugation patterns. We would expect *ho-{pronoun}-xpe*, and that is what we find in Kansa and Quapaw: 1sg *ho-á-xpe*, 2sg *ho-yá-xpe* 'you cough(ed)' (Kansa), 2sg *ho-dá-xpe* (Quapaw). In Dakotan, however, the verb is conjugated with the pronominals outside the incorporated noun: 1sg *wa-hó-xpe*, 2sg *ya-hó-xpe*.

It appears that Dakotan speakers have lost etymological awareness of the source of *hóxpe*, which is now treated as a monomorphemic root, and they have moved the pronominals accordingly. Position of the noun seems to depend on when, historically, the original compounding was done and/or degree of opacity of the result, in other words, degree of lexicalisation.

2.1.3 Order of locatives   Locative/instrumentive prefixes also present problems for any synchronic, invariant ordering proposals. They can double up, a second locative appearing outside of an earlier one to derive a new lexical verb stem. There are a great many examples of doubled or even tripled locative prefixes. When locatives are layered there appears to be no fixed order for them: the order is the one in which they were applied historically. Often one and sometimes both of the prefixes has been bleached of any clear locative meaning. The process and a variety of examples are discussed in detail in Boas and Deloria (1941: 43–5): *a-í-čapa* 'open mouth toward' < *í-čapa* 'open the mouth'; *i-á-kaška*[6] 'imprison' < *kaška* 'tie fast'; *a-ó-nathaka* 'lock in';

---

[6] Boas and Deloria write an initial glottal stop with all vowel-initials and also write a glide, [y] between the vowels. Both elements are predictable and have been omitted here for clarity. I have

o-á-š?aka 'be crusted inside'; *o-í-o-kpaza* 'it is dark all around' (three locatives) < *kpáza* 'dark'; *i-ó-sni* 'cool something (inside) with' < *-sní* 'cold'.

2.1.4 Locatives, instrumentals and pronominals One of the most convincing examples of difficulties with a templatic approach is Lakota *oyúspa* 'to arrest'. In the inflected form 'we arrested them' there are several conflicting ordering principles at work: (1) *wičha-* 'animate 3pl patient' is normally ordered after *o-* 'locative', (2) *ųk-* 'we' must be ordered after *wičha-*, but (3) *ųk-* must also be ordered preceding locative *o-*. Obviously there is a problem here: *o-* + *wičhá* + *ųk-* + *o-*, with a single locative *o-* having to be in two places at once. This paradox creates a class of exceptions and a problem that speakers must somehow solve. According to Rood and Taylor (1996: 468), they resolve the problem in either of two ways. Some speakers insert both pronominals in the proper order but must then repeat locative *o-* after *ųk-*: *o-wíčh-ųk-o-yu-spa=pi* 'we arrested them'. Others simply ignore the normative rule that *ųk-* must precede *o-* and say *o-wíčh-ų-yuspa=pi*.[7]

Diachronically, what has happened here is that two nouns, **wų́·ke* and *wičháša*, both meaning 'man/person', have been grammaticalised as pronouns at different times. *Wų́·ke* became 'first person inclusive' throughout much of Siouan, while *wichá* became 'third person animate patient,' but only in Dakotan. Each probably began its grammaticalisation as an incorporated noun, and each in turn was ordered with respect to the other prefixes or proclitics in the system at the time of incorporation. Ordering apparently became a problem in Dakotan as the pattern was extended to all transitive verbs and all dialect areas. The exact circumstances remain unclear.

2.1.5 Problems with infixing verbs Lastly, while most Siouan verbs are prefixing, some are genuinely infixing, with the pronominals placed between two halves of the verb root. These infixing roots may have been compounds at one time, but the parts no longer have individual meanings. Infixing verbs will be exceptions in any attempt at templatic morphology, since the first person dual inclusive prefix can come either prefixed or infixed, depending on the language and on the individual verb. If the inclusive is infixed, it obviously follows all the other prefix positions, whereas normally it is the left-most prefix. To make matters worse, Dakotan conjugates the verb one way but Omaha the other, while Quapaw does both. The verb 'walk' is found throughout Mississippi Valley Siouan (the 3sg is zero and reveals the bare stem):

also replaced Deloria's symbols for aspiration, *š*, *ž*, *č*, *x*, *y* and *?* with currently used symbols on a one-to-one basis.

[7] The Dakotan inclusive and first person plural pronominal has two allomorphs, [?]*ųk-* preceding vowels and [?]*ų-* preceding consonants. An analogous rule exists in Dhegiha languages.

	Dakotan (Buechel 1970)	Omaha (Dorsey 1890)	Quapaw (Dorsey 1890–94)
1sg	ma-wá-ni	mą -b-ðį́	a-mą́- b-dį
2sg	ma-yá-ni	mą-š-nį́	da-mą́- t-tį
3sg	ma- -ní	mą - -ðį́	mą- -nį́
1du	ma- ų́-ni	ą- mą́- -ðį	ą-mą́-ą-nį

These examples, plus the ones illustrating noun incorporation, further demonstrate that templatic morphology is not destined to work with Siouan languages. The semantics of locatives is especially problematic as they variably lose their locative meaning to one or another degree. At one time they were proclitics or independent words as they tend strongly to attract accent, and one of them, *i-* 'with, using', may appear as an independent word in Crow, suggesting recent grammaticalisation in the Mississippi Valley.

Certainly all of the forms cited above are grammatical words. The grammatical morphemes, both derivational and inflectional, within them occur together, not scattered throughout the clause. They also have the requisite conventionalised meanings. But the constituent grammatical morphemes do not occur in a consistent, predictable order, i.e., they cannot be thought of as generated by a simplistic set of quasi-syntactic rules.

> *2.1.6 Two kinds of incorporation* We have been using the terms compounding and incorporation more or less interchangeably, because it is not possible always to distinguish them on syntactic or phonological grounds, but it is useful to distinguish them semantically. Boas and Deloria (1941: 67), discussing this problem, state 'Each compound has only one primary accent... Compounding always expresses that the compound is a unit concept. There are however two degrees of such unity.'

In the first of Deloria's examples *thąka* 'be large' is a stative verb in an internally headed relative clause. 'Kettle' and 'large' are both independent phonological and grammatical words and both have primary accent. No compounding or incorporation is involved.

(8) čhéγa wą thą́ka kį hé ma-kʔú
     kettle a large the that me-give
     Give me the kettle that is large.

In the next example, *thąka* functions as a noun modifier, but it is not accented, and Deloria, an educated native-speaker of Lakota, writes a hyphen between the elements of the compound. This is her first type of conceptual unity.

(9) čhéγa-thąka kį hé ma-kʔú
     kettle large the that me-give
     Give me the big-kettle.

In Deloria's third example we are dealing with full incorporation in which the noun undergoes some phonological truncation, and accent is assigned by rule to the second syllable, which happens here to be the verb.[8]

(10)   čhex-thą́ka   wóhe?
          kettle-large   (3sg)-cooked
          She cooked a big-kettle-ful (i.e., she cooked for a feast).

Deloria's type 1 unity results in a compound that is transparently the sum of its semantic parts. She felt that both kinds of what she called 'unity' resulted in a single concept, so we probably want to say that it is a single grammatical word. Its single accent signals a phonological word. Deloria's type 2 unity results in a single phonological and, certainly, grammatical word with a unique meaning, not derivable from the sum of its parts. Additional examples of these patterns include, type 1: *čhéγa-zi* 'yellow kettle', type 2: *čhex-zí* 'brass kettle' (Boas and Deloria 1941:67); type 1: *sí čhola* 'lack feet' < *si* 'foot', type 2: *si-čhóla* 'be barefoot' (de Reuse 1994).

De Reuse too distinguishes what he calls syntactic compounds, Deloria's type 1 unity, from what he calls lexical compounds, Deloria's type 2 unity. Syntactic compounds for him are normally single phonological and, presumably, single grammatical words. Lexical compounds are very clearly single phonological and single grammatical words, although historically they often included, and sometimes still include, semantically analysable incorporated nouns (as well as other morphological elements, as discussed above).

De Reuse (1994: 215–18) also found a few instances of single words incorporating more than a single noun: *šų(g)-mní-kʔu* (lit. 'horse-water-give') 'to water horses'. Phonological truncation of *šų́ka* 'dog/horse' plus second syllable accentuation show that both nouns are incorporated within the verb. The entire construct is a single phonological word, defined by its stress pattern, and a single grammatical word, as strongly suggested by the truncated incorporandum. De Reuse says that the bracketing in such double incorporations is always [noun+[noun+verb]] and never [[noun+noun]+verb].

2.2   Missouri River Siouan affixal morphology

The same kinds of pronominal and instrumental morphology prefixed in Mississippi Valley Siouan are also affixal in Hidatsa and Crow in the northwest of the region. But noun incorporation in Crow is much more productive than in Dakotan. Apparently it always occurs with indefinite, non-specific direct objects

---

[8] Nouns are only truncated this way when their final vowel is of a certain sort (proto-Siouan *-e*), so with other noun-final vowels it may sometimes be difficult to tell the difference between Deloria's two degrees of unity. The best indicator here is accentual if the first word only has one syllable. If it is disyllabic so that accent falls on the first word whether or not it is a type 1 or type 2 incorporation, the best indicator of status would probably be semantic.

where the noun–verb combination refers to a habitual activity. In such cases it is not optional for speakers: *alápeechia* 'fight fire' < *alápee* 'range fire'+*chía* 'extinguish'; *ilúkduushi* 'eat meat' < *ilúka* 'meat' + *duushí* 'eat'; *binnaxchilía* 'fix fence' < *binnaxchí* 'fence' + *día* 'do, make'. It is possible that there is some semantic backgrounding present when objects are incorporated. In this type of object incorporation the active pronominal prefixes occur between the incorporated noun, 'meat', and the stem, e.g. 1sg *ilúk-b-uushi*, 2sg *ilúk-di-luushi*, 3sg *ilúk-duushi*.

There are even examples of incorporation of borrowed English nouns, which attests to its productivity:

(11)   *wíne*-isshiik
        he is drinking wine

(12)   ak-   *íce*-iiwaaiaschilee-sh   kala-híi- k
        AGENT-*ice*- sell-   DET   now- arrive-DEC
        the one who sells ice is here

(13)   ak-*bús*-chilakee
        bus driver

In the second example the accent is on 'ice', and the incorporated noun is part of an incorporated relative clause. These are all single phonological words. It is possible that we might wish to consider distinguishing *grammatical word* from *syntactic word* in such instances. If the latter term has any utility, surely it would be in cases such as these.

2.2.1 Body part statives There is another type of incorporation involving inalienably possessed body part nouns and stative verbs. *daásicchi* 'be happy' < *daasá* 'heart' + *ícchi* 'be good', *daásduupa* 'be uncertain, undecided' < *daasá* 'heart' + *dúupa* 'be two'. These are inflected with the possessive prefixes: *ba-lasícchi* 'I am happy', *da-lásduupa* 'you are uncertain', etc. With these verbs, then, the inflection precedes the incorporated noun rather than following it.

2.2.2 More templatic problems The notion of template tends to break down in Crow, just as in other Siouan languages.

(1) There is variability in the ordering of incorporanda and pronominal prefixes. For example, in the word/sentence given above in (3) as an example of polysynthesis, Crow speakers find an alternate order acceptable. The pronominal *dii-* 'you', the object of the verb in the subordinate clause, may either precede or follow 'Billings + GOAL':

(14) ak- dii- ammalapáshkuua-ss- aa- lee-waa- chiin-m- oo- k
      REL-2OBJ- Billings-   GOAL-PORT-go- 1ACTR- look.for-one-MODE-DEC
      We'll look for someone who [will] take **you** to Billings.

(15) ak- ammalapáshkuua-ss- dii- aa- lee-waa- chiin-m- oo-   k
      REL-*Billings*-   GOAL-2OBJ-PORT-go- 1ACTR-look.for-one-MODE.PL-DEC
      We'll look for someone who [will] take **you** to *Billings* (opposed to elsewhere).

The former represents the unmarked order, while the latter is pragmatically marked and contrasts Billings with other possible destinations. Thus, in Crow, the order of morphemes may be manipulated at the subword level in order to shift focus.

(2) With the future auxiliaries, the agent pronominals are postposed. That is, the order is PRO STEM PRO AUX except for *biá* 'want to, intend to, be going to', where the order is PRO STEM AUX PRO: *baa- lée-wia-waa-k* (1ACTR-go-FUT-1ACTR-DEC) 'I am going to go.'

(3) Crow, like other Siouan languages, has a number of verbs with genuinely infixed person markers. Note the distinct allomorphs with vowels, nasals and clusters.

	'steal'	'enter'	'know'
1sg	at-b-aalí	bím-m-aali	é-wa-hče
2sg	at-d-áali	bín-n-aali	é-la-hče
3sg	at--aalí	bil--éeli	é--hče

2.3   Summary of synchronic questions

Thus far we have seen that Siouan verbs do not fit well into templatic models because the many prefixes are ordered according to sometimes-conflicting principles. (1) Derivation is recursive in that locatives can be relatively freely concatenated in any order. (2) Nouns can be incorporated at more than one point among the prefixes. (3) Pronominals may be infixed within some verbs, and, if they are prefixed, their order can be disturbed by positioning of locatives. Reduplicated verb roots, although not discussed here, can be regarded as prefixes, as the process has grammatical functions, marking iteration in active verbs, intensity in stative verbs. Finally, the patterns illustrated above are quite typical of what is found across Siouan among fluent speakers. These are not examples produced by confused semi-speakers of moribund languages.

2.3.1 Implications of diachrony Grammatical words in Siouan include the root and all prefixed material. We might want to ask ourselves, however, whether we wish to treat transparent compounds like Lakota *sí čhola* 'be footless' (from *si* 'foot' and *čhola* 'be without') in exactly the same way that we treat opaque compounds like *si-čhóla* 'be barefoot' – both with the same status as grammatical words. Diachronically they are clearly later and earlier derivations from the same two roots. Such doublets, one a syntactic compound and the other a lexical compound, are not uncommon though, so the problem of their overall word status is a real one. Using the term *syntactic word* at least for clause-incorporating structures in Crow is one possibility.

The process of lexicalisation is slow, and it is not uncommon to find compounds near some mid-point along the diachronic lexicalisation continuum. Such partially digested compounds may ultimately resist attempts to distinguish subtypes of grammatical words on principled grounds. *Hóxpe* 'to cough' is such a verb when looked at across Siouan. Some speakers treat it as a *Gestalt* and have prefixed agent pronominals to the entire word; others still infix the pronominals, treating *ho* 'voice' as a noun. Enclitics (§4, below) provide additional examples of grammaticalisation by degree.

2.4   *Grammatical hierarchy*

The grammatical hierarchy includes inflectional and derivational morphemes (including incorporanda), roots and stems. The tradition among Siouanists is to consider the bare verb root as a stem, but to consider that root with each of its instrumental prefixes and each of its locative prefixes as stems as well. This is because the instrumentals and especially the locatives may possess bleached, or at least very general, meanings. Phrases are clear-cut, especially noun phrases. Verb phrases include among other things the lexical verb and any auxiliaries plus numerous possible enclitics. Clauses, sentences and perhaps larger organisational units round out the picture.

3   Phonological words

3.1   *Accent*

In Siouan languages accent yields one of the best approaches to determination of phonological words; there is normally a single primary accent per phonological word. Accent placement is variable but usually falls on one of the first two syllables.[9] Boas and Deloria (1941: 21) say of accent, 'We may distinguish between accented words and unaccented parts of speech, enclitics and proclitics and others so firmly united with the accented parts of speech that they may be written as suffixes or prefixes. Some of these enclitics may under special conditions become accented. Syllables bearing the main accent have a high

---

[9] Ken Miner (see Hayes 1995: 346–65 for a good summary) has shown that Winnebago accent has been shifted to the right, so that it is often a syllable farther from the beginning of the word than in the other Mississippi Valley languages.

pitch.' So although Deloria wrote many of our enclitics as independent words (see list, below), either she or Boas made a decision to continue calling them enclitics.

It is probable that accent was predictable in Proto-Siouan where it seems to have been a feature of the second syllable, or perhaps mora, of the word. We reconstruct Proto-Siouan with pitch accent of a basically iambic sort. If the initial syllable vowel was long, it was probably accented. Otherwise the second vowel was accented. Alternate vowels to the right of the accented vowel could bear non-distinctive secondary accent. Second syllable accentuation is perhaps the most common pattern in Siouan words today also, and it shifts leftward as prefixes are added. Examples from Lakota (Boas and Deloria 1941: 21): *lową́* 'he sings', *walówą* 'I sing'; *yazą́* 'he is sick', *ʔiyázą* 'he is sick on account of', *ʔimáyazą* 'I am sick on account of'.

However, this pattern was badly disturbed in Mississippi Valley Siouan languages by historical loss of many unaccented initial syllable vowels. Syncope in prefixes left a great many roots with initial syllable accent. In addition, a few prefixes actually attract accent – notably locatives. So accent does not really mark word boundaries in Siouan. There are, in fact, no phonological criteria that provide clear, unambiguous and consistent delimitation of word boundaries in Siouan. Several factors may furnish hints to speakers (and child learners) about boundaries however.

3.1.1 Other hints for boundary phenomena Dakotan has an epenthetic [ʔ] before word-initial vowels, but there are other glottal stops that do not signal word boundaries. Winnebago inserts [h] preceding word-initial short vowels, but there are also *h*s that are not at word boundaries. Hints about word boundaries in Dakotan and some other languages may also occasionally be had from the spread and extent of nasalisation. Historically, in many Siouan languages nasality spread leftward from a nasal vowel until it reached either an obstruent consonant or a word boundary. This is still the case in Mandan, but in Dakotan and Dhegiha the pattern now has many exceptions. In at least some Siouan languages all monosyllabic words of major lexical categories (noun, verb, adverb, etc.) must have a long vowel.

In Crow and Hidatsa [m, w, b] and [n, l/r, d] are allophonic variants, and only one phone each from the labial or dental sonorants may appear in word-initial position. Since many affixes begin with a sonorant, this can potentially provide a helpful hint. Unfortunately it does not always work in Crow, since initial [d] and [b] can also occur after an obstruent, and since the [w] and [l] allophones, normally intervocalic, may appear across word boundaries in a phrase, e.g. *hinné baapé* [hinnéẃaapé] 'this day', *hinné daláakbachee* [hinnéĺaláakbačee] 'this, your son'. Only if people are asked to repeat phrases like this slowly, do the [b] and [d] allophones appear. A Crow word may never begin with a consonant cluster, but clusters are common word-internally. Finally, a speaker may pause between words, but not word-internally.

Ignoring the problem of exact boundaries, however, it is possible to give a straightforward definition of 'word' in Crow and Hidatsa based on phonological properties: as in Dakota and Dhegiha, the word is the domain of a single primary accent. With few exceptions, lexical morphemes in Siouan languages are inherently accented, and in words composed of more than one morpheme, there are rules that reduce all the accents to one.

3.2   Pauses

Longer verb forms with their prefixes and incorporanda are not normally interruptible. This seems to include enclitics in Crow, but Dakotan is a more difficult call. We do not have first hand information at this point that would inform us about ability to pause before enclitics that Deloria tended consistently to write as separate words. These would mostly be the ones toward the bottom of the enclitic chart, farther from the verb root.

Verbs, certainly, can form a complete utterance, including stative verbs and nominal predicates. We take the position that there is no class of adjectives in Siouan. Some adverbials and other words can be utterances.

3.3   Phonological and grammatical congruity

While in everyday speech there is considerable congruity between phonological words and grammatical words, there are exceptions. Graczyk and Boyle, linguists working with Crow and Hidatsa, find the phonological definition of the word to be much more helpful than those of us working farther south with Dhegihan or Dakotan dialects. There, it is not possible to be categorical about pauses and accent among the outer clitics. Sometimes these enclitics may be accented according to available sources (Boas and Deloria 1941, Trechter 1995). If the phonological word is defined accentually, accented enclitics represent the primary source of mismatch between phonological and grammatical words in Dakotan.

Depending on how we treat the syntactic incorporations in Crow and Hidatsa, phonological words in Siouan languages may be made up of one or more grammatical words. In the more southerly languages, most grammatical words are simple monomorphemic or polymorphemic sequences, but in verbs (and trivially in possessed kin-terms) the grammatical words are inflected by prefixation. Thus phonological words may contain multiple inflections, one set for each grammatical word. In addition, grammatical verb words in particular may manifest a relatively complex polymorphemic derivational structure including compound verb forms, one or more incorporated nouns, or, in Crow and Hidatsa, entire incorporated relative clauses. The specific rules for these derivational structures must be rather complex. No Siouanist has been entirely successful in producing a detailed account of such a system.

3.4   The phonological hierarchy

Most Siouanists deal with phonemes by some definition, underlying (organic), surface, or both. There may still be differences over how to interpret ejectives and aspirates, but we will treat them as units in Dakotan and Dhegiha, where they are a prominent feature. So segmental units represent one domain. Syllables seem to be useful in some treatments of Dakotan reduplication and type-two (lexical) compounding, but there is not space to try to define them here. Feet play little or no role in definitions of the phonological word as it is used in this chapter. (But see Hayes (1995: 346–65) on Winnebago metrical phonology.) The phonological word is defined as the domain of a single primary accent, although this does not enable us to define exact word boundaries. Studies of sentence stress and intonation in Siouan are generally lacking. To the extent that single words can be sentences, a not infrequent occurrence, sentence stress coincides with word accent.

4   Enclitics

Siouan languages lack phonological words that have no syntactic coherence, i.e., we do not have clitics in the often used sense of unmotivated or accidental attachment of a light constituent to a chance neighbour. Siouan languages are known, however, for their numerous post-verbal grammatical elements. Unlike the complex, sometimes conflicting morphotactics of elements that precede the verb root, post-verbal grammar follows strict syntactic ordering principles. Sadock (1991) states that 'clitics generally display the behavior of bound affixes, but appear clearly to be distributed according to syntactic rules'. This is not surprising from a diachronic point of view, since the vast majority of Siouan enclitics are older, (mostly) uninflected verbs that have lost their status as distinct grammatical words and have merged with the greater phonological verb stems. Rood and Taylor (1996: 473) comment on these in Dakotan: 'Except in those instances when a conjunction stands last in the sentence ... post-verbal elements belong to the class here called enclitics. These words express aspect, tense, modality, and, in one case, number. In other descriptions of Lakota, enclitics have been variously treated as suffixes, adverbs, or auxiliaries, and indeed the decision to treat the most common of them as enclitics rather than suffixes is based on semantics and on native-speaker intuition rather than on phonological criteria. Speakers recognise these words as independent, isolable, and as meaningful. But one-syllable enclitics are frequently not stressed, so they do sound as if they are suffixed to the verb.'

It is a fact, however, that enclitics are often difficult to distinguish from suffixes on principled grounds. For example, *kta* 'potential mode' clearly forms a part of the phonological verb that precedes it; it causes/passes nasalisation just as if there were no major boundary present. Dakotan *kta* 'potential mode' is a (rare) nasalising morpheme. Thus we have the examples such as: *b-le* [ble] 'I go', but, nasalised, *b-le* + *kta* → [mnį́kte] 'I will/would go'. There are other sandhi rules that operate routinely between stems and enclitics that do not operate across other major category boundaries. But in other ways, several of these same traditional Siouan enclitics are hard to distinguish from independent words. For example, those with more than a single syllable may bear accent, something that most recognised clitics avoid (Trechter 1995).

4.1   Dakotan enclitics

Rood and Taylor's excellent sketch of Lakota (1996) has twelve enclitic positions. Arranging the orders vertically, beginning with the verb root and working rightward, these Dakotan clitics are listed below. Some of them were written as suffixes by Ella Deloria in Boas and Deloria (1941). Others were treated as distinct words by Deloria and written with a space before them. A few are found written both ways in the *Dakota Grammar*. We must assume that Deloria was conveying her native intuitions about their status with her use of hyphens and spaces.

Suffixes according to Deloria:
1. hą   'continuative aspect'
2. pi   'plural' (subject, animate object or both)
3. la   'diminutive'
4. ka   'somewhat'

Treated inconsistently by Deloria:
5. kta   'potential mode' (both word and suffix)
6. šni   'negative mode' (both word and suffix)

Treated as separate words by Deloria:
7. sʔa   'iterative aspect'
8. yo   'imperative, male speaking'
   ye   'imperative, female speaking'
   yethó   'familiar imperative, men'
   nithó   'familiar imperative, women' or
   įthó   'familiar imperative, women'
   ye   'imperative, request, men/women'
   na   'imperative, request, women only'

9. séča   'conjecture, "probably"'
   načhéča   'conjecture, "probably"'
10. kéya   'quotative'
    kéya-pi   'PL quotative'
11. lax   'emotional involvement of speaker', 'really'
    láxča   'emotional involvement of speaker', 'really'
    láxčaka   'emotional involvement of speaker', 'really'
12. More than twenty-seven additional particles marking interrogatives, suggestions, assertions, emphatic negation, narratives, etc. Disyllabic ones may bear accent.

4.2   Sources and stability of enclitics

To the comparative linguist there are some revealing items on this list. The potential mode enclitic in Dakotan and Dhegihan languages is part of a pan-Siouan cognate set: Crow *išši* 'want to', Hidatsa *hte* 'desiderative', Mandan *-kt-* 'future', Dakota *kta* 'potential', Winnebago *kǰe* 'intentive', Omaha *tte*, Kansa *tte*, Osage *hte*, Quapaw *tte* 'potential mode', Biloxi *te* 'want', Tutelo *ta* 'future' Proto-Siouan **kte* (Carter, Jones and Rankin, in preparation). From the distribution of meanings across Siouan, it seems fairly clear that this mode marker is descended historically from a verb meaning approximately 'want' (see Boyle 2000). This is not surprising, nor does it bear directly on our synchronic analysis of Dakotan *kta* or Dhegihan *tte*, but it serves as a warning that many of the post-verbal particles will be found along a continuum of grammaticalised and semi-grammaticalised verbs.

4.3   One word or two: enclitic or auxiliary?

A little farther along, in position ten, *kéya* and *kéya-pi* 'quotative' are reflexes of the common Siouan verb **k-e·he* 'say the preceding'.[10] And, although it is labelled an enclitic, it is still inflected for number with its own enclitic, *-pi* 'plural'. So an enclitic has its own enclitic, and *-pi* appears twice (2 and 10) in the ordering. Deloria consistently writes these as separate, post-verbal words. It is common for a quotative to be derived from a verb of saying, but might this still be a verb synchronically, perhaps an auxiliary? It is no longer inflected for person, aspect or mode, but it retains other verb-like characteristics and has its own internal structure, i.e., an incorporated, frozen deictic object and number marking.

In other Siouan languages there are indeed fully fledged auxiliary verbs denoting various kinds of *Aktionsart* and modality (imperfective, perfective,

---

[10] Most Siouan languages form quotative verbs and particles with **e-he* 'say' but in Dakotan this verb has become contaminated by the phonetically similar verb *iya* 'to speak'.

progressive, causative and negative in Dhegihan). The problem is that these auxiliaries, quasi-auxiliaries and enclitics can be found in varying degrees of grammaticalisation in a single language. They cease to be auxiliaries bit by bit, losing inflection one category at a time. At what point along this continuum do they become enclitics and/or suffixes? We know of no test that will allow us reliably and consistently to assign synchronic status to these partially grammat-icalised constructs. They may certainly form single phonological words with the verb stem in Dakotan and Dhegiha languages, but, as implied in Deloria's (sometimes inconsistent) treatment of them, they may also retain accent and be treated as distinct grammatical and phonological words. In some models their syntactic function may then be different, and they may simply be analysed as higher verbs. Most of what we have said about Dakotan enclitics applies to Crow and other Siouan languages, but in Crow, verbal enclitics apparently do not take accent, and their status as enclitics to a single grammatical and phonological verb is clearer.

4.4   Noun enclitics

Moving briefly to nouns, we find throughout Siouan definite and indefinite articles that attach to the right-most end of noun phrases and are clearly enclitics, as other noun modifiers intervene between the noun proper and the article. Although generally unaccented, articles may on occasion bear accent. Examples here are from Quapaw (Dorsey 1890–94) but are typical of what is found in all five Dhegiha languages: *žą́=khe* 'the.LYING log', *žą́=the* 'the.STANDING tree', *wak ʔį=the* 'the carrying of something', *mažą́ kówa=nįkhe* 'the.SITTING yonder (piece of) land', *kką́tte=ke* 'the.SCATTERED plums'.

4.5   Controversial nature of Siouan enclitics

Zwicky (1985) disagrees with Matthews (1965) as to the nature of the Hidatsa (and, by extension, other Siouan) mood markers. Matthews assumes that, since they are syntactic in nature, and are readjusted through transformations to form phonological words, they are clitics (although he does not use the term 'clitic' overtly). He says that the 'main clause is assured by the presence of the Mood constituent at the end, for only the clauses are followed by Mood' (Matthews 1965: 38). By calling the mood markers constituents, Matthews stresses their fundamental syntactic role. Further, Matthews states that 'constituents, includ-ing those that consist of a single morpheme [i.e., the mood markers], are the important units in Hidatsa syntax'. He contrasts this notion with a description of prefixes (and by extension grammatical suffixes), stating that 'syntactically each prefix is most closely associated with a specific constituent of the sen-tence...'(Matthews 1965: 54). Affixes, whether inflectional or derivational, are not constituents for Matthews, since they do not play a syntactic role. The mood markers, on the other hand, do play a syntactic role, however they cannot stand alone as grammatical words (Boyle 2000). As a result, they attach phonologically to the preceding verb and hence are clitics – syntactic elements that form a phonological word with the preceding verb (Matthews 1965: 267–72) rather than morphological words themselves. This was also Zwicky's (1985: 629) assessment of Matthews' view of the mood markers.

Zwicky argues instead that they are not clitics but affixes based on three criteria (see Zwicky and Pullum 1983): (1) that they belong to a 'relatively small closed system, one of whose members must always appear at the relative place in the structure' (Carstairs 1981: 4), (2) that 'clitics can exhibit a low degree of selection with respect to their hosts, while affixes exhibit a high degree of selection with respect to their stems', and (3) 'morphophonological idiosyncrasies are more characteristic of affixed words than of clitic groups' (Zwicky and Pullum 1983: 503–4).

Graczyk, however, looks upon several of these same phenomena, particularly morphophonological irregularities, as evidence that the mood markers are enclitics in the closely related Crow. The bond that exists between the mood markers and the verb is not as tight as the bond between a verb and an affix.

5   Definitional problems

Overall, one of the central problems here is the impossibility of trying to define a system in terms of itself. Every logical discipline proceeds from undefined terms or domains justified by external hand-waving. Geometry does not define points, lines and surfaces, for example, and grammar can ultimately only define sentences or grammatical words generatively or, less successfully, with nongrammatical clues. The pertinent domain (sentence, word, etc.) is supplied and we merely try to account for the supplied examples. But, given a phonological string, we always lack any really comprehensive set of criteria to characterise words beyond the rules and generalisations about them. Apart from rules, we have to depend on judgements such as 'the speaker felt that this example was not a whole utterance or word', or 'the speaker claimed this was two words, not one long one'. The speaker intuits this from some internal process that we hope our statements approximate.

It is not circularity to assemble examples of words and then claim that a grammar that generates them defines 'word'. It is approximation, if you will. The process of selecting some data that strike us intuitively as words and then seeing if we can account for things on that basis is certainly a case of iterative hypothesis refinement, but it is not circular. The real issue is whether identifying a target – words, affixes, enclitics, etc. – as a domain gets us anywhere. While admitting to some deficiencies in the concepts of word, affix or clitic, very few linguists have suggested the concepts should be rejected, even though there is no real way to define a word or enclitic except by rule (a statement true of perhaps most theoretical terms in linguistics). One may develop heuristic approaches to identifying words, like pauses for breath or thought, or evidential particles or glottal stops or certain allophones, but these will never be sufficient to define words. One cannot define a verb word in Siouan as 'everything between a glottal stop or aspirate and a final evidential'. At best one uses such things as clues during the period in which one has not developed enough of a grammar of words or sentences to be able to recognise them by parsing.

Alternatively one may rely on the native speaker or another, earlier linguist, like Dorsey (1890), Lowie (1930), Boas and Deloria (1941), Robinett (1955), Rood and Taylor (1960), Buechel (1970), Koontz (1985), Zwicky (1985), Graczyk (1991) or de Reuse (1994) and trust their judgement, but that, of course, is informed by their own grammars, however obscure or deficient, and not by their consciousness of where they pause to take a breath.

Ultimately, it is necessary to define grammatical words with a set of rules or templates (these latter will not work well in Siouan). Sooner or later we should be able to parse things in terms of them, or not, and then the case pro, or con, is closed. In short, if the rules finally work and seem to correspond to a reality in which speaker intuition and intra-grammatical considerations hopefully dovetail, they justify themselves. And, of course, that is the crux of the matter: does hypothesising that Siouan phonological words are made up of one or more grammatical words plus particular clitics and affixes get us anywhere? We maintain that it does. Using the concept of grammatical word we can write a simpler grammar, with fewer exceptions than if we try to generate or templatise whole phonological words.

5.1   Implications of linguistic change

Of course many of the kinds of problems discussed at length above remain. They require judgement calls by the individual linguist or speaker. For example, it is probably not the case that it will ever be possible to resolve all of the types and tokens of complex grammatical words into just three classes of objects – words, clitics and affixes – to anyone's satisfaction. The boundary between clitic and affix is inherently unclear in Siouan. We are faced with a *continuum* of affixed, incorporated, cliticised, partially or contextually cliticised, loosely juxtaposed and auxiliary elements, as shown in figure 1.

Syntactic and lexical compounds (or syntactic and lexicalised incorporation) are polar points on this scale, favoured implicitly by Boas and Deloria and by de Reuse. Likewise, inflected auxiliaries and uninflected, or semi-inflected, enclitics are at opposite ends of the continuum. But diachronic study shows that the processes of lexicalisation and grammaticalisation are gradual and that

Productive   Fossilised
syntactic ----------------------(time)-----------------→ lexical(ised)
compounds and   compounds,
conjugated   enclitics and
auxiliaries   affixes

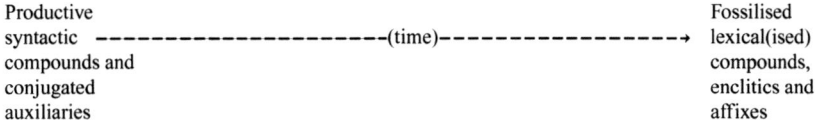

Figure 1 Temporal productivity continuum.

they affect both words and speakers one at a time. It is therefore inherently
unlikely that synchronic linguists, fond as they are of binary categories, will
ever be able to define a precise set of objective criteria that will enable them to
apportion all compounds or incorporations to one or the other category to either
their colleagues' or the speakers' satisfaction (much less both). In cases where
some post-verbal elements are still partially inflected as verbs, as they are in
the Dakotan quotative, it is safe to say that there will be plenty of instances in
which we cannot make a principled determination of their status. This follows
from the very nature of analogical linguistic change.

6   Speakers' concept of 'word'

People do talk about 'words' in their native languages and in English when
speaking about them or attempting to write them. This is not a topic about
which most Siouanists are fully conversant as necessary experimental evidence
is not available, but there is a written tradition at least in Dakotan beginning
with the translation of the Bible into that language well over a century ago and
extending to the sophisticated native analyses of Ella Deloria, in the grammar
she co-authored with Franz Boas (1941) and in her text collections (1932). No
doubt both these works contain the speakers' insights and the grammatical
prejudices of the Bible-translators or of Boas.

Those of us involved with language teaching programmes note that the post-
verbal elements we have described as enclitics tend to be written as separate
words by speakers writing their language for the first time (Kathy Shea, p. c.).
This dovetails fairly well with what Deloria seems to have favoured. The same
writing habits hold for the definite articles that are enclitic to noun phrases. There
does seem to be a certain lack of consistency to all of these efforts however.

The languages themselves do not contain a large variety of expressions for
linguistic elements. In the nine-hundred-page Omaha and Ponca text collection
by James Owen Dorsey, one of his consultants (Dorsey 1890: 134.16) refers to
a sentence as *íe* 'word(s)'. Another (194.11) refers to 'talk' or 'instructions' as
íe=khe 'the (HORIZONTAL) words'. And in the traditional story of Two Faces
(209.5) the narrator says: *Gisíðe=ama íe=the* 'he forgot the (STANDING) words'
in reference to the confusion that falls over Lodge Boy's mind whenever he tries
to tell his father that his secret twin, Spring Boy, has been about. All in all, no

distinction is made among words, sentences, messages, etc. All are *íe*, which may be either a verb or a noun according to position and usage, and which means simply 'speech' or 'to speak'.

6.1   Taboo

In Siouan this concept does not have the significance that it does in some varieties of Austronesian or in Australian languages. One or two observations can be made however. Historically in Siouan the terms for 'black bear' and 'snake' appear to have been the subject of taboo, or at the very least, of large-scale replacement. Most Siouan tribes also practise the mother-in-law taboo; historically, a male may not directly address his mother-in-law. Fletcher and La Flesche (1911) report cases of Omaha language conversations with in-laws carried out by addressing a child who is present. This might explain why the terms for parents-in-law are 'grandfather' and 'grandmother'. Boyle reports that in Hidatsa women and their fathers-in-law are similarly affected, but perhaps to a lesser extent.

7   Conclusion

In this chapter we have tried to present some of the complexities involved in the concept of 'word' in several Siouan languages. These languages possess the concept, perhaps most easily defined as a stretch of speech that has a single primary accent, but where the internal structure of the word is not easily amenable to generation by any extension of simple syntactic rules. Prefix ordering is complex, the product of a long history of incorporations and idiosyncratic layerings. Enclitic ordering is syntactically more systematic, but the status of enclitics is harder to determine on principled grounds because of the varying degrees of grammaticalisation and accentability found among them.

Anecdotally, from the tale of Two Faces, there is the briefest mention of language acquisition by Lodge Boy and his secret twin, Spring Boy (Dorsey 1890: 148.14–15).

(16)	kki	šígažíga	akkíwa	íe	wakką́dagi=
	and	children	both	to.speak	they.were.enchanted
	hną=	bi=	ama		
	HABIT.	PL	QUOTATIVE		

and they say both the children were enchanted in speaking

In this context *wakką́dagi* 'sorcerer, be enchanted' appears to mean just 'they were precocious in speaking'. This idiom is elsewhere applied to walking, sitting (of babies), running and using the bow. It seems to imply that precocity requires a spirit sponsor. Perhaps defining the word in Siouan does too.

References

Boas, F. and Deloria, E. 1941. *Dakota Grammar*, Vol. 23, 2nd Memoir, National Academy of Sciences. Washington: Government Printing Office.

Boyle, J. P. 2000. 'The Hidatsa causative and future markers: a parallel development?', Paper presented at the Siouan and Caddoan Languages Conference, Anadarko, Oklahoma.

Buechel, E. 1970. *A dictionary of the Teton Dakota Sioux language*, edited by P. Manhart. Pine Ridge: Red Cloud Indian School.

Carstairs, A. 1981. *Notes on affixes, clitics, and paradigms*. Bloomington: Indiana University Linguistics Club.

Carter, R. T., Jones, A. W. and Rankin, R. L., et al., eds. In preparation. Siouan comparative dictionary. Computer database.

Comrie, B. 1989. *Language universals and linguistic typology*. Oxford: Basil Blackwell.

Deloria, Ella. 1932. *Dakota texts*. Publications of the American Ethnological Society 14. New York: Stechert.

de Reuse, W. 1994. 'Noun incorporation in Lakota (Siouan)', *International Journal of American Linguistics* 60.199–260.

Dorsey, J. O. 1890. *The ¢egiha language*, Contributions to North American Ethnography 6. Washington: Government Printing Office.

1890–94. Quapaw texts, dictionary and grammar notes, ms. collection of the National Anthropological Archives. Smithsonian Institution, Washington, DC.

Dorsey, J. O. and Swanton, J. R. 1912. *A dictionary of the Biloxi and Ofo languages: accompanied with thirty-one Biloxi texts and numerous Biloxi phrases*, Bureau of American Ethnology Bulletin 47. Washington: Government Printing Office.

Fletcher, A. and La Flesche, F. 1911. *The Omaha tribe*, Bureau of American Ethnology Annual Report 27. Washington: Government Printing Office.

Graczyk, R. 1991. 'Incorporation and cliticization in Crow morphosyntax'. PhD dissertation, University of Chicago.

Hayes, B. 1995. *Metrical stress theory*. Chicago: University of Chicago Press.

Koontz, J. E. 1985. Omaha grammar notes, ms.

Lowie, R. 1930. 'Hidatsa texts – with grammatical notes and phonograph transcriptions by Zellig Harris and C. F. Voegelin', Prehistory research series, Vol. 1, no. 6. Indianapolis: Indiana Historical Society.

Matthews, G. H. 1965. *Hidatsa syntax*. The Hague: Mouton.

Mithun, M. 1984. 'The evolution of noun incorporation', *Language* 60.847–94.

Oliverio, G. R. M. 1996. 'A grammar and dictionary of Tutelo'. PhD dissertation, University of Kansas.

Rankin, R. L. 1986. Quapaw–English lexicon, ms.

1987. Kansa–English lexicon, ms.

Robinett, F. M. 1955. 'Hidatsa I, II, III', *International Journal of American Linguistics* 21.1–7, 160–77, 210–16.

Rood, D. S. and Taylor, A. R. 1996. 'Lakhota', pp. 440–82 of *Handbook of North American Indians*, Vol. 17, edited by I. Goddard. Washington: Smithsonian Institution Press.

Sadock, J. M. 1991. *Autolexical syntax: a theory of parallel grammatical representations*. Chicago: University of Chicago Press.

Sapir, E. 1921. *Language*. New York: Harcourt Brace.

Trechter, S. J. 1995. 'The pragmatic functions of gendered clitics in Lakhota'. PhD dissertation, University of Kansas.

Zwicky, A. M. 1985. 'Cliticization versus inflection: the Hidatsa mood markers', *International Journal of American Linguistics* 51.629–30.

Zwicky, A. M. and Pullum, G. K. 1983. 'Cliticization vs. inflection: English *n't,*' *Language* 59.502–13.

8   What is a word in Dagbani?

Knut J. Olawsky

Dagbani is a Gur language spoken by approximately five hundred thousand people (Dagbamba/Dagombas) in Northern Ghana. With regard to morphological typology, Dagbani can be described as agglutinative with some degree of fusion: certain combinations of morphemes may be obscured by phonological and morphophonological rules. Most affixes in the language occur as suffixes, with a few prefixes to verbs. Compounding of verbal or nominal roots is common; typically, the output will be a noun. Syntactically, Dagbani is strictly AVO, SV; however frontshifting of objects or other non-verbal elements is very common.

As far as the status of the word is concerned, the language displays a number of interesting features. These include the structure of possible minimal words (§1.5), the role of noun–adjective constructions which surface as morphological compounds (§2.1), and adjectival derivations that illustrate the phenomenon of 'bound words' (§2.2). Dagbani also has a number of proclitic and enclitic elements, which is interesting, since most languages that are predominantly suffixing tend not to have proclitics (see Aikhenvald in chapter 2).

The following sections describe how Dagbani words can be characterised with respect to their relationship to phonology, morphology and syntax/ semantics.

1   Phonological word

As pointed out in chapter 1, the distinction between grammatical and phonological word is often difficult to make. Among the criteria for the definition of a phonological word, some of the following have been suggested, although there are problematic cases:
- boundaries defined by stress or tone;
- pauses (e.g. in dictation);
- phonological rules specifically applying to a word.

These criteria are language-specific, i.e. a word in one language can be defined by certain criteria, and in another language, by others. A phonological word is usually composed of smaller prosodic units such as feet, syllables or moras (which in turn are built from combinations of segments).

In order to define the status of 'word' in Dagbani, several of these criteria can be employed. There are a number of phonological phenomena that can best be defined if one assumes the phonological word as their domain. Examples will be given below (§§1.1–1.3). Regarding the behaviour of Dagbani speakers with respect to pauses in dictation or natural fluent speech, no systematic data is available; therefore, I will not comment on this criterion. Stress is definitely assigned to a phonological word (cf. §1.2). Tone, in contrast, appears to be only marginally related to the word: while the syllable functions as the tone-bearing unit, there is also evidence that the morpheme plays an important role in tone assignment.[1] Further discussion will follow in §1.3.

1.1   *Syllable structure and word boundaries*

The basic syllable structure of Dagbani is (C)V(V)(N), with a few deviations from this (e.g. syllabic nasals occur) and some restrictions on coda consonants. The second V position represents vowel length; diphthongs occur only in loan-words. Most phonological words are disyllabic (e.g. 76 per cent of all simplex nouns), although monosyllabic words are very common as well (especially verbs). Words containing more than two syllables are less frequent.

In contrast to the structure of Dagbani syllables, the boundaries of a phono-logical word are subject to certain restrictions:
1. Whereas a word-internal syllable can end in [m, n, ŋ, l, r, b, ɣ], the only coda consonants allowed in word-final position are [m, ŋ] (with a small number of exceptions).[2]
2. At the beginning of a word, the distribution of consonants is also constrained: [r, h] are not found in this position (but this is also due to the fact that they are allophones of [d, s], respectively).

1.2   *Stress*

Stress in Dagbani is not contrastive and applies to syllables as units of the phonological word as its domain, rather than to morphologically defined struc-tures. A phonological word bears exactly one main stress which in Dagbani predictably falls on the penultimate syllable. This pattern applies consistently and holds for simplex and complex words of all categories. The regular penulti-mate stress pattern is illustrated below, applying to words of various categories, length and morphological structure.

---

[1] As the transcription of tones is not relevant to the discussion in this chapter, all examples are generally given in Dagbani orthography, which omits statement of tones.

[2] Note that not all of these sounds are phonemes; therefore, they are represented with their phonetic values. Specifically, [r] and [ɣ] are allophones of /d/ and /g/, respectively. The following is a complete list of Dagbani phonemes: /p, t, k, b, d, g, k͡p, g͡b, ŋm, n, m, ɲ, ŋ, f, s, v, z, l, ʋ, j/ and /a, e, o, i, u, ə/.

(1)   Penultimate stress

      a. Morphologically simple words

guŋa	['gu.ŋa]	'kapok tree'
kpuŋkpaŋa	[k͡puŋ.'k͡pa.ŋa]	'wing'
naanzua	[naːn.'zu.a]	'pepper'

      b. Compounds

bin-piel-li	[bən.'pjɛl.li]	(thing-white-sg)	'shroud'
dulim-bil-ga	[du.ləm.'bəl.ga]	(urinate-well-sg)	'urinating hole'
ashibiti-bil-a	[a.ʃib.ti.'bə.la]	(hospital-small-sg)	'clinic'

At first sight, some words seem to deviate from this regularity in that they display either final or antepenultimate stress. A look at the examples in (2) reveals that the difference is of a systematic nature: these nouns bear their stress on the antepenultimate syllable in the singular.

(2)   Antepenultimate stress on words containing an epenthetic vowel

chihili, chiha	['tɕi.hə.li, 'tɕi.ha]	'tribal scar'-sg, pl
sabisigu, sabisa	['sab.sə.gu, 'sab.sa]	'gecko'-sg, pl
gahindili, gahinda	[ga.'hin.də.li, ga.'hin.da]	'interesting'-sg, pl

However, they have something else in common: the singular forms of all these words contain an epenthetic vowel [ə] in the penultimate syllable. This vowel is transparent for stress assignment and is therefore disregarded. Evidence for the underlying penultimate stress pattern on the words in (2) is found when we look at the plural forms of these words. Since no epenthetic vowel is necessary in this context, the stress pattern is regular. The other type of words that deviate from the regular pattern are shown in (3). In contrast to other nouns, their singular forms are stressed on the final syllable.

(3)   Irregular stress on nouns ending in a nasal consonant or long vowel

niŋgbuŋ, niŋgbuna	[nəŋ.g͡buŋ nəŋ.g͡bu.na]	'body'-sg/pl
dachee, dachɛhi	[da.'tɕeː, da.'tɕɛ.hi]	'playmate'-sg/pl

Note that the plural forms consistently follow the penultimate pattern – a fact which demonstrates the underlying stress pattern for the singular as well. The deviations from the regular stress pattern can be understood if the singular forms of these examples are taken as 'shortened' versions of the underlying form. Although a word like *kunduŋ* /kun.dun/ 'hyena' is clearly disyllabic, its stress pattern reflects an underlying sequence of three syllables, as is demonstrated by its plural form *kunduna* /kun.du.na/.[3] Further evidence for underlying invisible

---

[3] Note that the underlying form of 'hyena' is /kundun/; there is, however, a velarisation rule that applies to word-final /n/, which leads to the realisation as [kunduŋ] (cf. §1.4.1).

units in Dagbani can be found in tone assignment, where nasals and long vowels function as tone-bearing units word-finally only (cf. §1.3).

Now supposing that a final 'empty' syllable belongs to the structure of words ending in a nasal consonant, a word like *kunduŋ* can be represented as /kun.'dun.X/, where 'X' represents the invisible prosodic unit, i.e. a syllable. Stress has access to this structure and is correctly placed on /dun/. Therefore, we can now claim for the above-mentioned nominal forms that a catalectic syllable in words ending in CVN or CVV provides the solution for the apparent mismapping of stress and syllabic structure.

The examples discussed above illustrate the consistency of penultimate stress assignment in Dagbani. In addition, it has been shown that we have to assume a more complex prosodic structure for certain lexical items in that they involve underlying units which have systematic effects on the prosodic realisation of the word.

1.3   Tone

As mentioned earlier, tone plays a secondary role in the recognition of a word in Dagbani. Most tonal rules indeed apply across word boundaries; one example of this is rightward High Tone Spreading (cf. Olawsky 1999). Nevertheless, there are a few cases that show how tone assignment interacts with word boundaries; I will mention just two here.

(1) On the prosodic level, there seems to be a constraint that disallows words with an all-Low tone pattern, so every word has at least one High tone. While High Tone Spreading generally applies from left to right across word boundaries, Hyman (1993) postulates a High Tone Anticipation rule where a High tone spreads leftward from a suffix to a toneless root. Olawsky (1999) proposes a different solution for toneless roots having a High tone, which is related to tone assignment by stress. However, while the two authors assume different kinds of processes are at work, both proposals operate with rules applying to the domain of the word.

(2) The discussion on stress in the previous section revealed that tone assignment is related to word structure in that suffix tones are placed on CVV and CVN syllables under certain conditions. Whereas a contrastive tone is never assigned to nasals and long vowels in CVN and CVV syllables word-internally, it is placed on the last syllable of the word.

1.4   The word as domain for phonological rules

1.4.1 Velarisation of final /n/ A look at the phonological rules related to the structure of Dagbani words reveals that many alternations apply to units smaller than the word. In most cases, they apply to the domain of the syllable. However, one example which applies to the phonological word will be mentioned here: words that underlyingly end in the nasal consonant /n/ are realised with [ŋ]. This velarisation rule applies exclusively at the end of a phonological word; *kunduŋ* 'hyena' is an example already mentioned in §1.2. This rule applies to all nouns and verbs.

1.4.2 Vowel harmony The other phenomenon that plays a certain (though peripheral) role in Dagbani phonology is cross height vowel harmony. Its effects are weaker in Dagbani than they are in some of its neighbouring languages; however, there is at least a tendency for root vowels to affect suffix vowels. This is described below.

In general, [−ATR] ('lax') and [+ATR] ('tense') vowels are not distinctive in Dagbani; they occur as allophones of each other, as two sets of [ɛ, ɔ, ʊ, ɨ] versus [e, o, u, i].[4] However, Kropp-Dakubu (1997) observes certain regularities in the distribution of [+ATR] and [−ATR] vowels in Dagbani which indicate a systematic occurrence of the two vowel sets with respect to the phonological word. In particular, she makes the observation that certain vowels in the root ('nucleus') of a word are followed by a second set of vowels in the suffix ('coda') of a word. Though Kropp-Dakubu only lists examples from disyllabic nouns, vowel harmony is also found in some words whose root is longer than one syllable. The following table illustrates the possible combinations of vowels in roots and suffixes. Thus, the root vowels [a, ɛ, ɔ, ʊ, ɨ] are followed by a member of the same set in the suffix so that the feature [−ATR] is found in both morphemes of the word. Similarly, the [+ATR] vowels [o, u, i] in the nucleus trigger a vowel of the same set in the coda. For [a], the contrast [+/−ATR] is neutralised.

(4)　　[ATR] vowel harmony in Dagbani

root	suffix	root	suffix
[−ATR]	[−ATR]	[+ ATR]	[+ATR]
[a]	[a]	[i]	[i]
[ɛ]	[ɛ]	[u]	[u]
[ɔ]	[ɔ]	[o]	[o]
[ʊ]	[ʊ]	([e])	[a]
[ɨ/ə][5]	[ɨ]		([e])

---

[4] According to Olawsky (1999), tense and lax vowels are not different phonemes, as they are not distinctive in any other context. An analysis involving two different sets of vowels that can both occur in a root, however, would have to postulate that all eight vowels could be underlying, and therefore could be phonemes. As a solution to this, it would be necessary to analyse the segmental environment for each vowel in the root. Olawsky (1999) makes some observations that can predict the occurrence of tense and lax vowels in a root at least tendentially.

[5] Kropp-Dakubu uses [ɨ] for schwa or a schwa-like vowel. Here, it will be represented as [ə].

In contrast to the examples that display cross height vowel harmony, there are words which do not feature this phenomenon. There are at least three contexts that exclude vowel harmony.

(1) Many disyllabic roots arbitrarily contain two vowels of different harmony sets, which may suggest that predictable vowel harmony in Dagbani is limited to combinations of monosyllabic roots with a suffix.

(2) Another instance is the blocking of harmony when an epenthetic schwa is inserted between the root and the suffix. Epenthetic schwa occurs with all root types, regardless of their feature value for [ATR], and it blocks vowel harmony. For instance, the root vowel of *bihili* /bih-li/ 'breast' is clearly [+ATR]; however, the suffix vowel tends to be realised [−ATR] (→ [bihəlı]), and the only visible trigger is the neighbouring epenthetic schwa.

(3) In compounds, each constituent's vowels keep their own [ATR] values, as is also confirmed by Kropp-Dakubu (1997). The word for 'hencoop', *nosɔɣu* /no-so-gu/ 'fowl-stall'-sg, is realised as [no.sɔ.ɣʋ], the vowel in the first part ('fowl') being realised [+ATR], and the second part ('stall') having [−ATR] vowels. Thus, Dagbani compounds represent single grammatical words with two 'vowel harmony units'. One cannot say that these are phonological words, as only one main stress is present.

The examples in (5) and (6) illustrate the distribution of [+/−ATR] vowels in words with monosyllabic and polysyllabic roots respectively.

(5)   Vowel harmony across morpheme boundaries: monosyllabic roots

	feature	root	suffix	example		gloss
a.	[−ATR]	[a]	[ɪ]	zali	[zalɪ]	'anvil'-sg
		[ɛ]	[ɪ]	biɛri	[bjɛrɪ]	'day'-pl
		[ɔ]	[ʋ]	yɔrigu	[jɔrgʋ]	'lid'-sg
		[ʋ]	[ɪ]	luɣili	[lʋɣlɪ]	'side'-sg
		[ə]	[a]	siliga	[səlga]	'cave'-sg
b.	[+ATR]	[i]	[u]	dirigu	[dirgu]	'spoon'-sg
		[i]	[o]	chibo	[tçibo]	'soap'-sg
		[o]	[o]	polo	[polo]	'side'-sg
		[u]	[o]	tumo	[tumo]	'messenger'-sg
		[u]	[i]	wuni	[ʋuni]	'god'-sg

(6)   Vowel harmony across morpheme boundaries: polysyllabic roots

	feature	V1	V2	suffix	example		gloss
a.	[−ATR]	[a]	[ə]	[ɪ]	kpakpuli	[kp͡akpəlɪ]	'tortoise'-sg
		[ɛ]	[ɛ]	[ɪ]	jenjɛni	[dʒɛndʒɛnɪ]	'type of coin'-sg
		[ʋ]	[ɔ]	[a]	dundɔna	[dʋndɔna]	'courtyard'-pl
		[ə]	[ə]	[ɪ]	bimbini	[bəmbənɪ]	'altar'-sg

b. [+ATR] [i] [i] [a]   pipia   [pipia]   'type of calabash'-sg
       [i] [u] [a]   nintua   [nintua] 'ring'-sg
       [o] [o] [i]   pololi   [pololi] 'frog'-sg
       [o] [i] [o]   dɔbino   [dobino] 'date fruit'-sg

When a root contains a long vowel (which is always realised [+ATR]), such as in *kpeeni* 'important', the final /i/ is realised as [+ATR] [i] as well, whereas the final /i/ in *nɛli* 'millstone' is pronounced as [−ATR] [ɪ] because it is preceded by the [−ATR] vowel [ɛ]. As mentioned above, lexical exceptions are mostly found with nouns that have disyllabic (or longer) roots; disharmony may be found inside the root, whereas the suffix usually takes the [ATR] value of the last vowel.

(7)   Vowel disharmony in disyllabic roots
    [i] – [ɛ] – [ɪ]   gbingbɛli   [ĝbinĝbɛlɪ]   'mud'-N
    [i] – [ɛ] – [a]   chinchɛŋga [tɕintɕɛŋga] 'kebab'-sg
    [i] – [ɔ] – [ɪ]   nyingoli   [ɲingɔlɪ]   'neck'-sg
    [u] – [ɔ] – [ɪ]   kukoli   [kukɔlɪ]   'voice'-sg

These examples, apart from the cases that are ruled out by epenthesis or complex lexical structure, lead to the following conclusion: while vowel harmony functions within certain contexts in Dagbani, its occurrence is predictable only for disyllabic nouns. In these cases, vowel harmony can be used to define a phonological word. As far as longer nouns are concerned, some follow the rule, whereas others show disharmonic behaviour.

1.5 The minimal word requirement in Dagbani

In many languages, there is a requirement that the minimal length of a phonological word be bimoraic. This usually applies to lexical categories, whereas grammatical markers or particles (which may be characterised as clitics in some cases) may be shorter than this. Regarding the structure of most nouns in Dagbani, one realises that Dagbani tends to have similar preferences: typical simplex nouns are at least disyllabic, including those surfacing as CVV or CVN, as mentioned earlier.

Non-lexical categories in Dagbani tend rather to be short, i.e. they typically have a CV structure, as those displayed in (8). This also includes a number of words which might be considered adverbials.

(8)   Some monomoraic non-lexical morphemes in Dagbani
    ku   /ku/   negative future marker
    sa   /sa/   proximality marker
    kpe   /k͡pe/   'here'
    gba   /g͡ba/   'also'

On the other hand, Dagbani has a small number of nouns which – despite their status as lexical categories – are clearly monomoraic. Some of these are listed below:

(9)   Monomoraic nouns
      ba   /ba/   'father'-sg; 'ride'
      ma   /ma/   'mother'-sg
      zo   /zo/   'friend'-sg; 'run'
      za   /za/   'millet'

The monomoraic status of these words is confirmed by the fact that *ba* and *ma* contrast with the same words with a long vowel *baa* 'dog, swamp' and *maa* (definite article). In addition to these nouns, there are many verbs which have the structure CV. Verbs like *di/ba/nyu* 'eat'/'ride'/'drink' are very common. Speakers have no difficulty in identifying these units as 'complete words'. But in spoken language, these verbal roots do not normally occur in isolation: in their citation form, they are typically accompanied by the prefix /n-/. In sentences, they occur in combination with a pronoun, and (often) with a suffix indicating the perfective or imperfective form (as all verbs do, regardless of their length). On the other hand, it must be assumed that these verbs, as well as the nouns mentioned above, are stored as monomoraic lexical entries in the lexicon. This leads to the conclusion that Dagbani phonological words tend to satisfy the minimal word requirement.

2   Grammatical word

The well-formedness of a word in Dagbani strongly depends on its category. All lexical categories fulfil the conditions for grammatical words mentioned by Dixon and Aikhenvald in chapter 1, in that they contain elements that always occur together. Secondly, lexical roots and their respective suffixes occur in fixed order and, thirdly, the combination of root and suffix has a conventionalised meaning. For instance, nouns and adjectives consistently contain a root and a number suffix which belongs to one of five classes. Abstract nouns do not have such a class suffix, but may display derivational suffixes. Several roots may be combined to form a compound which in turn will have exactly one class suffix. Similarly, most verbs also consist of a root and a suffix; a large number of verbs, however, have the structure CV or CVN and do not display any suffix (*lu* 'fall', *baŋ* 'know'). There are verbs of the structure CVCN that end in a nasal; these contain an epenthetic vowel (/bohm/ → [bɔ.həm] 'learn') which makes them disyllabic on the surface. The other type of verb has a CVV or CVC root and ends in the verbal suffix /-i/ (*gbaa-i* 'catch', *kul-i* 'go home').[6]

---

[6] Note that this vowel is not suffixed to CV and CVN verbs for partly phonotactic reasons. /i/ can neither follow a short vowel other than /i/ nor be preceded by /ŋ/.

2.1 Compounding

In the sections above, a (grammatical) word always consisted of one lexical morpheme and – in most cases – of an affixal extension of some kind. I will now turn to more complex structures which are still word-like, but are composed of different morphemes or even other grammatical words. In Dagbani (as probably in many other languages), compounds consisting of only two lexical roots are the most common compounds. Fewer, but still numerous compounds contain three roots, while words longer than that are rare. Three main types of compounds occur: noun–noun, noun–adjective and verb–noun.

One productive type of compound involves a noun root followed by an adjective. Plural is marked only on the morphological head: the singular of /bən-pjel-li/ 'shroud' (cf. (10a)), for instance, ends in /-li/ and therefore the word is inflected according to number class 1a, i.e., the plural will be /bən-pjel-a/ 'shrouds'. /ʋag-ze-gu/ 'type of snake' in (10b) pluralises as expected: as a class 4a noun, ending in /-gu/, its plural form is ʋag-ze-ri/.

(10)   noun–adjective
    a. binpiɛlli   /bən-pjel-li/   (thing-white-sg)   'shroud, white calico'-sg
    b. waɣiʒɛɣu   /ʋag-ze-gu/   (snake-red-sg)   'type of snake'-sg
    c. tikpilli   /ti-kpəl-li/   (medicine-round-sg)   'medical pill'-sg
    d. gbanpiɛlli   /gban-pjel-li/   (skin-white-sg)   'Western person'-sg

Noun–noun compounds, and words composed of a verb plus a noun, have a comparable structure. For example, the word for 'hail', *sakuɣili*, contains the elements /sa-/ 'rain' and /kug-li/ 'stone'(-sg). Similarly, verbs can form the initial part of a compound, as in /bagsi-kug-li/ 'grinding stone'(-sg), where /bagsi/ means 'grind'.

All Dagbani compounds have one main stress (which predictably falls on the penultimate syllable, cf. §1.2). This supports the view that they are each one phonological word as well as one grammatical word. On the tonal level, each root in a compound keeps its lexical tone (which may be altered by tonal rules, such as spreading). As previously mentioned (cf. §1.4.2) vowel harmony does not apply within compounds, as each root has its own [ATR] value.

Another property of compounds is that they are at least trisyllabic. This is consistent with the fact that they consist minimally of two roots (which each contain a syllable) and a suffix. The suffix, too, will usually contain a vowel; in some cases this vowel can be catalectic and surface only in the plural form, as was shown in §1.2.

I will not discuss all possible combinations here, although one merits particular interest. One may distinguish lexicalised and semantically transparent compounds. In lexicalised compounds, the single elements may not display their original meaning any more; their semantic structure is fossilised and the combination of both parts results in a new meaning for the whole. Note that the example in (10a), for instance, is lexicalised, but it may well occur as a spontaneously produced construction of noun plus adjective, referring to a 'white thing', and not necessarily to a 'shroud'. Such noun–adjective constructions are particularly interesting since these ad hoc combinations of nouns and adjectives in a nominal phrase containing an adjectival phrase are built in the very same way as lexicalised noun–adjective compounds – which may be a good reason to call these constructions 'compounds'. Accordingly, plural is only marked on the morphological head at the right word boundary. As mentioned above, adjectives have the same morphological structure as nouns, as they consist of a singular and a plural form which are characterised as belonging to a specific number class.[7] When an adjective and a noun are combined in any ad hoc construction, the noun (being in initial position) loses its class suffix; what remains is only the nominal root, followed by the adjective. The number specification of the phrase is determined solely by the class suffix on the adjective. The singular or plural suffix in this position is the inherent suffix of the adjective. For instance, the root *yil-* of the class 3 noun *yil-ga* 'horn'-sg, as illustrated in (11a), will be in first position of a construction with the (class 1) adjective *piɛl-li* 'white'-sg as the second element. The resulting form *yil-piɛl-li* 'white horn' has only one suffix, namely the class 1 suffix /-li/ of the adjective. Plural formation ('white horns') is realised according to class 1 of the adjective as well (*yil-kar-a*). While 'horn' in this example is clearly the semantic head, its morphological features are neutralised and unambiguously determined by the adjective, i.e. its suffix.

(11)   Noun–adjective compounds with canonical nouns

	a.	yil-ga, yil-si	'horn'-sg, pl	+	piɛl-li, piɛl-a	'white'-sg, pl
	→	yil-piɛl-li	'white horn'			
		yil-piɛl-a	'white horns'			
	b.	paɣ-a, paɣ-ba	'woman'-sg, pl	+	kasi, kasi-nima	'holy'-sg, pl
	→	paɣ-kasi	'holy woman'			
		paɣ-kasi-nima	'holy women'			

The same applies to noun–adjective compounds which involve a type B adjective (cf. note 7), as in (11b): the noun is realised in its root form, whereas the pseudo-adjective is unmarked in the singular. For plural formation, the default plural marker *-nima* is attached to the adjective. This final suffix marks the whole phrase as [+plural].

---

[7] This applies to canonical adjectives (type A). Dagbani has another type of adjective (type B) that is pluralised like loans and which differs from type A by various morphological and syntactic features. A detailed discussion of these differences is in preparation (Olawsky and Ortmann 2002).

The status of these constructions as morphological compounds is further supported by the fact that their structure corresponds to that of noun–noun compounds: given the case that *yil*-is combined with a second noun, the plural will be realised in the same way as in an noun–adjective compound, depending on the class membership of the second word. Additional evidence for the status of noun–adjective constructions as compounds can also be drawn from their stress pattern: similarly to lexical compounds, noun–adjective constructions also bear only one main stress. Their tonal behaviour further strengthens this view, though this cannot be discussed here (for further analysis, cf. Olawsky 1999).[8] Vowel harmony does not occur in noun–adjective constructions, which further supports the idea that they are compounds in which each component keeps its own [ATR] value (cf. §1.4.2).

2.2   *Adjectival derivations*

Another aspect of adjective compounding relates to the existence of a group of morphemes whose status appears to be intermediate between grammatical words and derivational suffixes. These elements have almost the same status as adjectives, since their ending corresponds to one of the number classes; as a result, they form their plural according to the respective class. The crucial difference is that these are bound morphemes, i.e. they cannot stand in isolation (while regular adjectives can). Semantically, they describe a closed class of animate referents, being translatable as 'male', 'female' or 'young', respectively. With some words, however, they also mean 'big' (for 'male') or 'small' (for 'female').

(12)   Adjectival elements for 'male', 'female', and 'young'

a.	/-la-a/ 'male'	naɣ-(g)u 'cow'-sg	→	naɣ-laa, naɣ-la-hi 'bull'-sg/pl
		lun-ga 'hourglass drum'-sg	→	lun-daa, lun-da-hi 'big hourglass drum'-sg/pl
b.	/-lo-gu/ 'male'	no-o 'fowl'-sg	→	no-lɔɣu, no-lɔ-ri 'cock'-sg/pl
		so-li 'way'-sg	→	so-lɔɣu, so-lɔ-ri 'main road'-sg/pl

---

[8] While NPs of the structure noun–adjective can be regarded as compounds on the basis of the above discussion, other elements that can be part of an NP, such as determiners or quantifiers, do not form part of it, as they follow the noun–adjective construction and form independent phonological and grammatical words, e.g. [noun–adjective] demonstrative *do-titan-a ŋɔ* 'these big men'.

c. /-ɲaŋ/   no-o   →   no-nyaŋ, no-nyam-a   'hen'-sg/pl
   'female'   'fowl'-sg

           nag-gu   →   naɣ-nyaŋ, naɣ-nyam-a   'female cow'-sg/pl
           'cow'-sg

/-sa-a/   nag-gu   →   naɣ-saa, naɣ-sa-hi   'young cow'-sg/pl
'young'   'cow'-sg

Similar to constructions with free adjectives, the plural formation of these compounds follows the inherent forms of the two suffixes /-la-a/ and /-lo-gu/ according to the number classes 3f and 4a, respectively; i.e., /-la-a/ has the plural /-la-si/ ([lahi]), whereas the plural of /-lo-gu/ is /-lo-di/ ([lɔri]). Plural formation for 'young' and 'female' functions accordingly.

The hypothesis that these constructions are to be characterised as both one phonological word and one grammatical word is further supported by the fact that only one syllable bears stress. At the same time they are compounds, as both components can have different [ATR] values (cf. §1.4.2).

The most interesting aspect is the intermediate status of the adjectival elements in these constructions: they are obviously not words, since they cannot stand in isolation. They are not clitics, since they are morphologically complex and with respect to other features are not comparable to the class of clitics (cf. §3). For the same reason, they cannot be defined as suffixes, as they are composed of a lexical (root) element and an ending that forms a plural, i.e. a suffix. Going back to their function and meaning, and comparing them to actual adjectives, the best way to characterise these elements is as bound adjectives – apparently a rare category of lexical item. As a unit, these bound words also display a significant mismatch between phonological and grammatical word: while they are grammatical words, they cannot constitute a separate phonological word.

In summary – leaving aside the matter of vowel harmony – all Dagbani compounds represent both one phonological and one grammatical word.

3   Clitics

The status of clitics is usually characterised as something 'between' an affix and a word. Whereas a clitic functions as a grammatical word, it usually lacks certain features of a phonological word:

(1) It does not bear stress.
(2) It is attached to a host phonological word, rather than occurring in isolation.

There is, in addition, a property that all clitic-like elements in Dagbani share: they do not engage in vowel harmony with their hosts. Their tonal behaviour can be very complex: as reported in Hyman and Olawsky (forthcoming), their tonal structure is strongly influenced by the tonal pattern that applies according to each grammatical construction (which will override the lexical tones).

Table 1 *Non-emphatic pronouns*

	pre-verbal	post-verbal
1sg	n, m	ma
2sg	a	a
3sg [+animate]	o	o
3sg [−animate]	di	li
1pl	ti	ti
2pl	yi	ya
3pl [+animate]	bi	ba
3pl [−animate]	di, ŋa	li, ŋa

3.1   Pronouns

Dagbani pronouns are good candidates for being considered clitics, as their structure seems to accord with the factors mentioned above. Dagbani has emphatic and non-emphatic pronouns, both of which distinguish person, number and animacy (third person only). The non-emphatic pre-verbal and post-verbal pronouns are shown in table 1. The shape and the distribution of the non-emphatic pronouns indicate that they should be regarded as clitics, as they display the following properties:

• They usually do not stand alone, but occur together with other words.
• The phonological structure of those pronouns which contain schwa (these are *də, lə, tə* and *bə*, but <i> is used in the orthography) does not correspond to a phonological word, since they can be characterised as consisting of a consonant plus transitional vowel, i.e. if we represent the third person singular pronoun as /d/, for instance, where the schwa is epenthetic. This makes /d/, /l/, /t/ and /b/ non-syllabic, which means that these have to be attached to a phonological host by some means.
• Apart from the fact that the non-syllabic pronouns cannot occur without a host, none of the non-emphatic pronouns can bear stress.
• The fact that vowel harmony does not apply across a clitic boundary further strengthens the view that they are not affixes (which also follows from syntactic evidence, as other non-prefixal elements can occur between pronouns and verbs).

These arguments suffice to justify treating the non-emphatic pronouns discussed in this work as proclitics.

It should be noted that the set of possessive pronouns (occurring in pre-nominal position) is identical to the pre-verbal pronouns. Another aspect worth mentioning is that pre-verbal and post-verbal pronouns are closely related in that they share the initial consonant. Whereas the unmarked (pre-verbal) pronouns tend to consist of a consonant plus schwa, the post-verbal pronouns end in the vowel [a], but have the initial consonant in common with their pre-verbal counterparts.

In summary, as non-emphatic pronouns can be regarded as grammatical words, but not as phonological words, they can be characterised as clitics.

3.2   *Pre-verbal markers*

A more controversial issue than the definition of non-emphatic pronouns as proclitics is the status of a number of so called 'markers' for tense, proximality, aspect and negation which are listed here:

(13)   List of pre-verbal markers
        /nə/, /ku/   future tense markers (affirmative, negative)
        /də/, /sa/, /da:/   proximality ('time depth') markers
        /bə/   negation markers (non-future)

One extreme would be to call these prefixes, as each of them can occur adjacent to a verbal root; on the other hand, one might regard them as independent words, since some of them are not necessarily unstressed or phonologically 'weak'. In the following, the status of each of these markers will be discussed.

   3.2.1 Tense markers Tense is expressed by elements which occur before the verb. More precisely, only future tense has such markers, *ni* (affirmative) and *ku* (negative), whereas past or present (= 'non-future') does not need any specific marking. A sentence without explicit tense marking may be past or present, depending on the context.

(14)   Use of future marker *ni* (/nə/)
        a. n   chaŋ   daa.
           1sg   go   market
           I went to the market.
        b. n   ni   chaŋ   daa.
           1sg   FUT   go   market
           I will go to the market.
        c. o   ku   chaŋ   daa.
           3sg   FUT:NEG   go   market
           He will not go to the market.

There are several typical features of a phonological word that *ni* and *ku* lack:
(1) phonological weakness of *nə*, whose nucleus is a (probably epenthetic) schwa, and which is reduced to [n] after vowels (i.e. almost always);
(2) both markers never bear stress and are therefore not phonological words;

(3) *nə* and *ku* always occur adjacent to a verbal root;

(4) neither can be used in isolation and no other elements ever occur between a future marker and the verbal root.

These criteria show that the future tense markers are also deficient as clitics, based on the assumption that clitics are grammatical words, but lack features of a phonological word. *Ni* and *ku* cannot be characterised as grammatical words as they do neither constitute units in isolation, but are always part of a verb. This leads to the conclusion that they are prefixes.

3.2.2 Proximality markers Dagbani has three grammatical elements which indicate the proximality, or 'time depth', of an event, being in the past or in the future.

(15)　List of proximality markers

　　　di [də]　　'earlier same day' (only with past)

　　　sa [sa]　　'one day away' (= 'yesterday' or 'tomorrow')

　　　daa [da:]　'two or more days away' (= the day before yesterday or earlier; the day after tomorrow or later)

These markers precede the verb or any tense/aspect or negative markers. For instance, in (16a), *sa* precedes the negative marker *bi*; in (16b), *daa* is followed by the future marker *ni*, and in (16c) by the aspect marker *yɛn*.

(16)　Use of proximality markers

　　　a. n　　sa　　bi　　gbihi　yuŋ　　la.

　　　　 1sg　PRX　NEG　sleep　night　DEF.ART

　　　　 I did not sleep last night.

　　　b. o　　daa　　ni　　chaŋ　Tamali.

　　　　 3sg　PRX　FUT　go　　Tamale

　　　　 He will go to Tamale after two days.

　　　c. o　　daa　　yɛn　　chaŋ　Tamali.

　　　　 3sg　PRX　about.to　go　　Tamale

　　　　 He was about to go to Tamale

All three elements are not 'complete' grammatical words as they do not occur in isolation. But while there is good reason to assume that they are clitics, they differ from the clitics described so far with respect to a few features.

(1) Unlike most pronominal clitics, *sa* and *daa* are phonologically more prominent (while *di* is realised with a schwa as syllabic nucleus). They both contain full vowels and are never reduced phonologically.

(2) All three markers can potentially bear stress under certain conditions. This is the case when the emphasiser /n-/ is prefixed to them. (/n-/ is usually attached

to verbs, having varied functions: it can function as an 'infinitive' marker, as a conjoining element in serial verb constructions and as a kind of emphasiser; in the latter case, it also co-occurs with the proximality markers. However, its exact function is unclear and will not be discussed here. Apparently, stress is only realised on proximality markers when they are preceded by /n-/, which shows that they are prosodically deficient and therefore not phonological words.

(3) The proximality markers are not always directly attached to the verb, since other elements may occur in between. These include the irrealis marker *naan* and the aspect marker *yɛn* (neither discussed here) and the negation marker *bi*, which is also a clitic (see §3.2.3 below). Vowel harmony does not apply in this context, similarly to the pronominal clitics.

As they function as grammatical words, it is evident that these elements should be regarded as clitics, though they are still different from other clitics. Following Zwicky (1977), one might classify them as 'simple clitics' as opposed to 'special clitics' (see also chapter 2 by Aikhenvald). While Dagbani speakers might say them in isolation when asked for 'the word that indicates past', for instance, they would not normally use them without a verb, e.g. in a response to a question.

3.2.3 Negation marker The clause negation marker in Dagbani is *bi* [bə], and it refers to non-future tense.[9] *bi* always precedes the negated element and can occur in combination with proximality markers; in this context *bi* is found between these and the verb.

Regarding its status, *bi* fulfils the phonological and grammatical conditions for a clitic: it is unstressed, does not occur in isolation and is always attached to a phonological host. As may be expected, vowel harmony does not operate. On the other hand, the negation marker is a grammatical word, rather than a prefix, as other elements can occur between *bi* and the verb.

3.3   Post-verbal emphasisers

Two other elements which are candidates for being considered clitics are the focus marker *la* and the emphasiser *mi*. In contrast to the examples discussed above, both occur in post-verbal position. Since their function is rather complex,

---

[9] Another marker related to negation is *ku*. However, there are reasons to classify *ku*, which clearly combines information about negation and future tense, as a future marker first and foremost. It appears in the same position as its affirmative counterpart *ni*, while *bi* occurs in a different position and has a different status, as shown earlier in this section.

it will not be discussed in detail here, but their distribution is definitely of interest.

On the one hand, the function of *la* is to focus on what follows the verb, while on the other hand, when *la* occurs with a verb in the imperfective form, it gives the verb a continuous meaning (without *la*, the interpretation would be habitual).

(17)   Particle *la* with continuous meaning in imperfective forms
        a. Fati   ba-ri-la   chεchε.
           Fati   ride-IMPFVE-FOC   bicycle
           Fati is riding a bicycle.
        b. m   bɔhin-di-la   Dagbani.
           1sg   learn-IMPFVE-FOC   Dagbani
           I am learning Dagbani.

la is generally found after the verb. However, there are certain restrictions on its distribution:
• it is never found when no word follows (or when a subordinate clause follows);
• it does not occur before non-emphatic pronouns (possibly because they cannot be focussed).

Interestingly, separation of the focus marker *la* from the verb is possible, as the examples in (18) show. Bawa (1978) mentions this type of construction as 'disjunctive occurrence' of *la*. The difference in meaning as compared to the unmarked position is hard to explain. Another aspect is that *la* also functions as a definite article so that the *la* in *saɣim la* (18a) may be interpreted as 'the (porridge)' rather than as the same particle occurring in *dila*. Speakers of Dagbani usually have difficulties assigning a precise meaning to *la* in this position. However, it attaches to a phonological host, forming a stress unit with it, which is ['saɣəmla] or ['dɔɣbala], respectively, in the examples below.

(18)   Discontinuous use of *la*
        a. Adam   di   saɣim   la.
           Adam   eat   porridge   (DEF.ART?)
           Adam has eaten (the?) porridge.
        b. o   daa   dɔɣi   ba   la   bi-hi   ata.
           3sg   PRX   give.birth 3pl   FOC   child-pl   three
           She gave birth to (them) three children.

The other marker found in post-verbal position is *mi*. It can be best described as an emphasiser, although its exact function is difficult to describe, similarly as for *la*. In a way, it is related to *la*, as it also implies continuous meaning when it co-occurs with the imperfective (cf. (19a, b)). It also occurs with perfective forms, where its function is simply emphatic, rather than affecting the interpretation of aspect (cf. (19c)). The crucial difference between *mi* and *la* is that *mi* occurs only with intransitive clauses.

(19)   *mi* in intransitive clause

    a. o   daa   di-ri-mi.
       3sg   prx eat-IMPFVE/EMPH
       He was eating.

    b. n   di   ku-ni-mi.
       1sg   PRX go.home-IMPFVE/EMPH
       I was going home.

    c. bi-hi   maa   di-la   sayim.   bi-hi   maa   di-mi.
       child-pl DEF.ART eat-FOC   porridge child-pl DEF.ART eat-EMPH
       The children have eaten porridge.   The children have eaten.

Also similarly to *la*, *mi* can be separated from the verb in transitive sentences. The examples in (19) show that *mi* cannot be followed by an object. Nevertheless, *mi* occurs in the clearly transitive sentences; in this case it is separated from the verb and inserted after the object phrase to indicate emphasis. Bawa (1978) characterises this occurrence of *mi* as discontinuous form again. Comparing it with *la* in this position, the analysis of this form is ambiguous, as there is another particle *mi*, meaning 'also', which may occur in the same position (20e).

(20)   Discontinuous occurrence of *mi*

    a. o   nyu-ri   kom   mi.
       3sg drink-IMPFVE water EMPH
       He is drinking water.

    b. o   puhi-ri   ma   mi.
       3sg greet-IMPFVE me   EMPH
       He is greeting me.

    c. o   gbihi-ri   pumpɔŋɔ mi.
       3sg sleep-IMPFVE now   EMPH
       He is sleeping now.

    d. o   gbihi-ri-mi   pumpɔŋɔ.
       3sg sleep-IMPFVE/EMPH now
       He is sleeping now.

    e. o   puhi-ri   naa   mi.
       3sg greet-IMPFVE chief also
       He is also greeting the chief (because it's the chief's turn).

The difference between sentences (20a–d) and (20e) is unclear, as in the former, the interpretation 'also' is obviously not given, whereas this translation seems to be valid for (20e). Another aspect to consider is that (20a) and (20e) are

Table 2 *Features of Dagbani clitics*

	segmentally salient	can bear stress	attached to a phonological host	variable word order	occur in isolation
words (general)	+	+	−	+	+
affixes (general)	(some)	−	+	−	−
future tense markers	(one)	−	+	−	−
negation marker	−	−	+	+	−
personal pronouns	(some)	−	+	+	−
post−verbal emphasisers *la, mi*	+	−	+	+	−
proximality markers	+	+	+	+	−

transitive sentences, but as mentioned above, *mi* typically occurs with intransitives. This raises the question whether *mi* in (20a) and (20e) is actually the same as the emphatic marker. Note also that the position of *mi* is variable when the complement involved is not a direct object, but an adverbial, as in (20c, d). In any case (whether it is an emphasis marker or means 'also'), *mi* is not a phonological word, as it always is an unstressed part of a stress unit.

The discussion above raises the question of how *la* and *mi* should be characterised regarding their categorisation as 'word' or 'clitic'. What is certainly remarkable is their ability to shift to phrase-final position under certain conditions. Phonologically, both lack the status of a word, since they do not bear stress. Their varying position within the sentence further supports the view that they are clitics. Since we have already observed different kinds of clitics in Dagbani, the question will be to what category *la* and *mi* can be assigned. The best way to answer this is to view them in a table that compares the various features of all 'markers' between 'word' and 'affix' that have been discussed in this chapter. Note that one criterion is 'segmental saliency'. By this I mean the degree of phonological prominence, e.g. an epenthetic schwa is less salient than a 'full' vowel. Table 2 clearly indicates the gap between proximality markers and other clitics (or affixes), as the former display certain features that show a closer relationship to words than to affixes. I conclude that Dagbani has a variety of clitics, which may have different properties. Some are obviously closer to affixes, whereas others share more features of words.

4 Relationship between grammatical and phonological word

In many instances, the grammatical and the phonological word in Dagbani coincide. A morphologically complete grammatical word is always a phonological word, with the exception of clitics, as was discussed in §4: if proclitics which

consist of a (non-nasal) consonant only are grammatical words, but are phonologically 'complete' only when attached to a host (which involves epenthesis
of a vowel), we must speak of two grammatical words contained in one phonological word. Note that phonological and grammatical words also coincide in
compounds: since a compound may contain several roots, but only one suffix,
only the whole will be acceptable as a grammatical word. This coincides with
the fact that compounds have only one primary stress, namely on the penultimate syllable, while each of the roots involved would bear stress on its penult
if it stood in isolation. Even reduplications, which are grammatical words in
many languages, containing more than one phonological word, do not match
the criteria: many reduplicated words in Dagbani are inherently reduplicated
ideophones and not duplicates of one word that otherwise occurs in isolation.
Examples like /bjela-bjela/ 'slowly' are not decomposable into two meaningful
units; on the phonological side, the word has only one primary stress. Another
type of construction that also shows a mismatch between grammatical and
phonological word is represented by bound adjectives (cf. §2.2). On the one
hand these are phonological words in that they can bear stress; on the other, they
cannot occur in isolation, as would be expected from grammatical words. Their
status as a category 'between' complex suffix and word makes them particularly
interesting.

Various examples cited in this chapter have shown that the concept of 'word'
is an important psychological reality in Dagbani. Even though this is not manifested by a term used specifically for 'word' in the vocabulary, Dagbani speakers
have a strong idea of what are 'words' and what are not.

Appendices

I   *The word for 'word' in Dagbani*

Dagbani uses several lexical items in order to refer to 'word' (listed in (21)).
The contextual use of three of these is illustrated by the compounds in (22)
and (23).

(21)   Dagbani words for 'word'
         a. *bachi*   (derived from English 'A, B, C'), used in the sense of
                          grammatical word
         b. *nangbani* (lit. 'lip'), used in a contextual sense
         c. *yɛligu*   (lit. 'say-thing'), used in the sense of 'statement',
                          'utterance'
         d. *yɛlitɔyili* (lit. 'say-speak-thing'), meaning 'word', 'speech',
                          'conversation', 'sentence'

(22) Compounds related to *nangbani* 'lip'

nangban-kpeeni	('strong lip')	'argument,dissension,dispute'
nangban-maliŋ	('sweet lip')	'blabbermouth'
nangban-malisim	('lip sweetness')	'sweet words'
nangban-tɔɣu	('bitter lip')	'hunger, involuntary fasting'
nangban-yini	('one lip')	'unity'

(23) Compounds related to *yɛligu* 'word' and *yɛlitɔɣili* ('word, speech')

yɛli-kpeeni	('strong word')	'concern'
yɛli-kurili	('old word')	'custom'
yɛli-maŋli	('true, real word')	'truth'
yɛli-muɣisirili	('bothering word')	'problem', 'pressing matter'
yɛli-niŋdili	('happening word')	'event'
yɛli-wumsa	('say-hear thing')	'hearsay, rumour'
yɛlitɔɣa balibu	('language bundle')	'dialect'
yɛlitɔɣi-kaha	('unripe language')	'vulgar language'

II   Psycholinguistic experiments on the acceptability of pseudo-words

An experiment conducted with ten Dagbani speakers demonstrates that morphological and specific phonological factors play a role in the well-formedness of a Dagbani noun. In a rating test, the participants were asked to evaluate each of 292 given pseudo-words with regard to acceptability. The results show that a noun must have a suffix. In addition, word length plays a role in the well-formedness of a Dagbani word, whereas other factors, such as vowel length and vowel epenthesis are less relevant (cf. Olawsky 1998).

III   The word in Dagbani orthography

A complex system of rules determines the separate or joint writing of Dagbani words. These rules frequently, but not always, follow the morphological structure. When the phonological or morphological structure of a word is violated, this will be indicated in the orthography. When a phonological unit (typically a vowel) is missing, it is replaced by an apostrophe. This also applies when a morpheme is missing, for example, in the noun–adjective construction. These constructions, which I called 'compounds' above (cf. §2.1), are distinguished from lexicalised compounds in their written form: while the latter, 'true' compounds are written jointly, nouns and adjectives in ad hoc constructions are separated from each other by an apostrophe:

(24)   Ad hoc and lexicalised noun–adjective compounds in Dagbani
         orthography

a. *paɣ'viɛlli*	/pag-vjel-li/	('woman-nice'-sg)	'nice woman'
do' suma	/do-sum-a/	('man-good'-pl)	'good men'
b. *zuɣisuŋ*	/zug-suŋ/	('head-good'-sg)	'good fortune'
suhipiɛlli	/suh-pjel-li/	('heart-white'-sg)	'happiness'
paɣipiɛliga	/pag-pjel-ga/	('woman-white'-sg)	'virgin'

References

Bawa, A-B. 1978. 'Collected notes on Dagbani grammar', ms., Ajumako.

Dagbani Orthography Committee 2000. *Dagbani sabbu zalisi – Rules for spelling Dagbani*, as fixed by the Dagbani Orthography Committee at the 2nd Conference on Dagbani Orthography, 28–29th November 1997. Tamale: Ghana Institute of Linguistics, Literacy and Bible Translation Press.

Kropp-Dakubu, M. E. 1997. 'Oti-Volta vowel harmony and Dagbani', pp 81–8 of *Gur Papers / Cahiers Gur* 2: Actes du 1er Colloque international sur les langues gur du 3 au 7 mars 1997 à Ouagadougou, 1ère partie: Généralités et phonologie.

Hyman, L. 1993. 'Structure preservation and postlexical tonology in Dagbani', pp 235–54 of *Phonetics and phonology*, Vol. 4: *Studies in lexical phonology*, edited by S. Hargus and E. Kaisse. San Diego, Calif.: Academic Press.

Hyman, L. and Olawsky, K. forthcoming. 'Dagbani verb tonology', to appear in *Proceedings of the 31st Annual Conference on African Linguistics*, Boston, 2–5 March 2000.

Olawsky, K. J. 1998. *Psycholinguistic experiments on Dagbani novel nouns*, Arbeiten des Sonderforschungsbereichs 282, 'Theorie des Lexikons' 108. Düsseldorf: Heinrich-Heine-Universität.

1999. *Aspects of Dagbani grammar – with special emphasis on phonology and morphology*. Muenchen: LINCOM Europa.

Olawsky, K. J. and Ortmann, A. 2002. 'Dagbani adjectives', ms., University of California, Berkeley and Heinrich-Heine-Universität, Düsseldorf.

Zwicky, A. M. 1977. *On clitics*. Bloomington: Indiana University Linguistics Club.

9 The word in Georgian

Alice C. Harris

Georgian is a language of the Kartvelian (South Caucasian) language family; this family appears to be unrelated to North East Caucasian and North West Caucasian language families. Georgian is spoken by some five million speakers in the Republic of Georgia, formerly part of the USSR, but now independent.

The notion 'word' (Georgian *sit'q'va*) is very much recognised in Georgian culture. The society is deeply literary, with the Georgian alphabet having been invented in the fourth or fifth century AD, and with texts dating from that time. Georgians have strong intuitions about what is a word, and this corresponds to orthographic practice, with few exceptions.

1 Summary of the typology

Like other languages of the Caucasus, Georgian has a large number of consonants (twenty-eight) and a modest number of vowels (five). Georgian is famous for its consonant clusters, which may contain up to seven consonants, e.g. *mc'vrtneli* 'trainer', *vprckvni* 'I peel it'; clusters are not punctuated by epenthetic vowels. Traditional work in Georgian has identified so-called harmonic consonant clusters, which are characterised by (a) shared laryngeal properties (roughly, all voiceless, all voiced or all ejectives), (b) a structure in which each successive consonant is articulated further back in the mouth (e.g. *pt*, *pk*, *tk* are harmonic clusters, but *kp* and *tp*, while allowed, are not harmonic) and (c) a first segment that is a stop or affricate and a second that is a stop, affricate or fricative; see Vogt (1958) and Mač'avariani (1965).[1] Vogt (1958) and others have argued that harmonic clusters in Georgian are actually complex segments, not consonant clusters; if this is correct, it would push the number of consonants in the language much higher. However, Chitoran (1994) presents acoustic data

---

[1] Axvlediani, who may have been the first to analyse harmonic clusters, lists them (1951: 113) as the following:

p'k'	pk	bg	p'q'	px	bɣ
t'k'	tk	dg	t'q'	tx	dɣ
c'k'	ck	ȝg	c'q'	cx	ȝɣ
č'k'	čk	ǯg	č'q'	čx	ǯɣ

227

that show that harmonic clusters are true clusters of consonants, not complex segments.

The morphology is predominantly agglutinative, but there is some fusional morphology. A simple verb paradigm illustrates both the agglutination that characterises most of the language and the fusion.

(1)   singular   plural
        1   v-xedav   v-xedav-t   'see' PRESENT
        2   xedav   xedav-t
        3   xedav-s   xedav-en

An interesting (and potentially confusing) feature of the morphology is the widespread use of circumfixes and other linked morphemes, beside prefixes and suffixes. Some examples of circumfixes are given in (2).

(2)   sa--o   sa-kartvel-o 'Georgia'   kartvel- 'Georgian (person)'
                 sa-megrel-o 'Mingrelia'   megrel- 'Mingrelian (person)'
                 sa-st'umr-o 'hotel'   st'umar- 'guest'

        sa--e   sa-katm-e 'chicken coop'   katam- 'chicken'
                 sa-sapn-e 'soap dish'   sapon- 'soap'

        u--o   u-švil-o 'childless'   švil- 'child'
                 u-ʒm-o 'brother-less'   ʒma 'brother'

        m--ar   m-tav-ar- 'chief, head'   tav- 'head'
                 m-xat'v-ar- 'painter'   xat'av- 'paint'
                 m-k'vlev-ar- 'researcher'   k'vlev- 'research'

While these examples are relatively simple, the morphemes of the verb combine in complex ways to indicate tense – aspect – mood (TAM) categories.

2   The grammatical word in Georgian

2.1   *Basic criteria*

The first three criteria stated in chapter 1 apply in Modern Georgian:

> A **grammatical word** consists of a number of grammatical elements which
> (a) always occur together, rather than scattered through the clause (the criterion of cohesiveness);
> (b) occur in a fixed order;
> (c) have a conventionalised coherence and meaning.

In Old Georgian, non-verbal elements, such as conjunctions, often occurred between a pre-verb and the rest of the verb form (Cherchi 1994 and other sources), and this phenomenon is well known in other languages; it does not, however, occur in the modern language. Although deviations from a single order are known even in some neighbouring languages, such as Udi (Harris 2000), there are no such deviations in Georgian. The parts of a word in Modern Georgian always occur together, in a fixed order, with a conventionalised meaning.

2.2   Recursion

Some derivational circumfixes appear to be recursive, but in my view are not true examples of recursion. This is true, for example, of *sa--o*, which forms words identifying a place or an intended function. For example, we find *sa-dil-i* 'dinner' (where −*i* is the nominative case marker), from *dila* 'morning'; based on *sadili*, we have *sa-sa-dil-o* 'dining room'. Notice that *sa-dil-i* 'dinner', is based on *sa--∅*, instead of *sa--o*. Apparently from *zɣva* 'sea', we get *sa-zɣv-ar-i* 'border' (formed with a related circumfix, *sa--ar*), and from that, *sa-sa-zɣv-r-o* 'relating to the border, for use at the border'. It is difficult to view these as true recursion for two reasons. First, although the first elements of the circumfixes are the same (*sa-* in each instance), the circumfixes used in any one word actually are different from one another. I am not aware of any examples where the final element, *-o* or *-ar* (or one of the others used with *sa-*), is repeated. In order to consider the examples cited here formally recursive, we would have to treat *sa--o*, *sa--ar* and *sa--∅* as different forms of the *same* circumfix. Second, it is likely that the 'inside' forms have been reanalysed. If speakers use *sa-sadil-o* 'dining room', without connecting its base with *dila* 'morning', then the formation is not productively recursive. (Note in this connection the related word *sa-dila-o* 'relating to morning'.) In sum, from a synchronic point of view, no category in Georgian is clearly truly recursive. Nevertheless, the fact that the sequence *sa-* (and perhaps prefixal portions of other circumfixes) can repeat makes it difficult to apply this effectively as a criterion for wordhood.

2.3   A single inflectional affix per word

The Latin criterion of a single inflectional affix per word does not characterise the word in Georgian in the same way. For example, within limits, verbs may bear non-zero marking of both subjects and objects: *g-elodeb-a* 'she waits for you',[2] where *g-* marks the second person object, and *-a* the third person singular subject. Nouns may bear both a case and a number marker (*d-eb-s* 'to the sisters', where *-eb* marks plurality and *-s* marks the dative case) or two case markers (with or without a number marker, *d-eb-isa-s* 'to something belonging to the

---

[2] Georgian does not distinguish gender in pronouns or in verbal forms; third person singular pronouns and the subjects of third person singular verb forms in this chapter are translated with a feminine pronoun.

sisters', where *-isa* marks the genitive). A compound such as *t'ol-amxanag-i* 'comrade(s) of the same age', composed of *t'ol-* 'person of the same age group' and *amxanag-* 'comrade', can be identified as a single morphological word because here the first constituent, *t'ol-*, cannot occur as an independent word without its own case marker (*t'ol-i* 'person of the same age group-NOM').

2.4   *Pausability*

In Georgian pausing is permitted between phonological words. There cannot ordinarily be a pause inside a phonological word composed of a host and a clitic, whether the clitic is non-syllabic, such as ʒ*ma=c* 'brother (NOM)=too', or syllabic, as in *ak=ac* 'here=too'. However, to aid a foreigner, a speaker may sometimes spontaneously pronounce a troublesome word with a short pause between syllables. For both reasons, this is not an effective criterion for distinguishing the morphological word in Georgian.

2.5   *Complete utterance*

In Georgian, verbs are commonly complete statements, as long as the referent of each argument has been identified in discourse. For example, *iq'ida* 'she bought it' is a complete utterance, as long as we already know who the referent of the subject is and what the referent of the object is. Other major parts of speech can stand alone as an utterance in answer to a question or under certain other contextually defined circumstances. For example, (3) might be used to identify a contact lens to someone who had never seen one, or (4) might be said to someone moving a heavy object; (5) might be used as an afterthought.

(3)   lens-i
       lens-NOM

(4)   ak 'here'

(5)   samc'uxarod 'unfortunately'

   Major parts of speech may be used with the enclitic form of the verb 'be' to form a complete statement, as long as the referents of the arguments have been identified in discourse:

(6)   ekimi=a
       doctor=is
       She's a doctor.

(7)   č'k'viani=a
       smart=is
       She's smart.

These are phonological words, grammatical phrases (clauses).

Most clitics, including those that cliticise only optionally, cannot be used alone (e.g. *rom* 'that', *tu* 'if', *=ve* 'again', *=ode* 'approximately', *=ze* 'on', *=ši* 'in'). However, *ara* 'not' and forms of 'be' *can* be used alone. No non-clitic conjunctions of any kind can be used alone (e.g. *da* 'and', *an* 'or', *tumsa* 'although', *rodesac* 'when').

2.6   Circumfixes

Circumfixes provide a possible criterion for wordhood in some problematic instances. This criterion would be based on the assumption, which may prove to be untrue as a universal, that words can be formed only on the base of roots or words, not on the base of phrases. If accepted as a criterion, the use of the privative circumfix *u--o* in *u-da-ʒm-o* 'without siblings, siblingless' would argue that *da-ʒma* 'sibling(s)', literally 'sister-brother', is a single (compound) word, not a phrase. Indeed, this is the commonly accepted view in this instance, and the orthographic norms require this to be written with a hyphen, not a space.

However, there are instances where this criterion gives results that other criteria call into doubt. For example, formants of some participles are circumfixes, and the verb is within the semantic scope of the participial circumfix, yet the pre-verb is located physically outside the circumfix; compare (8) and (9), which illustrate use of the participial circumfix *m--el*.

(8)   mo-m-svl-el-i
        hither-PTCPL-move-PTCPL-NOM
        coming

(9)   mi-m-svl-el-i   (Tschenkéli 1958: 540)
        thither-PTCPL-move-PTCPL-NOM
        going

Such examples are not limited to circumfixes, since the pre-verb is also 'outside' the agreement markers and so-called character vowels, yet is within the semantic scope of all of these (see Ackermann and Webelhuth 1998 for discussion).

A similar kind of problem is presented by the bracketing paradox in (11). Ordinal numbers are formed with the circumfix *me--e*. Cardinal numbers between twenty and forty, forty and sixty, etc. are formed with *da* 'and' as in (10) and are widely considered compound single words. (The orthographic norm requires that they be written without hyphens or spaces, though hyphens are used here.)

(10)   oc-da-or-i
        20-and-2-NOM
        twenty-two

Clearly the entire cardinal is within the semantic scope of the formant of the ordinal, but it is not within its phonological or morphological scope, as shown in (11).

(11)   oc-da-**me**-or-**e**
        20-and-ORD-2-ORD
        twenty-second

Note that a similar bracketing paradox is found both in the Modern English translation of (11) and in the archaic *four and twentieth* (Zechariah 1:7).

In the end we must conclude that a circumfix may encompass a unit that *may* be smaller than a word; that is, its status is still to be established on other grounds. Nevertheless, it is probable that units larger than a word cannot be encompassed by a circumfix.

2.7   Conclusion

The most reliable criteria for identifying a grammatical word in Georgian are the basic ones quoted above from chapter 1: cohesion, fixed order of elements and conventionalised meaning. Other criteria can play a supporting role.

3   The phonological word in Georgian

In Georgian the word may consist of a single syllable; this is true not only of conjunctions and particles, such as *rom* 'that' and *xom* (roughly) 'isn't it?', but also of nouns, such as *da* 'sister' and *k'u* 'turtle', and verbs, such as *č'ris* 'she cuts it' and *var* 'I am'. Alternatively a word may consist of many syllables, such as the noun *mo.na.di.re.e.bi.sa* 'hunter (GEN)', the adjective *mra.val.mar.cvli.a.ni* 'polysyllabic' or the verb *ga.da.u.tar.gmni.ne.bi.na* 'she made him translate it'.

For Georgian, segmental features are not helpful in distinguishing a word, but a number of phonological processes are.

3.1   Stress

Stress in Georgian is very even, and according to phonologists its position is not entirely predictable (Tschenkéli 1958: lix–lxi; Vogt 1971: 15–16; Žɣent'i 1963). Very frequently it is the first syllable that is (lightly) stressed, regardless of the length of the word and regardless of whether or not the first syllable is a prefix: *déda* 'mother', *kálak-i* 'city', *sá-tval-e* 'eye-glasses', *gá-mo-a-cx-o* 'heated', *mó-nadir-e* 'hunter'. It is not unusual for the antepenult to be stressed (*amxánag-i* 'comrade, acquaintance'), and other syllables may be stressed (*sa-st'úmr-o* 'hotel', *me-ótx-e* 'fourth').

Compounds may have a single primary stress or one per constituent-word: *šúa-mta* name of a monastery (lit. 'between mountains'), *mk'áta-tve* 'July' (lit. 'month of mowing'), *káli-švili* 'daughter, girl, virgin', *svet'i-cxóveli* name of a cathedral (lit. 'living column'), *sxva-da-sxvá* 'various', *dá-ʒma* 'sibling(s)', but *t'ól-amxánagi* 'comrade(s) of the same age', *púr-íremi* 'female deer'. Neither the number of stresses nor the position of the primary stress appears to be determined by the type of compound; in particular, compounds formed of two nouns of equal semantic weight (i.e. neither modifying the other) may have stress on the first constituent-word, on the second or on both: *dá-ʒma* 'sibling(s)' (lit. 'sister-brother'), *ded-máma* 'parent(s)' (lit. 'mother-father'), *t'ól-amxánagi* 'comrade(s) of the same age' (lit. 'person of the same age – comrade'. Because stress is not fixed, it is not a reliable gauge of either end of a word.

Phrases may be distinguished from similar compounds by the number of stresses assigned.

(12)   a. d-ís   sáxl-i
           sister-GEN   house-NOM
           [her] sister's house
        b. d-ís-švil-i
           sister-GEN-child-NOM
           niece, nephew

(13)   a. gívi-s   xíl-i
           Givi-GEN   fruit-NOM
           Givi's fruit
        b. zét-is-xil-i
           oil-GEN-fruit-NOM
           olive

In (12–13), the (a) examples are phrases consisting of a noun in the genitive, followed by a noun in the nominative; each word has a primary stress. The (b) examples are similar, consisting also of a noun in the genitive, followed by a noun in the nominative, but the (b) examples are considered compounds and have a single primary stress. Because some words that on morphological grounds are considered compounds have dual stress, there is sometimes a mismatch between the phonological and the morphological word.

3.2   *Phonological processes and syllable structure*

In Georgian a syllable may consist of a nucleus alone (*a̲.ra* 'no, not', *ga.a̲.k'e.ta* 'she did it'), an onset with a nucleus (*da* 'sister'), a nucleus with a coda (*ik* 'there') or an onset, nucleus and coda (*mas* 'her DAT'). Either onsets or codas or both may consist of consonant clusters (*mc'vrtne.li* 'trainer', *tbi.li.si*

'Tbilisi', *a.kebs* 'she praises it', *msxverp'ls* 'victim DAT'). Sonorant consonants never serve as the nucleus of a syllable in Georgian.

A basic principle of syllabification is that the first segment in a consonant cluster is syllabified with the preceding vowel, subsequent consonants with the following vowel: *ʒaɣ.li* 'dog', *iɣ.ba.li* (Žɣent'i 1960: 141; Uturgaiʒe 1976: 137).

In general, in compounds, the two constituent words are syllabified separately: *da.-ʒma /*da-ʒ.ma* 'sibling(s)' (lit. 'sister-brother'), *t'ol.-am.xa.na.gi /*t'o.l-am.xa.na.gi* 'comrade(s) of the same age' (lit. 'person of the same age – comrade'), *xar.-i.re.mi /*xa.r-i.re.mi* 'male deer' (lit. 'bull-deer'). Thus the constituents of the compound are each phonological words.

Specialists have given inconsistent analyses of syllabification in Georgian. For example, Šaniʒe (1974: 21) divides the narrative case of *k'ac-* 'man' as *k'ac.ma*, while Axvlediani (1938) and Žɣent'i (1960)[3] divide the same form as *k'a.cma*; Šaniʒe (1974: 21) indicates *var.debs* 'roses DAT', while Axvlediani (1938) gives both *var.di* and *va.rdi* 'rose NOM'.

In general, enclitics are syllabified in the same way suffixes are, as illustrated in (14).

(14)   *mo.-d-i.-a.n=o /*mo.-d-i.-an.=o* 'they are coming'
      so.p-e.l-i=c 'the village too'
      dɣe=m.de /*dɣe.=mde. 'until today'

Bush (1997) argues that *consonant devoicing* is a productive rule that applies in word-initial position. For example, while *mta* 'mountain' may be phonetically [m̥ta], *šua-mta*, the name of a monastery, cannot be [*šua-m̥ta].[4] This devoicing is more likely to occur at moderate and rapid rates of speech than at slower ones. According to Bush, devoicing is not simply a matter of assimilation, as it applies also in words such as *mdgomareoba* 'situation'; yet devoicing is more likely when the potential target segment is followed by a voiceless consonant, as in *mta* 'mountain'. Thus, presence of devoicing provides evidence of the initial boundary of a phonological word.

According to Hewitt (1995: 21), consonant devoicing also occurs at the end of words, with words such as *rusul-ad* 'Russian [language] ADV' optionally pronounced [rusulat]. Historically this has resulted in words such as *egret* 'thus' from **eg-r-ed*. In principle, this can provide evidence of the final boundary of the word, but in practice both types of devoicing in Georgian are weak and difficult to identify.

---

[3] Axvlediani (1938) is not available to me, but Žɣent'i (1960: 141–2) summarises and accepts Axvlediani's position; in subsequent pages he elaborates on it and illustrates it.

[4] Bush (1997) states that *mta* is pronounced [ta] and that 'it is actually a rather moot point whether the nasal is devoiced or actually deleted...' Compare Robins and Waterson (1952: 62), who claim that Georgian /m/ is devoiced only before voiceless consonants and imply that it is not deleted.

Bush (1997, 1999) argues that a rule he calls Monosyllabic Lengthening (ML) applies to monosyllabic words. According to Bush, ML applies when the last word of a yes-no question is monosyllabic, as in (15).

(15)   k'art'opils   prckvniîs?   (Bush 1997: 9)
          potato   he.peel
          Is he peeling the potatoes?

In (15), the last syllable of *prckvnis* rises, as in other Georgian yes-no questions, and as indicated here by the double acute accent; in addition, because it is the last word of a yes-no question and is monosyllabic, the vowel is lengthened (indicated here by doubling the vowel, contrary to the orthographic norms).[5] All vowels (i, e, a, o, u) are subject to ML. The *-i* in (15) is usually analysed as a suffix; ML also applies if the vowel of the monosyllabic word is in the root (e.g. *daǎ?* 'sister?') or in a prefix, as in (16).

(16)   aǎkvs?   [morphologically,   a-kv-s]
                                        cv-have-3sg
          Does she have it?

However, if the last 'word' of the yes-no question is a clitic, ML does not apply, as I show below.

(17)   a. ak=veّ? /*ak=veeّ?
             here=again
             Here again?
          b. ak=ǎc? /*ak=aǎc?
             here=too
             Here too?
          c. xe=ǎ? /*xe=aǎ?
             wood=is
             Is it wood?

In each instance, ML is ungrammatical. If we assume that the clitic and its host are a phonological word, ML applies only where the phonological word is monosyllabic.

---

[5] Though not noted by Bush, there are sentences in which a word meets the two criteria of being final in a yes-no question and being monosyllabic and yet the word does not get ML, as in (i).

(i)   c'avidǎ   šeni   da?
          she. leave   your   sister
          Did your sister leave?

Here the rising question intonation is on *c'avida*; the end of the sentence may have either falling tone or rising, but it cannot have ML. See also K'iziria (1991: 97).

3.3   Conclusions

A phonological word in Georgian has a single primary stress. Syllabification can distinguish an enclitic from an independent word, but cannot discriminate between a clitic and a suffix. Although devoicing may help to identify either end of a word, in practice it is not a reliable diagnostic. A monosyllabic phonological word undergoes ML.

4   Clitics

Georgian makes use of a variety of clitics, both proclitics and enclitics.

The neutral negative particle *ar(a)*, the prohibitive *nu* (used in negative imperatives) and other negators occur immediately before the verb in predicate- or sentence-negation and optionally cliticise.[6] Stress often shifts to the proclitic, but may fall instead on the verb or on both the verb and the proclitic.

(18)   a. merab-i   ekim-i   ár   áris
            Merab-NOM   doctor-NOM   NEG   he.be
            Merab is not a doctor.
        b. merabi ekimi ár aris

(19)   a. (Are you a doctor?)
            ékimi   vár
            doctor   I.be
            [Yes,] I am a doctor.
        b. (Are you a doctor?)
            ékimi   ára   var
            doctor   NEG   I.be
            [No,] I'm not a doctor.

(20)   a. puli   ára   m-akvs
            money   NEG   1sg.OBL-have
            I don't have any money
        b. puli ara mákvs
        c. ara mákvs puli

When the same particle negates a single word or phrase, it may immediately precede or follow the constituent negated. If the negative precedes, it does not normally cliticise.

---

[6] Either *ar* or *ara* may cliticise, and either may fail to cliticise; the first is not a clitic form of the latter. The full form, *ara*, is used before present tense forms of 'be' (*ara var* 'I am not', *ara xar* 'you are not', etc.), including the reduced form of the third person singular, *ara=a* 'she is not', but not with the unreduced forms of the third persons, *ar aris* 'she is not' (**ara aris*). It is also used with the present tense of 'have (inanimate object)': *ara makvs* 'I don't have it', *ara akvs* 'she doesn't have it', etc.

(21)   ára   mérabi,   aramed   irak'li   c'avida   amerik'a=ši
        NEG   Merab,   rather   Irakli   he.go   America=in
        Not Merab, but Irakli, went to America (It was not Merab, but
        Irakli, who went to America.)

On the other hand, if the negative follows the word it negates, it does ordinarily
(en)cliticise, and the stress shifts to it.

(22)   merabi ára –   (aramed)   irak'li   c'avida   amerik'a=ši
        Merab NEG   (rather)   Irakli   he.go   America=in
        (same as (21))

Georgian also possesses two clitics that are positioned in an unusual way:
rom 'if, when, that, because, etc.' and *tu* 'if, whether'. *Rom* may be said to
be an all-purpose clausal conjunction, because it can mark almost any kind of
embedded clause. However, when it marks clauses that occur as the complement
of verbs such as 'say' or 'believe', it is simply initial in the clause and otherwise
has properties different from those discussed below. In its other functions, it
may occur first, but in speech more often occurs in second or later position.
In languages such as Serbo-Croatian, second position may be understood as
following the first word or as following the first phrase. That is not the issue
here; *rom* can follow one or more sentence constituents:

(23)   a. merabi   sakartvelo=ši   rom   iq'o,   me   ik   ar   vq'opilvar
           Merab   Georgia=in   THAT   he.be   I   there   NEG   I.be
           When Merab was in Georgia, I [contrastive] was not there.
        b. merabi rom sakartveloši iq'o, ...
        c. ??rom merabi sakartveloši iq'o, ...

Rom must, however, come before the verb; it can never follow the verb:

(24)   *merabi iq'o rom sakartveloši, ...
        *merabi sakartveloši iq'o rom, . . .

In each of its possible positions, *rom* is proclitic, and its host may be any type
of constituent; unlike *ar(a)*, it does not attract stress:

(25)   [ro=íq'o] (from (23a) above)
        [*ró(m)=iq'o]

Tu 'if, whether' occurs in a position similar to that of *rom*.
    There are two morphemes of the form =*ve*; one of these may be enclitic to a
noun, pronoun, postposition or adverb in the sense 'again, same'.

(26)   a. ík=ve 'in the same place, there'
        b. ák=ve 'in the same place, here'

The second =*ve* means 'all' and occurs only with numbers.

(27)   a. or-i=ve
             two-NOM=all   'both'
        b. sam-i=ve
             three-NOM=all   'all three'
        c. otx-i=ve
             four-NOM=all   'all four'

=*ve* does not bear word stress.[7] Not only are the meanings of these two homophonous enclitics and the hosts to which they attach different, their distri-
butions in the word are also different. The morpheme =*ve* in the meaning 'all'
(illustrated in (27)), appears to be undergoing reanalysis from an enclitic to a
derivational suffix. Speakers in some instances accept both the order CASE-*ve*
and the order *ve*-CASE, as in (28) (see also Jorbenaȝe, Kiobaiȝe and Beriȝe 1988:
165–6); in other instances they accept only one or the other, as in (29–30). (In
the first variant of (28), I assume that *ori* functions as the stem, with -*ve* reanalysed as a suffix, followed by a dative case suffix, which deletes before -*ši*
'in'.)

(28)   ór-i-ve-s   / ór-sa=ve   vxedav
        two-NOM-all-DAT   two-DAT=all   I.see.it
        I see both.

(29)   c'q'ali   šemovida   ór-i-ve=ši   / *ór-sa=ve=ši
        water.NOM   it.came.in two-NOM-all=in   two-DAT=all=in
        The water came into both.

(30)   merabi or-i-ve-s=tana=a   / *or-sa=ve=tana=a
        Merab two-NOM-all-DAT=with=is   two-DAT=all=with=is
        Merab is with both.

It is the order CASE-*ve* that was used in Old Georgian, while the order *ve*-CASE
seems to be preferred today. In the meaning 'again', on the other hand, as
illustrated in (31–2), =*ve* is certainly an enclitic; for example, it follows the
dative case marker in (31) and the postposition -*ze* 'on' in (32).

(31)   dɣe-s=ve / *dɣe-ve-s
        day-DAT=again
        on the same day

---

[7] In yes-no questions, stress shifts to the last syllable of the last word; if this happens to be an
enclitic that otherwise does not bear stress, it does so in this situation. For example, 'in the same
place (remote)' as a statement or part of one is [ík=ve], not [*ik=vé]; as a yes-no question, or as
the last word of a question, however, it is [ik=vé̋], where the double acute accent indicates stress
and the special rising tone found in Georgian only in yes-no questions. This seems to be true also
of all other enclitics in Georgian.

(32)   ima=ze=ve
        it.DAT=on=again
        on the same one

=(a)c 'too, also' can be enclitic to any one of a variety of hosts – noun, pronoun, deictic, adjective. (The vowel occurs after a consonant.)

(33)   a. šeni   da=c
           your   sister=too
        b. man=ac
           she.NAR=too
        c. ak=ac
           here=too

The forms of the verb 'be' may occur as distinct phonological words, as in (19a) above; this occurs when they represent the copula in a clause with a predicate complement. In certain TAM categories, forms of 'be' occurred historically as auxiliaries with all verbs (or all of a particular category). In this function, some linguists analyse the forms synchronically as enclitics, while in the opinion of others they have been reanalysed as suffixes. An example is the perfect, also known as the first evidential; one of the uses of this TAM category is to indicate past tense of unintentional action under negation (contrasting with past tense of intentional action under negation, indicated by the aorist).

(34)   a. ik   ar   v-q'opil-var
           there   NEG   1sg-be-1sg
           I haven't been there (unintentional).
        b. ik   ar   Ø-q'opil-xar
           there   NEG   2sg-be-2sg
           You (sg) haven't been there (unintentional).

The third person singular of the verb 'be' in the present tense, unlike any other person–number combination or TAM category, has a special clitic form. Reduction (with cliticisation) is optional, but failure to reduce gives emphasis to the statement.

(35)   a. merabi saxl=ši   aris
           Merab   house=in   he.be
           Merab is in the house. (slightly emphatic)
        b. merabi saxl=ši=a
                   house=in=a
           Merab is in the house.

The special clitic, or the suffix derived historically from it, is used in the formation of the TAM categories mentioned above; (36) is parallel to (34) above.

(36)   ak   ar   q'opil-a
         here   NEG   be-3sg
         She hasn't been here. (unintentional)

With the caveat stated in note 7, =*a* does not bear stress; we find, for example, [sáxl=ši=a] from (35b) and [q'ópil=a] from (36).

There are three quotatives: *metki* 'I said', =*tko* 'you should say', =*o* 'she said, they said, they say'. The second is literary and so infrequently used that some consultants have even told me that it is not Georgian. The other two are commonly used in conversation and in writing. The example below, where the quotative co-occurs with a verb of speaking, shows that this is really a quotative, not (synchronically) a verb of speaking.

(37)   c'avedi   mepes=tan   da   vtkvi,   mdidari   k'aci   ara   var,   metki
       I.went   king=with   and   I.said   rich   man   NEG   I.am   QUOT
       I went to the king and said, 'I am not a rich man.'

As the example above illustrates, *metki* 'I said' occurs at the end of the sentence; its scope is commonly a clause, broadly understood, but it may be even greater. The scope of =*o* is the same in principle, but in conversation it is often 'repeated' earlier in the clause.

(38)   mepem   mitxra: ara=o,   tkven=o   puli   ar   gč'irdeba=o
       king   he.said.me   no=QUOT   you=QUOT   money   NEG   you.need.it=QUOT
       The king said to me: 'No, you [emphatic] don't need money.'

There are additional clitics in Georgian, but I have covered here many of those that are used most frequently, with the exception of postpositions.

To summarise, Georgian has both proclitics (e.g. *ar(a)*= NEG) and enclitics (e.g. =*ve* 'again', =*var* 'I am', =*o* QUOT). Some cliticise optionally (e.g. *ara*= NEG, =*var* 'I am'), and others obligatorily (e.g. =*ve* 'again', =*o* QUOT). Some may attract stress (e.g. *ar(a)* NEG); others never bear stress (e.g. *rom*= 'that'), or do so only if they are sentence-final in yes-no questions (e.g. =*ve* 'again; all'). Some enclitics are hosted by the narrow constituents, usually single words, that are in their scope (e.g. =*ve* 'again', =*(a)c* 'too'). Either proclitics (e.g. negative and affirmative particles, subordinating conjunctions) or enclitics (e.g. quotatives) may have scope over an entire clause. In this case the negative and affirmative particles are positioned relative to the verb, the quotatives relative to the end of the clause (or quoted material). Positioning of the subordinating conjunctions, on the other hand, takes into account both the beginning of the clause and the position of the verb.

5 Conclusion

The basic criteria stated by Dixon and Aikhenvald in chapter 1 – cohesion, fixed order of elements and conventionalised meaning – are the most reliable ones for identifying the morphological word in Georgian. The phonological word can be identified as having a single primary stress. Syllabification and Monosyllabic Lengthening treat a host with its enclitics as a phonological word.

In some instances there are mismatches between the criteria for the morphological word and those for the phonological word. As noted in 3.1, some compounds have two stresses, generally a characteristic of a two-word phrase (e.g. *t'ól-amxánagi* 'comrade(s) of the same age', *púr-íremi* 'female deer'). Yet the fact that the first component of each of these has no case marker indicates that it is not an independent word, and consequently that the whole is a compound.

References

Ackerman, F. and Webelhuth, G. 1998. *A theory of predicates*. Stanford: CSLI.

Axvlediani, G. 1938. *Zogadi da kartuli enis ponet'ik'is sak'itxebi* [Questions of general and Georgian language phonetics]. Not seen.

1951. 'Dve sistemy garmoničeskix smyčnyx v gruzinskom jazyke', pp 113–16 of *Pamjati akademika L'va Vladimiroviča Ščerby (1880–1944): Sbornik statej*. Leningrad: Universitet.

Bush, R. 1997. 'Georgian syllable structure', *Phonology at Santa Cruz* 5.1–14.

1999. 'Georgian yes-no question intonation', *Phonology at Santa Cruz* 6.1–11.

Cherchi, M. 1994. 'Verbal tmesis in Georgian', *Annali del Dipartimento di Studi del Mondo Classico e del Mediterraneo Antico Sezione linguistica* 16.33–115.

Chitoran, I. 1994. 'Acoustic investigation of Georgian harmonic clusters', *Working Papers of the Cornell Phonetics Laboratory* 9.27–65.

Harris, A. C. 2000. 'Where in the word is the Udi clitic?' *Language* 76.593–616.

Hewitt, B. G. 1995. *Georgian: a structural reference grammar*. Amsterdam: Benjamins.

Jorbenaʒe, B., K'obaiʒe, M. and Beriʒe, M. 1988. *Kartul enis morpemebisa da modaluri element'ebis leksik'oni* [Dictionary of morphemes and modal elements of the Georgian language]. Tbilisi: Mecniereba.

K'iziria, N. 1991. 'Int'onacia da c'inadadebata t'ip'ebi [Intonation and types of intonation]', *Macne* 3.96–101.

Mač'avariani, G. 1965. *Saerto-kartveluri k'onsonant'uri sist'ema* [The Common Kartvelian consonant system]. Tbilisi: Universit'et'i.

Robins, R.H. and Waterson, N. 1952. 'Notes on the phonetics of the Georgian word', *Bulletin of the School of Oriental and African Studies* XIV, Pt. 1, 55–72.

Šaniʒe, A. 1974. *Kartuli enis gramat'ik'is sapuʒvlebi*. [Fundamentals of the grammar of the Georgian language]. Tbilisi: Universit'et'i.

Tschenkéli, K. 1958. *Einführung in die georgische Sprache*, Band 1. Zürich: Amirani.

1960–1974. *Georgisch–Deutsches Wörterbuch*. Zürich: Amirani-Verlag.

Uturgaiʒe, T. 1976. *Kartuli enis ponemat'uri st'rukt'ura* [Phonemic structure of the Georgian language]. Tbilisi: Ak'ademia.

Vogt, H. 1958. 'Structure phonémique du Georgien: Étude sur le classement des phonèmes et des groupes des phonèmes', *Norsk Tidsskrift for Sprogvidenskap* 18.5–90. Reprinted pp 344–429 of *Studia Caucasologica*, II: *Hans Vogt: Linguistique caucasienne et arménienne*, edited by Even Hovdhaugen and Fridrik Thordarson. Oslo: Norwegian University Press, 1988.

1971. *Grammaire de la langue Géorgienne*. Oslo: Universitetsforlaget.

Žγent'i, S. 1960. *Kartvelur enata šedarebiti ponet'ik'a, I: Marcvlis agebulebis p'roblema* [Comparative phonetics of the Kartvelian languages, vol. 1: The problem of the structure of the syllable]. Tbilisi: Universit'et'i.

1963. *Kartuli enis rit'mik'ul-melodik'uri s'trukt'ura* [The rhythmic–melodic structure of the Georgian language]. Tbilisi: Codna.

10   The word in Modern Greek

Brian D. Joseph[1]

1   Introduction

Despite centuries of sophisticated grammatical analysis of the Greek language (see, e.g., Robins 1993 and Koerner and Asher 1995 on the Greek grammatical tradition), we are no closer, perhaps, to a fully satisfactory account of what a 'word' is in that language than what the syntactically based definition given by the Hellenistic grammarians (Robins 1993: 57) has to offer:

(1)   perì léxeōs: léxis   estì   méros   toû   katà
       about word+GEN word-NOM is-3sg part+NOM ART+GEN concerning
       súntaxin   lógou   elákhiston
       syntax /ACC expression+GEN least/NOM
       On the word: a word is the minimal part of a syntactic construction

Moreover, the characterisation of the linguistic construct 'word' is, as far as Modern Greek is concerned, as vexed an issue as in other languages, despite some attempts in the literature at resolving it (e.g. Philippaki-Warburton and Spyropoulos 1999). Nonetheless, as the other chapters in this volume show, some progress can be made towards developing both a working definition and a suitable set of heuristics that might permit the identification of proper units of analysis that instantiate the 'word', understood in some appropriate sense. In this chapter, this issue is explored in detail, and such a set of criteria for determining 'wordhood' for Greek is developed. In addition, a full discussion is offered of the attendant problems with these criteria and this determination.

[1] The many participants at the International Workshop on the Status of 'Word' offered lively discussion of the issues contained herein and comments that I benefitted greatly from. I would like to thank Amalia Arvaniti and Giorgos Tserdanelis for their help with some of the data and Rich Janda for healthy criticism of various notions presented here; also, the editors of this volume provided useful comments on an earlier version. The usual disclaimers as to their complicity hold.

2   Some important preliminaries

2.1   *The theoretical framework*

Many of the relevant issues pertaining to the identification of 'word' in Modern Greek hinge on the treatment of what might be neutrally referred to as 'little elements', what have been called 'clitics' in the literature.

The literature on 'clitics' is enormous (see Nevis et al. 1994 for relevant bibliography) and in this vast amount of scholarship, one finds incredibly varied ways in which different linguists have used the term 'clitic'. Some take it almost to be any short word-like entity that has some grammatical function and some prosodic deficiencies, and more tellingly, perhaps, relatively few linguists justify the use of the term for any particular element in the language under examination, as if it were always self-evident that a given element was a 'clitic'.

There is a solution in this terminological and analytic morass. As argued by Arnold Zwicky, in a number of works (but especially Zwicky 1985, 1994), the use of the term 'clitic' is most uninformative. He suggests that 'clitic ... is an umbrella term, not a genuine category in grammatical theory' (1994: xiii). Moreover, noting that many 'phenomena [that] have appeared under the clitic umbrella ... merely have marked properties in one or more components of grammar' (xv), Zwicky claims that instead of recognising 'clitic' as a primitive element in the vocabulary of grammatical description, all that is needed is the more restrictive typology of just 'word' versus 'affix', and the recognition that there are typical and atypical words as well as typical and atypical affixes. If we want to use 'clitic' as a cover term for atypical words and atypical affixes, so be it, but it need not be a grammatical primitive, a construct required by the grammar (so also, Everett 1996, 2000).

This is a view that I personally find very appealing, not only for its elegance and economy but also for its precision. Accordingly, in this chapter, I generally avoid the use of the term 'clitic', and instead attempt to show that considerations of typicality, as suggested by Zwicky, are of great benefit in bringing some clarity to some often confusing data.

Since 'clitics' and such 'little' (i.e. clitic-like) 'elements' in general provide most of the direct challenges to any attempt to unambiguously identify words, all of the ensuing discussion of these elements clearly has a bearing on how the notion of 'word' is to be defined and determined for Modern Greek. In addition, some other tests relevant to this determination are examined.

2.2   *Range of clitic-like phenomena in Greek*

Modern Greek actually has a fairly large number of potential candidates for 'clitic' status; while these are typically treated as if they were words (in some sense) or 'clitics' (whatever the term might mean), some (especially those with grammatical functions) may instead be analysable as affixes (possibly inflectional in nature). A full enumeration of these elements is given in (2).

(2)   a. elements modifying the verb, clustering obligatorily before it (when they occur), marking:

subjunctive mood (general irrealis):	na
subjunctive mood (hortative):	as
future (and some modality):	θa
negation (indicative):	ðe(n)
negation (subjunctive):	mi(n)

     b. elements marking argument structure of verb ('object pronouns'), occurring as the closest element to verb (i.e. 'inside of' modal etc. modifiers above), positioned before finite verbs and after non-finite verbs (imperatives and participles); 'ACC' stands for direct object markers, 'GEN' for indirect object markers:

person	SG.ACC	SG.GEN	PL.ACC	PL.GEN
1	me	mu	mas	mas
2	se	su	sas	sas
3m	ton	tu	tus	tus
3f	tin	tis	tis	tus
3ntr	ta	tu	ta	tus

     c. weak third person nominative (subject) markers (with two – and only two – predicates, ná '(t)here is/are!' and pún 'where is/are?', always after the predicate and inseparable from it):

person	SG	PL
3m	tos	ti
3f	ti	tes
3ntr	to	ta

     d. 'weakened' (different from weak forms, cf. below) nominatives (i.e. subjects):

person	SG	PL
1	γo	mis
2	si	sis

     e. attitudinal marker (of impatience), dé, always phrase-final (except for one fixed expression, dé ke kalá 'with obstinate insistence')

     f. pronominal marking of possession within noun phrase (so-called 'genitive' pronouns, typically occurring at end of noun phrase after noun; identical in form with weak indirect object markers but not in all behavioural aspects (see below)):

person	SG	PL
1	mu	mas
2	su	sas
3m	tu	tus
3f	tis	tus
3ntr	tu	tus

g. definiteness within the noun phrase (the so-called 'article'):

case	M.SG	F.SG	NTR.SG	M.PL	F.PL	N.PL
NOM	o	i	to	i	i	ta
ACC	ton	tin	to	tus	tis	ta
GEN	tu	tis	tu	ton	ton	ton

h. locative/dative preposition *s(e)* 'to; in; on; at', always phrase-initial, attaching to whatever occurs next in noun phrase (but not necessarily always 'clitic'; see below).

Examples of these elements are given in (3), with the relevant elements underlined:

(3)   a. <u>ðe</u>   <u>θa</u>   <u>ton</u>   páte   <u>s</u> <u>to</u> spíti <u>su</u>
          NEG FUT   him+3sg+ACC go+2pl+PRES to the house your
          You won't take him to your house

      b. <u>as</u>   <u>min tus</u>   <u>ta</u>   púme <u>ta</u> néa <u>mas</u>
          SUBJUNC NEG them+GEN them+NTR+ACC say+1pl the news our
          Let's not say our news to them

      c. <u>na</u>   <u>su</u>   éɣrafe
          SUBJUNC   you+GEN write+3sg+PST+IMPFVE
          He should have written to you

      d. pés   <u>to</u>   <u>dé</u>
          say+IMPV.SG it+ACC   de
          So say it already!

      e. pún   <u>dos</u>?   Ná   <u>tos</u>!
          where.is he+WK+NOM here.is he+WK+NOM
          Where is he? Here he is!

      f. kséro   <u>ɣó</u>
          know+1sg   I+NOM(WKNED)
          How should I know?

In the sections that follow, after a brief typology of Modern Greek, the issue of how to characterise some of these elements with regard to wordhood or affixhood – or in-between status, if such is warranted – is addressed in the context of a general consideration of tests and parameters in Greek that might define the word for this (stage of the) language.

2.3   A quick typology of Modern Greek

A brief overview of Modern Greek from a typological standpoint is useful by way of setting the stage for understanding the data and argumentation to follow. Accordingly, it can be noted that Greek has a reasonable amount of inflection – in the verb, in the noun and pronoun and in the adjective – more so than any 'standard average European' language (but not as much as Ancient Greek, for instance). The categories in (4) are the relevant ones:

(4)   a. NOUN: case, number, gender (plus declensional (stem-)class)
       b. VERB: person, number, tense, voice, aspect, mood
       c. ADJECTIVE: case, number, gender (plus possibly comparative/
                      superlative)

The way categories are expressed reveals Greek to be a fusional–synthetic language, with individual endings encoding several different grammatical categories all at once, e.g. the verbal ending *-es* = second person and singular and past, the verbal suffix *-θik-* = past and non-active and perfective, nominal ending *-us* = accusative and masculine and plural (and *o*-stem), but not to an extensive degree (i.e. Greek is not polysynthetic). Still, there are some seemingly agglutinative structures in the language (e.g. (3a), if all the pre-verbal elements are affixes (see §3)) as well as some analytic formations that move Greek away from being a perfectly well-behaved fusional–synthetic language. For instance, the perfect tense is formed periphrastically, consisting of the verb 'have' (Greek *éxo*) plus a perfect formative (an invariant non-finite form), e.g. *éxo lísi* 'I-have untied', and these parts can be separated, as in (5):

(5)   éxi   o   jánis   lísi
       have+3sg   the   John+NOM   untied+PERF
       John has untied

Similarly, there are occasional bipartite verbs, consisting of, for instance, the verb *káno* 'make' plus a nominal form, that describe a unitary activity/event and are even paralleled in some cases by monolexemic verbs, as in (6):[2]

---

[2] There are two other types of ostensible multiword units that deserve mention here, though they will not be treated systematically. First, as John Henderson has reminded me, Greek has word-level units, discussed first by Rivero 1992, that are composites of noun or adverb stems with verbs, e.g. *ksanavlépo* 'I-again-see' (i.e. 'I see again') (cf. *vlépo ksaná* 'I-see again'). These are best treated simply as lexically derived compounds (Smirniotopoulos and Joseph 1998); they behave with respect to inflection (e.g. with the grammatical 'little elements' or with person/number marking) just like non-compound verbs. Second, there are nominal compounds that consist of two nominal words (not stems), each of which is capable of inflection, e.g. *xóra-mélos* 'member-country (e.g. of an alliance') (lit. 'country – member'), whose nominative plural form is *xóres-méli*, with both parts inflected. These are admittedly difficult to analyse as to their word-level status; see Joseph and Philippaki-Warburton (1987:227–8) for discussion, including the fact that some such compounds show inflection only on the first member.

(6)   a. ðen ton   káno   γústo
           not him+ACC make+1sg taste
           I don't care for him
        b. ðen ton   γustáro
           not him+ACC like+1sg
           I don't care for him

For the most part, though, the characterisation of Greek as synthetic–fusional gives an accurate picture of the general structure of words and the expression of grammatical categories.

3   Various types of 'word' and relevant criteria and tests

We are now in a position to begin to investigate various criteria and tests that might be brought to bear on the identification of 'word' in Modern Greek. It is assumed here that for Greek, the construct 'grammatical word' is based on 'word' as listed in the lexicon, representing major syntactic categories: noun, e.g. *spíti* 'house'; verb, e.g. *lín-* 'untie'; adjective, e.g. *árosto-* 'sick'; preposition, e.g. *apó* 'from'. Admittedly, the bipartite verbs such as *káno γústo* in (6) above meet some of the criteria for grammatical word status discussed by Dixon and Aikhenvald in chapter 1 (§7), including cohesiveness, in that the parts always occur together, and fixed order. Even so, though, such combinations typically involve two forms that occur independently in other contexts, and the meaning of the combination is roughly compositional (e.g. *káno* 'make' + *γústo* 'taste' = 'have a taste (i.e. a liking) for'), contrary to the criterion of conventionalised meaning. Thus, except for such verbal units, which could after all simply be treated as Verb + Object idioms, there is no reason to posit a level of 'grammatical word' different from 'lexical word' plus other independently needed machinery (e.g. inflections) for Greek.

In such an approach, however, there are some representational issues that need to be addressed. First, with regard to inflection, following Lyons 1968, the lexical listing is stem (i.e. lexeme – see also the discussion by Dixon and Aikhenvald in chapter 1 (§4.1)) and inflected forms (where they exist) are then the grammatical words. A relevant question here is the representation of the vexing 'little elements', many of which have grammatical function (as with the markers in the verbal complex) and thus could be considered inflection, and thus properly part of a grammatical word. Alternatively, one needs to consider instead if they are separate grammatical words in their own right, with their own lexical listings. Moreover, besides grammatical word as delineated here, one has to entertain the possibility that there may be a distinct level of phonological word, though this depends to some extent on how all the 'little elements' with grammatical values are analysed; if they are inflectional affixes, then much of what might be called a 'phonological word' is simply created by regular word-formation and inflectional processes.

It is thus appropriate to begin an examination of tests and criteria pertaining to wordhood with various aspects of Greek phonology, in particular with regard to the segmental level, to phonotactics, to morphophonemics and to suprasegmentals and especially word accent. Moreover, these areas constitute the most interesting and fruitful lines of evidence for relevant criteria, since, as §3.6 indicates, morphological evidence alone is inconclusive.

3.1   Phonological factors – segmental

As suggested by Dixon and Aikhenvald in chapter 1 (§6a), word domains and boundaries in some languages place restrictions on segmental distribution, so that a first consideration towards defining 'word' concerns examining the segments of Greek and especially which segments can occur where and in which types of words. The segmental inventory of Greek is given in (7):

(7)   p b f v   t d s z θ ð t^s d^z k g x γ   r l m n   j   a e i o u

However, all of these sounds can occur utterance-initially, so there is no test for wordhood based on possible initial segments. For final segments, the situation holds more promise, as there are some restrictions, although loan words now interfere with the probative value of such final segment restrictions. Still, a generalisation can be formulated as in (8) regarding final segments for words that have been in Greek for more than about a hundred years[3] and not from the archaising high-style katharevousa register:[4]

(8)   Only -s, -n, and *vowels* are allowed word-finally in Modern Greek (for certain classes of words).

The extent to which recent loans and learned borrowings have altered that generalisation is evident from the forms in (9) with other final segments:

(9)   a. foreign loans: *mát^s* '(football) match', *zéniθ* 'zenith', *tést* 'test', *fílm* 'film', *asansér* 'elevator', *básket* 'basketball'
          b. learned borrowings: *ánθraks* 'coal', *íðor* 'water'

---

[3] The reason for this temporal parameter is that in the twentieth century, presumably owing to different attitudes on the part of native speakers of Greek with regard to nativisation of loanwords, literally hundreds of loans, especially from French in the first half of the century and later from English, entered the language with only minimal phonological adaptation.

[4] This distinction is necessary owing to the sociolinguistic situation prevailing throughout most of Post-Classical Greek period but with particular intensity in the nineteenth and twentieth centuries, in which an archaising, high-style form, 'katharevousa' and a more colloquial, stylistically lower form, 'demotic', competed in a classic diglossic situation (see Ferguson 1959). To some extent, both this distinction and that concerning the age of a loan mentioned in note 3 reflect a linguist's somewhat omniscient perspective, not necessarily a naive native speaker's.

Moreover, there is even a class of native Greek words (or word-like forms) with a wider range of possible word-final sounds, namely interjections, onomatopes, clippings and acronyms, as in (10), which, like borrowings, violate (9):

(10)   *matˢ-mutˢ* 'kissing noise'
         tˢak 'cracking noise'
         ax 'Oh, ah!'
         prokat 'pre-fab (houses)' (clipped from *prokataskevasména spítia* 'pre-fab(ricated houses)')
         PASOK (acronym for <u>pa</u>nelínio <u>so</u>sialistikó <u>kí</u>nima 'Pan-Hellenic Socialistic Movement')

However, it is not entirely clear that all such forms in (10), especially the onomatopes, should be treated as 'words'.[5] Thus the segmental level proves inconclusive regarding a characterisation of 'word'; accordingly, we turn to the next level up in a phonological hierarchy, namely that of clusters.

3.2   *Phonological factors – phonotactics of clusters*

Examining consonant clusters is somewhat more promising, since some clusters are found only utterance-internally and never utterance-initially or utterance-finally, e.g. ... *atlázi* ... could not be lexically segmented into ... *a#tla* ... or ... *atl#a* ... or (except for the case of recent loans and acronyms) ... *at#la* ... , and so could only be *#atlázi* ... 'satin ... ', while ... *atmí* ... could be *-a#tm-* (since word-initial *tm-* occurs, cf. *tmíma* 'department', thus possibly *(mikr)a tmí(mata)* 'small departments') or ... *#atmí* ... (e.g. *atmí* 'vapours') but not ... *atm#í-*.... Still, it seems unlikely that one would want to define 'word' in Greek as that entity which begins with sounds other than **tl-* (etc.) and/or ends with something other than **-tl, -tm* (etc.). It seems, therefore, that the level of phonotactics of clusters does not lead anywhere productive, and the restrictions on clusters may be simply descriptive generalisations that have little import in the characterisation of 'word'.

3.3   *Morphophonemics*

Even though clusters in general, viewed from a phonotactic standpoint, offer little insight here, there is one particular type of cluster that holds more promise:

---

[5] One can of course legitimately ask whether forms such as *matˢ-mutˢ, ax*, etc. are 'words'. While they can stand as independent utterances and in some sense are 'minimal syntactic units', they are functionally different from *spíti, lín-*. A functionally based characterisation of 'word' that would exclude interjectional utterances might be problematic, since some (apparent) interjections are 'quasi-grammatical', e.g. the one-word prohibitive utterance *mi!* 'Don't!', which shows a synchronic connection (in a complicated way – see Joseph and Janda 1999, Joseph 2001c) to the bound subjunctive negator *mi(n)* (see (3b)).

combinations of nasals plus stops. Examining these combinations leads into a consideration of morphophonemics and 'wordhood', addressed in this section.

3.3.1 Nasal-induced voicing The basic relevant facts concerning stops and nasals are as follows. The status of the plain voiced stops [b d g] in Greek is rather tricky. At the lexical level (what corresponds to 'grammatical word' in traditional terms), for many (now generally older) speakers, excluding recent loans, [b d g] occur by themselves only word-initially and occur medially only after a nasal; thus _brostá_ 'in front' but _émboros_ 'merchant' (not *_éboros_). Moreover, again excluding recent loans, there are no cases word-internally of a nasal + voiceless stop (i.e. no cases of *VmpV*). But even for (some) such speakers, the initial stop can sometimes (perhaps rarely) be lightly pre-nasalised in some words, and medially, the preceding nasal consonant can be quite 'weak' and sometimes even absent (all subject to a complex of factors including addressee, style, speech rate, etc.),[6] i.e. [ᵐbrostá] / [éᵐboros]~[éboros], and for some (mostly younger) speakers, the nasal is (almost) categorically absent. This distribution, even for older speakers, has been somewhat disrupted by loan words, so that for some speakers, [robót] 'robot' has only a voiced stop and [sampánja] 'champagne' shows no medial voicing (while for others, there can be voicing in such loans, e.g. [sambánja], and for yet others borrowed medial voiced stops can be 'propped up' with a nasal, e.g. [rombót] or [roᵐbót]).

This situation is complicated by facts bearing involving combinations of the 'little elements' of (2) with a 'host' element, for in these, final nasals induce voicing on following voiceless stops at boundaries (and the nasal undergoes place assimilation); e.g.:

(11)   /ton patéra/   → [tom batéra]
        the father/ACC
        /tin píraksa/   → [tim bíraksa]
        her I-teased
        /ðen pirázi/   → [ðem birázi]
        not it-matters

Optionally (again subject to a complex of factors), the nasal can be weak or even absent, but also, for some speakers, sporadically, there is no voicing whatsoever and sometimes just deletion of the nasal, e.g. [ti(n) píraksa] 'I-teased her'.[7]

---

[6] All of the hedging in these statements is necessary due to the complex sets of sociolinguistic conditions attendant on the nasal + stop realisations; see Arvaniti and Joseph 2000 for some discussion and literature. Given the variation, it is difficult to describe the status of [b d g] for the Modern Greek speech community taken as a whole.

[7] Such forms probably reflect the effects of hypercorrective pressures (see Kazazis 1992) or even spelling pronunciations, but such explanations alone of their occurrence are not enough to warrant discounting them.

Some linguists take the voicing in these combinations as evidence that a level of phonological word must be recognised, combining grammatical (lexical) words into phrases in which certain phonological effects are located, and note that the voicing effects, while similar to what is found word-internally, are not identical (the [ti píraksa] outcome is not found in medial position); for such linguists, the 'little elements' are 'clitics'. Alternatively, if the 'little elements' are affixes, one could point to the similarity of the 'boundary' phenomena to word-internal combinations with voiced stops, and treat the [ti píraksa] outcome as part of the idiosyncrasy of affixal combinations (thus considering the construct as a morphological word or perhaps morphosyntactic word, with the affixes as the realisation ('spell-out') of various features, such as [+negation] or [+3SG.F.DIR.OBJ])

Still, some voicing can be induced by what must be a word in any approach. For instance, for some speakers (maybe only in fast speech), the complementiser *án* 'if' can trigger voicing on a following stop, as in /*án pó*/ 'if I-say' → [*ám bó*]. Such facts might tip the balance in favour of the (grammatical-words-combining-into-a-) phonological-word approach and against the affixal/morphological-word approach, although counterbalancing the possibility of voicing here is the further fact that for some speakers as well, the usual outcome of /*án pó*/ is [*ám pó*], definitely not a word-internal type outcome. Moreover, in any case, it can never have the nasalless realisation *[a *bo*], even for speakers who usually do not have a nasal with a voiced stop word-internally. Therefore, there is indeed *some* difference between combinations with articles, pronouns, etc. and combinations with more clear-cut grammatical words (contrast *(na) ti(m) bó* 'should I-tell her' with *ám pó*). This might well be taken by some as evidence for an intermediate construct such as 'clitic' or simply as atypical word- or atypical affix-behaviour.

Yet, there is another way to view all this, in the light of still further facts. The genitive weak pronoun used for marking indirect objects is formally identical with the genitive weak pronoun used for marking possession (cf. (2b, f)), but they show different behaviour vis-à-vis nasal-induced voicing. In particular, the object pronouns (which are affix-like in showing idiosyncrasies, high selectivity, strict ordering, etc. – see Joseph 1988, 1989, 1990) are voiced post-verbally after the imperative singular of *káno* 'do, make', the only context where a weak object pronoun occurs after a nasal-final host in the standard language, as in (12):

(12)   kán   tu   mja xári → [ká(*n*) *du* ...]
        do+2sg+IMPV   him+GEN   a-favour
        Do a favour for him!

However, the homophonous possessive pronoun *tu* 'his' in *ton anθrópon tu* 'of his men' (lit. 'of.the.men+GEN+PL of.him') does not undergo voicing – *[ton anθrópo(*n*) *du*] is impossible (for many speakers, though some variation is to be found). Most treatments label both of these instances of *tu* as 'words' (e.g. 'clitic words'), but their differential behaviour here is reason for separating them, despite their homophony, and thus possibly also reason for treating the object pronouns as affixes and the possessives as words (admittedly an atypical kind of word, a prosodically weak 'bound' word). One can note further that the possessives are unaffix-like in being able to move around within the noun phrase without altering meaning, thus showing a reordering that is only stylistic in nature (see the discussion by Dixon and Aikhenvald in chapter 1 (§7)). For instance, both *o kalós fílos tu* 'the good friend of.him' and *o kalós tu fílos* 'the good of.him friend' are acceptable for 'his good friend'. At the very least, then, voicing should probably be separated into a couple (or more) (sub-)processes, and one possible generalisation for voicing is that prosodically weak words cannot undergo post-nasal voicing (maybe more specifically, not induced by a verbal 'host').[8]

Thus, nasal-voicing in Greek, a phenomenon which has been taken by some to motivate a level of phonological word and analyses in which there is a class of 'clitics' distinct from affixes and grammatical words, need not be interpreted in that way. Some of the behaviour is in fact consistent with a view that starts just with words and affixes, though recognising the possibility of atypicality for some instantiations of these, so that the morphophonemics of nasal voicing can be treated rather as evidence of affixal status for some of the 'little elements'.[9]

3.3.2 Morphophonemic irregularities One further issue pertaining to morphophonemics and what they may say about wordhood in Greek is the claim made by Philippaki-Warburton and Spyropoulos (1999: 65) that 'in Greek... there are no... special irregularities in the morphophonology of the clitic[pronoun]s'. The presence of various sorts of idiosyncratic features is characteristic of affixes and morphological combinations, and less expected with syntactically distributed elements (i.e. words), as noted by Zwicky and Pullum 1983, so Philippaki-Warburton and Spyropoulos use their claim as an argument against treating the weak pronouns as affixal; they say that since there

---

[8] This generalisation is admittedly not overly broad, but it does differentiate possessives from weak object pronouns. If accurate, moreover, it allows for a determination of the status of the weak nominatives (cf. Joseph 1994, forthcoming b), e.g. *tos* (cf. (2c, 3e)), since the *t*- of *tos* can, and in fact must, be voiced in its post-nasal occurrence with the predicate *pún* 'where is/are?', i.e. *pún dos* 'Where is he?' (not **pún tos*). It would thus *not* be a prosodically weak word (i. e. *not* a clitic) and therefore is best treated as an affix (thus a new verbal inflection, for subject, in the language, though with two and only two predicates).

[9] A level of *phonological phrase*, however, is a different matter; the nasal-induced voicing and regressive assimilation seen in *am bo* would reflect a phrase-level ('post-lexical') set of processes. That they duplicate in some way the word-internal morphophonemics with the addition of (weak-pronouns-as) inflectional affixes is a consequence of the analysis argued for here, but since the word-internal and the phrasal phenomena are not point for point identical (recall **a bo*), no analysis can collapse the two environments.

is no idiosyncrasy, these elements are not affixal. However, their argument fails in two ways. First, it is not the case that all affixes necessarily show idiosyncrasies – the presence of idiosyncrasies may be probative but their absence says nothing in and of itself. Second, it turns out that there in fact are various irregularities in the morphophonology of the weak pronouns that Philippaki-Warburton and Spyropoulos overlook.

For instance, in the combination of 2sg.GEN *su* + any third person form (necessarily accusative since two genitives cannot co-occur), the *u* may be elided, thus: *su to stélno* 'to-you it I-send' may surface as *sto stélno* 'I send it to you'. However, there is no *general* process of Standard Modern Greek that elides (unaccented) *-u-* in such a context; there is a regular process eliminating unaccented high vowels in northern dialects, but in the Standard language – based on a southern dialect – there is deletion of unstressed high vowels only in fast speech. Thus, one might imagine that some form of that process is at work in *su to stélno* → *sto stélno*, but that cannot be the case. A deleted *u* typically leaves a 'mark' on a preceding *s* in the form of rounding, e.g. /sutárizma/ 'shooting' becomes [sᵂtárizma]; importantly, though, this rounding never happens in the reduced form of the indirect object marker *su*, i.e. [sto stélno] but not *[sᵂtostélno]). Thus the elidability of the *-u-* in combinations like *su to (stélno)* is not attributable to a general property of Greek phonology but rather is a feature of the particular combination of *su* with a third person pronoun, i.e. it is a morphological irregularity associated with *su*, contrary to Philippaki-Warburton and Spyropoulos' claim.

So also in the combination of any third person form with the markers *na* and *θa*, the initial *t-* of the pronoun may (optionally, with considerable idiolectal variation) be voiced to [d]; thus *θa to stélno* 'FUT it I-send' can optionally surface as *θa do stélno* 'I'll be sending it', even though intervocalic *t* in Greek is not usually distinctively voiced and *na* and *θa* do not canonically end in *-n* (the typical voicing element in Greek – see above in §3.3.1); *θa* did end in a nasal in earlier stages of Greek but *na* never did and in any case there is no sign of a nasal before a vowel (where it would be expected if there were one with these forms canonically) – the contrast of *θa stélno* 'I will be sending' but *θa alázo* 'I will be changing' (not *θan alázo*) with *ðe stélno* 'I do not send' but *ðen alázo* 'I do not change' (not *ðe alázo*) is instructive in this regard. Thus the voicing triggered by *na* and *θa* on third person weak pronouns is an idiosyncrasy of these combinations, countering Philippaki-Warburton and Spyropoulos' claim about the pronouns.[10]

Therefore, there is indeed morphophonological idiosyncrasy associated with the weak pronouns. Moreover, Philippaki-Warburton and Spyropoulos (1999: 65 n.5) themselves do recognise that there are ordering restrictions, as

---

[10]   Moreover, the triggering of voicing here can also be considered an idiosyncrasy associated with *θa* and with *na*, and thus constitutes evidence suggestive of affixal status for these elements. See also note 13 below.

well as combinatorial restrictions; for instance, first and second person combinations cannot occur (i.e. there is no way of saying 'He is sending you to me' using weak pronouns). All of these observations therefore point to an affixal analysis, and thus are consistent with the general approach taken here and with the conclusions in §3.3.1 above concerning nasal voicing and §3.5 below concerning accent placement.

3.4   A further segmental phenomenon

There is one further segmental phenomenon in Greek, referred to by Philippaki-Warburton and Spyropoulos (1999: 54) as 'euphonic -e', that is worth considering here, since they give it as an argument for taking some of the 'little elements', specifically the weak pronouns, as words and not as affixes. This turns out to be particularly interesting to consider, for a wider range of data indicates that just the opposite interpretation is called for.

Philippaki-Warburton and Spyropoulos claim 'there is a strong preference for open syllables in word-final position [see (10) above]. When a word terminates in final -n, there is a tendency for a euphonic -e to be added after it in order to obtain a word final open syllable', e.g. milún/milúne 'they speak'. Observing further that 'affixes . . . have no need for such a constraint nor do they show such a tendency' and noting that 'clitic [i.e. weak] pronouns may appear with such final euphonic -e', e.g. tone vlépo 'him I-see' (acceptable also: ton vlépo), they offer these facts as an argument for word-level status for the weak pronouns.

However, there is an unsettling vagueness in the reference to a 'tendency' – Philippaki-Warburton and Spyropoulos themselves admit that 'not all words ending in -n will add a euphonic -e' – as well as an their unfounded assertion as to causality when they state that 'those that do are *clearly* [emphasis added] motivated by this preference for word final open syllable'. More important, though, their argument can be countered empirically.

First, there are indeed words ending in -n that never take 'euphonic -e', e.g. betón 'cement' (never *betóne), endjaféron 'interesting/NTR.SG' (never *endiaférone), as well as grammatical elements which the authors themselves want to call words that do not take -e, e.g. the indicative negator ðen 'not'. Thus, it is not at all clear that 'euphonic -e' is a useful indicator of wordhood.

Second, the real generalisation is not that words can take this -e but rather that inflectional morphemes do, or rather can, since not all actually do. The best cases of euphonic -e come with various verbal and nominal grammatical endings, e.g. 3PL.PST -an, 3PL.PRES -un and GEN.PL -on (among some others). Therefore, 'euphonic -e' would provide an argument that accusative singular weak pronouns ton/tin are inflectional morphemes instead of words. And this generalisation would explain why betón and endjaféron do not take the -e, since the -n in those elements is part of the word-stem, and not part of an inflectional marker; the underlying stem in 'interesting' is arguably endjaférond-, given the genitive singular *enðjaférond-os*, whereas *betón* is an indeclinable loanword (from French *béton*), so that the *-n* simply is a part of the lexical stem. Moreover, the failure of negative *ðen* to take *-e* would instead be an index of idiosyncrasy, and thus would be consistent with, and even argue for, an affixal analysis of negation (as argued also in Joseph 1990, on different grounds).

While there are other phonological phenomena involving segments that might be investigated, most seem to be inconclusive at best.[11] However, an area of considerable interest, as well as controversy, involves Greek suprasegmentals, in particular, the placement and nature of the stress accent in combinations involving the 'little elements'.

3.5   Suprasegmental issues

The basic facts about accent in Modern Greek are as follows: in general, there is at most a single main stress accent in a grammatical (i.e. inflected) word, underlyingly (in its lexical form), and it must fall on one of the last three syllables. The feminine nouns in *-a* show all the possibilities: *peripétia* 'adventure' versus *ðimokratía* 'democracy' versus *omorfiá* 'beauty'. When a clear inflectional suffix is added to a stem, it can trigger a rightward accent shift in a stem that has (lexical) antepenultimate accent, e.g.:

(13)   ónoma   name (NOM/ACC)
        onóma-tos   of a name (GEN)

Such facts have traditionally been treated (e.g. in Joseph and Philippaki-Warburton 1987) as consistent with a principle that the accent in a grammatical word can be no farther from the end of the word than the antepenultimate syllable. When a pronoun (including the possessives) is added to the end of a word with antepenultimate accent, however, it triggers the addition of an accent, which becomes the primary accent, on the syllable before the pronoun, and a

---

[11] For instance, the potential location of *pauses* (as discussed by Dixon and Aikhenvald in chapter 1 (§5)) says little, since pauses (or really the Greek equivalent of pausing, the filler sound [e] or the protraction of a vowel) can occur within traditionally defined grammatical words, e.g. *enðiaaa¶ féronda* 'interesting things/NTR.PL'. Moreover, a prosodic definition of *minimal word* yields an 'almost' argument for some types of words, but close is not good enough: statistically, by far, most nouns, verbs and adjectives contain at least two syllables, but there is a non-negligible number of monosyllabic forms, rendering this 'test' unreliable. These include nouns, e.g. *jós* 'son/NOM', *jó* 'son/ACC' (and even more if loanwords are taken into account, e.g. *jót* 'yacht', *gél* 'sex appeal', etc.); adjectives, e.g. *blé* 'blue', *móv* 'mauve', etc.; and verbs, e.g. imperatives such as *ðés* 'see', *pés* 'say', *bés* 'enter', etc., all of which can occur by themselves as one-word utterances, imperfectives with surface diphthongal nuclei, e.g. [páw] 'I-go', [páj] '(s)he goes', [kléj] '(s)he cries' (though these are almost certainly disyllabic underlyingly, and possibly so in careful speech) and perfectives such as *pó* 'I-say', *ðí* '(s)he sees', etc., which, while not able to occur by themselves as one-word utterances, and so always co-occur with some other element (e.g. *ópote ðí* 'whenever he-sees'), nonetheless occur with forms that are clearly separate words (e.g. *ópote* 'whenever').

concomitant reduction of the (lexical) antepenultimate accent to a secondary accent:

(14)   to ónoma the name / to ònomá tu the name his (i.e., his name)
         kítakse! Look! (IMPV.SG) / kìtaksé me Look-at me!

Such facts have also traditionally been treated as induced by a ban on accent farther from the end of a word than the antepenultima, with the reduction triggered by a ban on more than one main stress in a word.

For linguists inclined to treat pronouns as word-like entities of some sort (e.g. 'clitics', with their own maximal projection in the syntax), these facts have motivated a higher level construct such as 'prosodic word' (implicit, e.g., in the accounts of Arvaniti 1991, 1992) or 'clitic group' (e.g. Nespor and Vogel 1986), or perhaps simply 'phonological word', since the pronouns behave differently from clear affixes (which shift accent) and from clear word combinations (which have no accentual effect); recall also §3.3.1 regarding nasal-induced voicing and how that can be used as a basis for defining 'phonological word', e.g. with article + noun (and other) combinations.

Still, these accentual facts in and of themselves, despite their being consistent with non-affixal status for the weak pronouns, are not conclusive evidence for that categorisation, and in fact can just as well be taken as evidence for the opposite classification. That is, there are several different idiosyncratic accent requirements with affixes, e.g.:

(15)   a. the neuter GEN.SG -tos requires accent placement two syllables to
            the left of -tos, e.g. 'name' ónoma / onómatos, 'verb' ríma / rímatos
         b. the neuter GEN.PL -ton requires accent placement one syllable to the
            left of -ton, e.g. 'name' ónoma / onomáton, 'verb' ríma / rimáton
         c. the IMPERF marker -ús- always attracts the accent onto it (whereas
            the alternate IMPERF marker -ay- does not necessarily attract the
            accent, being accented only if antepenultimate), e.g. filó 'I kiss' /
            filúsa ~ fílaya 'I was kissing' (cf. 1pl filúsame ~ filáyame 'we were
            kissing')
         d. the 1pl -me is never accented and requires no particular accent
            placement, i.e. it is accentually inert

This range of accentual effects associated with affixes means that the accent addition with weak pronouns, if affixal, could simply be one such idiosyncratic effect an affix can have.

The argumentation needs some further development, but the case can be made. Admittedly, the possessive pronouns also provoke accent addition. Thus, if they are 'clitics', or atypical, i.e. prosodically special, words, one could argue that the weak pronouns should fall into the same category. Otherwise, the argument would go, the grammar would have duplication through the multiple statements needed for accent addition, in that some affixes would do it and so would 'clitics' (or some words, as the case may be).

However, what makes this an interesting case is that there are some differences between weak pronouns and possessives, for instance with regard to nasal-induced voicing, as shown in §3.3.1 by the difference between *ká(n) du* 'do for–him' (cf. (12)) and *anθrópon tu (*anθrópo(n) du)* 'of his men'. Thus somehow these two elements need to be differentiated in the grammar: if accent addition with the possessives and weak pronouns is consistent with their both being words, the post-nasal voicing facts are consistent with their each being a different kind of element. Of considerable importance here is the fact that there are prosodically weak words, e.g. the attitudinal marker *dé* (cf. (2e) and (3d) above) with different accentual properties. In particular, *dé* always 'leans' on the end of a host but never provokes accent addition (e.g. *ðokímase* 'try!' (IMPV.SG) / *ðokímase dé* 'try already!' / **ðokìmasé de*); therefore accentually, *dé* and the possessives like *tu* have to be differentiated, so that even within the class of words, accentually distinct behaviours must be stipulated. If one were to say that possessives are 'true' clitics, based on their accentual behaviour, then presumably weak pronouns belong in the same class, since they behave accentually like the possessives. What then of the post-nasal voicing differences (cf. (12))? Should the grammar recognise four (or even more) distinct morphosyntactic elements: word versus possessive-type 'clitic' versus weak-pronoun-type 'clitic' versus affix?

A solution here is to follow the strict categorisation schema outlined in §2.1 and to recognise only affix and word as basic constructs, while at the same time setting some tokens apart within those categories by way of recognising different behaviours and realising that affixes can show various idiosyncrasies. This approach may also mean that one should give up on trying to generalise over accentual behaviour as a way of differentiating basic morphosyntactic element types, though recognising differences within larger types.

Of interest here, but not, strictly speaking, relevant for Standard Modern Greek is the fact that some dialects (but not Standard Greek) have accent addition with some disyllabic forms that ostensibly are affixes. For example, in northern Greek one finds *érxu-mi* 'come/1sg'/*érxu-másti* 'come/1pl' (versus Standard Greek *érxome* / *erxómaste*). While one could of course say that these endings have been reanalysed as clitics, that would seem to be begging the question of how to identify such entities in the first place.[12]

---

[12] See Joseph 2001b for discussion of relevant dialectal facts concerning the status of 'word'. Not only are the accent addition facts quite different in some regional dialects, but so are the accent placement facts; Crimean Greek, for instance, allows words with the lone accent five syllables from the end, as in *timázanandini* 'they were preparing' (Standard Greek *etimázondan*); see Delopoulos 1977 and Newton 1972 for examples.

Thus, the upshot regarding accent and wordhood is that while it does admittedly provide a basis from which one might motivate an affix versus clitic distinction, or a grammatical word versus phonological word distinction, it is not a clean basis. The relevance of this observation for a general theoretical framework for dealing with such elements is taken up in §4.

3.6   Some possible morphological criteria

With various phonological criteria for wordhood examined, it is possible to move up the grammatical hierarchy to see if there are any purely morphological criteria that are relevant here. As it happens, some of the observations from the previous sections can be 'tweaked' a bit to yield a morphological generalisation about wordhood that is limited in scope but not completely unrevealing.

First, it should be noted that there are some borrowed nouns and adjectives that are invariant with no inflection whatsoever, e.g.:

(16)   to ble jot   tu ble jot   ta ble jot
        the blue yacht+NOM   the blue yacht+GEN   the blue yacht+PL

However, there are no uninflected verbs. Therefore, a finite set of verbal endings (marking person, number, tense, etc.) allows for verbs to be uniquely identified, at least paradigmatically (i.e. in relation to other forms). Thus while [pó] could conceivably be a noun (cf. [jó] 'son+ACC'), once it is linked with [pís]/[pí]/[púme] etc. (2SG/3SG/1PL), it is clearly identifiable as a verb, as a member – specifically 1sg – of the paradigm of the perfective forms of 'say'. Moreover, if one ignores uninflected nouns and adjectives, a generalisation is possible about the shape of a subclass of words, namely *inflected* words:

(17)   All inflected words in Greek end in -s or -n or a vowel.

Still, however valid (17) may be, ending in -s or -n or a vowel is not in itself an identifying mark of a word, since many clear inflectional and derivational affixes end in -s or -n or a vowel (cf. 2sg -s as in *pís*, 1pl -me as in *púme*, etc.), and some *uninflected* words do too, e.g. *tóte* 'then', *méxris* 'up to', etc.). It is not at all obvious therefore that morphological considerations offer a significant generalisation that has any validity for determining or defining (or refining) the notion of 'word' for Greek.

4   Summation regarding wordhood

The most controversial – and thus the most interesting – aspects of the determination of wordhood in Greek hinge on the analysis of the various grammatical elements presented above in (2) and (3). Some of those elements – in particular the verbal elements θa, *na* and $\partial e(n)$ (from (2a)), the weak object pronouns (from (2b)) and the third person weak subject pronouns (from (2c)) – have been examined here to varying degrees and have been argued to be affixes, and not independent or even prosodically weak words, whereas others – in particular the attitudinal marker *dé* (from (2e)) and the possessives (from (2f)) – give evidence of being prosodically weak or deficient words. Further arguments for the affixhood or wordhood for these elements are possible, as is a determination concerning the word or affix status of all of those not systematically treated here, i.e. the weakened nominative pronouns (from (2d)), the definite article (from (2g), and the locative/dative marker (from (2h)).[13] Still, the evidence discussed here concerning the weak pronouns especially gives a glimpse of what can be done with a highly restrictive set of assumptions about wordhood. This is so even if some of the resulting analyses – as with accent placement – are a bit messy, so to speak, in that some stipulations are needed, e.g. as to accent addition being one of several accentual effects associated with affixation rather than a feature that falls out automatically from some other sets of facts.

It can be argued, though, that even with some messiness on the side of the word-and-affix-only approach, it is not at all clear that there is anything to be gained by adopting an analysis that is based on the multiplication of the number of basic morphological entities that linguistic theory must recognise. That is, there is a trade-off between, on the one hand, the neater, more constrained system one has with the recognition of only word versus affix as basic morphological constructs and the few stipulations that are needed in such a system, and, on the other hand, a system with a greater number of basic morphological entities but perhaps fewer stipulative statements. It may not be an even trade-off, though, since one can argue that the default assumption in all instances should be to avoid multiplying basic units – since some stipulation is always needed – until it is convincingly demonstrated that such an approach cannot work. That is, recognising a third type of element, e.g. 'clitic', as a basic morphological construct should always be at best a last resort, a highly marked – and thus 'costly' – analysis.[14] I would argue that the Greek facts do not compel one

---

[13] Regarding additional argumentation, see, for instance, Joseph (1988, 1994, forthcoming b) and Nevis and Joseph 1993 for arguments for the various pronominal elements as affixes, Joseph 1990 concerning the indicative negator and Joseph 2001a, on the future marker. Additional evidence beyond these considerations, as well as arguments concerning many of the other elements, is discussed in Joseph (forthcoming a). As for the elements not discussed here, my inclination is to treat the locative/dative marker *s(e)* and the definite article as (bound, i.e. prosodically weak) words, though the jury may still be out on them, and the weakened subject pronouns as nothing more than phonologically conditioned variants of the strong forms (see Joseph forthcoming b).

[14] This is essentially the view taken by Zwicky 1994, a position with which I agree wholeheartedly. It is perhaps significant to note here that, as ubiquitous as 'clitic-like' elements seem to be (so that some linguists see them everywhere!), there are languages that do not have any such elements; as Dixon argues in chapter 5, Jarawara is just such a language, with no grammatical elements that might be called 'clitics'.

to recognise such a marked construct; all relevant facts can be accounted for under a system with just words and affixes, and the independently needed scale of typicality within each construct.

It may well be, of course, that more distinctions among elements are needed, and indeed, even the approach advocated here, with words and affixes, and degrees of typicality for each, recognises that on the surface, there can be more than two kinds of entities. Underlyingly, however, even an atypical element, it is claimed, must be categorised as either an affix or a word, however much it may deviate from other members of its category. Under this approach, this merely reflects the 'messy' reality, but the grammar has to make the difficult decisions, so to speak, and give definitive classifications. That in effect is the job of the grammar. The situation described here is thus analogous to what is done routinely with regard to sounds: it is often the case that numerous and physically diverse surface phones are categorised as the same at an abstract level of analysis referred to as the 'phoneme'; that is, the grammar imposes discrete category membership on elements with superficially different properties. So also with the classification of what are here, e.g., called typical and atypical affixes as members of a single basic morphological type.

5   Conclusion

In addition to all the foregoing argumentation, with its synchronic analytic basis, an entirely different area of linguistic investigation, that of diachrony and the examination of language change, can be mined for some added perspectives concerning 'word' as a grammatical construct. As it happens, there are three lines of evidence that emerge from the way languages change that can be brought to bear on the identification of 'word'. These are discussed here, by way of conclusion, with illustrative examples from Greek where possible.

First, the notion 'word' might have some value in contact situations, in terms of helping to define what is borrowed. Although phrases can be borrowed (e.g. Greek has borrowed Turkish *anadan babadan* 'from-mother from-father' as *anadam babadam* meaning 'from way back, for generations'), borrowing of individual words is by far the most common type of borrowing. Moreover, while affixes can be borrowed (e.g. Greek borrowed an Italian diminutive suffix and hellenised it to give *-utsiko-*; the Turkish occupational suffix *-cI* / *-çI* was borrowed as *-tsis* / *-dzis*; and the English plural *-s* has been borrowed), the medium for borrowing of affixes is most likely the *word*. For example, the *-s* plural in Greek is restricted to words of English origin, e.g. *ta tests* 'the tests', and there are also some cases of *-s* being borrowed and used as a part of the stem, as with *to klips* for '(the) clip' (singular!). While it is true that borrowed affixes can appear on words other than the original word that brought them into the language, so that *-tsis/-dzis* (from the Turkish occupational suffix) is highly productive in Greek now and not just limited to originally Turkish words (note, e.g., *o taksi-dzís* 'the taxi-driver'), the occurrence of an affix in such novel contexts need not be taken to mean that the affix by itself was borrowed; rather, it can be viewed as resulting from the extraction of the affix out of particular instances of the affix attached to a borrowed word, i.e. as a perfectly ordinary case of morphological segmentation and analogical spread based on the analysis by speakers of word-level units in their language (whatever their ultimate origin). Thus the distinction between words and affixes seems to play a role in language contact.

Second, the notion of 'lexical diffusion' (Wang 1969, among others) claims that the vehicle for the spread of sound change is the word, or rather, the lexical entry; morphemes could be intended here as something that fits the bill, since sound changes are found in endings, prefixes and roots, as well as in unanalysable units, but the claims of Wang and others have focussed on the 'word'. There is no relevant evidence from Greek here, but generally speaking, it can be argued that there need not be a separate mechanism of change, i.e. 'lexical diffusion' – distinct from analogy and dialect borrowing – that has to be recognised; that is, analogy and dialect borrowing together can give a diffusionary effect in the realisation and spread of sound change, thus relegating a putative process such as lexical diffusion to epiphenomenal status (see Joseph 2001a). However, if one believes in lexical diffusion, then such a process may offer a useful handle on defining/determining 'word'.

Third, and finally, there are many sound changes which come to be restricted to occurrence at word boundaries. While that in itself might be taken to suggest an importance for 'word' as a theoretical construct, it may well be that such conditioning on sound changes does not reflect the original state of affairs with any given change. That is, following the Neogrammarian view that sound changes are not in and of themselves conditioned by non-phonetic factors, and given that word boundaries are not phonetic entities, any instances of a word-boundary-conditioned sound change would have to be the result of reanalysis and generalisation of the change. One possible source for such reanalysis and generalisation is from utterance-final (or utterance-initial) position to word-final/initial position; utterance edges are phonetically defined (e.g. by silence, by the vocal folds standing at rest, etc.) and word edges of course can coincide with utterance boundaries. Another source is an original syllabic basis for change, since word onsets necessarily give possible syllable onsets and word-initial position can be utterance-initial position where no resyllabification is possible. Thus, even if a sound change might originate in such a way as to be oblivious to word boundaries (per Neogrammarian principles), it seems that speakers often impose a word-boundary basis onto the effects of a sound change, altering (i.e. reanalysing) the original basis for the change; often also, linguists studying the aftermath of a change only see the results of the reanalysis and generalisation and formulate (erroneously) the historical statement of the change in terms of word boundaries.[15] An example from Greek is the loss of *-n* in word-final position – since *n* before some consonants, particularly the fricatives, was lost word-internally, as in *nífi* 'bride' from Ancient Greek *númphē* or the widespread *áθropos* 'man' from earlier *ánθrōpos*, the loss of word-final *n* (as in earlier *peðín* 'child' → *peðíØ*) can be understood to be the generalisation of an original loss of *-n* before word-initial fricatives (e.g. *to peðín fandázete* → *to peðíØ fandázete* 'the child imagines') to a broader set of contexts.

What all these cases show is that words really do seem to matter to speakers; therefore, linguistic theory must take them into account, and the question of how to identify and delineate this construct in general is a serious challenge to linguistic theory that cannot be ignored. The present examination of these issues in individual languages such as Modern Greek is thus offered here as a (partial) contribution to what must be an on-going cross-linguistic investigation.

References

Arvaniti, A. 1991. 'The phonetics of Modern Greek rhythm and its phonological implications'. PhD dissertation, University of Cambridge.

1992. 'Secondary stress: evidence from Modern Greek', pp 398–419 of *Papers in laboratory phonology*, Vol. 2: *Gesture, segment, prosody*, edited by G. Docherty and D. R. Ladd. Cambridge: Cambridge University Press.

Arvaniti, A. and Joseph, B. 2000. 'Variation in voiced stop prenasalization in Greek', *Glossologia, A Greek Journal for General and Historical Linguistics* 11–12. 131–66 (preliminary version in *Ohio State Working Papers in Linguistics* 52.203–33 (1999)).

Delopoulos, G. 1977. 'To vório iðíoma sti mesimvriní rosía' ['The northern dialect in southern Russia'], pp 263–304 of *A' Simbósio ylosolojías tu vorioelaðikú xóru*. Thessaloniki: Institute for Balkan Studies.

Everett, D. 1996. *Why there are no clitics: an alternative perspective on pronominal allomorphy*. Dallas: Summer Institute of Linguistics.

2000. 'Why there are no clitics: on the storage, insertion, and form of [phi]-features', pp 91–114 of *Lexical specification and insertion*, edited by P. Coopmans, M. Everaert and J. Grimshaw. Amsterdam: John Benjamins.

Ferguson, C. 1959. 'Diglossia', *Word* 15.325–40.

Hock, H. 1976. 'Review Article on Anttila 1972', *Language* 52.202–20.

Joseph, B. 1988. 'Pronominal affixes in Modern Greek: the case against clisis', pp 203–15 of *Papers from the 24th Regional Meeting, Chicago Linguistic*

---

[15] See Hock 1976 for a discussion of cases where formulations of sound changes in terms of word boundaries are actually better analysed as based on syllable structure or utterance-finality. Posner (1996: 290) states the conditions for *e-* prosthesis in Romance languages to have been based on word boundaries (#sC- → #esC-) when in fact, as recognised by Lausberg (1956 ff), the original basis for this development was syllable-shape in connected speech (i.e. 'Satzphonetik' or sentence-sandhi), as seen in the standard Italian facts that Posner herself notes, namely that 'prosthesis is limited to postconsonantal contexts' (e.g. *la scuola* 'the school' versus *in iscuola* 'in school').

Society, edited by L. MacLeod, G. Larson and D. Brentari. Chicago: Chicago Linguistic Society.

1989. 'I erminía merikón voríon típon tis prostaktikís katá ti simeriní morfolojikí θeoría ['The interpretation of several northern forms of the imperative according to current morphological theory'], *Eliniki Dialektolojía* 1. 21–6.

1990. 'The benefits of morphological classification: on some apparently problematic clitics in Modern Greek', pp 171–181 of *Contemporary morphology*, edited by W. Dressler, H. Luschützky, O. Pfeiffer and J. Rennison. Berlin: Mouton de Gruyter.

1994. 'On weak subjects and pro-drop in Greek', pp 21–32 of *Themes in Greek linguistics (Papers from the First International Conference on Greek Linguistics, Reading, September 1993)*, edited by I. Philippaki-Warburton, K. Nicolaidis and M. Sifianou. Amsterdam: John Benjamins.

2001a. 'Is there such a thing as "Grammaticalization"?', *Language Sciences* (Special Issue – *Grammaticalization: a critical assessment*, edited by L. Campbell) 23(2–3).163–86.

2001b. 'Dialect evidence bearing on the definition of "word" in Greek', in *Proceedings of First International Conference on Greek Dialects and Linguistic Theory*. Patras: Department of Philology, University of Patras.

2001c. 'Is Balkan comparative syntax possible?', pp 17–43 of *Comparative Syntax of Baltic Languages*, edited by M. Rivero and A. Ralli. Oxford: Oxford University Press.

2002. 'Morphologization from syntax', in *Handbook of historical linguistics*, edited by B. Joseph and R. Janda. Oxford: Blackwell.

forthcoming a. 'Defining "word" in Modern Greek: a response to Philippaki-Warburton and Spyropoulos 1999'. To appear in *Yearbook of Morphology*, 2001.

forthcoming b. The Modern Greek weak subject pronoun to *τος* – its origins and implications for language change and language structure: a study in grammatical change, to appear in Innsbrucker Beiträge zur Sprachwissenschaft series, Universität Innsbruck.

Joseph, B. and Janda, R. 1999. 'The Modern Greek negator μη (ν)(-) as a morphological constellation', pp 341–51 of *Greek linguistics: proceedings of the 3rd International Conference on Greek Linguistics*. Athens: Elinika Gramata.

Joseph, B. and Philippaki-Warburton, I. 1987. *Modern Greek*. London: Croom Helm.

Kazazis, K. 1992. 'Sunday Greek revisited', *Journal of Modern Greek Studies* 10(1).57–69.

Koerner, E. F. K. and Asher, R. E. 1995. Editors of *Concise history of the language sciences: from the Sumerians to the cognitivists*. New York: Pergamon.

Lausberg, H. 1956–62. *Romanische Sprachwissenschaft*. Berlin: de Gruyter.

Lyons, J. 1968. *Introduction to theoretical linguistics*. Cambridge: Cambridge University Press.

Nespor, M. and Vogel, I. 1986. *Prosodic phonology*. Dordrecht: Foris.

Nevis, J. and Joseph, B. 1993. 'Wackernagel affixes: evidence from Balto-Slavic', *Yearbook of Morphology* 1992.93–111.

Nevis, J., Joseph, B. Wanner, D. and Zwicky, A. 1994. *Clitics: a comprehensive bibliography 1892–1991*, Amsterdam Studies in the Theory and History of Linguistic Science, Series V: Library & Information Sources in Linguistics 22. Amsterdam: John Benjamins.

Newton, B. 1972. 'The dialect geography of Modern Greek passive inflections', *Glotta* 50(3–4).262–89.

Philippaki-Warburton, I. and Spyropoulos, V. 1999. 'On the boundaries of inflection and syntax: Greek pronominal clitics and particles', *Yearbook of Morphology* 1998 45–72.

Posner, R. 1996. *The Romance languages*. Cambridge: Cambridge University Press.

Rivero, M-L. 1992. 'Adverb incorporation and the syntax of adverbs in Modern Greek', *Linguistics and Philosophy* 15.289–331.

Robins, R. H. 1993. *The Byzantine grammarians: their place in history*, Trends in Linguistics, Studies and Monographs 70. Berlin: Mouton de Gruyter.

Smirniotopoulos, J. and Joseph, B. 1998. 'Syntax versus the lexicon: incorporation and compounding in Modern Greek', *Journal of Linguistics* 34.447–88.

Wang, W. 1969. 'Competing changes as a cause of residue', *Language* 45.9–25.

Zwicky, A. 1985. 'Clitics and particles', *Language* 61(2).283–305.

   1994. 'What is a clitic?', pp xii–xx of Nevis et al., 1994.

Zwicky, A. and Pullum, G. 1983. 'Cliticization vs. inflection: English *n't*'. *Language* 59(3).502–13.

11   What can we conclude?

P. H. Matthews

1   Introduction

The problem of the word has worried general linguists for the best part of a century. In investigating any language, one can hardly fail to make divisions between units that are word-like by at least some of the relevant criteria. But these units may be simple or both long and complex, and other criteria may establish other units. It is therefore natural to ask if 'words' are universal, or what properties might define them as such. Dixon and Aikhenvald set out admirably in chapter 1 the terms in which these questions, among others, might be discussed. I am not sure, however, that the way I have just posed them is of much help.

Other chapters make clear not just that criteria conflict, but that different linguists may resolve some kinds of conflict very differently. In chapter 10, for instance, Joseph offers a solution for the so-called 'clitics' in Modern Greek that is evidently resisted by most other specialists in the language. For students of Romance his chapter may recall especially what Bally said, in different terms, about French (1965: 287ff). Bally used the term 'word' only in inverted commas, as did Martinet, also a French-speaking linguist, in his textbook (1960). But we may equally be tempted to describe the sentence in (1) as one word, not, as the orthography would have it, as six.

(1)   je-ne-l-ai-pas-vu
        1sg+NEG$_1$+3sg+AUX.1sg+NEG$_2$+see.PP
        I didn't see it

Our problem, as it is often presented, is to determine whether this or some competing treatment is right. We are therefore urged to seek a universal theory, whether of words or of some other unit such as Bally's 'molécule syntaxique', which will rigorously determine what the truth about each language is.

But it is no easier, as we well know, to establish that such theories are themselves right. The 'truth' about Greek is that, in its ancient form, the word was not a problem. Some forms were accentually enclitic: in (2), for example, *tis* is an enclitic that is said to 'throw back' a high pitch onto the final syllable of what would otherwise be *nê:sos*:

(2)   nê:sós   tis
       island+NOM.sg   some specific+NOM.sg
       an island

But enclitics were themselves words: *tis*, for example, was the nominative singular in a paradigm like that of many nouns. In Modern Greek the forms called 'clitics' pose a problem which the inherited orthography undoubtedly disguises. We can explain objectively, in terms of facts that are undoubtedly relevant, both where it lies and what the alternative solutions might be. The most obvious truth is therefore that this problem exists. If it were resolved in one way Greek would still seem to be 'flexional'; but a typologist who relied on this might associate it misleadingly with languages for which the facts encourage no other answer. In the alternative view, its inflectional type might tend more towards that of Cup'ik, as described by Woodbury in chapter 3. But that statement too cannot be swallowed without qualification. The true type is simply that of other languages in which the nature of our difficulty is similar.

In taking this view I am inspired by an inaugural lecture by Bazell (1958), little noticed and well worth rereading. Linguistics in the west has roots, however, in the analysis of languages in which the word itself was not a problem. Of these Latin, in particular, still influences our thinking: not least that of scholars who write introductions to morphology, such as my own (1991). It may therefore help if I begin with a brief look at its structure, both as seen in antiquity and in the terms that Dixon and Aikhenvald propose.

2   The word as established in Latin

Latin had inherited words for 'word' and 'name' related etymologically to those of English. *Nomen* 'name' was then used by the grammarians for a 'noun' in general, following the development of the corresponding word in Greek. *Uerbum* 'word' became their technical term for 'verb'. But, in ordinary usage, to say something in one word was still to say it 'in one *uerbum*'; to express it differently was to use 'other (plural) *uerba*'.

For 'word' itself the grammarians had instead a term of art, whose form was calqued directly on a similar term in Greek. The origins of ancient grammar are in part obscured (see, for instance, Matthews 1994); but the Greek term (*léxis*) was a nominalisation of the root for 'say' (*leg-*), adapted to this usage not more than a century before the Romans took the technical concept over. Latin *dictio* 'way or act of speaking' was a similarly transparent nominalisation of the root *dic-* and, as the term for 'word', was defined by the same formula that Joseph cites in Greek at the beginning of his chapter. An 'utterance' (*oratio*) was defined physically, as a stretch of vocal sound (*uox*) formed, in ancient accounts, by air set in motion. As speech, it was articulated ultimately into spoken 'letters': as many have remarked, the ancient term for 'letter' (*litera*) might as easily be translated by 'speech sound' or 'phoneme'. The *dictio* 'word' was thus the smallest unit from which such a stretch of speech was formed directly. In (3), for example, the whole would have been a single 'utterance' or sentence:

(3)   Romam   deleui
       Rome+ACC.sg   destroy+PERF.1sg
       I destroyed Rome

It was made up of two words, or as the grammarians also said, two 'parts of an utterance'. Each was in turn composed of syllables (*ro, mam, de, le, ui*), which were themselves composed of letters with their phonetic value (*r*, long *o*, and so on).

The grammarians defined no units but these: no other into which words were divided, none intermediate between it and the sentence. For any word the first task was accordingly to ask 'what part' or 'what part of an utterance' (*quae pars?* or *quae pars orationis?*) it was. *Romam*, for example, belonged to the 'part of speech', as we now call it, noun. One would then ask what were its 'accompanying' or 'contingent' properties (Greek *parepómena*, Latin *accidentia*): thus *Romam* was, among other things, a proper noun, in the accusative case, and singular. The next 'part', *deleui*, was a verb and, among other things, one which was active. So, in the light of this, these two 'parts' could stand in a transitive relation. This system was, of course, not that of specialists only; but was literally beaten into educated citizens throughout the empire.

It was also suited to the language. There is no doubt, first, that 'parts' like those in our example were both morphological and syntactic units. They were grammatically complex and, in broad terms, it is possible to distinguish stems from variable 'endings'. For example, *deleui* could be divided into a verb stem (*de:le:-*) and inflectional ending (*-ui:*). In terms of our criteria these were totally cohesive: there was no construction in which stems and endings could be separated. Their order was again fixed: there was no form such as *ui:-de:le:*, and, if there had been, it would have had an unrelated meaning. They undoubtedly had 'a conventionalised coherence in meaning'. Our division between stems and endings is not ancient: in English, both terms were first used in this sense in the nineteenth century. The grammarians classed certain forms as compound. *Suburbanus*, for example, was composed of *sub* 'under' and *urbanus* 'of the city+MASC.NOM.sg'; hence its meaning 'close to the city+MASC.NOM.sg'. They included compounds in which component words were said to have been altered: for example, in *agricola* 'farmer+NOM.sg' we can distinguish forms related to ones with the meanings 'field' and 'cultivate', but not identical to them. In our eyes, the relation is between a stem *agr(i)-* and another stem *col-*. But semantic units smaller than the word were not identified.

By contrast, most 'parts' were themselves quite mobile. Their order in (3) was not subject to rule: it was also possible to say *deleui Romam*. 'Parts' that stood in a close syntactic relation were not necessarily adjacent: (4), for example, illustrates a pattern in which the copula verb (*erat*) splits a modifier (*magno*) from its immediate head (*periculo*), which are in turn split by a governing preposition (example from Adams 1994: 22):

(4) tum   magno   erat   in   periculo   res
     then   great+ABL.sg be+IMPERF.3sg   in   danger+ABL.sg   thing+NOM.sg
     Then matters were in great danger

If the 'morpheme' was not obvious to ancient linguists, neither was the 'phrase'. But the 'grammatical word', as seen by these criteria, would have stared them in the face.

Virtually the same 'parts' were distinguished phonologically. We know from ancient sources that an accent fell in positions determined, in part, by grammatical boundaries. In *Rómam* and *deléui* it would fall, as shown, on the penultimate syllable: so too, for example, in *Márcum* 'Marcus+ACC.sg' or *respóndit* 'answer+PERF.3sg'. This was so for any such form in which the penultimate was heavy: that is, either open with a long vowel (*ro:*, *le:*) or closed (*mar*, *pon*). If the penultimate was light it would fall on the syllable preceding: thus *uítulus* 'calf+NOM.sg'. This rule has been widely discussed (notably by Allen 1973), and the only problem, as we will remind ourselves in a moment, was that the boundaries of grammatical and phonological words, as defined by our criteria, did not coincide entirely. Most 'parts' ended either in a vowel or in a very restricted range of consonants: *m*, *s*, *r* or *t*. This was, to be more precise, a restriction on the phonology of inflectional endings. Other facts are not recoverable entirely. But we know, for example, that in verse a sequence such as *Roma et . . .* 'Rome+NOM.sg and', or indeed *Romam et*, counted as two syllables and not three. For an interpretation of the evidence see Allen 1978: chapter 4); but it is clear that the rule again refers to the same boundary.

We can therefore talk in ancient fashion of a single unit, implicitly 'grammatical' and 'phonological'. The exceptions seem to have been few, and are not all of the same type.

The best known are three forms classed in antiquity as 'enclitic'. One was the neutral interrogative particle, *ne*; the others one of the 'and' coordinators (*que*) and one of the 'or' coordinators (*ue*). They were the only monosyllables that end in short *e*, and, in contrast, short vowels elsewhere in a monosyllable were lengthened. They were also unaccented and in, for example, (5); the accent on *populus* was where it would be if *que* was part of the same phonological unit: *populúsque*, not *pópulus que*.

(5)   senatus   populus=que   romanus
       senate+NOM.sg   people+NOM.sg=and   Roman+NOM.sg
       the senate and people of Rome

That much is clear, though for the rule in general and for certain other possible 'clitics', our evidence is less secure (Allen 1978: chapter 5). At the same time these were units in syntax, attaching to a variety of 'hosts' and, in the case of *ne*, at varying positions in the sentence. They were also felt as separate. Our practice in writing spaces is a medieval innovation (charted by Saenger 1997). But the ancient abbreviation for (5) was precisely 'S.P.Q.R.'.

Other exceptions involve, for example, the preposition *cum* 'with', which in combination with a pronoun might be represented as in (6):

(6)   pax   uobis=cum
       peace you (pl)+NOM.pl=with
       Peace be with you!

There were also forms that dictionaries describe as either one word or two. The form *quousque* 'how far?' could alternatively have the order *usquequo*, and would thus fail one of our criteria. *Quomodo* (literally 'in what way?') would fail another when interrupted by *que*: *quo=que modo* 'and in what way?'. But the qualifications truly take up more space than they deserve. The word in Latin never was a problem; and, although the language was originally described by reference to a prior analysis of Greek, it does not seem likely that we would ourselves have had much difficulty if we had come to it cold.

The problems lie in justifying any other kind of unit. For morphemes, in particular, the difficulty is not simply that there was 'fusion'. In many other languages there is quite striking fusion; nevertheless the underlying forms of roots and affixes can be established without disagreement. In one like Latin that is just where we have difficulty. For the Roman grammarians, a noun like *puella:rum* 'girl+GEN.pl' was derived by adding the syllable *rum* to the corresponding ablative singular: *puella:* 'girl+ABL.sg' → *puella:rum*. This was their standard technique, whose application to, for example, Italian is still worth exploring (Matthews 1996). But if we look for morphemes we will find it hard to say how such forms should be analysed. Is the genitive, for example, *puella:-rum*, with an underlying stem *puella:-*? This stem would then be shortened in forms like *puella-m* 'girl+ACC.sg'. Or is it *puella-:rum*, with *-:rum* lengthening a stem whose underlying vowel is short? Is the ablative then *puella-:*? Or is there perhaps an underlying form *puella-e*, with an *-e* found in some other ablative singulars?

In contrast, it was very easy to establish paradigms. The word in ancient grammar was not formally a lexeme: on this point it might be wise to amend the remark by Lyons (1968: 197) cited by Dixon and Aikhenvald (chapter 1).

But *puellarum* (to return to the usual spelling) is unproblematically opposed, as plural, to the corresponding genitive singular, and as genitive, to forms in other cases. Every word that enters into such a paradigm must then be characterised by the meaning of a common lexical unit, however we define it.

3   How can general linguists help?

Since our conception of the word originates in the description of Ancient Greek and Latin, it is not surprising that they now seem to approximate to an ideal case, in which all our criteria agree. A language such as Georgian, as described by Harris in chapter 9, is another in which the identity of words is not traditionally a problem: its type is different from that of Latin mainly in that their internal structure is agglutinative. But the pattern may be ideal only in that that is how we have historically perceived it.

One conclusion that emerges clearly from this volume is that a grammatical 'word' does not also have to be a phonological 'word'. There is no 'logical reason' (Matthews 1991: 215) why it should: nevertheless, at that point, I implied that, when such units coincide, it is in some way more significant than when, for instance, morphemes happen also to be syllables. If the latter had coincided in the classical languages, we might happily have inherited a single term for both. The term 'syllable' referred in Greek to letters 'taken together'; and, in the case that we might then see as ideal, they would be 'together' both as sounds and in meaning. The 'problem of the syllable' would arise in languages in which 'grammatical syllables' are at variance with 'phonological syllables', in which 'phonological syllables' are clear but 'grammatical syllables' not easily identified, and so on.

Is our ideal of the word more valid? However confident our answer, it is a wise precaution to insist, with Dixon and Aikhenvald in chapter 1, that grammatical and phonological units should be distinguished. But two further properties of words in Latin are worth underlining.

The first is that they did not, or they did not obviously, form syntactic 'phrases'. The properties of phrases are, in many languages, in part those of grammatical words: thus in English, in *the old house*, the constituents occur in a fixed order, and the whole is cohesive in that the unit can be interrupted only by other constituents directly or indirectly subordinate to its head. Still less can *the*, *old* and *house* be 'scattered', as Dixon and Aikhenvald put it, 'throughout the clause'. These are among the criteria for, in general, a grammatical unit, which do not themselves define what kind of unit it is. In this light, a peculiarity of Latin is that they were met by just one, which had, in addition, almost every other feature, positive and negative, that we now perceive as 'word-like'. But in other cases both these properties may hold of smaller and of larger units.

We might therefore envisage a language in which the 'word' would in reality be no more than a minimal phrase. Within it smaller elements could form compounds, and in that sense some at least could be described as having, by our third criterion, a 'conventionalised coherence in meaning'. But larger phrases could likewise include what we would then call 'idioms'. Words would also include grammatical morphemes: those like, say, an invariant plural morpheme, which we would describe as bound at that level. But other single morphemes, of the type of English *of* or the conjunction *that*, would enter, and in a similar sense be 'bound', into larger constructions. There might be reasons why such morphemes should in turn be called 'words'; or, so far as our particular language is concerned, there might not. 'Words' might again have certain phonological properties; but larger phrases might in turn have others. It is by extrapolating from, for example, Chinese that one can perhaps see how a structure like this might be realised.

The second property is reflected in the way in which words are conventionally identified. Most again form paradigms: as Lyons and I have put it, they are characterised on the one hand by a lexeme and, on the other, by specific inflections. Something like the same point can be made for many other languages. As Dixon and Aikhenvald have put it in chapter 1, most grammatical words are 'centred on a root', or, in the case of compounds, 'on a combination of roots'. Exceptions, or at least perceived exceptions, are rare. Thus Dixon notes one instance in Jarawara (chapter 5, example (10)) where a word has, for specific reasons, no root.

But could there be a language which was radically different? Let us imagine, for example, that word boundaries in French fell clearly where they fall in writing. The form *les chauves-souris* could thus be represented as in (7):

(7)   l-e   ʃov-suri
        DEF+pl   bald+mouse
        the bats

Now we are used to saying that *les* is 'the plural of the definite article', just as, in the case of Latin, *illi* was a nominative plural of a demonstrative pronoun. But *illi* was part of a paradigm in which the categories, and many of the actual endings, were identical to those of nouns. There was thus good reason for describing it in that way. But there are no motives of that kind in French. The pattern would be simply one in which two 'morphèmes' or grammatical elements from closed classes, [l] 'definite' and [e] 'plural', form one word: schematically $g_1 g_2$. Two lexemes, or 'semantèmes', form another: $l_1 l_2$.

Could there then be languages in which a pattern such as this was general? Some words would consist of one or more grammatical elements: $g_1 \ldots g_n$. Others would be simple words or compounds formed from lexical elements:

$l, l_1 l_2$, possibly $[l_1 l_2] l_3$, and so on. I leave this as a question, since I have not heard of such a language. But the example from French reminds us that establishing 'roots' is in part a matter of perception. There are many cases, in particular, where words are formed from various affixes and what is classified as an 'auxiliary'. In most we have good reason for describing the auxiliary as a root on which the whole is centred. Thus, in particular, the same affixes attach to roots of main verbs. But in other cases the 'auxiliary' could, in reality, be just one of a sequence of grammatical morphemes.

What general 'theory' is then possible? I am not sure that I understand what every linguist means by this term. But one kind of 'theory' would propose constraints on what a language can in principle be like: for example, it could not be, even predominantly, of the type that I have just described. Now one proposition which is certainly implicit is that any language must have units into which an utterance may be organised, which, whatever semantic status they may or may not have, are not always semantically simple. There would accordingly be no language which did not have words or phrases, grammatical or phonological, of any kind. One issue, then, is whether more specific constraints can be justified.

If not, there are still ways in which general linguists can contribute. What has often been called a 'theory' is, in reality, more like a descriptive linguist's tool bag. Different types of language differ in the problems that they raise, and we naturally find that forms and methods of description which work well for one are of no help at all for others. An excellent instance is the demonstration by Rankin and his colleagues (in chapter 7) that, in their words, 'Siouan languages really do not lend themselves to description in terms of templatic morphology'. Others, of course, may. Dixon (in chapter 5) remarks in passing that in Jarawara, as in 'many other South American languages', there is no useful role for the distinction between inflectional and derivational processes. Now that distinction is bound up with the traditional conception of a paradigm: derivation is a relation between different lexemes, inflection between forms of the same lexeme. It is not primarily, as some writers carelessly imply, between two kinds of affix. When we have grasped that, it is clear that there will be cases where a language cannot be described successfully unless we have this tool in hand, and others where we will return it to our bag quite quickly.

This image is not new. But we need to be reminded that there are many general concepts that should not be generalised beyond the point at which their application is illuminating. In most languages the syllable, for instance, seems unproblematic. It is transparently so in languages that are described as 'syllable-timed', like Spanish; and, in this volume, it is only in Harris' account of Georgian (chapter 9), and Henderson's of Arrernte (chapter 4), that its character is an issue. Many indeed claim that the unit is universal, and that its properties are universally constrained.

'Universal' is another term, like 'theory', that is often obscure. But the concept of the syllable is one that we can certainly pull from our tool bag, and we all know cases, at least marginal, where its application is not easy. Southern British English *gardener* is represented, in the latest revision of Jones' pronouncing dictionary, as, alternatively, [ˈgɑː.dᵊn.əʳ], with three syllables, or [ˈgɑːd.nəʳ], with two (Jones 1997). The raised schwa indicates a possible syllabic nasal: thus [ˈgɑː.dn̩.əʳ]. But where lies the difference between that and a dissyllable? *Partner*, in contrast, is represented only as [ˈpɑːt.nəʳ]; but could it never instead be trisyllabic [ˈpɑː.tn̩.əʳ]? These are questions which we might be expected to answer if the syllable were posited as universal. But it is not clear that there is any other reason why they should be asked. We know that *gardener* is morphologically *garden-er*, and how *garden* itself can be realised. We know too that *partner* is not likewise *partn-er*. Any difference in the ways they can be realised is explained directly by that. If there is a schwa in *garden-*, *gardener* is three syllables; otherwise, does it matter whether, in either form, the [n] is called syllabic or not? I cannot pretend to any feel for Georgian, or for other Caucasian languages in which the syllable has been seen as problematic. But the notion that syllables are 'a universal' often carries with it the specific assumption that, in any language, they must be identified exhaustively. This may, in some, create more difficulties than it solves.

The problem in Arrernte is that the 'syllable' as identified by patterns of prosodic morphology is in general not a 'syllable' by phonetic criteria. The patterns themselves are clearly demonstrated; and, just as other rules in other languages 'count syllables', it would be hard to say that it is any other unit that is being counted here. It merely does not have a CV structure of a kind that syllables usually do have. Now we might well argue that, ideally, a 'metrical syllable', or syllable that is in one way or another counted, ought to correspond to a 'phonetic syllable'. It at least seems more like an ideal than the case where grammatical words are also phonological words. But the example is a warning not to mistake an ideal for a universal. For phonetic reasons we do not expect that syllables will have obligatorily a structure VC(C). But so what, once we recognise that other criteria may apply?

The issue for us is whether the word has any other status. No criterion is either necessary or sufficient, as Bazell, who is cited in chapter 1 by Dixon and Aikhenvald, made clear long ago. But they are relevant insofar as, in particular languages, they do tend to coincide. A form which is cohesive need not logically consist of elements whose order is fixed. I have already cited an exception in Latin; but, in Latin itself, it is precisely an exception. Nor do units which have 'a conventionalised coherence and meaning' logically have to be cohesive. A familiar example is that of separable verbs in German: infinitive *ausbleiben*, literally 'out-remain'; finite *bleibt* (...) *aus*. But, although this is a pattern systematic for verbs of that class, it too is exceptional within the language.

Otherwise forms meeting one criterion also meet the other: thus, with the same initial element, a noun like *Ausland*, literally 'out-country'. We have taken care to qualify 'words' as grammatical or phonological, and, in particular languages, we do find regular discrepancies. Dixon (in chapter 5) has identified three such in Jarawara: one, for example, holds for compounds. Another discrepancy involving compounds is reported by Henderson for Arrernte. But, within these languages, these are again exceptions to a general tendency in which such units, to quote Dixon, 'almost always coincide'. It is in that sense that both implicitly are 'words'; not, like the morpheme and the syllable, different units altogether.

Exceptions within languages are one thing; languages that would themselves count as 'exceptions' are another. The implication is again that of an 'ideal', from which such languages depart. But can we take it, firstly, that a language has 'ideally' words of both kinds?

There seems no reason, in particular, why we should always find it helpful to distinguish words in phonology. The criteria, as Dixon and Aikhenvald make clear in chapter 1, are specific to particular languages. Different kinds of evidence are relevant, and none need always be available. There are languages, for instance, which have no restrictions on the vowels or consonants with which word-like units may end. Some kinds, at least, may also be evidence for phrases: thus, especially, that of accentuation. What then is the relevant unit in, for instance, French? Examples (1) and (7) would normally have accents on their final syllable: *je ne l'ai pas vú*; *les chauves-sourís*. Neither can be partitioned into smaller units that are phonologically word-like: on that at least all analysts seem likely to agree. But what we actually call them will depend, in practice, on combined criteria from both grammar and phonology. If (1), for example, is a phrase in syntax we can agree that it is also a 'phrase' in phonology. The crucial evidence for that view of the grammar is that adverbs such as *encore* can be inserted before *vu*: *je ne l'ai pas encore vu* 'I've not yet seen it'. If it were instead a word grammatically we could agree that it was also a 'word' phonologically. Now in many languages there is a distinction in phonology between 'words' and 'phrases'. We have no reason, however, to claim that it is 'universal'.

Can we even take it that, at either level, our criteria will not regularly conflict? A specialist in Bantu languages might well feel that this situation was precisely that faced when, in practice, different ways of writing them became established. But let us assume, for argument's sake, that languages 'ideally' have words both in grammar and in phonology. Are both units then, 'ideally' at least, exhaustive? In the traditional account of Latin, all 'parts of the sentence' are words, clitics included. But, of the terms used in the preceding chapters, 'clitic' is the one that leaves me most confused. For it seems that, in an alternative view, a sentence may consist not wholly of words; but in part of 'words' and also in part of 'clitics', which are not 'words'.

4   'Clitics'

Let me begin at least by keeping the term in inverted commas. For it may be
that no single kind of unit is referred to.

The words in Greek originally called 'enclitics' were, to repeat, words. Some
were morphologically simple, and to that extent were also like affixes. But
others, such as *tis* in (1), were inflected ('some specific+NOM.sg'), and, in the
paradigm of the verb 'to be', some forms, such as *esti* 'is', were enclitic, while
others were not. In such words we could say, of course, that what was 'clitic'
was the root: *ti(n)-* (compare oblique forms such as genitive singular *tinos*), or,
in *esti*, a suppletive clitic alternant *es-*. But these too would be no more like an
affix than the root of any other lexeme. In Latin a unit such as *=que* 'and' was
again 'affix-like', as it was also 'root-like', in being morphologically simple.
But its status as a word has never been disputed. Affixes were elements specific
to word classes: thus a nominative singular morpheme, if that is what we want
to call it, was found only in nouns, pronouns, adjectives and participles. But the
enclitic in *populus=que* 'people+NOM.sg=and' could be attached to words at
the appropriate point in any form syntactically coordinated with another. These
points may seem obvious. But, as Woodbury's criteria for Cup'ik (in chapter
3, §6.2) also briefly remind us, the varieties of 'host' to which a 'clitic' can
be added may be crucial to the reasoning by which we call it 'clitic' in the
first place. Affixes too can have accentual peculiarities: thus, in Italian, the first
plural ending in (8) could similarly be said to 'move' an accent to the syllable
before it: third singular *mandá-va*, first plural *manda-vá-mo*.

(8)   manda-va-mo
       send+IMPERF+1pl
       (we) were sending

The difference between Italian *-mo* and Latin *=que* is that the forms to
which *=que* was attached were not limited morphologically.

In the traditional account *=que* was, accordingly, a word; it was merely not
like other words in its phonology. Its status seems to have been stable for a
long time, since its cognates in both Greek (*=te*) and in Sanskrit (*=ca*) patterned
similarly. Nor, in passing, does it have a reflex in the Romance languages. Now
we could, in principle, reserve the term 'word' for the forms that were not
enclitic. Thus, in Latin, *populus=que* could be represented not exhaustively,
as two words, but as a word *populus* plus another element that is neither a
word nor part of a word. The definition of a 'clitic' would then be as a residue.
In our example from Ancient Greek, the word *nê:sos* 'island+NOM.sg' could
similarly be said to combine, in its phonology, with a residual non-word *tis*.

In neither language may it matter greatly which way we decide to put it. But
for many linguists 'clitics' can be characterised more generally as, in the words

of another contributor, 'something "between" an affix and a word'. Is it possible that, for other languages, this second way of talking is more helpful?

There is no doubt that, in many, it is the difference between 'affixes' and 'clitics' that is difficult. One telling observation, in the account by Rankin and his colleagues in chapter 7, is that certain elements in Siouan have been classed by different linguists either as inflections or as enclitics, 'for almost the same reasons'. In their own account, the boundary between these categories is 'inherently unclear'. But, even if it were not, a Siouan 'clitic' would seem, if one may speak loosely, more like a peculiar kind of affix than, as in Ancient Greek or Latin, a peculiar kind of word. There are also languages like English in which 'clitics' are perhaps more literally intermediate. One can argue forever about the status of possessive -'s, vowel-less -n't and others. For these two, the issue is whether they should count as 'clitics' or as affixes. But I am not sure that the distinction is any easier between 'clitics' and words that are not 'clitics'. Some might well talk of a 'cline' in which -'s is at least more affix-like than word-like; the conjunction [ðət], among others, the reverse.

In this light, a typology of 'clitics' must explore the forms of reasoning that lead specialists in particular languages or families to make use of this term. Some, for example, use it only of a unit that is morphologically simple. That is one reason given by Olawsky (in chapter 8) for not applying it in Dagbani to what he calls 'bound' adjectives. These are, in themselves, 'grammatical words' that 'cannot constitute a separate phonological word', and may well be 'clitic' by some general definitions. But they do not have the properties of the elements that Olawsky does so classify. The term might also be applied to units that are merely unstressed or have a reduced or no vowel: thus, in English, [(ə)v] (*of*) or the article [ðə]/[ði]. We might not feel a need to argue that in, for example, *heaps of diamonds* the 'clitic', as we would call it, 'leans' in the traditional sense as either enclitic to the word before or proclitic to the one after. Some 'clitics', unlike =*que* in Latin, are a product of 'grammaticalisation'; hence, it is tempting to say, they can be indeterminate. But here too we should generalise with caution. Delbrück remarked, a century ago, that if we did not know the history of -'s in, for example, *the King of England's* we could easily imagine that it must have come from what had been an independent element (1901: 45f). For some languages, our earlier records do show changes in which words become more 'clitic'; or a 'clitic', in turn, more affixal. But in many cases we must rely entirely on techniques of reconstruction. These tend inevitably to take forms that are more 'grammaticalised' and manufacture from them 'earlier' forms that are more independent.

How much might all 'clitics' have in common? The term is generally applied when the criteria that usually identify a unit conflict. It does not follow that a clitic must be a third kind of unit. It may simply be that, in a particular language, a few forms which are either affix-like or word-like nevertheless do not have every property that affixes or words in general do have. But, with that proviso, our inverted commas may perhaps be tentatively suppressed.

The term is thus traditionally applied when, as originally in Ancient Greek, successive units are described as words in grammar but are not separate in phonology. It is not usual when, in contrast, one grammatical word is treated as two phonological words: thus again in Dixon's examples in Jarawara (chapter 5) or in Henderson's in Arrernte (chapter 4). But there are many tricky cases where we cannot expect consistency.

One, in particular, is where we might speak of two levels of inflection. (9), for example, illustrates the usual analysis of Modern Greek:

(9)   ton   sinántise
         3sg+MASC.ACC.sg   meet+PAST.ACT.3sg
         He/she met him

The verb *sinántise* is assigned to a verb paradigm; *ton* to one which is in part like those of nouns. Since the only accent is on *sinántise* the 'pronoun' is then said to be 'proclitic'. But in calling *ton* a pronoun one is clearly begging questions. We could, for example, add an object noun phrase: *ton sinántise ton patéra mu*, literally '...the father my'. If *ton* is a 'pronoun' this is then a case of so-called 'clitic doubling', which in Greek would be syntactically optional. But it is clearly not a pronoun in the sense that, for example, *him* in English is a pronoun. It does not, like *him*, have the syntax of an object noun phrase. If the so-called 'doubling' were obligatory, and *ton* morphologically simple, an unbiassed analyst might describe it without hesitation as an object prefix.

There is no need for me to repeat Joseph's arguments (chapter 10). It is worth remarking, however, that a recent grammar of Modern Greek defines a clitic pronoun as both 'structurally and accentually dependent on another word' (Holton, Mackridge and Philippaki-Warburton 1997: 506). One might equally well say that, in English *girls*, *-s* is 'structurally' as well as phonologically 'dependent on' *girl*. The problem in Modern Greek is that these forms are indeed, in that way, 'affix-like'. But at the same time they are still, in their internal structure, 'word-like'. The genitive singular *mu*, in *ton patéra mu*, can be analysed easily into a 'root' *m-* 'first person' and a genitive singular 'ending' *-u*. For the ending compare, for example, the forms traditionally represented as in (10):

(10)   t-u   anθróp-u
         the+GEN.sg   man+GEN.sg
         the man's

The analysis of (either) *ton*, as can be seen in part from Joseph's paradigms, is merely less straightforward. Are these words, then, which are in turn affixes within larger words? Or must we argue that, since *m-u* is a grammatical word, *ton patéra mu*, of which it is a part, cannot also be a grammatical word? Or do we say that, while *patéra* and *sinántise* are grammatical words, *mu* and *ton* are complex units that are neither parts of words nor yet words in themselves?

In my dictionary of linguistics, I defined a clitic as, in part, 'a grammatical element treated as an independent word in syntax' (1997: s.v.). But the 'treated as' is crucial: a definition cannot be expected to determine, for a linguist faced with a particular language, whether it 'has' clitics, or whether a specific unit, simple or complex, 'is' one. A clitic word is then defined as 'forming a phonological unit with the word that precedes or follows it'. This definition as a whole respects the ancient origin of the term 'enclitic', and, as Aikhenvald notes at the beginning of her discussion of Tariana (chapter 2), the term does 'typically' refer to 'morphological elements' which are like that. But she does not say 'words'; and in, for example, =*yanà-pe* 'pejorative-pl' (early in the text of §2.4.2), the clitic is, I take it, *yanà* itself. This is perhaps like saying that in Modern Greek, in an analysis I have not explored, *ton patéra mu* consists of a root *pater-* accompanied equally by affixes and proclitic and enclitic morphemes: *t=o-n-pater-a=m-u*. Now our 'ideal', which has already been partly questioned, is that sentences can be divided exhaustively into words, and words exhaustively into roots and affixes. On my interpretation, which is sharpened considerably by my reading of Aikhenvald's analysis of Tariana, the term 'clitic' is liable to be applied whenever we have any kind of difficulty in meeting it: in saying that a form is unequivocally a word; or unequivocally an affix; or, it should now be added, unequivocally a 'sémantème' or root. If the traditional definition is to be replaced, I cannot yet hazard anything more specific.

5   Are units like words necessary?

One putative 'universal' is, again, that every language will have words or continuous phrases of some kind. It is therefore fair to ask why this is so; or, if we are ultra-cautious, why we should expect this.

The answer usually implied is that sentences are more easily produced, and understood, if organised into such packages. If we try to elaborate this, we can easily lapse into waffle. But Zeshan's discussion of sign language (chapter 6) may perhaps inspire us to reflect, by contrast, on the nature of the vocal medium. For many linguists, 'languages' are systems realised equally by either gestures or speech; these include theorists, such as Lyons (1991), who command respect. But it does seem possible that, in part, the systems are themselves structured differently.

On the one hand Zeshan's 'compounds', for example, are like compounds in such languages as English, and exist for the same reasons. They too can be said to combine either 'words' or what might equally be called 'lexemes'. Her 'clitics' can again be seen as units that are 'word'-like but whose realisation is dependent on a host. But, on the other hand, it is not pedantic to query notions of 'phonology' in sign language. Phonology is defined by its place in a system of double articulation, in which languages are structured independently on two levels. This does not merely facilitate a multiplicity of 'signs', as Martinet originally remarked (1960); it also guarantees, or is one factor guaranteeing, the redundancy that is so clearly necessary, in the spoken medium, if forms are not to be misheard. This is familiar to phoneticians, and in grammar both syntactic rules in general, and rules forming larger units, contribute to the same end. In terms dating from the 1950s, these involve restrictions on the average probabilities of transitions from one morpheme to another, and probabilities that vary within and between sub-sequences (compare, in a much later formulation, Harris 1991). We can thus expect 'packaging', though not always, as the preceding chapters have shown, of the same kind. Now Zeshan makes clear that the roles of simultaneity and sequencing are different in the medium of hand gestures; so too that of iconicity. There is also no precise equivalent, at a still more elementary level, of a speaker's need to breathe at appropriate places. It then seems reasonable to ask what level of redundancy is necessary. Are the factors that potentially interfere with signed communication similar to those in spoken language, and of similar intensity?

Some similarities that link gestural to spoken 'language' may, of course, be due to influence from it. This does not mean that sign language is merely derivative. That would not only be politically incorrect, but indeed wrong. It is possible, however, that human sign language might not have some properties that it does have if spoken language had not evolved, whether (to avoid fractious speculation) earlier, or later, or in parallel.

References

Adams, J. N. 1994. *Wackernagel's law and the placement of the copula* esse *in Classical Latin*. Cambridge: Cambridge Philological Society.

Allen, W. S. 1973. *Accent and rhythm*. Cambridge: Cambridge University Press.

1978. *Vox latina*, 2nd edn. Cambridge: Cambridge University Press.

Bally, C. 1965. *Linguistique générale et linguistique française*, 4th edn. Berne: Francke.

Bazell, C. E. 1958. *Linguistic typology*. London: School of Oriental and African Studies.

Delbrück, B. 1901. *Grundfragen der Sprachforschung*. Strasbourg: Trübner.

Harris, Z. S. 1991. *A theory of language and information*. Oxford: Clarendon.

Holton, D., Mackridge, P. and Philippaki-Warburton, I. 1997. *Greek*. London: Routledge.

Jones, D. 1997. *English pronouncing dictionary*, 15th edn, by P. Roach and J. Hartman. Cambridge: Cambridge University Press.

Lyons, J. 1968. *Introduction to theoretical linguistics*. Cambridge: Cambridge University Press.

1991. *Natural language and universal grammar*. Cambridge: Cambridge University Press.

Martinet, A. 1960. *Éléments de linguistique générale*. Paris: Colin.

Matthews, P. H. 1991. *Morphology*, 2nd edn. Cambridge: Cambridge University Press.

1994. 'Greek and Latin linguistics', pp 1–133 of *History of linguistics*, Vol. 2: *Classical and medieval linguistics*, edited by G. Lepschy. London: Longman.

1996. 'Morfologia all'antica', translated by D. Bentley, pp 191–205 of *Italiano e dialetti nel tempo*, edited by P. Beninca', G. Cinque, T. de Mauro and N. Vincent. Rome: Bulzoni.

1997. *The concise Oxford dictionary of linguistics*. Oxford: Oxford University Press.

Saenger, P. 1997. *Spaces between words*. Stanford: Stanford University Press.

Index of authors

Index of languages and language families

Index of subjects

accent 9, 12–13, 16, 31, 42, 47–48, 58, 80,
  181–83, 188–98, 189n8, 192n9, 202,
  235, 249, 256–60, 258n12, 266, 269,
  275–78
  see stress
adposition 54–57
agglutinative language 8, 11–12, 24, 49, 57,
  80, 83, 101, 125, 180–83, 205, 228, 247,
  271
aktionsart 56, 61, 64, 67–68, 71, 156, 160–61,
  175, 197
analytic language 3, 11, 101, 140–43, 247
article 26, 29–30, 36–37, 45, 48, 142, 198,
  201, 221, 246, 252, 260n13, 272
aspect 52, 56, 60, 108, 119, 142, 156,
  175, 195–97, 218–22, 228, 239,
  247
aspiration 14–16, 49, 58, 68, 195
auxiliary 19, 22, 28, 44, 46, 53, 56, 56n10,
  72–74, 129–40, 134n4, 136n6, 136n7,
  143–51, 144n11, 147n13, 191–92,
  195–201, 239, 273

borrowing 34, 155, 249–50, 261–62
  see loanword

clitic 1, 9–10, 13, 13n8, 19, 24–28, 35–37,
  42–78, 101, 107–21, 126, 159–67, 176,
  195–200, 216–23, 230–31, 235–240,
  236n6, 244–46, 252–60, 253n8, 260n14,
  266, 270, 276–79
  boundary 19, 26, 43, 49–51, 50n7, 68, 93,
    100n2, 217
  enclitic 12, 19, 26–28, 42–78, 80, 89–97,
    108, 181, 181n4, 192–202, 205, 230,
    234–241, 238n7, 266–69, 276–79
  endoclisis 44, 53, 60
  host 25–6, 36, 43–51, 46n5, 54–57, 61–64,
    67–73, 91, 111–13, 164–67, 176, 217,
    220, 224, 230, 235, 239, 253, 258,
    270, 276
  mesoclisis 44, 74

proclitic 25–26, 43–44, 44n3, 47, 50–55,
  51n8, 58–63, 67–71, 188, 192, 205, 218,
  223–24, 236–37, 240, 279
compound 21–23, 28–30, 35–36, 51, 56, 59,
  101, 107, 113, 128–29, 147, 159–63, 167,
  173, 177, 184–89, 192, 195, 201, 205–7,
  210–16, 215n8, 224–26, 233, 241, 247n2,
  268, 272, 275, 279
consonant 14–15, 20, 25, 35, 49, 95,
  101–7, 110–12, 127, 182, 193,
  206–9, 227–28, 233–34, 239, 250–53,
  269, 275
constituent order 19, 57, 101, 191, 271

deictic 26, 56, 144, 164, 166, 197, 239
dependent-marking 57, 80
determiner 23, 56, 166, 215n8
dictation 2, 12, 31, 206
diphthong 14–15, 29–30, 36–37, 104–5, 206,
  256n11

evidentiality 60–61, 64, 67–68, 71, 73, 131,
  239

foot 12, 31, 80, 91–95, 98, 102–3, 205
fusional language 2, 11, 80, 83, 125, 180–83,
  205, 228, 247

gender 21, 33, 44, 53, 59, 64, 67, 73, 125–26,
  132, 229n2, 247
grammatical unit 1, 9–10, 31, 91, 161, 271
grammatical word 1–2, 8–13, 17–37, 43, 48,
  51–54, 59–71, 69n15, 79–98, 101, 107–8,
  112–14, 119, 123–32, 125n1, 138–48,
  147n13, 156–66, 176–77, 183–95,
  198–200, 205, 212–20, 215n8, 223–24,
  228–32, 248, 252–53, 256, 256n11, 259,
  269–74, 277–79
  criteria for 1–2, 6–13, 13n8, 18–28, 32–7,
    59, 63, 81, 84, 88, 98, 107–8, 123, 128,
    143–45, 160–61, 167, 228–29, 232, 248,
    272–75

Printed in the United Kingdom
by Lightning Source UK Ltd.
125651UK00002BC/232-237/A